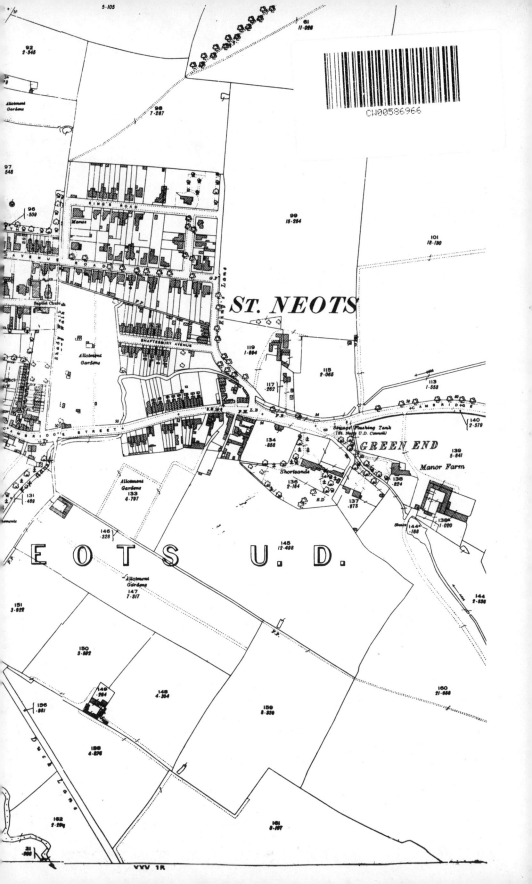

ST. NEOTS

GREEN END

EOTS U. D.

ST. NEOTS
The History of a Huntingdonshire Town

ST. NEOTS

The History of a Huntingdonshire Town

C.F. Tebbutt

PHILLIMORE

First published 1978 by
PHILLIMORE & CO. LTD.
Shopwyke Hall, Chichester, Sussex, England

CORRECTED REPRINT 1984

ISBN 0 85033 270 2

Printed and bound in Great Britain by
BILLINGS BOOK PLAN
Worcester, England

CONTENTS

LIST OF ILLUSTRATIONS

PREFACE

WHATEVER FAULTS this book .may contain, and I am sure there are many, I feel great satisfaction in dedicating it to the people of St. Neots and Eynesbury, where I was born and lived for 56 years of my life. I am fully conscious that what it contains is largely the work of others and that my part in it was in searching and collecting what lay hidden in a great many places, including the memories of people now dead. I have no claim to be a historian but what skill i have as an archaeologist has been used in piecing together evidence to make a story. I have, however, gone beyond what would have been permitted by the historian or archaeologist. Many stories, from locally printed or verbal sources, have been included, and often I have had no idea if they be true, false, or exaggerated. I have included them, without apology, because I consider them to be important as folk tales, and the sort of stories that interested, amused, or shocked people in the 19th century, the stories they *wanted* to believe were true ... I can however assure the reader that none have been invented by me.

Although my main theme has been to present a picture of 19th-century St. Neots I have not stuck too rigidly to this period. Much of St. Neots and Eynesbury, particularly as to plan and architecture, can only be understood by going back much farther in their history, and I have tried to include what I considered necessary to fulfil this aim. Some 19th-century business firms and institutions have their origins well beyond 1800 and I have tried to trace them to their source. Others have carried on into this century and I have therefore followed them into more recent times.

This brings me to the main source of my material, other than the obvious ones in the church safe, public and local record offices and libraries, of which the Norris Museum and Library, St. Ives, was perhaps the most fruitful. A mine of information was found in the files of the local weekly newspapers, generously and conveniently put at my disposal by Mr. Colin Ledrum at the *St. Neots Advertiser* offices. There I went carefully through all the local papers, which date from about 1850, to the editions of about 1910, filling many notebooks with items of interest, and finally indexing them.

The treasure trove from this research was a number of letters and articles recording memories and reminiscences of the writers. Medbury Joyce, writing under the pseudonym of 'Townborn', wrote letters from 1866 to 1892, vividly descriptive of his early days in St. Neots. He was born there in 1812, and emigrated to North America in 1833. However he soon returned to his native town and set up as an architect and surveyor, leaving again in 1863 to practise his profession in London. D. R. Tomson, owner and editor of the *St. Neots Advertiser*, published in that paper, in 1909, an article describing all the people who lived or had business premises on the market square when he first opened his own shop there in 1848. In 1930/31 Arthur Chapman wrote a series of articles about townspeople and events of the period 1860-70, and in 1932 John Batsford, then aged 86, wrote similarly about his memories, going back to about 1855.

I am particularly pleased to include some of the vast amount of material collected by Joseph Wright, who died tragically in 1934, at the age of about 90, when his house in East Street was burnt together with most of his large collection of books, papers, and notes relating to St. Neots, that he had spent a lifetime in collecting. A small part only was saved and it fortunately included his MS. copy (now in the Norris Library, St. Ives), of the minutes of the town commissioners, of which the whereabouts of the original is now unknown.

Many old people, too numerous to mention, have told me stories of 'the old days', and a few, not so old, have remembered things that their parents or grandparents told them. I must especially mention George Harvey (1879-1966), my neighbour at Eynesbury, with whom I spent many happy evenings in 1962, taking down his vivid memories of the period 1890-1910.

I am also grateful to the many friends who entrusted me with the ancient deeds of their houses and property to copy, and the account books of their business houses to peruse. I cannot remember a refusal.

The only printed source of local history that I must specially mention is *The History and Antiquaries of Eynesbury and St. Neot's in Huntingdonshire, and St. Neot's in Cornwall*, by Rev. G. C. Gorham, published in 1820. The author was born in a house on the Market Square in 1787, the son of a merchant family, educated at Queens' College, Cambridge, took Holy Orders, and became a Fellow of his college. The book contains a wealth of detail, from MS. sources, about St. Neots Priory and displays the scholarship, learning and accuracy of the writer to a degree that subsequent researchers have failed to fault. Unfortunately he did not include much about the town at the time of his publication, a fault about which I have the least right to complain.

INTRODUCTION

BEFORE PROCEEDING with any account of the 19th-century St. Neots, which occupies my main study, I feel that I should try to picture what the town was like in the opening years of that century. Firstly it was a small town in 1800 with only 1,750 people, living in 370 houses, and a further 575 people in Eynesbury. This number was to grow to 3,320 at St. Neots and 1,340 at Eynesbury by 1861 and to decline to 2,850 and 1,120 in 1901.

Administratively both parishes, in 1800, were governed separately by their churchwardens, with limited powers to levy rates or make bye-laws, and having the heavy burden of looking after their own poor. In 1819 however, by Act of Parliament, St. Neots was taken over by Town Commissioners, who were able to effect great improvements, but the two parishes did not become one unit of local government until 1876.

The agricultural part of St. Neots parish was enclosed in 1770, an early date for the district, and this was probably part of the reason why it retained its common (few later enclosures did). Before the enclosure most farmers, in this part of England, lived in the towns or villages in their parishes, and in 1800 many of the older large houses in the town were still, or had been, farmhouses. In contrast the south and west sides of the Market Square were occupied by merchants' houses and yards directly connected with the navigation of the Ouse and Hen Brook. They lived on the premises.

Thursday market day was undoubtedly the most important day of the week in the town, and corn the most important commodity sold there. In good harvest years much corn was exported by barge destined for the North of England or the Continent. 'Corn shops' to store grain were scattered all round the vicinity of the square, in inn yards and other odd places. The market provided much permanent and casual employment.

For the numerous visitors and workers in the market there were inns of all types in which to transact business and buy food and refreshment. Several were stagecoach stops. On the Square one could choose between the *King's Head*, the *Queen's Head*, the *Bull*, the *Bear*, the *Falcon*, the *Half Moon*, the *Cross Keys*, the *White Lion*, the *Angel*, the *Fox and Hounds*, the *Golden Ball* and the *Wrestlers*.

For shoppers there was Shop Row, occupying the north side of the square (originally established under the Priory wall), and shops had gradually extended along High Street up to the Cross. This street was planned to be wide enough to act as an overflow from the market, hence its old name of Sheep Street. Here were mainly small shops who often displayed their goods on stalls outside. All these business premises faced the menace of floods although the Square had been raised by up to four feet in former times.

The inhabitants then all lived in that part of the town comprising the Square, High Street, Huntingdon Street, Cambridge Street as far as Shady Walk, Church Street, Brook Street, and South Street. The richer merchants, farmers, and professional classes held their balls and routs at the Assembly Rooms at the corner of High Street and Huntingdon Street. The poor lived in the 'borough' in Huntingdon Street and the 'yards' and 'courts' behind the shops and inns, where little two- and four-room cottages crowded. The aged and helpless poor were put in the workhouse in Church Street.

Eynesbury parish was not enclosed until 1830 and remained governed by its churchwardens until 1876. Most of its farmhouses were in the village which consisted of St. Mary's Street, Berkeley Street (with houses on the east side only) as far as the green, Montague Street, and Montague Square.

In these days of mass production, and manufacture of nearly all articles in everyday use, it is astonishing to find how self-supporting every little town was in the 19th century, employing great numbers of individual craftsmen and their apprentices, each doing satisfying work for customers they knew personally. Unfortunately there is no comprehensive directory for the beginning of the century but the variety of tradesmen listed in the *History and Gazetteer of Huntingdonshire* (1854), is probably not very different from that of 50 years before. For the two parishes they comprise: one each of whitesmiths, higglers, hucksters, staymakers, parchment-makers, pig dealers, millwrights, marine store dealers, tobacco pipe makers, basket-makers, comb-makers, horse dealers, razor-grinders, sausage-makers, letter carriers and glovers, turners, coach builders, master watermen, straw plait dealers, machine men, dyers and scourers, iron founders, curriers, also two blacksmiths, 16 bootmakers, 13 bakers, five brewers, five maltsters, six bricklayers, 15 carpenters, four brickmakers, two millers, 10 butchers, four coopers, two rope-makers, two sadlers, three stonemasons, two tallow chandlers, 15 tailors, two upholsterers, three watch and clock makers, four milliners and dressmakers, four wheelwrights, six painters, plumbers and glaziers, three printers, 26 inn-keepers, 28 beer retailers, three carriers, and two lace dealers.

How did the town look to a stranger entering it for the first time at the turn of the century? Not very favourably I fear. One contemporary writer described it as 'dirty', and the Hon. John Byng, in 1794, wrote it down in his *Torrington Diaries* as a 'dull place', although he found it rather more lively at his next visit which coincided with the May Fair (see Fairs and Feasts). He found the whole district depressing, and particularly the condition of the poor. He thus describes his journey from St. Neots to Cambridge at about the same date: 'thru a vile dreary country with nothing to see or amuse I came to the village of Eltisley, a place as deplorable as I hope to see unmatched in Britain. Are we fighting for the wrong of France, are we to preserve Holland, are we to think of nothing but trade, and to brag of our numerous ships, when our land is desolate, our poor oppressed, and the interior of our country threadbare, to finance a tinsel fringe, an exterior of Trade, that bane of comfort, that selfish unfeeling monster? To two human male beings, whose nakedness was not concealed by rags, who held my horse, I gave my loose halfpence. Never had they known such treasure. Covering for head and feet they had never known. They seemed to be about 12 or 14 years of age'. The above would probably have described some of the poor at St. Neots at that time.

APPENDIX TO INTRODUCTION

Census Returns

	St. Neots	Eynesbury
1801	1,752	575
1821	2,272	903
1841	3,123	1,003
1861	3,321	1,341
1881	3,136	1,398
1901	2,851	1,127

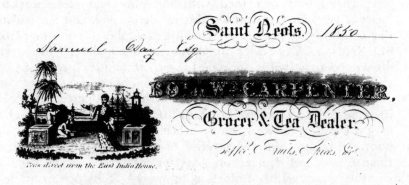

Tea direct from the East India House.

II
PREHISTORIC AND HISTORIC BACKGROUND

AS SO MUCH of what happened to St. Neots in the 19th century, and indeed what is happening today, has depended on its long historic past, a brief outline of how the town and its twin parish of Eynesbury came into being is not out of place. Indeed few small town sites can boast of such a proven long period of continuous occupation.

We now know that the whole valley of the Ouse, in Huntingdonshire and Bedfordshire, was intensively farmed in pre-historic and Roman times, but where people actually lived was probably dictated by such considerations as high unfloodable land near the river, shallow hard-bottomed fords, places where ancient trackways crossed at such fords, and, of course, the presence of easily-worked farm land. It is probable that such conditions obtained at St. Neots and Eynesbury. The road to Cambridge is almost certainly a prehistoric east-west trackway and the name Eaton Ford preserves a memory of the ford there before the present river crossing was bridged in the 12th century. Both St. Neots and Eynesbury have some land near the river above flood level, the flood plain being only built over at a relatively late date historically.

Stone and Bronze Age
Evidence of the earliest occupation comes from Eynesbury. Gravel pits dug just south of Montague Square, in the late 19th century, produced polished stone axes and 'beaker' pottery of the early Bronze Age.

Iron Age
The early part of the Iron Age (probably before 500 B.C.) was represented by a pit, containing pottery, found. by the author

in what is now the playing field of Eynesbury School, behind the old rectory. People of the later Iron Age had a settlement near Howitts Lane. They were Belgic tribesmen from the Continent who conquered this part of the country in the century or so before the Roman invasion, and brought with them improved farming techniques.

Evidence from this site, as from many others, proved that these people remained undisturbed by the invasion and must have peacefully accepted Roman rule.

The Roman period

During the Roman period (43-410 A.D.) the Eynesbury settlement expanded and seems to have moved nearer the river, occupying the area round about the church and the Coneygear, and from these extended south of the present village on land just above the river flood plain. Sites of at least two houses with hypocaust central heating have been located in this area. People here may have been partly engaged in loading agricultural produce on to barges for shipment down river. Many archaeologists think that the whole of this area was organised as an imperial farm to supply food for the army in the north. Support for the idea that Eynesbury had a trading post or administrative centre was the existence of a small defensive earthwork at the Coneygear, now largely destroyed. Excavations here by the writer, in 1933, proved that it was constructed about the late 2nd century A.D., a time when many such defences were being constructed. Could it be possible that the old story recorded by Gorham, of a giant on Eynesbury Coneygear throwing missiles at another giant at Eaton Socon may retain a folk memory of a Roman military catapult once set up here?

Besides its navigation Eynesbury also had good road communications in Roman times. The Sandy to Godmanchester road passed not far to the east, and from it branched a lesser road to Eynesbury. The line of this is still preserved in the Half Mile Meadow public footpath, Howitts Lane, and Berkeley Street.

On the St. Neots side of Hen Brook settlement seems to have been minor. Pottery and ditches of this period have been found near the *Woolpack* inn, and in gardens behind the vicarage. A small excavation by the author showed that the public footpath leading from Duck Lane towards Wintringham, east of the railway, was actually on the line of a metalled Roman footpath, and pottery was found near it. (Grid ref.: TL 200591)

The Pagan Saxon period

The mystery of what happened to the people of Roman Britain after the withdrawal of the legions in 410 A.D. will perhaps never be solved. However we do know that there was, in the 6th century, a settlement of the pagan Saxons, probably on both sides of the Hen Brook. In Eynesbury there were dwellings of some sort on, or near, the Roman village as clay loom weights of this period were found in the course of gravel digging on the Coneygear in the 19th century. Also from Eynesbury is a decorated narrow-necked pottery vessel, now in the Museum of Archaeology, Cambridge, dated by Dr. J. N. L. Myers as probably 7th-century.

At St. Neots a cemetery of this period, containing both cremation and inhumation burials, was found on the south side of Avenue Road, at the west end, when it was being first developed in 1886. Some relics from this cemetery are in the Norris Museum, St. Ives.

The Late or Christian Saxon period

The events of the long Dark Ages remain as dark here as elsewhere and it is not until the late 10th century that there is recorded what was, in its consequences, the most important event in the town's history. This was the founding, by a Saxon landowner named Leofric and his wife Leoflaed, of a small monastery on his land in the parish of Ernulph's Bury (Eynesbury). To add prestige to the new foundation the miracle-working bones of the Cornish Saint Neot were by some means obtained, and enshrined in the monastery church.

The site of the Saxon monastery is not certainly known and some local historians have been led astray in their speculations, not appreciating the fact that at that time the parish of Eynesbury included that of St. Neots. The writer thinks that the site is most likely to be that of the later Norman priory. This was built on one of the few flood-free sites near the river and, as the priory took over with enthusiasm the cult and shrine of St. Neot, there would be a strong pull to the old sacred site so long as it was architecturally suitable. However, when the writer was excavating the foundations of the priory no trace of the earlier monastery was found. This was perhaps not surprising as the buildings were probably of wood and all signs of them would probably be destroyed in constructing the stone buildings of the priory. Further it is not clear, from the records, if the monastery was ever fully restored after its destruction in the Danish war of 1010 A.D.

From discoveries and excavations by the author we now know that there was also a civilian community living, not far from the monastery, on land just above the flood plain, east of Church Street, and between it and the small brook that crosses Cambridge Street. Here, in gravel pits being dug in the grounds of Hall Place in 1929, were found sunken huts containing tools and pottery of this period, and now thought to date from the 10th century. The type of pottery found was here first identified as belonging to this period, and is now known as 'St. Neots Ware'. In the 1950s further excavations were undertaken by P. V. Addyman, on behalf of the Ministry of Works, on an adjoining site behind the vicarage, threatened by building operations. Here were the plans of large barn-like wooden buildings of the late Saxon period, as well as pits and ditches and plentiful pottery.

In 1964 the author, excavating where shops had been pulled down at the corner of Church Street and Cambridge Street, found a large ditch which ran roughly parallel with Cambridge Street, under the building line, and at the corner turned south similarly along Church Street. Its line was later picked up by Messrs. Rudd and Daines in a section dug just inside gardens on the east side of Church Street opposite the church. It had been deliberately filled in in the late 12th century.

The two lengths of this ditch would appear to enclose the north and west sides of the late Saxon settlement and it is probable that Hen Brook, and its tributary from Cambridge Street form the other two sides of a defensive earthwork.

The above facts show that the town of St. Neots had an origin in Saxon times and did not, as previous writers have suggested, grow up as an adjunct to the post-Conquest priory.

The Norman Conquest and after

After the Conquest, in 1066, the manor of Eynesbury came into the possession of Richard of Clare who, probably through the influence of his wife Rohais, decided to hand over the little Saxon monastery to the great and important Benedictine monastery of Bec in their homeland of Normandy. This was another momentous step in the town's history as Bec was one of the leading intellectual and cultural centres of northern Europe. Bec had produced as its abbot Lanfranc, William the Conqueror's first Archbishop of Canterbury, and he was followed at Bec by Anselm, afterwards to succeed Lanfranc in his high office in England. This Italian monk, who rose from humble origins to the highest ecclesiastical office, was by nature gentle, simple, but with the highest intelligence and quite fearless in denouncing even the King when he felt the Church and its religious standards were threatened.

As Abbot of Bec, Anselm visited its new possession, then called Neotsbury, in 1078, and it would appear that he at once took a special interest in the place. This interest was probably in the saint himself, a man after his own heart. It is recorded that he carefully examined the shrine and satisfied himself that the bones of St. Neot were indeed there, and he even abstracted his jawbone to take back to Bec where ever after the Festival of St. Neot was annually celebrated.

Anselm, later to be canonised as St. Anselm, then determined to create a new Benedictine priory here and to make it the most important possession of Bec in England. To this end about 18 monks, no doubt specially chosen for this task, were sent from France, and always replaced, when necessary, from that source. Wealth was the next requirement and the power of Anselm's recommendation and patronage, which he still continued after becoming Archbishop, soon produced large gifts of money, land, and livings, to the new foundation. Thus, while other Bec possessions in England became mainly revenue-producing estates, St. Neots was from the first a favourite child, only paying a nominal annual tribute and always staffed by men from a background close to the full stream of European culture.

We must now, therefore, state very briefly what these educated and farseeing men did with the wealth, patronage, and opportunities at their disposal.

The first task would have been to build their church and the conventual buildings necessary to a Benedictine establishment. This was done, using the navigational facilities to bring stone from Barnack and Bedfordshire. Thereafter the sequence of events is not clear, but we do know that a charter to hold a weekly market and fairs was obtained from Henry I and confirmed by Henry II. Also sometime in the 12th century (before 1180) a wooden bridge was built to replace the ford or ferry across the Ouse. These two advantages must have influenced the decision to plan a new town to attract pilgrims and commerce.

The Medieval town plan

The town centre was marked by a cross, the Cross of St. Neot, placed just outside the N.W. corner of the ditch of the late Saxon village, and on the ancient road from Cambridge to the river crossing. From the Cross two streets were laid out approximately at right angles, Huntingdon Street to the north and the present Church Street to the south. This latter followed just outside the Saxon ditch and pointed to the ford, later a bridge, crossing Hen Brook to Eynesbury. Later, probably in the 15th century, this road had to be 'bent' to allow the new St. Neots church to be built, which presumably took up more space than its predecessor. Hence the 'kink' in this road. Huntingdon Street led to the road to Huntingdon and Godmanchester, and at the end of the town was a branch to Toseland known as the St. Ives Way. High Street originally had dwellings only at its east end, probably because floods often came up to half way along it.

The Market Square, one of the largest in the country, was laid out by the French monks to accommodate the markets and fairs that they hoped to encourage so as to increase their rents and tolls. Its position and extent was a stroke of genius and optimism for which we should today be grateful to them. The square must then have been subject to frequent flood for its original surface was then between two and a half and four feet below that at present. The north side of the square was formed partly by the south wall of the Priory church and partly by its precinct wall. Against these, facing the market and the sun, small shops and workshops were allowed to be built, on payment of rent. This became known as 'Shop Row'.

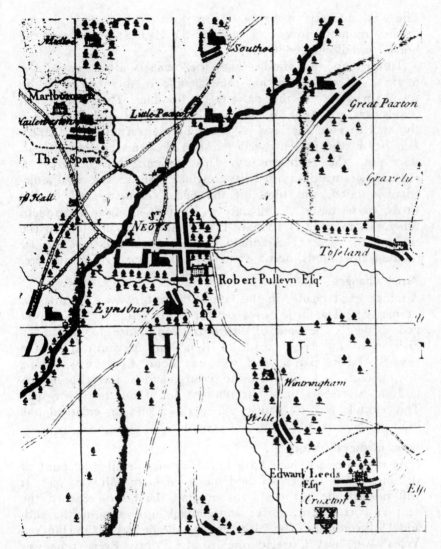

Gordon's Map of 1730

The west side was probably at first open to the river, and open ditches running along each side of the High Street crossed the Square and discharged here.

Throughout the Middle Ages the business attraction of the market and the navigation drew people to these areas of the town, in spite of the dangers of flooding. Their answer to floods was gradually to dump soil, gravel and rubbish all over the area to raise the level. A study of the pottery found stratified below the present surface shows that this process did not start until the 14th century. This tendency for the town to expand westwards caused its original plan to become somewhat lopsided, and some of the occupied areas, east of the Cross, to be deserted and only to be built up again in modern times. There appears to have been medieval occupation on the site of the present Sandfield U.D.C. estate and revealed by building operations, and a coin of Hardicanute was found here.

Parish changes

Another great change in the late 12th century was the division of parishes. The little town on the Priory side of Hen Brook had evidently become of sufficient importance to warrant a division of the large parish of Eynesbury to form from it a new St. Neots parish, and this was done. Eynesbury had its own church, belonging to the Priory, and a new church was built at St. Neots on a site allowed for it on the town plan. This church was of course pulled down and an enlarged one built on the same site in the 15th century.

Later medieval history

It is not intended here to give a long and detailed account of the history of the Priory and the town in the Middle Ages. It will perhaps be sufficient to say that the Priory reached the zenith of its wealth, power, and perhaps inspiration, in the 12th and 13th centuries. The 14th century, the period of the Hundred Years' War, was a tragic one for the Priory. Every time war with France was declared the Priory and all its revenues were seized by the King, and the monks given only a small living allowance. Buildings and estates fell into such decay that full recovery was impossible even when it became English, after the tie with Bec was finally severed in 1409. Conditions seem to have slightly improved just before the Dissolution in 1539.

Surviving documents also throw some light on conditions in the town and its inhabitants. It would seem to have started as a thriving village community with a market and navigational facilities to become one of the most important ports in the country. In the 13th century there were a number of craftsmen, including goldsmiths, and a fuller. The 14th century, when the Priory was declining, saw an expansion of trade, and a considerable expansion in the 15th and 16th centuries. At some time, it is not quite clear when, there was considerable new commercial development on the south side of the square and along the Hen Brook as far as Eynesbury Bridge. Also Hen Brook has, at some time, been deepened and canalised and Brook Street and Brookside raised by dumping material. One would suspect that this took place after locks were built on the river in the early 17th century. However there are merchants' houses on the south side of the Square that must date from the 15th or 16th centuries.

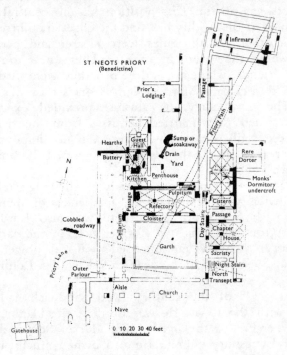

III
SOCIAL CONDITIONS

Victorian Class Society

As elsewhere in the country St. Neots, in the 19th century, inherited a fairly rigid class structure which did not begin to break up before 1914. Within the separate classes, comprising the aristocracy, the upper, upper middle, lower middle, and lower classes, there were, of course, minor power and prestige struggles, and between some classes the barriers were easier to pass than between others. This position has not entirely gone today, but much of the rigidity has, and the edges are blurred.

In the Victorian era the rules were clearer and people at least knew where they were in society. They knew too where to find their friends, where to find help if they were in trouble, and where to find charity. Marriage out of one's class was almost unknown. The aristocracy, as always, provided exceptions. When impoverished they married heiresses from the rich merchant class, especially Americans, or even, if not impoverished, beautiful actresses. In both cases they termed it 'marrying beneath them'.

The aristocrats were represented locally by the long established Earls of Sandwich at Hinchingbrooke, and Dukes of Manchester at Kimbolton. For a short time there was also Lord Esmé Gordon at Paxton Park. The two former had, in the early part of the century, virtually monopolised political power in all south Huntingdonshire, but this was ended by the Reform Act of 1832.

In the first half of the century Lord Sandwich had many connections with the town. He was Lord of the Manor, which gave him ownership of the market and Market Square and lay rectorship of Eynesbury church. He also owned much property and land in St. Neots parish, including Manor Farm. Most of this represented old Priory property. During the century this was nearly all sold, mainly in 1848, and the manor, market, and Manor Farm bought by the Rowleys of Priory Park.

The Manchesters had little direct influence on the town, but undoubtedly added colour to its rather drab life by their patronage of hunting (meets were often held on the Market Square) and their entertainment of Royalty and distinguished political and aristocratic figures of the day. These often travelled to Kimbolton from St. Neots station and did their shopping in the town. The lives of the Dukes at Kimbolton Castle, their extravagances, near bankruptcies, and marriages to American heiresses provided plenty of gossip in the town.

Lord Esmé Gordon entered enthusiastically into the field sports of his class and gave his patronage and encouragement to the sports clubs in the town.

Below the aristocrats came the land-owning squires of whom the Rowleys of Priory Hill, within the parish, were by far the most important. Coming to St. Neots at the very end of the 18th century their influence was felt throughout the 19th century and well into the 20th. For them the 19th century was a progress of increasing wealth and power. Their original estate was greatly increased in size until they owned almost all the land east of the urban district. Their unwillingness to sell any land prevented any development in that direction. From Lord Sandwich they acquired the manor of St. Neots and the Market Square, and from the Crown the advowson of St. Neots church. They were successful in steering the railway away from their park which resulted in the station being built a mile from the town centre.

With the exception of one member of the family, who had a scientific bent, the main interests of the occupants of Priory Park were in managing their wealth and estates (they held another in Rutland), public service in local government at county level, in the administration of justice, and in the welfare of St. Neots church. Their main recreation was the rearing and shooting of game on their estates. The nearness of their estates to the town was a continual source of friction between them and the inhabitants, due to poaching and the claims of public rights of way over their land.

Neighbouring squires were the Reynolds of Paxton Hall, some members of which had lived in the town and taken part

in its affairs. The Alingtons of Little Barford, who came early
in the century, and the Stanleys of Paxton Park, took little
part in St. Neots life except as patrons of sport.

The upper middle class were represented by the prosperous
and often quite wealthy merchants, brewers, and manufacturers,
who were particularly numerous in St. Neots because of its
favourable position as a market town with long established
navigational links with the sea, and later a main line railway
station. Some of these men were also engaged in banking and
farming, and some bought land. The ownership of land had
great social prestige value and a man able to buy an estate
could hope to launch his son into the squire class. Many of
the St. Neots merchants, however, seem to have invested their
profits in risky ventures which came to grief. Of such prominent 18th-century merchant names as Wye, Bainton, Hatley,
Bailey, Billet and Fowley, few survived into the 19th century,
and the Ingersoles, Rix, Fosters, Stevens, of the early 19th
had disappeared by the middle of the century. Exceptions
were the Paines, Days, and Toogoods.

These men were often quite wealthy and their businesses
were very important to the prosperity of the town but they
were 'in trade' and thus rigidly excluded from close social
contact with the landowning class above. Mr. Toogood, owner
of St. Neots Paper Mill, was a close acquaintance of Mr. Standley
but was never invited to a meal or social occasion at Paxton
Park. Few St. Neots people ever visited Priory . Park house,
except on business.

Almost without exception the merchants originally lived at
or near their business premises, and their homes formed much
of the pleasing façade of the south side of the Market Square.
In the latter part of the century, however, the prosperous
merchants and manufacturers moved away to large houses in
the town or district, which they surrounded with spacious
lawns, gardens and greenhouses, needing the employment of a
large indoor and outdoor staff. These premises were usually
readily lent for such public events as school treats and fêtes.

From this class were chosen the Town Commissioners who
administered the town government from 1816 to 1876, and
they appeared to have acted with foresight and imagination
within the limits allowed them in the Act. Unfortunately when

they were superseded by a democratically elected Local Board, and later an Urban District Council, men from this class with a few exceptions were either not elected or decided not to stand, perhaps for class reasons.

Equated with the upper middle class, but in a way separate, were the small band of professional men, then confined to lawyers, doctors of medicine, and ministers of religion. Some of the clergy were rather differently placed when they were the younger sons of aristocratic or squire families. Nearly all this group had had university training and formed the nucleus of the intellectual life of the town. Both nonconformist and church ministers did much to found and maintain schools, and the doctors gave devoted service to the poor without reward.

The stratum below contained the lower middle class, and consisted of shopkeepers and small business men. It ranged from the craftsman, with one or more apprentices or assistants, to the builder with a dozen or so men working for him; and from the one man shopkeeper to the large shopkeeper with a dress-making establishment. Lawyers' clerks and merchants' office managers also came into this class. At the lower end of the scale the small shopkeeper often lived in real poverty but he had what he valued most, his independence, and he felt 'a cut above' the wage-earning class below him. A great many of this class were Liberal in politics and Nonconformist in religion. If they had money to invest they bought old house property in the town. Many of this class were elected to the new councils and their outlook was decidedly prejudiced against rate expenditure on town improvement, such as sewerage and water.

This class was being continually added to from the lower class below. Craftsmen in all trades would save money to start their own small businesses, daughters would set up as dress-makers, and wives as shopkeepers. It was also a two-way traffic and failed or bankrupt business men sank to become wage earners.

The lower classes were the great amorphous class of wage earners, both skilled and unskilled, working for a master, with perhaps an elite of 'pen pushers' from business offices. Their security of employment was slight, at the most a week's notice. In the case of a craftsman working at an hourly rate, only an hour's notice was necessary, plus time to sharpen his tools.

There was, of course, no Labour Exchange or unemployment pay, and a small weekly sum as sick pay only if contributions had been made to the 'club'.

Wages for the unskilled were only just above starvation level and, if the family was large, the wife and older children had to contribute by work of some kind. Daughters, lucky enough to be able to produce good references, might find work as servants in upper middle class homes. Housing conditions were often deplorable with chronic overcrowding and no security of tenure. For much of the century this class had no vote either in parliamentary or local elections.

To add to their burdens this class had also to suffer from being vigorously preached at on the subject of alcoholic drink. Many men, faced on their return from long hours of work by a single room, full of screaming children, drying laundry, and an understandably short-tempered wife, sought relaxation in one of the many public houses. Here, in spite of the cheapness of the beer, they often spent money that the family could ill afford. A further temptation was the long opening hours. They were even open when the men went to work in the morning. All this often resulted in the humiliating sight of wives waiting outside their husbands' place of work, on pay days, to try to extract enough money for the family's weekly budget, before they called at the pub on the way home.

With the near impossibility of saving enough to keep them in their old age (there was no old age pension) the unskilled labourer and his wife had little future prospect but the workhouse, where they would of course be separated. Large families were thus often thought of as providing not only child labour to add to the family income, but adults who would, later on be willing (as they usually were) to keep their parents out of the workhouse. After education became compulsory in 1880, one of the commonest cases brought before St. Neots court was that of parents not sending their children to school. The excuse was always that they could not afford to lose the wages their children were earning. One result of the conditions above was that very many of the more enterprising young men of the lower class emigrated to North America or Australia.

An interesting sub-class of the lower class were those who worked for no master but provided a small, and often menial,

service to the public. Their financial reward must often have
been less than that of the unskilled labourer, but what was to
them important was that they were independent, and had no
regular hours of work, and could use their intellect and powers
of persuasion to scrape a meagre living. One such sold soft
river water to housewives on washing day, and another tarred
waterbutts. Others were pedlars carrying baskets from door to
door or crying their wares in the street. Among goods sold were
bloaters and herrings, rabbits, cows' heels, and muffins. The
author remembers as a child acquiring a toy windmill, made
by a pedlar, in exchange for a glass jam jar. A few of these
casual workers achieved a measure of prosperity. The rat-
catcher Baldock had a horse and cart and a plot of market
garden land. John Franks, the wealthy furniture dealer, had
started as a pedlar, and the Wren family built up their business
by hawking fish round the markets and villages.

A few of the itinerant ballad mongers seem to have survived,
at least as late as 1871, when some pedlars were brought before
St. Neots court for hawking songs without the required licence.
Evidence was given that they had toured the town singing dog-
gerel songs, copies of which they sold for a penny. They were
said to have reaped a rich reward with verses composed on the
late murder at Little Staughton. The press published 'a sample
of the rubbish hawked' as follows:

> If William Bull is guilty found
> Of this atrocious crime,
> A murderer's fate will be his doom,
> And short will be his time,
> When he must stand before his God,
> Who unto him will say,
> 'You guilty man, your murd'rous hand
> Did Sally Marshall slay'.

Although there was a constant upward movement by a few
from the lower to the lower middle class this was only accomplished under strict social rules. To qualify one had to carry
on a business in fixed premises and if possible employ some
labour. The rules relating to social mixing came out perhaps
most noticeably in the pub, as different classes had their own
pubs. G. Harvey once described to the author how he, as a
young and employed man about 1900, was taken by his uncle,

an employer of labour, to his favourite pub for a drink. As they entered there was instant silence and everyone stared at him. This continued all the time he was there and he was glad to finish his drink quickly and leave the hostile atmosphere.

The laws of etiquette were perhaps strictest among the middle classes with all the complicated procedure of 'calling' and the leaving of cards. Those relating to proposal, engagement, and marriage were some of the most rigid. A delightful example was quoted in the *St. Neots Advertiser* in 1872, in reporting a local breach of promise case. The prospective bridegroom had written to the girl who was suing him as follows:

> Madam. I now venture to write what the timidity of honorable passion has hitherto prevented me from expressing in your presence. Your beauty and accomplishments have captivated my heart. While I thus avow myself your true lover, my fear lest some happier man should prove a successful rival overwhelms me with sorrow. Nor, I fear, are these apprehensions groundless for who, permit me to say, can enjoy the pleasure of your society without feeling respect, adoration, and tenderness. Yet as I am convinced that cruelty can never be an intimate of your fair bosom, I am encouraged to hope you will reward my virtuous attachment with mutual affection. An early answer will relieve from anxiety your sincere admirer.

One wonders if the young man really made this up himself or did he copy it from a book on etiquette?

IV
LOCAL GOVERNMENT

LOCAL GOVERNMENT, as we know it today, did not exist in St. Neots before 1819. Before that date the town was no better off, in this respect, than any of the surrounding village parishes. This obviously leads to the question why Huntingdon and Godmanchester had self government, by achieving borough status, and St. Neots and Ramsey had not. It is a long story to explain the success of the first two towns but the reason why the two latter never became boroughs lies in the dominance of their local monastic establishments, as lords of the manor.

Thus during the Middle Ages St. Neots was governed by the Priory officials, through their chief bailiff, with his headquarters in the Court Hall on the market square. After the Dissolution the new lay Lord of the Manor carried on the same system. If there was ever any demand by the citizens to be granted a charter for borough status it must have been strongly and successfully resisted.

By the 18th century local government in parishes, other than boroughs, had devolved onto the churchwardens, and this was the case in both St. Neots and Eynesbury. The churchwardens had the power to levy rates and they administered their parish through their Clerk, Overseers of the Poor, Surveyor of the Highways, and Parish Constables. While this system got by in many rural parishes it was patently inadequate in expanding market towns where the churchwardens had neither the resources nor the legal powers to run a town efficiently. Examples of these inadequacies are apparent in the new powers granted in the 1819 Act (see below).

In the case of St. Neots it is apparent that leading citizens were deeply disturbed at the town's prospects under the existing régime and therefore promoted a Parliamentary Bill to improve the town's government, after careful consideration of what it should contain to make it locally effective. In judging their foresight it would be fair to say that the new form of local government when introduced ran with reasonable effectiveness for 57 years. An interesting point in the Bill was the general acceptance, at that time, that the best body of men to govern a town was a board of commissioners originally selected, presumably by the promoters, from among leading citizens, and thereafter perpetuated by new members selected by that same body.

Eynesbury was not included in the area covered by the Bill, and remained under its churchwardens until 1876 when, much against its will, it was joined to St. Neots under a local board. The administration of the Poor Law in both parishes remained with the churchwardens until taken over by Poor Law Guardians in 1836.

The Town Commissioners

The St. Neots Paving and Lighting Act 1819 came into force in the same year. In the preamble to the Act it states 'Whereas the Streets, Lanes, public Passages, and Places of the Town of St. Neots . . . are not properly paved, cleaned, or lighted, and are subject to various Encroachments, Nuisances, and Annoyances: and whereas it would tend greatly to the Benefit, Convenience and Safety, not only to the Inhabitants of the said Town, but to persons resorting thereto, if the said Streets, Lanes, and public Passages and Places were properly paved, lighted, and cleansed, and if certain Encroachments and Annoyances were removed; and Provision made for preventing the same in the future; but in such Purposes cannot be effected without the Aid and Authority of Parliament: may it therefore please your Majesty that it be enacted: . . . That Samuel Allvey M.D., William Abbott the elder, Charles Banks, John Day, William Day, William Foster, Samuel Fairey the elder, George James Gorham, William Ingersole, Thomas Ingersole, James Livett, The Reverend Thomas Morell, William Alexander Peppercorn, John Paxton, Richard Pamplin, Ousley Rowley, David Rowley, Francis Rix, Octavius Marmaduke Saunders, Joseph Savill, Robert Sabine, Matthew Towgood the elder, Thomas Thorns, the Vicar of St. Neots for the time being, and William Wiles the elder (Cornfactor), and several other persons from Time to Time elected and appointed in manner herein after mentioned, shall be and are hereby appointed

Commissioners for putting this Act into Execution'. The Act goes on to say that new commissioners are to be elected by the surviving commissioners at a statutory meeting attended by not less than five commissioners. Meetings are to be held at the *Falcon* inn, or in some other convenient house, or in the vestry of the parish church, on the second Tuesday in January, April, July, and October, and can be adjourned. The quorum was to be five.

The commissioners were required to appoint a clerk, collector, treasurer, and receiver of rates; the clerk and treasurer to be different persons.

They were given power to purchase, by agreement, buildings or erections that encroached over footways or carriage ways, or for the purpose of widening streets or lanes. They were required to have the highways in the town (not being turnpike roads) repaired and footways paved, and to cause streets, lanes etc. to be cleansed, lighted and watered. They were empowered to cause to be made drains and sewers, and to fill up or arch over existing drains and sewers. They would assume all the powers of the present Surveyor of the Highways, including the levying of rates. They were empowered to fix lamps to walls and buildings, and pay persons for lighting and attending such lamps. They could appoint watchmen to be employed within the streets and lanes at night, and provide them with proper arms, ammunition, weapons, and clothing, and erect watch-houses and watchboxes.

The commissioners were empowered to purchase compulsorily certain properties, subject to the right of the owners to have the price settled by a jury. Included among these were the following:

Messuages, buildings, and ground extending from St. Neots Bridge to the Market Place, the property of the Earl of Sandwich and in the occupation of Richard Slade and Joseph Northern.

So much of the messuages, buildings and ground opposite the above, also the property of the said Earl, in the occupation of Eliza Norman, widow, and John Brown; as shall not exceed five feet in width from the present bridge and road.

Buildings and ground belonging to the said Earl, and in the occupation of Sarah Danns, laying on the west side of New Lane.

Buildings and ground, the property of Samuel Fairey, and in the occupation of Jas. Fairey, adjoining to the Fighting Cocks and Bulls Head. Also property adjoining the last mentioned premises and the Brook, the property of John Day. Part of the Churchyard of St. Neots,

on the east and south sides, extending from the entrance gate on
the south west corner; but not to exceed in width at any one part
10 feet, and not to be taken without the consent of the Bishop
of Lincoln.

Three messuages belonging to the churchwardens and Overseers of
the Poor.

The purpose of taking the first two of these properties was
clearly to widen the entrance to the bridge, and the next the
entrance to New Lane (New Street), which was then beginning
to be developed as a residential street. The reference to property near the *Fighting Cocks* is more obscure as this inn was
at No. 22 High Street.

A number of bye-laws were included in the Act, the most
important being set out below:

For preventing accidents by fire, no stack of hay or straw, rush or
faggot, to be set up within 40 yards of any dwelling house situated
within two furlongs of St. Neots Churchyard; unless covered by lead,
copper, metal, slate, or tile. No person shall drive a coach, cart,
wagon, dray, wheelbarrow, or any carriage whatever, over any foot
pavement.

No person shall permit any beast to wander about any street.

No person shall kill, slaughter, singe, scald, dress, or cut up, any
beast; or allow blood to run from any Slaughter House on to the
highway.

No person shall hoop, cleanse, wash or scald, any casks, hew or saw
any timber, bind or make a wheel or shoe; bleed, dress, or farry
any horse; set, place, or expose for sale any goods on footways or
carriage ways.

Nor make fires, called Bonfires, or set fire, or let off, or throw, any
Squib, Rocket, Serpent, or Firework; or play football, or any other
game, nor sift screen, or slack any line, on a highway or footway.

No wagon, cart, or dray shall be left to stand on the highway, with
or without horses, for longer than reasonable for loading or unload-
ing, nor any stage coach than is reasonable for taking up or setting
down passengers.

No dung, ashes, or rubbish to be thrown on to any highway.

Beasts found wandering on the streets to be put in the Common
Pound, and not released until the owner pay a sum not exceeding
20s. If not paid within seven days the Pound Keeper may sell the
beast, giving two days notice to the owner, if known.

In case of a slaughter house, hog stye, or other noisome building,
carrion, blood, offal, soil, or dung, being near a highway and offensive to the inhabitants, the Commissioners may give notice in writing
for the nuisance to be removed, and if not removed within two days,
the offender shall pay a sum, not exceeding 40s., for each day the
same be unremoved.

From the passing of the Act all persons occupying houses, buildings, shops, warehouses, yards, gardens, and stables, in or against any street, shall cause to be swept and cleansed, the footways, paths, and pavements, the whole length of their property, between the hours of 7 and 10 o'clock of the forenoon, twice or oftener each week. With a penalty of not less than 5s. and not more than 10s. for every neglect.

When a building or house standing upon a street, and projecting beyond the regular line of that street, be taken down and rebuilt, the Commissioners may direct that it be set back to such regular line, and make compensation to the owner.

Rates shall be levied once or oftener each year on property as judged needful, in any sum not exceeding in one whole year 1s. 6d. in the pound on all property as assessed for the Relief of the Poor.

The mansion house of Ousley Rowley Esq., and the St. Neots Water Mills, now occupied by Matthew Towgood Esq., not to be assessed at a greater annual value than £40. No property beyond one mile radius from St. Neots church to be rated. Poor persons excused from Poor Rate, not to be rated.

Empty houses to be charged half.

Appeals against rates or assessments may be made to the Justices of the Peace.

The Commissioners have the power to borrow money, or mortgate and pay interest, and to reward informers.

The original minute books of the Town Commissioners have disappeared but a complete copy in pencil, made by the late Joseph Wright, is in the Norris Library, St. Ives. From this some of the more interesting items are given below.

The first meeting of the new commissioners was held at the *Falcon* inn on 23 June 1819, there being 15 commissioners present, all took the prescribed oath and Ousley Rowley was voted to the chair. William Day was appointed clerk, and Francis Rix treasurer. They then decided to call on a quarter of the 'subscription'. This referred to loans promised by individual commissioners, mainly individual sums of £100 but later increased to £120, and amounting to a total of £1,720.

They then decided to advertise for a surveyor and rate collector, at salaries of £20 a year, and print notices to the inhabitants informing them of the bye-laws relating to roof coverings of stacks erected in the town, and to cattle wandering in the streets.

A number of statutory and adjourned meetings were held in 1819, at which various people took the chair, there being no permanent chairman elected throughout the whole period of the commissioners. Attendance at meetings was often not good, and they had often to be adjourned for lack of a quorum.

One of the first acts in 1819 was to start negotiations with Lord Sandwich to purchase the property mentioned in the Act, adjoining the bridge. Lamps and lamp-posts were next considered, and a sample lamp in copper, with a tin top, submitted by Mr. Carrington, fully glazed at 10s. each and with a lamp iron at 5s., was accepted.

At another meeting James Kirby, watchmaker, was appointed surveyor and rate collector, and instructed to employ poor persons in the workhouse to clean the streets. John King, the town crier, was made pinder (pound keeper), and ordered to impound any beasts found wandering in the streets. At the same time the clerk was asked to write to Mrs. Simpson, who had rescued her husband's hogs from being driven into the Pound, and threaten prosecution. Householders were reminded of their obligation, under the Act, to sweep and clean the footpaths and pavements along their frontages, twice a week, so that the surveyor could cart away the rubbish.

The erection of street lamps started, and by September there were nineteen. John Cook was appointed lamplighter. Nine of the lamps were to be lit from sundown to 1 a.m., and the remainder until 4 a.m. This would be for seven months of the year only, and none were to be lit on the six nights preceding, and one night after, full moon. The total limit of lamps in the town was to be 90, and John Cook signed a contract at 16s. a lamp, for the year.

Finance at once claimed serious attention. Mr. Gorham, one of the old Highway Surveyors whose responsibilities had now been taken over by the commissioners, attended a meeting and stated that a considerable sum was due to him for road works. William Day, the clerk, also produced a bill for Parliamentary expenses in getting the bill drawn up and passed, amounting to £324, plus his own expenses, as agent, of £244. He agreed to accept £500 in full settlement. It was agreed to levy a rate of 9d. for the half year, and thereafter, throughout the whole period of the commissioners, an annual rate of 1s. 6d., the maximum allowed in the Act, was demanded.

In 1820 the commissioners interviewed a Mr. Bevan regarding the making of a common sewer. Plans and estimates were accepted and a large order for bricks was divided between the three local brickmakers, Messrs. Rix, Gorham, and Banks. The new sewer ran from Cambridge Street, (near Shady Path) to the High Street and Market Square, discharging into the river just above the bridge. As the sewer had only a fall of three feet six inches over its whole length a weir was made to raise the level of the brook at its east end, from which the sewer could be flushed. The contractors were John Warren and James Rich (of Brook Street) at a price of 3s. 6d. per yard.

Meetings now began to be held either in the *Cross Keys* or the church vestry. In early November 1820 the town crier was ordered to announce that bonfires and fireworks were not allowed in the streets.

In the same year a committee was appointed to confer with the trustees of the North Road and of the St. Neots and Cambridge Road trusts, the two turnpike authorities having roads through the town, to arrange a plan whereby the commissioners would take over parts of their roads through the town. Tempsford bridge was then not built and the North Road ran through the town to Huntingdon, while the Cambridge turnpike started at the corner of Priory Park in Huntingdon Street. Agreement was reached with the trustees to pay the commissioners £40 a year to take over the one and a quarter miles of their roads in the town.

In 1821 a Mr. Groom of Boston attended to explain the best method of paving the town, and a contract was made with him for paving with cobbles at 9d. a square yard. It was decided to start on the Market Square and a supply of pebbles was bought at 4d. to 6d. a bushel. However the quantity available was not sufficient and enquiries were made of Lynn shippers as to obtaining Spurn Point cobbles. The reply stated that owing to the lateness of the season and the dangers of the coast, none would be got this year with any certainty. The probable cost at the proper season would be 10s. a ton at Lynn plus 7s. 3d. a ton freight to St. Neots. It was decided to wait until the next spring.

Negotiations with the Earl of Sandwich having been completed the cottage property on either side of the bridge was pulled down, enabling the entrance to be widened and steps made down to the river on the south side.

The problem of obstructions in the streets was now fackled, and free-standing sign posts in front of the *Bear*, *King's Head*, and *Golden Ball* inns, were ordered to be taken down. It was also ordered that Mr. Lewis's blacksmith's shop be altered so that it did not open directly on to the pavement.

In 1822 John Day (of the Priory Brewery) offered the commissioners a cast iron pedestal with four arms to receive lamp brackets, for erection in the centre of the Market Hill, provided that the commissioners would supply and light the lamps. The offer was gratefully accepted and Thomas Ingersole was asked to furnish a suitable inscription for casting on the monument, at the expense of the donor. Three years later the stones at the base of what had then become known as the 'Obelisk' were found to be decaying, and granite blocks were ordered to replace them, with an iron railing to protect the base.

Nutters Lane (Bedford Street) was now beginning to be developed, and it was ordered to be curbed and gravelled. In 1823 a water cart was ordered for street watering, when necessary, to suppress the dust.

In 1824 a financial crisis began to develop, and in 1825 the surveyor was ordered to reduce his staff to two men in winter and three in summer. This was done in spite of complaints of horses roaming loose in the streets and rubbish and filth accumulating on the streets and pavements. A further reduction of expenditure was necessary in 1826, and it was ordered that the street lamps be only lit for five months, i.e. from 17 October to 17 March. More remarkably William Day, the clerk, offered to have his salary reduced from £5 to £4, and the surveyor, Jas. Kirby, from £26 to £20.

In 1829 Jas. Kirby, the first surveyor and rate-collector, died and his son Richard was appointed in his place, at the reduced salary of £20 a year. He proved unsatisfactory, and in 1832 he was replaced, at the same salary, by John Shrives. He, however, was required to find a £100 bond in respect of his rate-collecting activities.

In 1833 it was resolved that, to provide extra supplies of water for fire fighting and watering the streets, a drain from the Brook leading to a pump near Mr. Lewis's blacksmith's shop near the Hog Market (the present Electricity Board's offices) be continued to the Cross and into Huntingdon Street, to fill a large brick underground storage tank there, near the town pump (near the Wesleyan chapel).

In 1834 it was agreed to take over Russell Row as a public highway. By this year finances seem to have improved, and it was decided that in 1835 watchmen would be appointed to serve during the winter months, i.e. from 10 October to the end of street lighting, although in 1837 the time was reduced to a period of four months from 1 November. There is no record of who was appointed, but in 1848 the watchmen were William Hall and John Baxter. Neither is their equipment mentioned except an entry authorising new greatcoats in 1837. In 1849 William Hinds was appointed in place of Hall, who had left to join the Bedfordshire Rural Police Force.

In 1850 it was stated that the watchmen were, in future, to be called special constables, but the old name continued. In the same year Samuel Day asked for the watch box to be removed from its position near his property (the present Salvation Army Citadel). In 1851 a watchman was badly assaulted and the commissioners agreed to pay the prosecution fees against his assailant. Perhaps as a result of this attack two new watchmen were appointed later the same year, John Bath and Chas. Tokins. In 1853 John Bath had to be reprimanded for being drunk while on duty and improperly assaulting one Bransom, a sawyer. As a result, perhaps, a watch inspector, Chas. Sibley, was appointed at a salary of £5 a year.

In 1854 the watchmen's wages were raised by 2s. a week, 'owing to the high price of provisions and bad weather', and in 1855 they were ordered to go on duty on Sunday evenings, owing to Sunday rowdyism, and their wages raised to 13s. a week. Following the formation of a police force watching was discontinued in 1856, but Chas. Sibley was kept on for other duties.

In 1836 Windmill Row was declared a private road, and a request to light it refused. In 1838 John Day, of the Priory Brewery, asked permission to rebuild the *Queens Head* inn, and offered to sell the commissioners a strip of land from the Market Place corner to the Brook, to widen Bell Lane (Brook Street). This was agreed to.

In 1839 the commissioners considered the desirability of widening the entrance to the town by New Lane, and it was agreed to confer with Lord Sandwich, who owned the property on the west side. However nothing came of this and another approach was made in 1841, Mr. Medland being paid £2 2s. for a plan and survey of the proposed alteration. Lord Sandwich agreed to sell the property, with an offer to repurchase any parts of the site found later not to be required. By April 1843 the buildings on the site had been removed and the road widening done.

The commissioners now entertained a more ambitious scheme for the surplus land. They decided to build a fire engine house, lamp house, and other store houses, on the ground floor, with a public room above, (the present Wade Gery and Brackenbury offices). Tenders were asked for and that of Samuel Charlton of St. Neots, in the sum of £368, was accepted. Medbury Joyce, whose published reminiscences have added so much to this book, was appointed architect at a fee of £17 10s. Money to build the 'New Rooms' was found by borrowing £380 from the Overseers of the Poor, at four and a half per cent. Mr. King, the town crier, was made caretaker at £1 11s. 6d. a year. On 24 April 1846 the commissioners held their first meeting in the new building, and in 1847 the County Court paid £12 a year for its use on court days.

In 1849 the commissioners received a deputation from the committee of the St. Neots, Eaton Socon, and Eynesbury Mechanics' Institute, to discuss hiring the 'New Rooms', with the use of smaller rooms below, and the liberty to put up shelves. The small room to be open from 6 to 10 each evening, except on Sunday, Good Friday, and Christmas Day. There is no record of the result of the application, but there was probably no agreement.

In 1852 Mr. Medland (who lived in the present Constitutional Club house, New Street) attended a meeting and submitted a proposal for building a much larger public room on land next to, and south of, the river bridge, on condition that the commissioners disposed of their 'New Rooms'. They must have already found their own premises inadequate for they readily agreed to the proposition and asked Mr. Medland, who was an auctioneer, to sell their 'New Rooms' by auction. The property made £315, which was applied to paying off the loan. Arrangements were made to hold their meetings in the new 'Public Rooms', and store their equipment in the yard and cellars there.

In 1839 came the first suggestion for introducing gas lighting in the town. A Mr. Malam proposed to erect gasworks provided that the commissioners would give him a contract for all the street lighting. The commissioners decided against the proposal and called a meeting of inhabitants to confirm their decision. The meeting was announced for Friday 6 December at 10 a.m. at the *Cross Keys*, (surely a place that could accommodate few people, and a time when few could attend). The result is not recorded, but presumably the decision was confirmed.

In 1842 a Mr. Baslow, of Stepney Green, wrote to propose erecting gasworks, and on attending in person was told that the commissioners would not entertain the idea at present.

In 1845 a report was received from a Mr. Culyer, agent to Mr. Atkins of Bicester, on lighting the town with gas, and an estimate of the probable cost. The commissioners resolved 'that it was desirable to light the town with gas, and that a meeting of inhabitants be called at the 'New Rooms' on 30 September'. The result must have been favourable for, on 24 April 1846, they met Thos. Smith Darnell and Saml. Fairey, directors of the new St. Neots Gas and Coke Co., who offered the following:

> To light as many public lamps, with burners not consuming less than 4 feet and not more than 5 feet per hour, as may be required of them; to burn for not exceeding 7 hours a night between 10 October and 24 March, except 6 nights before and one night after full moon; for a sum not exceeding £2 a lamp.

This offer was at once accepted. In 1841 Francis Rix died and was replaced by Thomas Smith Darnell. Besides being an original commissioner and the first treasurer he was a well-known local doctor and antiquarian. In 1844 William Day, the first clerk, resigned and was replaced by Samuel Day.

In 1843 it was decided to remove the old town pump from the Market Street, near the *Cross Keys*. The well serving this pump was rediscovered in the 1960s and filled in. It was found to be stone lined and was almost certainly medieval.

In January 1845 a meeting of inhabitants was called to support the commissioners in their opposition to a proposed new railway. The agenda item was, 'To consider and determine upon the best steps to be taken effectually to oppose the proposed Line of Railway from Ely to Bedford, which proposes making an embankment across St. Neots Common and Meadows as will Flood the Town and neighbourhood to a Ruinous Extent'. We are not told if it was the town's opposition, or for other reasons, that the scheme was abandoned.

In 1846 a meeting was held 'to consider the injury and danger arising from a Steam Mill, about to be erected by Henry Medlock, and the nuisance occasioned thereby, not only to the inhabitants resident in the immediate neighbourhood but to the town at large'. The site was in Back Lane, near the corner of New Street, and immediately adjoining the commissioners' New Rooms. It was resolved 'that the means of conducting water from the commissioners' sewer to the works, as now existing, be at once stopped, and that every means in the power of the commissioners, both as a body, and as individuals, be taken to stop further progress of the work. If the work be completed to cause the removal thereof by indictment or other proceedings at law'. A committee was to confer with owners and occupiers in the vicinity, and a copy of the resolution sent to John Medlock and his son Henry.

After taking these rather militant steps, the commissioners must have found that their legal powers were not as strong as they had thought for we next find them discussing with John Medlock the amount of compensation to be paid to him for removing his buildings. The final amount agreed was £120, of which £50 was found by the commissioners and the rest by neighbouring owners; the steam mill was then removed to Nutters Lane.

In 1847 the cost of lighting the town with gas was £96, and the roadmen were given a weekly increase of 1s. Cottagers in Duck Lane were ordered to cease their practice (a long-established medieval one) of throwing their slops out of doors on to the street. In the same year Snowdens, the ropemakers, were required to cease using Church Lane (Church Walk) as a ropewalk.

In 1851 the Corn Exchange was about to be built and the commissioners had various ideas as to its construction and use. They offered a rent of £40 for the ground floor, and the use of an ante-room for their meetings; the ground floor to be used as a fowl and butter market. This was rejected by the Corn Exchange Co.

In 1853 the commissioners agreed to make a footpath (pavement) from the end of the town to the junction with the Railway Company road to the new railway station, provided that the company continued the path to the station. Priory Road and Back Lane were accepted as public roads.

In 1854 there were serious public complaints as to the neglected state of the footpaths and road crossings. The surveyor and his scavengers were called in and cautioned to be more efficient, the wages of the scavengers being raised 2s. a week, 'in consideration of the high price of provisions and bad weather'. The work of John Shrives, the surveyor, continued to be unsatisfactory, and he resigned in 1855. Advertisements for a new surveyor produced no applicants.

The Nuisance Removal Act of 1855 produced another financial crisis. Under the Act the commissioners were required to appoint an Inspector of Nuisances. Thos. Smith Darnell was appointed, but continued to act as treasurer and collector, at £20 a year, and temporarily as surveyor, at £15 a year. The poor rate assessment, on which their own rating was based, was felt to be very inaccurate, and the overseers were asked to review it. As a further measure of economy the street lighting cost was reduced from £110 to £70 a year, and the services of the watchmen discontinued.

In 1857 the North Road Turnpike Trust declined to continue to pay £40 a year for the repair of their roads through the town, and offered £25, which was accepted.

In 1857 it was minuted, 'that in consequence of the gross irregularities of the men having conduct of the engine at the late fire at the *Cross Keys*, the Surveyor had decided to appoint an entirely new body of men'. Watering of the streets was discontinued as no money was available.

The attention of Mr. Peppercorn (Lord Sandwich's agent) was drawn in 1859 to the state of the pound, with a request that it be repaired. Finally the commissioners found the labour and he the material. The pound was next to the near Common Gate, on the east side.

In 1859 another serious financial blow occurred when Thos. Smith Darnell, then acting as treasurer, rate collector, nuisance inspector, and surveyor, made a deed of assignment to his creditors and was found to owe the commissioners £250 for rates collected. He attended a meeting and stated that he had neither funds nor friends to help him, and no chance existed of any payment. Darnell finally paid 1s. 6d. in the pound.

New officers appointed in 1859 were Francis Maddison, as surveyor and rate collector, and Frederick Emery (bank manager) as treasurer. To accept this office the latter had to resign as a commissioner. The scavengers' wages were again raised by 1s., and street watering was stopped.

In 1861 Mr. Medland asked that the tenancy of the cellars under the public rooms be given up, and suggested that the old 'Lockup' in the High Street (the site is now no. 14) might be used to store the water cart, lamps etc. The 'Lockup' was no longer used as a prison since the police station had been built in New Street. On enquiry Mr. Peppercorn stated that he was not aware that the lord of the manor had any interest in the lockup, and it was therefore adapted to its new use.

In 1862 T. Gale and James May were appointed pinders (pound keepers) to prevent cattle straying on the streets, but next year Richard Barker, the new Superintendent of Police, was made pinder.

In 1867 the owners and occupiers of the east side of the Market Square subscribed £20 towards the total cost of £22 15s., to have Caithness stone used on their pavement.

Each year handbills were being printed for distribution warning against bonfires and fireworks on the streets on 5 November.

In 1869 the Petroleum Act came into force, and in 1870 applications to store petroleum were received. Those granted were Messrs. Barford and Mole, three barrels each of 20 gallons, Mr. Fisher, six barrels of 36 gallons, and John Lynn, one barrel.

In 1870 it was thought necessary to warn that persons playing hockey or other games in the streets were liable to a fine of 40s.

In the same year Saml. Day resigned as clerk and was elected a commissioner in place of C. R. Wade Gery, who resigned to become clerk.

In 1872 East Street was accepted as a public highway and given lamps. In this year too the country began to be concerned with public health with the passage of a Public Health

Act. Under this the commissioners became an Urban Sanitary Authority and had to subscribe £10 a year towards the £800 a year salary of a County Medical Officer of Health. At the same time they expressed concern at the sanitary conditions in the parish and their view that Eynesbury should now be included in their area. A letter was received from the Local Government Board stating that they would consider an application to repeal the 'Act of 39 George II, St. Neots', if accompanied by a map showing the proposed boundaries of a new district. The commissioners agreed to do this, thus taking the first step towards their own extinction.

In 1874 Francis Maddison asked to be allowed to resign as rate collector but remain as surveyor. However it was decided that the offices could not be separated, and he resigned both. John Martin was then appointed nuisance inspector, rate collector, and surveyor at a salary of £40 a year. At the same time the following new bye-laws were passed:

1. No field pipe to be used for polluted water, only glazed pipes of not less than four inches diameter.
2. Foul drains from houses to be trapped and ventilated.
3. No cesspools to be made where they can be avoided.
4. Water closets only to be put in with the approval of the Sanitary Authority.
5. Privies, *ditto*.
6. Ashpits, *ditto*.
7. No new buildings to be erected before plans had been submitted.

Another very important step was taken this year when G. S. Bower, a very progressive commissioner, was authorised to see a Mr. Hennell with a view to preparing a scheme for waterworks and sanitary drainage of the town.

Mr. Hennell, in his report dated 1874, first reported on the present state of the town, and it was, to our ears, very alarming. Some extracts are given below:

There is no sewerage, properly so called, i.e. no drains intended for the passage of excremental or other foul matter.

There is a main drain through the town from east to west of ample dimension with an inlet at its commencement from the brook near Green End, and so is well flushed after every considerable fall of rain.

There are drains of about 200 yards in length in Huntingdon Street, and 66 yards in Church Street (not flushed) and a cesspool under the street at the junction of the three drains. These are the only

drains of considerable size in the district. There are smaller surface
drains under most other streets, mostly merely a brick on each side
with one laid flat on top. Many of these are quite blocked up and
merely spread the liquid to soak away, in many places.

The provision made for excremental matter throughout the town is
by cesspools. A few of these, belonging to the better class of houses,
are constructed so as to be watertight, or nearly so, and provided
with overflows to the main drains. The majority are built of bricks
in mortar, or partly dry, and merely retain the solids, leaving the
liquids to percolate freely into the soil.

In the case of houses on the south side of the Market Place, and in
Brook Street, the sewage passes directly, or almost directly, into
the Brook; other sewage goes into the Ouse at River Terrace and the
Priory.

With regard to water, the present supply is entirely from private wells
sunk in gravel. In the southern part of the town however, it appears
that there is an intermediate stratum of clay, and that some of the
wells pass through this into gravel below; these may yield water of
fair average quality.

The majority being in gravel of no great depth are necessarily con-
taminated with anything that soaks in at the surface.

In New Street, Russell Row, Huntingdon Street, and elsewhere, wells
and cesspools are often close together and there is practically no drainage; all liquid matter sinks almost directly into a subsoil whence water
is drawn.

I was shown houses where there were cases of typhoid fever and should
be surprised if it be ever long absent while such a state of things
continues.

Mr. Hennell also produced a scheme for a new sewerage
system and a piped water supply for the town, to cost £6,000,
which could be borrowed at three and a half per cent from the
Public Works Loan Board. The commissioners ordered that his
whole report be printed and distributed to ratepayers.

The next step taken was to call a town meeting to discuss the
proposals. At this there was almost unanimous opposition to the
scheme by leading tradesmen and property owners, including
Mr. Peppercorn and Mr. Toogood; in fact, at the meeting only
Mr. Bowker spoke in favour. The idea was therefore shelved.

A new blow to the commissioners' finances was the expiry
of the St. Neots and Cambridge Turnpike Road Act, which
threw on them the upkeep of about three miles of road,
indeed they had immediately to buy 70 tons of Mountsorrel
granite for the length of Station Road to the Cross.

Meanwhile urgent letters were being sent to the Local Government Board to have the 1819 Act repealed, as it was quite impossible for the commissioners to carry out their statutory duties on the product of a 1s. 6d. rate. They also strongly urged that any new authority formed should include in its district both Eynesbury and Eaton Socon. There was however great opposition to this both at Eynesbury and Eaton Socon. The efforts at last bore fruit and a Provisional Order was received setting up a Local Board, to include Eynesbury but not Eaton Socon.

The last meeting of the commissioners was held on 19 September 1876. At this Mr. Wade Gery, the clerk, was voted 40 guineas for his extra work in connection with the Provisional Order. Mr. Martin the surveyor had proved unsatisfactory and was given the alternative of resigning or receiving notice. He claimed, however, that he could not be dismissed until 1877, and asked for extra salary for work on the roads taken over from the turnpike trusts. He was given £5.

All the vehicles and stock in trade belonging to the commissioners were handed over to the new Local Board together with a cash deficiency of £37.

The Local Board

The election, in 1876, for the first members of the new Local Board caused little excitement in St. Neots and Eynesbury, although Eynesbury felt rather apprehensive as a numerically inferior partner, only ratepayers were eligible to vote. Altogether 36 candidates were nominated for the 12 seats, and the election was spread over three days. Those elected, with their votes, were as below:

James Brown	630	Joseph Wilcox	483	D. R. Tomson	386
Wm. Paine	551	James Paine	445	George Bower	364
Rev. Maule	495	Samuel Wright	405	Ed. Squire	358
Samuel Day	484	W. H. Hall	402	H. Harvey	346

The Board unanimously elected G. Bower as chairman, and repeated this for the next 12 years. Retirement of members was staggered, to the extent of four members every three years. Mr. Wade Gery was appointed clerk, Mr. Emery, treasurer and Mr. Martin, surveyor. The committees were 'Financial and Assessment', 'Sanitary' and 'Highways, Paving and Lighting'.

In 1877 the population of the area was 4,598, and a rate of 1s. produced £553.

While the new board seems to have carried on the town's affairs with reasonable efficiency, for example, gas street lighting was immediately extended to Eynesbury, they seem to have done little to improve health standards in spite of the efforts of their chairman. Many members were house owners whose chief concern was to keep down the rates and avoid having forced on them improvements that would not bring in greater rents.

In 1885 a government inspector visited the town and, after warning the board to prepare for a possible cholera outbreak, visited some of the small properties. He found and reported not only appalling conditions in the older houses, but the bye-laws being disregarded in new houses being built. Some examples are:

> *Day's Court* [probably off south east end of High Street]. The court badly paved, the cottages dilapidated, no windows in the bedrooms except looking into the court. In the court are foul privy pits, a few years ago these were converted to earth closets, but were again altered back to privy pits. No accommodation for scavenging.
>
> *Rowley's Court, Huntingdon Street* [probably immediately north of the *Limes*]. Similar conditions as in Day's Court. Some of the cottages have floors below ground level which are damp, upstairs rooms are only five feet high, and drain gullies are defective.
>
> *East Street* New houses have had drains laid in unsocketed pipes and as a result sewer gas is escaping into some of the houses. Privy vaults in the gardens are only emptied every six months. Houses now in course of construction have unsocketed and unventilated drain pipes, and wells dug only 12 feet from their privy pits.
>
> Everywhere nuisances are being allowed to be perpetrated, and people are really drinking their own excrement. Many slaughter-houses should never have been licensed in their present state. It is essential that the town should have a public water supply. He had to admit that the present death rate was a low one, but in the last month of 1880 there were 30 cases of typhoid in the town.

The report had a hostile reception at a meeting of the board, almost the only member expressing agreement with it was the chairman, G. S. Bower.

In 1884 the board ordered that all houses be numbered. This did not, apparently, proceed very fast, for in 1887 it was reported that 22 people in East Street had refused to have numbers on their doors.

In 1887 there was a further visit and report from a Local Government Board inspector, in which the Local Board were plainly told that they should at once order that all privy pits, cesspools, and middens be removed, and a pail system be adopted to prevent soakage. Pails to be emptied at least once a week. All yards to be paved and traps put on all gullies.

It is interesting to note that in 1892 the Board decided to support the Local Boards Association in opposing the National Telephone Co. Bill to give them the power to erect poles and put in underground cables in any district. In the same year the market was hired from Lord Sandwich for £25, and a rate of 1s. 9d. levied, producing £1,056.

In 1893 they were involved in an issue that roused the town. This concerned a public footpath, known as Shady Walk, that started from Cemetery Lane, heading in a northerly direction to cross Cambridge Street and Avenue Road, and entered the Rowley Estate along the end of the present Kings Road. From this point it turned north east, across two fields, until it reached the outside of the Priory Park fence and then followed round the fence, along the line of the ancient St. Ives Way, to the Priory Hill road. From this road another public footpath crossed Hawkesden Leys Common to Toseland.

This path was obviously much disliked by the Rowley family at Priory Hill as it gave the public the right to walk near their house and park, and was probably an easy access for trespassers and poachers. As a result Mr. Fydell Rowley asked the Board if they had any objection to the path being diverted, from a point at the south end of the Lime Avenue, east along a hedge line to the railway, and then north along the west side of the railway to the public road. The Local Board members all agreed, except Mr. Elgood, and permission was given.

This decision at once produced letters of protest in the press claiming that the new footpath offered was already an ancient right of way to Loves Farm, across the railway.

The next dramatic move was by Mr. Amos Abraham who sued the Local Board at Quarter Sessions for giving permission to close the old path illegally. He claimed that people from Yelling, Gravely and Toseland used the path to get to St. Neots

market. Wm. Wills of Toseland gave evidence that he used to
go to chapel that way, and John T. Bull that the short route
was important when he had to carry seven gallons of milk
from Hawkesden Leys. Several people from Yelling also gave
evidence of their use of the path. Mr. Abraham also produced
a petition of protest with 1,000 signatures. The jury at Quarter
Sessions found against the Local Board.

However Mr. Rowley was still unwilling to admit defeat,
and, no doubt after legal advice, started a new legal process
to get his way. This took the form of the Local Board calling
a public meeting in the Corn Exchange, early in 1894, to try
to get a vote for the proposal. The meeting was a rowdy one,
and among many speakers Mr. Joseph Wright (the antiquarian)
reiterated that what was being offered was already a public
path, and he remembered that when the railway line was built
steps and a stile were provided to cross it to Loves Farm. The
result was an almost unanimous rejection of the proposal. The
matter was then dropped but bitterness on all sides remained
for a long time.

The Local Board had great hopes of getting a water supply
for the town from the East Hunts. Water Co., with wells at
Old North Road Station, who offered a supply in bulk at 6d.
per 1,000 gallons. However the water proved deficient in quality and quantity, and the offer had to be withdrawn.

The Local Board, most of whose meetings were held in the
Magistrates Court Room in New Street, came to an end in
1894 with the transfer of its authority to an Urban District
Council, which took office on 1 January 1895.

The Urban District Council

Although this afterwards became its name, it was known at
first as the St. Neots and Eynesbury District Council. At the
first election 33 candidates contested 13 seats and all electors
now had a vote. Those listed below, with the votes they received,
were elected.

T. Ellwood	314	W. Carter	207	D. R. Tomson	181
I. Hall	246	S. Hinsby	203	G. Brown	178
J. Wright	244	S. Huckle	201	A. W. Barker	178
Rev. Hodgson	212	C. Malden	185	P. Lovitt	176
G. Flawn	207				

It was interesting that the new council exercised their right to elect, as chairman, a non-elected member of the council, namely John McNish, and continued to use the Magistrates' Court Room for their meetings. The following committees were set up: 'Finance and Assessment', 'Buildings', 'Sanitary', 'Highways, Lighting, Watering and Tolls', and 'General Purposes'. Mr. Wade Gery remained as the clerk and Mr. Jackson as surveyor.

The pressing need in the district was for a piped water supply, but the council were in no hurry to move. In 1896 a 'further letter' on the subject from the Local Government Board was ordered to 'lie on the table', although at the same meeting they agreed to install a fountain on the Market Square, with water from a well at Paine & Co.'s yard. Meanwhile parliamentary agents enquired of the council if they intended to construct waterworks themselves, and if not a private company were considering a Bill to do so. The council replied that they had no intention of undertaking such a project. In view of this reply the St. Neots Water Co. Bill was drawn up and submitted to the council for their observations, which were almost all hostile or critical. Indeed they engaged counsel to oppose the Bill and did their best to get it thrown out. Part of the objection was to the site of the proposed wells (the present waterworks site west of the Little Barford road). They maintained, in the face of much expert advice to the contrary, that these would be polluted from the river, and from manure on the surrounding fields. Their bitter opposition did not prevent the Bill passing, but they did get a clause inserted reducing the capital of the company from £12,000 to £9,000 and an option compulsorily to take over the company at the end of two years, on payment of their costs plus 10 per cent. The Bill was passed in 1898, after heavy legal costs to both the Council and the company.

As a result of all this the company got off to a bad start, in spite of finding an excellent water supply at their wells, and the council, in the opinion of many people, continued a policy of harassment against them in revenge for their victory in Parliament, which added greatly to their capital costs. A pumping station was erected at their wells on the Little Barford road and water was pumped to a reservoir above the town on the road to Gamlingay. From this mains were laid all over the town area. In 1899 the new waterworks were ceremonially opened, the U.D.C. refusing to take any part or attend.

It is difficult at this length of time to form judgement on the motives of the U.D.C., but the writer has heard of the supposed prejudice of members who were large property owners, and who wished to put off supplying their cottages with water. This, they thought, would inevitably lead to sewerage improvements also, to be compulsorily imposed. An even meaner motive suggested was that if the Water Company could be driven into bankruptcy the Council could take over the undertaking at a cheap rate. Confirmation of this could be surmised in their strenuous opposition, in 1899, when the Water Company wished to promote a further Bill to increase their capital by £6,000 and extend their area of supply to include Eaton Socon, Roxton, and Little Barford.

About 1906 what some people had perhaps hoped for happened. The St. Neots Water Company went into liquidation, and was taken over by the U.D.C.

One interest of the U.D.C., that does not seem to have survived, was in the town charities. In 1896 a committee reported that the Joan Cromwell, Hugh Wise, J. Dryden, Joseph Eayre, E. Smith, and Mary Musgrove charities (recorded on the charity board in the church) appeared to be non-ecclesiastical, and they appointed two members, to act with the vicar, as trustees to administer them.

V
LAW AND ORDER

AT THE BEGINNING of the 19th century the Justices of the Peace, mainly local squires and clergy, had, besides their duties of law enforcement, great power in both county and local administration. Sitting at Quarter Sessions they administered all county affairs and had locally to approve the running of the Poor Law. This latter power was mainly lost to them in the 1840s, but it was not until 1870 that the first county councils took over county administration from Quarter Sessions. Thereafter until the end of the century, with a few exceptions, the duties of J.P.s were almost entirely confined to dealing with breaches of the criminal law.

The criminal law itself saw great changes throughout the century. In 1815 the death penalty could still be imposed for 220 offences. However for many of them the consciences of judges, and the refusal of juries to convict, made its application rare. Reforms came slowly and even in 1808 Parliament, while reducing the penalty for pickpocketing from hanging to transportation for life, refused to repeal the Act imposing death for stealing 5s. from a shop. It was not until 1832 that the crimes of housebreaking, sheep stealing, and forgery ceased to be capital offences.

Law Enforcement

'T' tells us that about 1820 the only magistrates in the Toseland Petty Sessions Division functioning were Ousley Rowley of Priory Hill and Rev. Palmer of Eynesbury, and that they held a court at the house of Mr. Wells the attorney at Eynesbury (probably Church House, 3 Berkeley Street). Later it was held at the clerk's office (that of Wilkinson and Butler) at the Cross, St. Neots, until the court in New Street was built about 1856.

About 1850, when local newspapers started to appear, court cases began to be reported, and from that time it would appear that sentences on adult offenders were not usually unreasonably harsh. An exception was a man sent to prison, in 1888, for stealing two turnips, which he claimed were all he had for his Sunday dinner. It is also a little surprising to read that, as late as 1897, a man fined 20s. for disorderly conduct was ordered to be put on the treadmill at Cambridge Jail for failing to pay his fine.

It is in reading how the St. Neots justices dealt with children that one is now most shocked. A few examples will illustrate this.

In 1864 two children, aged 11 and eight and a half, were convicted of stealing a muff, a shawl, and other oddments. They were sent to jail for 21 days. In 1870 three boys, aged 14, 15 and 16, were caught stealing sweets from Wildman's shop in St. Mary's Street, Eynesbury, and were sent to jail for six weeks' hard labour. The worst example happened in 1875 when a girl of 13, from Yelling, was charged with stealing two oranges, 43 marbles, eight thimbles, a length of ribbon, and a piece of cake, from a shop. She was one of a family of six with no mother. She was sent to reformatory for five years to be preceded by a month in jail.

The Police

It is difficult now to realise that until the middle of the 19th century there were no police, as we now know them, anywhere except in London. Law and order were only enforced by the parish constables and in some places, as at St. Neots, the night watchmen. The parish constables were private citizens, elected annually at the vestry meeting, and if they were unable to cope with any disorder it was clearly understood by everyone that they could call on all able-bodied citizens to assist them. If trouble was really serious the army could be called in. Arrested persons were temporarily placed by them in the local lockup. In St. Neots this was in the High Street. For certain minor offences prisoners could be put in the stocks or whipped at the whipping post. These were on the east side of the churchyard in St. Neots, and at Eynesbury near the north churchyard gate.

The first police, as a full-time professional body, were formed by Sir Robert Peel in 1829, but were for London only. The idea was not copied in the counties until about mid-century.

The first Huntingdonshire County Police Force seems to have been founded in 1848, and the Police Station and Magistrates Courts opened in New Street about 1856, followed by the retirement of Chas. Sibley, the head parish constable. The first constables wore white duck trousers.

The railway was then being built and one of their first duties was to deal with the large influx of railway navvies. On one occasion 20 navvies were caught poaching on the Croxton estate and, after being charged at the Court (at Wilkinson and Butler's office), were sent by wagon to Huntingdon Jail. The police then learnt that a large body of their mates had set out to intercept the wagon and rescue the prisoners. This attempt was foiled by sending the wagon round by Eltisley. Greater mobility was gained when bicycles were issued in 1898.

Private Protection

Crime was said to have increased after the disbandment of the armies following the Battle of Waterloo in 1815, and many people in country districts felt the need for greater protection than that provided by the authorities. This led, in Huntingdonshire and elsewhere, to bodies, such as local landowners, forming their own Local Defence Association. These offered mutual defence against crime, help in prosecutions, and rewards for information. (See Eynesbury Hardwick Farm, below.)

Even after the formation of the county police force these associations were still thought to be necessary. In 1873, for instance, a Huntingdonshire Farmers' Defence Force was advertised, mainly in fear of violence from striking agricultural labourers. In 1880, due to pilfering from gardens and allotments, the Eynesbury Garden Protection Society was formed. Members paid a subscription of a halfpenny a week and held an annual dinner. One garden owner, however, tried out the effectiveness of putting up a notice, as follows: 'God helps those who help themselves, but God help those that I catch helping themselves from my garden'.

VI
HOUSING AND SANITARY CONDITIONS

THE HOUSES of the upper middle class, in the 19th century, were always well appointed and comfortable, even if somewhat cold in winter by present day standards. There were plenty of servants to bring in coal for fires and hot water for baths. Gas became available in 1846 and was used mainly for lighting.

Soon after the Town Commissioners were appointed in 1816 they ordered the laying of new main sewers in the town which discharged direct into the river at the bridge. It was probable that not long before that there were still open sewerage ditches along each side of the High Street.

Water was never a problem as most of the town is built on water-bearing gravels in the Ouse flood plain. All the middle class houses had their own shallow wells and pumps. The lower class were served by public pumps, set at intervals about the town, from which water had to be fetched by pails. It was not until 1899 that a private company made piped water available, after the U.D.C. had successfully delayed the scheme for several years.

The means by which sewage was conveyed from the houses to the main sewer was the most serious health risk. Cesspits were seldom waterproof and connections to the sewer mains were by porous unglazed and unsocketed field pipes. Both cesspits and drains were often quite close to the drinking water well and the ground between saturated with sewage.

For centuries, no doubt, people, and particularly children, had died of water-borne diseases; and they continued to do so throughout the 19th century. Why more did not die can only be explained by a natural immunity that must have been acquired by the survivors, over many generations. Such evidence as we have comes only from the latter half of the century. Hennell, in his report on the town in 1874, mentions typhoid being present in the Russell Street, New Street, and Huntingdon Street area, where there was almost no drainage fall to the sewers, and implies that it was endemic in that area. In that same year the vital statistics showed that 43 per cent of all deaths were of children under ten. At one time, in 1880, there were 30 cases of typhoid in the town. There was an outbreak of smallpox in 1895, and the school log books covering this period record the deaths of many young children.

The compulsory appointment of local Medical Officers of Health, towards the end of the century, did much to improve health, but they had an uphill battle against the prejudices of the local councils and the non-enforcement of health bye-laws. Perhaps the greatest direct advance, affecting the lower and lower middle classes, was the formation of a District Nursing Association, which included Eaton Socon, in 1898. In the first year £100 was raised by subscriptions, and Mrs. Fydell Rowley of Priory Hill was appointed chairman. Under the scheme poor households could have home nursing in return for a minimum subscription of 2d. a month. A succession of dedicated nurses gave devoted service in the district.

Housing

The housing conditions of the lower classes throughout the century, were, to modern eyes, one of the most disgraceful sides to Victorian life. This was partly due to the fact that lower class house property was the favourite investment of the lower middle class. They built, or bought, the long terraces of low standard houses each consisting of 'two up and two down' with a detached washhouse and earth closet at the back but with, of course, no bathroom or indoor sanitation. Russell Street, St. Neots and Luke Street, Eynesbury were typical examples. There were also 'courts', even smaller and slummier houses built round a central court.

Eynesbury too had its problems of overcrowding. In 1870 it was reported that a father, a son aged 16, and two daughters aged 14 and 20, were all sleeping in one room on beds of straw with a cover of ticking and no blankets. In another house five people were sleeping in a room of eight by ten feet and only five and a half feet high.

The Homeless

The plight of homeless families could be grim. What must have been an extreme case occurred in late October 1874, and was reported in the local press. John Walton, who had been to jail several times for failing to support his children and whose eldest son had been sent to an Industrial School, had been ordered by the court to contribute 1s. a week towards his son's maintenance. He had left the district and had not been seen for two or three weeks. On Sunday he, with the two children and the woman with whom he co-habited, left St. Ives workhouse, where they had stayed as casual paupers, and walked to Eynesbury. They arrived too late to be admitted to the workhouse, and could find no lodgings. They spent the night in the porch of the *Dog and Duck* inn.

The next morning they ate a small quantity of bread which they had begged, and walked about the streets. A relative in the town gave them some refreshment at dinner time. Returning to Eynesbury the man, goaded by misery and desperation, and fearful of being again apprehended for not paying for his son's maintenance, decided to end his existence. With his last 2d. he bought some beer, which he shared with his children and the woman, and proceeded to the river. After taking off his cap and jacket he jumped in. At this spot it was only three feet deep so he lay down, with his head under water, and drowned. The woman, although standing only four feet away, made no attempt to save him and chided the children for 'knocking up such a row', saying 'he is dead now and was very little good when he was living'.

He was buried in Eynesbury cemetery and a portion of the burial service was read, omitting 'in the sure and certain hope of the resurrection to eternal life'. The body was not taken into the church.

Tramps

Tramps were a common sight on all main roads before 1914, sometimes solitary and sometimes in small bands. They chose the routes where workhouses could be reached in a day's march, for they were only allowed to stay for one night. In the morning they had to do some work, such as stone-breaking, before being allowed to leave. Part of the day they spent in begging for money with which to buy beer; the offer of food was often rejected. It was said that they marked, with secret signs, the gateways of houses to denote the kind of reception likely to be met there. A total of 871 tramps were admitted to St. Neots workhouse in 1898.

Public Charity

It would seem that towards the end of the century the condition of the poor began to arouse greater sympathy. For instance in 1888, a year of widespread unemployment and distress, a concert was given to raise money, and a soup kitchen provided. In the same year indignant letters appeared in the local press following the death, from starvation and neglect, of an old woman at Stonely. An officer from the Guardians had visited her but refused relief on the grounds that she was too ill to be moved to the workhouse.

Another unusual story of what could happen to the poor came from the obituary notice of the death of 'Long Robin', who died in the workhouse in 1887. He was actually born in the pesthouse in 1804, his real name was Robert Linford and he was six feet tall. He married a Miss Ayres from a cottage in Bell Yard, South Street, but deserted her and enlisted in the Guards. Soon he deserted from the army and returned to St. Neots, but was arrested and after the subsequent court martial was flogged so severely that he carried the deep wound scars to his grave. After discharge from the army he again rejoined but again deserted and for this second offence was transported to Australia for 14 years.

For some years he corresponded with friends in St. Neots but this ceased and for many years they heard nothing. A visit of the Duke of Edinburgh to the colony reminded him of home and he again wrote to a Samuel Page of St. Neots who, with others of his still faithful friends, collected enough money to pay his passage back. On his return to St. Neots, now an old man, he was paid an allowance of 7s. a week by his sister. However, he drifted into bad ways and the allowance was stopped, forcing him to spend the last 10 years of his life in the workhouse. A terrible scar on his head was the result of a boomerang thrown at him by an Australian aborigine.

VII
SCHOOLS

St. Neots Church of England School

The origins of this school, once known as the Charity School, go back very far, possibly to before the Dissolution, for we know that there was once a school at St. Neots Priory. Gorham says that a charity school was held in the Jesus Chapel of St. Neots church from the Reformation until 1745, when the chapel was thrown open to the north aisle, and the school presumably moved elsewhere.

The Jesus Chapel was once the property of the Guild of Jesus, and had belonging to it a number of local properties, to provide for its endowment and maintenance. These were all seized by the Crown during the reign of Edward VI. At that time it was not uncommon for such assets to be used to found a grammar school, although no evidence has come to light that this was done at St. Neots. However there is evidence that there was a grammar school and, according to Gorham, that it was held in the Jesus Chapel. In 1556 one Faucet was both priest and schoolmaster at St. Neots, and two well-known brothers, John and Francis White (1570-1615), sons of the vicar of Eaton Socon and St. Neots, are recorded as being educated at St. Neots Grammar School. The first became Bishop of Ely, and the second chaplain to James I.

That the school continued is proved by £20 being allowed out of church property to pay a schoolmaster, during the Commonwealth in 1658.

A hundred years later a St. Neots man, Loftus Hatley, who died in 1757, left by his will £40 to be used to educate poor children who were constant attenders at divine service. Later his son Richard, who died in 1789, left in his will £400 to produce annually £10 towards the pay of a schoolmaster and £10 12s. 6d. for clothing for seven poor boys from St. Neots and three from Eynesbury.

In 1760 there died in Leicester Alderman Newton who, although he had no apparent connection with Huntingdonshire, left money to a number of schools there. St. Neots was one of these, and the minister and churchwardens were to receive, annually, £26 out of lands in Leicester 'for the clothing, schooling, and educating of 25 boys of indigent and necessitous parents of the Established Church, between the ages of 7 and 14 years'. He goes on to specify that the clothing shall consist of green jackets, breeches, and waistcoats. The actual outfit supplied has been described as a jacket and breeches in a green baize kind of cloth, pale blue stockings, green 'Tam o'Shanter' hat with a red tassel, and a green waistcoat with brass buttons. The school thus became known as Green Coat School.

The intentions of the donor were no doubt good and fitting in the 18th century, but a hundred years later the 'green linnets', as they were nicknamed, were singled out in their uniforms as 'charity boys' and objects of ridicule. There is a record of 25 green suits made to contract by Chapman, a tailor of Eynesbury, in 1872, at 26s. 6d. each. In 1888 the Ministry of Education gave the school managers permission for the money to be used instead in grants to students and apprentices to buy books and tools. However the memory of the 'green linnets' lingered on, and the author has heard people, with some green in their clothing, so described.

A headmaster of the school, in 1784, was John Bewsher, M.A. He was also the curate and as schoolmaster he was paid £10 a year. He was appointed vicar of St. Neots in 1796 and died in 1806 aged 54.

The benefits that the school was to receive from the Alderman Newton Charity were for a long time in doubt as, after a number of payments had been paid, the heir at law tried to prove that the will was invalid. As a result between 1780 and 1803 payment was withheld. Accumulated arrears amounting to £598 were paid in 1803, and this sum was used to build a schoolhouse on land in Church Walk and buy the conveniently-near medieval timber-framed house at the north corner of Church Walk for the headmaster.

'Townborn' remembered James Wise, who was headmaster and living here in the first two decades of the 18th century.

He used part of the house to take in boarders. He was notorious as a stern disciplinarian and would chain boys to their desks as a punishment. On one occasion their friends smuggled in a file with which they released themselves.

Whatever accommodation was provided in 1803 was very soon found to be inadequate, and even after the building of the Girls and Infants School in Huntingdon Street, in 1840, there was gross overcrowding. In 1853 the churchwardens were again receiving rent for the use of the Jesus Chapel, and it seems probable that this was once more used as a school.

Either new, or additional, premises were brought into use in Church Walk in 1860, but the headmaster's log book still records overcrowding, as well as lack of both heating and ventilation, up to the end of the century, although another classroom was added in 1883.

Some extracts from the log book are given below. These books are now fortunately preserved in the County Record Office, and provide one of the most valuable MS. records not only of schooling but of social and health conditions, and life generally in the late 19th century.

1865	*St. Neots Charity and National School. Walter Cooper Headmaster.*
29 Jun. '63	Cricket Match on the Common Kept many boys away.
18 Feb. '64	A 1st class boy presented with a nomination to a Probationry Clerkship on the Gt. Northern Railway.
3 Mar. '64	Headmaster's birthday. Allowed boys 10 minutes extra play.
19 Sep. '64	New scale of payment came into force.
	Each boy whose parents are rated at £15 or upwards. 10s. qrtrly.
	Each boy whose parents are rated at £10 and under £15 7s. 6d. qrtrly.
	Each boy whose parents are rated at under £10. 5s. qrtrly. Sons of labourers as before 2d. weekly.
7 Jan. '67	James Bennett commenced duties as Headmaster.
1 Apl. '67	All Fools Day, boys troublesome.
14 Oct. '67	Night School opened.
9 Feb. '69	Shrove Tuesday, half holiday.
16 Dec. '70	Boys allowed to see performance of Punch and Judy in the playground.
29 May '71	Royal Oak Day, half holiday. Some boys went to a cricket match and others to see the 1st H.R.V.C. at Battalion Drill on the Common.
2 Oct. '71	Scarlet fever prevalent in the town (lasted until Jan. 1872).
2 Feb. '72	Outbreak of smallpox.

20 May '72	Whit Monday. Very poor school, owing to visit of His Grace the Duke of Manchester's Light Horse for their Annual Drill.
5 May '73	Little boy taken ill typhoid fever.
2 Jun. '73	Another death from typhoid fever.
29 Sep. '73	Taleur and Hutchinsons circus interfered with school, also visit of Mr. Spurgeon.
22 Jun. '74	Capital school this week, 144 on Monday. One boy walked from Buckden.
7 Jun. '75	School poorer in numbers this week owing to hay harvest, corn weeding and wet weather.
14 Jun. '75	Small pox in the family of a boy attending school. Boy not allowed to attend during the illness of his sister. Disease caughts from filthy rags at the Paper Mill.
26 July '75	School much lower last week owing to heavy floods in various parts of the town. Green End, Eaton Ford, Common cut off from the town.
25 Oct. '75	School empty on Friday on account of floods. Water very deep in Market Square, High Street, Cambridge Street impassable, also Eaton Ford, Russell Row, Brookside, and Duck Lane.
15 Nov. '75	Obliged to cancel attendances p.m. to allow children to get home. Town flooded again.
21 Feb. '76	Many boys all coughs and colds, whooping cough prevalent. Outbreak typhoid fever.
16 Oct. '76	Boys who have been at work very troublesome. 40 boys in night school.
18 Dec. '76	School not so good except on Break-up Day. Each child received a present of nuts and an orange. Boys gave an entertainment on 21st and prizes were distributed in the Corn Exchange.
18 Jun. '77	School spoilt for past week by marriage festivities of Miss Day.
11 Oct. '77	Reported case of a Free boy, who left three months ago and refused to give up last new suit of clothing. Order made for instant return, or proceedings will be taken.
5 Nov. '77	Five 1st class boys stayed away to take round a Guy Fawkes.
14 Jan. '78	Good school. Too full. More than 20 above accommodating space of school. 190 present out of 196 on books.
13 Feb. '78	Mr. Watts, Sanitary Officer called with printed notices for houses and children infected with fever. Such instruction much needed here, e.g. a fortnight ago a woman kept her two eldest boys at school for some days although their younger brother was dangerously ill with scarlet fever. Another case was that of a woman who admitted 12 day scholars to view the corpse of her child who had died after eight days illness of fever.
29 Apl. '78	Crowded school this week. Heat unbearable. Worked one class outdoors.

---

24 Jun. '78   School excessively hot this week. 90° registered in cupboard in coolest corner.

29 May '79   Stopped boys bringing nettles to sting those without oak. [Oak Apple Day celebrated the Restoration, and Charles II's escape in the oak.]

2 Jun. '79   Whitmonday. Headmaster took number of boys to London, and Regents Park Zoological Gardens.

4 Aug. '79   Bank Holiday. Poor school a.m., 70 boys absent. Many kept away through floods which entered houses to depth several feet, roads impassable in many places. Caused by terrific thunderstorm from 9.30 p.m. Sat. to 4 a.m. Sun. School premises flooded.

1 Dec. '79   School not full owing to skating on the Common.

31 May '80   School not so full. Many boys left for work. Great relief to have comfortable school as regards numbers.

9 Aug. '80   Excursion to Skegness. Upwards of 40 boys went with their parents.

8. Oct. '80   School closed on account of floods. Water in nearly every street. Omnibus could not run to the station in the evening, as the water reached to the knees of the inside passengers.

15 Nov. '80   Mumps and typhoid fever among children, owing to flood water in the houses.

6 Dec. '80   Typhoid fever thinning the school. 18 cases opposite the premises in High Street.

8 Oct. '83   Good numbers, but many stay away through lack of room, used master's house as school room for two Standards.

30 Jun. '84   Frederick Harrison takes charge of this school (St. Neots Boys Free) today.

13 Oct. '85   Many boys late owing to some Nigger Minstrels in the street.

13 Feb. '88   Gave notice no children need come for next six weeks. Fever on school premises.

13 Jan. '94   School closed Thursday and Friday owing to streets flooded from the Cross to half way up to Market Hill.

12 Jan. '95   Many boys away with whooping cough, skating kept many away Friday afternoon.

20 Mar. '95   A tremendous hurricane having blown many trees down, kept many boys away 'sticking' on Monday.

14 Sep. '95   Liberal Fête kept many away.

11 July '96   Closed school on Thursday owing to very severe storm and heavy rain. Streets and many houses flooded.

26 Jun. '97   School closed on Tuesday for H.M. Queen Victoria's Jubilee, which was celebrated by a dinner to those over 60, and a tea to all children over four and under 15, with sports and other amusements. Each child received one 1897 sixpence.

19 Feb. 1900   All streets flooded, children unable to get to school.

3 Mar. 1900   Closed school on Friday p.m. in celebration of 'Relief of Ladysmith'.

1 July '05	The Headmaster, having completed 21 years service in this school, entertained the boys to tea at 5.30, followed by a gramophone and magic lantern entertainment. The Vicar, on behalf of the Managers, children, and Teachers presented him with a gold chain in memory of the occasion.
28 May '10	Poor attendance on Tuesday p.m. owing to May Day celebrations at Eaton Socon.
29 July '11	Very hot week. School over 80°. Last Friday 87°.
12 Feb. '14	Lovely weather. Attendance good. School closed on account of a menagerie.

James Bennett was an outstanding headmaster, who died in 1885, a year after his retirement. Some readers will remember his daughter as the wife of Thomas Spencer, solicitor. At an inspection in 1870 there were at his school 140 boys, aged seven to 15, taught by one certificated and one assistant master, with three pupil teachers. The 85 girls (the number had risen from 50 in one year) had one certificated mistress and two pupil teachers. In the Infant School 200 children had one certificated and one assistant mistress and three pupil teachers.

Eynesbury Church of England School

No record has been found of a school at Eynesbury before the beginning of the 19th century, although under the Alderman Newton Charity of 1760 provision was made for three Eynesbury boys to attend St. Neots Charity School and have free clothing. (See above).

The memorial in the vestry of Eynesbury Church to Rev. Palmer (Rector 1808-1851) records that he establishèd, and maintained, for many years, a school for the poor of Eynesbury.

There seems no doubt that this school was held in a building at the south end of Luke Street bordering the Green. It was built at right angles to the street facing north across a yard. Many people will remember it as converted into a long low terrace of slum-type cottages, known as the 'Old School Yard', and pulled down in 1960. Once when repairs were being carried out to the end cottage, on the west, the author saw, when plaster was being taken down on the outside, an inscription over the doorway 'Suffer the Little Children to Come unto Me'.

It is almost certain that until sometime shortly before 1830 this building had been the parish workhouse, but, in 1830, Rev. Palmer was the tenant of it. *Pigot's Directory* of that date records a Free School at Eynesbury, with Ann Clark as mistress.

Sometime later the 'Old School Yard' premises were given up and Rev. Palmer moved the school to the rectory stable and coach-house block. The infants, however, could not be accommodated here and met in a 'rod barn'. This was probably one of the two large barns on either side of Luke Street, or even the old part of the building recently used as the Infant School, in St. Mary's Street, opposite the west end of the church.

'Townborn' wrote in praise of Eynesbury School at this time, calling it 'the best in the county' and producing the best choir. Mr. W. Chapman of Alma Cottage, Howitts Lane, has a relic of this school in the form of a sampler, on which is worked 'Ann Pattison Peck. Eynesbury School. Aged 10. 1836'. In 1840 the National School had 110 pupils.

Following Rev. Palmer came Rev. Maule (Rector 1851-90) He was at once disturbed by the condition of the school and its premises, and began to form plans for a radical improvement. In 1854 it is recorded that James Phillips was headmaster, with 90 pupils of both sexes, who each contributed a small weekly sum for their education.

Rev. Maule at once began to collect money from public and private sources to build a new school on part of the rectory glebe land opposite the west end of the church. He is said not to have asked the parish for any of this. The building was opened by the Bishop of Ely in 1868. In the bell tower was placed a bell dated 1851, which must have come from the old school. A further classroom was added in 1892.

Meanwhile the infant's school was either moved to, or remained in, the old building in St. Mary's Street, referred to above, with an additional room added.

Throughout his long incumbency Rev. Maule never lost his deep interest and enthusiasm for the school and its welfare, himself giving personal religious instruction to the pupils. Recalcitrant pupils would often be sent from the school to the rectory for admonishment and even punishment.

When he resigned the living, in 1890, Rev. Maule left the school in the very capable hands of A. E. Jennings as headmaster who had been appointed in 1876 and was to stay until his retirement in 1917. He was remembered by many generations of pupils with special affection and respect, and was regarded as the ideal village schoolmaster with the right mixture of human and scholastic virtues. In 1919 his old pupils subscribed nearly £100 to found the Jennings Memorial Fund, the interest from which was used to aid pupils from the school who wished to train as teachers.

Wesleyan School

The natural desires of the Nonconformists that their children should receive religious teaching and instruction in their own faith led to the setting up of Sunday Schools attached to each nonconformist chapel or meeting house. For the needs of general education there was, of course, no alternative for the children but to be privately educated, which many members could not afford, or attend one of the Church of England schools where the catechism of that church was taught.

The first attempt to remedy this state of affairs was the opening of a school in the old disused chapel behind the south frontage of 20 High Street in 1844. This 'British School' was under a joint committee of Independents (Old Meeting), Baptists and Wesleyans, but for an unknown reason came to an end in 1862.

Meanwhile the Wesleyans had started their own Day School on their own chapel premises (there was probably already a Sunday School room) in Huntingdon Street. No evidence has been found as to exactly when this school was started, but it was in existence in 1852, under Mr. A. Arundal, who was the first headmaster.

Probably due to the success of this school, and lack of space to expand it, a movement started to build an entirely new school on a new site. This had the ready support of other nonconformist bodies and in 1868 the foundation stone was laid of the new Wesleyan School on a site west of New Street, now known as Priory Road.

Under a succession of dedicated headmasters this school soon achieved a high reputation for academic success, and support from government education grants.

In this century, however, it became increasingly more difficult for the voluntary bodies concerned to maintain the school and bring it up to modern standards. As a result, about 1926, it was handed over to the County Council, becoming the first

'Council School' in the town. This change from a denominational status fortunately did nothing to lower the high reputation in which it was held.

The British School

This school, referred to above and about which almost nothing appears to be known, was held in the old disused chapel built behind No. 20, on the south side of the High Street, just east of the *New Inn*. It was founded in 1844 and run by a committee formed from members from the Baptist, Wesleyan and Old Meeting (Congregationalists) chapels. Pupils attending contributed a small weekly sum of money, and those from Eynesbury approached by a private path from Brook Street, just east of Brook House.

The headmasters known are, 1850 Wm. Stuckey; 1852 Robert Handford (also postmaster); 1854 Jonathan Oliffe. The school closed in 1862, after the Wesleyans had established their own school in Huntingdon Street about 1850.

Mr Shruis

HIGH STREET, ST. NEOTS,
(Adjoining the Corn Exchange).

Bought of S. S. EKINS, *Xmas*

CABINET MAKER AND UPHOLSTERER;
General Cabinet Furniture, Carpet, Bedstead, & Bedding Warehouse.

A LARGE STOCK of Superior IRON BEDSTEADS, Plain and Fancy CHAIRS, Chimney and Toilette GLASSES, Portable DESKS, WORK-BOXES, CADDIES, &c. Travelling BOXES and BAGS, PERAMBULATORS; Cocoa, Manilla, and Indian MATTINGS, Seasoned FLOOR-CLOTHS for Halls and Passages, MATS, HASSOCKS, BED-SACKINGS, Upholsterers' TRIMMINGS, FEATHERS, FLOCKS, &c., &c.

PIANO FORTES ON SALE OR HIRE.

OLD FURNITURE TAKEN IN EXCHANGE; Ditto REPAIRED AND FRENCH POLISHED; Sofas, Chairs, &c., RE-STUFFED AND COVERED; LADIES' WORK MOUNTED; PICTURE FRAMES in Gold and Fancy Woods; Wire-gauze, Venetian, and Roller BLINDS; BEDDING Purified and Re-made.

Furnishing Orders promptly executed.   Accounts due Midsummer & Christmas.

1869
Jan 28 3ft 6in Mahog Chest Drawers   2. 15. —
Apl 3   1 Doz White Balloon Chairs   2. 14. —
*   4ft 6in Iron French Bead   1. 3.*
*   2 Feather Pillows   10. —*
May 6   Mahog toilette Glass with Box   1. 6. —

VIII
ST. NEOTS PARISH CHURCH

ST. NEOTS parish church (plate 2) is undoubtedly the most important historic building in the town and architecturally its chief glory, well deserving its title of the cathedral of Huntingdonshire. It is also a rather rare example of a church belonging almost entirely to one period, the late 15th century. There can be no doubt that it replaced an earlier church, probably built in the 12th century, as the north wall of the chancel is of the 13th century, and the east wall of the north chapel 14th century.

The north and south chapels were both almost certainly built as guild chapels, the north, or Jesus Chapel, being associated with the known guild of Jesus in the town, and the south chapel was dedicated to Our Lady. The fine low pitched roof of the nave has on it, inside, many carvings of real and mythical animals that can hardly be seen without the aid of binoculars. Over the south porch is the Dove chamber, reached by a narrow winding stair. This contains a small library of early theological books and was probably named after Rev. Dove (Rector 1617-22). The tower is a very beautiful example of its period and stands 128 feet high to the top of the pinnacles. From it an extensive view of the town and surrounding countryside can be obtained. It contains eight bells, some originally made by Joseph Eayre, the St. Neots bellfounder, but all later recast.

The use of towers for secular purposes is well known and it is said that the town fire engine used to be kept there, thus accounting for the large doors at the west end. Another secular use of the church was for the annual meetings of the Common Right Proprietors, ordered by their Act of 1771 to be held in the parish church. During the Civil War both sides made a practice of using churches to accommodate troops and there is a strong tradition that St. Neots church was so used at the time of the Battle of St. Neots in 1648.

The church stands on ground normally above the level of floods but was inundated to the depth of two feet in the great flood of 1823. The original churchyard surrounded the church on all sides except the north which was by popular belief the unlucky, or Devil's side, and its use for burials did not start before the 19th century. Until recently only the south door was used for weddings.

A detailed account of the architecture of the church, its fittings, and the many monuments it contains, can be found in the *Victoria County History, Huntingdonshire*, and the *Royal Commission on Historic Monuments, Huntingdonshire*.

Besides what is recorded in the above the writer has found a number of items of interest, mainly in the church's own records, which do not appear in these works. Some are given below:

1689   An hour-glass was bought for 8d., and 'the Dutchman' was paid 15s. for making a clerk's desk, 15s. for making forms and desks for the children, and £2 7s. 6d. for a velvet and shag cushion.

1712   Lawrence Thompson gave to the church a silver communion plate, and Elizabeth Reynolds (of Little Paxton) a silver candlestick for the altar. Also in this year died Charles Baynton, draper and citizen of London, who had had the floor raised in the chancel, and provided a new altar and rails. (The Bayntons were a St. Neots family).

1718   The following expenses were incurred at a confirmation, *viz.* four bottles of sherry and one bottle of sack, 10s., two bottles of claret 3s. 4d., biscake 1s. 4d., a chamber pot 7d., two white wands 8d., and for the ringers 2s. 6d.

1734   A new desk and clerk's pew ordered.

1735   The new clock and chimes repaired. Undoubtedly the church clock then had chimes that played hymn tunes, and the earliest reference to these is in 1688. Later, in the early 19th century a subscription was raised for a new set, to be made by Robert Taylor the bellfounder, but not enough money was forthcoming. He therefore restored and reinstated the old set, which, we are told, played *Gramachree*. These seem to have been taken down when the church was restored about 1845, but for some time after the cylinder was lying about in the church. There is thus no truth in the suggestion that the existing Great Gransden church chimes came from here.

1738   The first reference to a 'Singing gallery' at the west end of the church, and in the same year Elizabeth Baily died leaving £100 to pay an organist.

1748   The ceiling of the gallery was taken down. This was probably to fit in a new organ as, in 1754, when Cole visited the church, he noted that a 'new and exceedingly handsome organ' was put in about

five years before. [See Cole MSS. Brit. Museum Add. MSS. 5837 f.127.]
Money was also spent in this year on varnishing the organ case and
'gilding the crown and two mitres', also 145 feet of the church floor
was paved at 4d. a foot.

1749   An account was paid for 'watering the new planted trees in
the churchyard', 18 times at 8d. a time.

1805   Half acre of land added to the churchyard on the north side.

1844   In this year, during the cure of Rev. Appleton, a scheme of
restoration was started. The north porch, then of brick, was taken
down and a new stone porch built. Three feet of soil was removed
from the north side of the church. Inside, on the north side, the wall
plaster was removed, and the stones revealed and pointed. New finials
were put on the roof and windows reglazed where necessary. A church
rate was raised.

1845   Restoration continued. First the south porch was restored. It
must have been at this time that two sundials, just under the roof apex
and depicted on a painting of about 1812, were destroyed. More interior
plaster was taken down and some windows, previously blocked by
masonry, reopened. Land on the north west of the church was purchased by subscription.

1847   The organ was brought down from the gallery and installed
in the Jesus chapel. It seems likely that at this time the gallery itself
was destroyed. Also, about this time, it was said that Rev. Appleton
instructed Robert Rich, who was parish clerk and also a painter, to
wash over the south front of the church with yellow ochre. After a
time this disfigurement wore off and was not renewed.

1855   The organ was exchanged for a new one at a cost of £530.

1854-65 During the time of Rev. Vaughan the first artificial heat was
put into the church when gas was substituted for oil lamps.

c. 1878   Rev. Meade, who had given the church a new altar table, gave
away, apparently without authority, the old altar table to Offord Darcy
church. It was said to date from about 1600 and had been stored in the
Dove Chamber over the south porch, and taken to pieces to get it up
the narrow winding stairway. At Offord the finely-carved oak legs were
gilded. Charles Rowley, of Wintringham Hall, was furious when he
heard the facts, and the matter was raised at the next Bishop's Visita-
tion. It was claimed that the removal was illegal and the table should be
returned. Offord agreed to this, on a faculty being procured, and Mr.
Rowley sent one of his farm wagons for the table and paid for its
restoration. On its return Rev. Meade suggested that it be put in St.
Mary's chapel, but this was opposed on the grounds that it was illegal
and popish to have more than one altar in the church. It is now used as
a communion table.

1884   A fire in a cupboard at the vicarage completely destroyed the
communion service, in silver gilt, and altar candlesticks. They were not
insured. These may have been those given to the church in 1712.

1896   A silver chalice, designed by Sir Arthur Bloomfield, presented.

Samuel Hawkesford, who was clerk and sexton from 1897 to 1961, told the writer in 1959 that of the four carved wooden figures at the west end of the stalls, he remembered when there were only three. Mrs. G. F. Rowley carved the north-east figure to match the others. The actual stalls were given to the church, those on the north side having once been in the possession of Dr. Evans, the antiquary, of Brook House. He also said that the Rowley memorial was of Italian workmanship and when first done had no grille. One day Charles Rowley came into the church and saw a woman fingering the ring on the finger of his mother's effigy; the ring being painted to represent gold with a precious stone. He was so upset at the idea of the public touching his memorial that he at once ordered a grille to be put on front of it.

In the Dove Chamber is a broken stone grave cross, probably 13th century. This was found while digging a grave just inside the south-east churchyard gate, and was saved by Mr. Hawkesford from being reburied.

An inscription on a buttress on the south side of the nave, and west of the south porch, has deteriorated during the writer's lifetime and is now nearly illegible. It runs 'Here lyeth the body of Wm. Heath who departed this life the thirtyeth day of August 1676. Stay mortal stay, depart not from this tombe untill thou hast pondered well thy day of doome. My boew stands bent if yt thou canst but see aimeing to shoote and it may lighte on thee. Prepare to walk in duste take home this line the grave that is opened next it may be thine'.

The bells and their ringers

The primary reason for the splendid tower at the west end of the church was, of course, to hold bells that would ring and throw their melody as far afield as possible. The ringers used to be considered privileged people who rang appropriate peals, not only at normal church occasions, but as messages of thanksgiving and warning, and even as messages to mark the time of events. This was very necessary among people often without watches or clocks. Ringing was thirsty work and the churchwardens were always ready to allow money from the rates to give to the ringers for refreshments. These payments therefore appear in the churchwardens' accounts. The ringers appeared to have been very loyal citizens from the few examples given below:

In 1685, on 21 December Thomas Attwood and Benjamin Dixey were given 4s. for ale 'ye day ye king came to his crown' (James II). In the same year the ringers Bax and Dixey had 1s. for ale at the 'thanksgiving for victory over ye rebels' (Monmouth). In 1688 they were ringing in thanksgiving for a prince being born, and later 'in order for to pray for the prince'. Loyalties soon changed for in 1689 they were ringing for the Coronation Day of William of Orange. In 1715 they celebrated the 'Kings Accession', (George I), and on 27 August 1718 'ringing two times for victory over the Spanish' (a naval battle in the Straits of Messina). In 1746 they rang for 'the Duke's birthday' (Cumberland?), and later 'for gaining a victory over the rebels' (Culloden). On 29 May 1752 they were still ringing to mark Charles II's Restoration (Oak Apple Day). In the same year, on 11 June, they rang to mark George II's 'inauguration', and on 24 October his coronation, refreshing themselves afterwards at the *Bell* and the *Angel*. In 1753 they rang for the King's birthday, on 10 May, and afterwards went to the *Wrestlers*.

At a number of other occasions single bells were rung, probably by the sexton, some of them daily to mark important times of day.

There was the early morning bell at 4 a.m., no doubt to get people up in time for work; this ceased in 1808.

The dinner bell was rung regularly by Sam. Hawkesford, every weekday, at 1 p.m., until 1939, when all bell ringing was ordered to cease, except to announce invasion. Another ringing, important for the poor, was the gleaning bell. This was rung at 7 a.m. each morning after harvest, when the farmers, or the most part of them, had cleared their fields of corn shocks. The gleaners could then go in but, to be fair to all, not before the gleaning bell had rung. It rang again at 7 p.m., when all gleaners must leave the fields. This bell was still being rung in 1898.

Another special event was marked by the pancake bell, rung at 11 a.m. on Shrove Tuesday, and discontinued between 1850 and 1856. In pre-Reformation times this bell was probably intended to call the faithful to church for confession and to be shriven before the holy season. Also on this day all eggs and butter in the house had to be cleared up before Ash Wednesday. Traditionally they were used to make pancakes, what better way, and the bell and the pancakes long survived the shriving.

On 5 November bells were 'clashed' or 'fired', all together at intervals, called 'shooting the bells' and starting at 8 a.m. Special ringing that has survived until recent times is on Christmas Eve and 'ringing in the New Year'.

Before the installation of fire alarm sirens the church bells were rung to give the public alarm and call the volunteer fire brigade. For this purpose the bells were 'rung backwards', starting with the smallest and finishing with the largest.

In 1832 the great bell, cast by Joseph Eayre in 1764, was cracked. This was said to have happened at the wedding of the daughter of Wm. Wiles, a merchant of 24 Market Square, to J. Sharp, a wealthy young London man. He was over-generous to the ringers, giving them £10. As a result they indulged too freely before the ceremony and rang the Treble Bob Major with such violence that the Great Tenor was fractured. A Mr. Austin, the workhouse master, persuaded the churchwardens to have the fissure filed free of contract, which he declared would restore the bell and its tone. This was quite an expensive job and a complete failure. The bell was then sent by water to Dodsons of Downham Market, a firm originating from that of Joseph Eayre of St. Neots, for recasting.

The Jesus Chapel

The Jesus chapel in the north aisle was undoubtedly once the private chapel of the St. Neots Guild of Jesus, whose property was seized by the Crown at the Reformation. It was not uncommon for some or all of such confiscated property to be used for the founding of schools. No proof has been found that this happened here, but it is significant that after the Reformation this chapel was used as a charity school. Gorham says that this use ceased in 1745, but the churchwardens' accounts show that rent was being received for the chapel in 1853, and it is possible that school use started again when the schoolhouse in Church Walk became overcrowded, before new buildings were erected in 1883.

IX
NONCONFORMITY

IN THIS DISTRICT the beginnings of nonconformity, in the
17th century, seemed to follow a pattern of great social interest
that would repay further study. The start would always be made
in the smaller villages, and from there spread to other villages,
before coming to market towns such as St. Neots. The reason
for this may have been that, in the smaller centres involved,
there was less hostility or effective opposition from either a
squirearchy or from a Church of England living of low value
or one held in plurality.

However, from the beginning members of the newly founded
'Meetings' were by no means all village people, and from the
first, within this district, a prominent part was played by people
from St. Neots. The next stage was for town members to start
small subsidiary meetings in their own town and, if these were
successful, to found another independent meeting house there.
Perhaps, with increasing age, the ardours of travel were an
incentive encouraging to this move.

At first the Congregationalists, or Independents, and the
Baptists seemed to worship happily together, but by the beginning of the 18th century they had split up. The Quakers likewise established themselves in the surrounding villages, but
never got further than the outskirts of St. Neots parish.

In the late 18th and 19th centuries the pattern changed.
The Methodist, or Wesleyan church, was founded in St. Neots
as a direct result of visits from Wesley himself, and a century
later the Salvation Army came to the town as a branch of a
national organisation. With both the Congregationalists and the
Baptists there were, perhaps the inevitable, schisms.

In the 17th and 18th centuries the pastors were usually
local men, fully employed in a trade or profession, and often
a menial one. They were often almost illiterate, and were chosen
by their fellow members because of their obvious sincerity and

gift of preaching. By the beginning of the 19th century they had become professional, full time ministers, and were required to be well educated.

The rise of a powerful nonconformist element in St. Neots in the 19th century was responsible for a social pattern that might be described as a vertical cleavage, across the normal horizontal class layers. In St. Neots it hardly reached up to the upper and professional classes, who had always supported the Church of England, but the Congregational and Wesleyan churches included among their members many prosperous farmers and shopkeepers, and even some of the wealthiest local businessmen.

It was to be expected that there would be more social intercourse between members of one church, but this fellowship also extended into the field of business, and church members were expected, where possible, to deal with shopkeepers and tradesmen of their own faith. This even went as far as doctors, and the writer remembers hearing a medical man described as 'the Nonconformist doctor'. A new minister coming into the town was quickly told by his deacons where his wife should do her shopping.

An amusing story concerns Wm. Bartlett, of the long established St. Neots butchers firm, and famous for his honesty and conscientiousness. Although a Wesleyan he was seen by a fellow member leaving Eynesbury church one Sunday, and rather strongly reproached. He answered, 'Well you see, Mr. Palmer, the Rector, called at my shop last Friday and bought a fine wether leg of mutton, so I thought that one good turn deserved another'.

The Congregationalists or Independents

A religious community or 'Meeting' of this faith was founded at Keysoe, in Bedfordshire, about 1657, with John Donne as pastor. He had been, on account of his faith, a fellow prisoner with John Bunyan in Bedford jail. A member of his congregation was Ralph Luke, of the Luke family of Eynesbury. In 1691 Luke became the first pastor of a new 'meeting' at Hail Weston, an offshoot of Keysoe, which he may have done much to start. From the beginning at Hail Weston, besides Ralph Luke, there were a number of members from outside the village, such as Oliver Bigg yeoman, Thomas Paine baker, John Nutter sieve-maker, and Daniel Eaton hatter, from St. Neots; also Silvester Addington of Eaton Ford.

The 'Meeting' met in a barn at Hail Weston, and during Luke's pastorate had a membership of 122, namely 54 males and 68 females. It appears from the minute book that the baptism of children was permitted if the parents wished it. After Luke's death in 1701 he was succeeded by Richard Rawlins of Linton, and it was during his time that the move to St. Neots took place. It is not clear from the surviving documents if the move was made on account of a doctrinal split on the question of baptism, or simply a desire of the St. Neots members to have a Meeting House nearer home, plus the offer of a site by Messrs. Paine and Bigg. However there is no record of a Baptist Meeting having started in Hail Weston for another 50 years, and the property there remained in the possession of the new St. Neots Meeting. Indeed they went on using the original minute book.

The new Meeting House in St. Neots was probably built in 1718, or soon after, well back from the north side of the High Street, and approached by a narrow passage, probably under an archway at the east side of *The Pigeon* inn; it was built in the style of the day, in red brick, and survived, although greatly altered, until destroyed by fire in 1969. Adjoining ground was purchased for a graveyard in 1839 and closed in 1881. Between 1846 and 1851 the Meeting House was added to, but without much taste, in white brick, and the old seating replaced, the main object being to provide a Sunday School.

In 1885 the 'Old Meeting', as it came to be called, was thought to have a defective roof, and in any case was not large enough for the congregation. By this time the Nonconformists were no longer ridiculed or persecuted, and wished for more showy places of worship, to rival parish churches, and no longer hidden away in back alleys. Among the St. Neots congregation were two wealthy members, Wm. Paine, almost certainly of the same family as the original Thomas Paine, and Joseph Wilcox who was a deacon for nearly 30 years. The former retired to live at Hastings in 1882, but bought, and presented to the chapel, as it was then beginning to be called, a block of property at that time occupying the

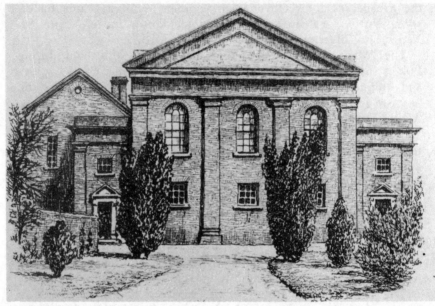

Independent Chapel, St. Neots. This was originally built in 1743

frontage of the present chapel building, besides giving other contributions towards a new chapel. Joseph Wilcox contributed a large part of the £2,500 which was the cost of building the chapel, designed by Edward Paine, and opened in 1888. This is the present building.

Of the original founders of the St. Neots Independent or Congregational Meeting, in 1718, John Nutter of St. Neots, Thos. Cooper of Colmworth yeoman, John Moon of St. Neots baker, John Piller of St. Neots cordwainer, Thos. Smith of Caxton yeoman, John Parrell of Hail Weston blacksmith, Thos. Measures of Brampton blacksmith, and Wm. May of St. Neots sieve-maker, were all from the Hail Weston Meeting; to them were added James Benson grocer, Benjamin Potter clothier, Wm. Luke fellmonger, all of St. Neots, and Thos. and Henry Ward tanners, of Eynesbury. They appointed Wm. Bennett to be minister of their new 'Tabernacle or Meeting House'.

There followed a succession of ministers of which perhaps the most notable was Dr. Wm. Gordon who was at St. Neots

1789-1802. He was born at Hitchin in 1720, and after several pastorates emigrated to America in 1770 and became a minister at Roxbury. Here he actively supported the revolution and had a price put on his head by the British. He was proposed as chaplain to General North's forces but instead became a close associate and private secretary to Washington. Later he took a D.D. degree at New Jersey College. After peace in 1788 he returned to England and wrote a four-volume work, *The History, Rise, Progress, and Establishment of Independence in the U.S.A.* He again left for America but found his political views not acceptable and returned here in 1789 to become pastor at St. Neots Old Meeting. He died in 1807.

In 1827, when Stephen Dobson was minister, a serious split occurred, which apparently could not be healed. As a result Dobson left, part of the congregation following him. They were able to raise money to build another chapel on the south side of the High Street behind premises now No. 20, which came into use about 1831, with Dobson as minister. After a few years of use, however, it lost support and was closed, its remaining congregation returning to the Old Meeting. In 1844 a joint committee, representing the Wesleyan, Baptist, and Independents, hired this chapel and opened a British School there, which closed in 1862.

In 1857/58 leading Independents in the town were engaged in a bitter struggle over church rates, in common with others about the country, refusing to pay the 'unrighteous tax' which St. Neots church vestry were attempting to collect for the repair of St. Neots church. Once more the old latent bitterness between the Church of England and Nonconformity came to the surface, as the churchwardens sued James Paine for 10s. 1½d., and the Nonconformists issued a pamphlet entitled *The Extraction of Church Rates from Nonconformists is Robbery.* On appeal the case went to the Court of Arches in 1858, and the verdict went to the defendant, with costs. St. Neots Nonconformists thus became pioneers in the successful struggle to abolish church rates. Much detailed history of the church can be found in *History of the Old Meeting House, St. Neots, 1691-1890* by R. D. Cooper (1890) and *Centenary St. Neots Congregational Sunday School, 1798-1898.*

Thé Baptists

The Baptists in this neighbourhood seem to have come from the same dissenting communities as the Congregationalists and Independents, and only to have split into separate churches early in the 19th century. Indeed as we have seen above at the Independents Meeting at Hail Weston baptism was optional, but when that church moved to St. Neots, about 1718, the Baptists were left behind. It is not exactly known what happened to these Hail Weston Baptists but they probably joined Meetings in other villages. About 1857 however a Baptist Meeting was started at Hail Weston and a chapel built, and from this came the founding of the present Baptist chapel at St. Neots.

The inspiration of this Hail Weston community, and its spread to St. Neots, was due almost solely to a remarkable man named William Joyce. He was born in 1720, probably at St. Neots, but was certainly living there as a young man. He was described as a hedge carpenter and hurdle-maker, and as being rude and illiterate. He was, however very sincere in his dissenting faith and determined to exercise his obvious natural gift for preaching. It would seem that there were attempts among the dissenting committees to restrain or suppress him, as he was continually changing his place of attendance at meetings. Finally his determination won through and he was successful in founding his own church.

In 1744 he began to attend the Independent Meeting at Keysoe, but soon left and joined that at Kimbolton. In 1746 he asked leave of this meeting to be allowed to preach at Little Staughton, where he was then living, but this was refused. In defiance he started a Meeting there in his own home, claiming that floods frequently prevented him and his friends getting to Kimbolton. This excuse was not accepted and Joyce resigned his membership, joining the Cambridge Baptist church as a member, but continuing to worship with others at Little Staughton, in a barn procured there in 1754.

By 1757 the Little Staughton Meeting was flourishing, with attenders coming from Eaton Socon and Hail Weston, and it was agreed to start a Meeting at the latter place, services to be held at each place on alternate Sundays. Joyce was officially appointed pastor at Hail Weston, and a chapel was built there in 1759. In 1762 the Little Staughton Meeting was discontinued and all services thereafter held at Hail Weston.

Some time after these events took place Joyce went to live at St. Neots, taking a draper's shop, said to have been next to Newman, the grocer, two doors east of the *Cross Keys*. Here, besides fulfilling his duties at Hail Weston, he started to preach to small gatherings, probably in his own house.

In 1793 he resigned his pastorate when 'God deprived him of his mental powers'. This precipitated a crisis at Hail Weston, some visitors wishing to appoint a new pastor, and others saying that this should not be done while Joyce was alive. The latter faction, presumably the minority, left their church and fitted up a small place of worship in some old cottages in what was then known as Kidmans Yard, at the back of No. 36 on the south side of St. Neots High Street. Here Joyce was occasionally able to preach, but at other times the services were taken by a Mr. Rand, from Needingworth, an unsuccessful candidate for the Hail Weston pastorate.

Meanwhile a Mr. Alcock was appointed pastor at Hail Weston but chose to live at St. Neots. On Sundays he held services at his chapel in the morning and afternoon, and also started a small evening service at St. Neots, both on Sundays and some weekdays. This was attended by Isaac Arnold of St. Neots who provided a first floor room, with an outside staircase, owned by him in the yard behind the *Fox and Hounds* inn, on the north side of the Market Square (plate 3).

Confusion now reigned between the two rival Baptist communities in the town, and this was added to when Arnold left the 'Alcock Church' and joined the 'Rand Church', denying the former the use of his room. Some Hail Weston members also became dissatisfied with Alcock and started services again in the *Fox and Hounds* room, presumably under Rand. They were vulgarly nicknamed the 'tally ho' Baptists.

Alcock died in 1801, and a successor was appointed in 1802. While in St. Neots he lived in the old vicarage in Church Street (pulled down in 1970). William Joyce died in 1799, and was buried in St. Neots churchyard, the inscription on his tombstone (now illegible) was:

Here is deposited the mortal part of
William Joyce
of affliction he departed this life
April 25, 1799   aged 79
A crumb of Jacob's dust lies here below
Richer than all the mines of Mexico
Its lying in these ruins does not prove
The Lord's neglect, nor yet decay of love
T'will rise and shine when Nature's works are o'er
Bright as the firmament for evermore.
It ever was and is the Lord's delight
And ne'er was put a moment from his sight.

Mr. Rand was apparently still preaching in St. Neots in 1810, when the Hail Weston church demanded his dismissal. It is not quite clear which sect it was that built the chapel in New Street in 1816, one of the first buildings in that street, or whether its first pastor, the Rev. G. Murrell (1784-1871), came to the town in 1808 or 1810, but it is perhaps significant that Isaac Arnold was one of the trustees.

He was undoubtedly a remarkable figure who stamped his image on the church over the period of 58 or 60 years that he was pastor. He was noted for his outspoken speech, and one example of this has been recorded. In a sermon preached in 1817 he said, 'some people may be disappointed that I am not preaching a sermon for the late Princess Charlotte. All that I can say is that those not converted to the grace of God will go to Hell. Of Princess Charlotte I know nothing . . . and if other people chose to preach a funeral sermon for a cat there is no reason why I should'.

In his last few years as a pastor he had to help him a co-pastor, the Rev. Wyard, who did not succeed him when he retired in 1868, a Rev. Bax being appointed. There was evidently a schism in the church over this appointment and part of the congregation decided to leave, together with Rev. Wyard, and found a new chapel (see East Street Baptist chapel).

The trust deed of the New Street Baptist chapel or Meeting House is in the Public Record Office (C54/9691. 6.) and bears the names of the first trustees as under: Saml. Fairey the elder, St. Neots; Peter Wildman, Eynesbury, baker; Jas. Kirby, St. Neots, watchmaker; Wm. Law, Eaton Socon, shopkeeper; Jas. Fairey, St. Neots, fellmonger; Thos. Thorns; Isaac Arnold, Eynesbury, cornfactor; Jas. King, Eaton Socon; Saml. Fairey the younger, draper; Jas. Topham, Eaton Socon, farmer; Thos. Hewitt, Eaton Socon, baker; Joshua Wildman, Eynesbury, baker; John Read, St. Neots, grocer. Land on which to build the Meeting House was bought for £30 from Thos. Thorns, being the north-west part of his garden in New Lane.

Much of the above information comes from the MS. church books of the various Baptist chapels concerned.

Evidence as to the attitude of the establishment to nonconformity at St. Neots is difficult to come by, but the following incident is of interest. The Grand Jury at a Quarter Sessions Court at Huntingdon in 1815 brought in a verdict of 'No true bill' against Daniel Griffin and John Mehew on a charge of 'wilfully, maliciously, or contemptuously did disquite and disturb a congregation of H.M. Protestant Subjects, dissenting from the Church of England, assembled for religious worship in their Meeting House . . . of which the Rev. Thomas Morell is minister'. They were alleged 'to have committed the offence by driving or forcing into the Meeting House a certain black dog with a tin saucepan tied to his tail, crying and howling during the time of Divine Service'.

The East Street or New Baptist chapel

As can be seen above, this breakaway sect left the New Street Baptist church, with its former co-pastor Rev. Wyard, about 1868. Services were at first held in the Corn Exchange, until a new chapel was built in East Street in 1873, at a cost of £900. The opening service was taken by the famous Rev. C. H. Spurgeon, and the principle families associated with the foundation were those of Dring, Fairey, Ellwood, and Ekins. It survived well into the present century, but is now a Roman Catholic church.

The Gospel Hall

Very little seems to be known about the Gospel Hall on the west side of New Street, or what it stood for. It was built and opened in 1867, with Rev. Newman as pastor (plate 31), and he was still there in 1902. He was said to have once been a Church of England parson. Branches of this chapel were built and opened at Staploe and Southoe. It is now used as a factory.

The Quakers

From early records of the Society of Friends (Quakers) in the Cambridgeshire Record Office, it would appear that the spread of Quakerism in Huntingdonshire was fairly rapid, following the visit of George Fox to Huntingdon in 1656, where he was favourably received by the mayor. By the end of the century Meetings had been started in many places throughout the county. As pointed out in the introduction nearly all Nonconformist Meetings in this district were first held in small village communities, and in fact no Quaker Meeting was ever established in the town itself.

In a list, dated 1689, there was a Meeting at Hardwick, in the parish of St. Neots. This must be Monks Hardwick, where Thomas Laundy a prominent Quaker lived and farmed. Like nearly all the other Meetings, this would be held in a private house. In 1724 it was proposed that if possible a suitable barn should be purchased in St. Neots in which to hold Meetings. This seems to indicate that numbers had increased, but there is no record that a barn was ever bought. Among those offering to subscribe to its cost was Stephen Scarborough, who must be a St. Neots man. In 1746 Joseph Liversidge of St. Neots was dismissed from membership of the Society for making a 'mixed marriage' with someone not a member, and being married by a priest.

Quakerism went into a slow decline in the county in the 18th century, and it would appear that the Meeting at Monks Hardwick, together with those at Midloe, Stirtloe, and Little Paxton (Wray House) all died out before the end of that century.

The Methodists or Wesleyans

The foundation of the Methodist church in St. Neots came about in quite a different way from that of the other Nonconformists, being the direct result of visits by John Wesley himself. From Wesley's own *Journal* we learn that he visited the town a number of times and was always enthusiastically received. The first visit was in 1776, coming from Bedford, and he writes, 'I dragged on through miserable roads to St. Neots, and preached in a large room to a numerous congregation. Understanding that all the Methodists had left the Church I earnestly expected them to return to it'. This seems to show that at that time there was no idea of forming a separate church. The 'large room' would almost certainly be the Assembly Room, at the corner of High Street and Huntingdon Street. He came again at the end of the same year, and next in 1778 when he comforted a young woman dying of consumption. For the date 3 December 1781 he writes, 'I preached in the evening to a larger congregation than I had ever seen there before'. The next visit was in 1782, and again soon after when he wrote 'I preached at St. Neots to the largest congregation that I ever saw there, and I know not that I ever saw them so affected. It seemed as if God had touched all their hearts'. His last visit was on 20 November 1788, when he said, 'We had a lovely congregation at St. Neots, who seemed ripe for the promises . . . .'.

Besides the Assembly Room, mentioned above, there are strong local traditions of Wesley preaching in the Old Malting in Cambridge Street, and in Ropers Barn, that stood on the east side of Huntingdon Street near the East Street corner.

From this strong beginning was founded Wesleyanism in the town, and the chapel was built in Huntingdon Street in 1794, on land formerly part of the yard of the *George* inn, to which was added a manse for the pastor in 1802.

Like other Nonconformists the Wesleyans did not like having to send their children to the Church of England schools, and first started a small day school in their own Sunday School, and in 1844 they joined with the Congregationalists and Baptists in running a day school in the old chapel behind the south side of the High Street. Their own Wesleyan School was opened in Priory Road in 1859.

The Salvation Army
The Salvation Army came late on the scene in comparison with the other Nonconformist churches, and suffered a great deal of ridicule and persecution in its first few years, possibly more than the others on account of holding its services in the open street and having no headquarters of its own for a number of years.

The first reported appearance of the Army was in 1883 when three defendants were brought before the St. Neots justices for 'an assault on Arthur Hite, a member of what is

now recognised by the inhabitants as a branch of the Salvation
Army. A dozen members singing and preaching in Duck Lane
were hustled by the three defendants. Col. Humbley, in the
chair, said it was a pity that they did not secure a room to
hold their meetings in, instead of thrusting their religious views
upon the public in the ostentatious manner they did.'

The next notice in the local press was in 1887, when what
were probably the inaugural meetings of the new branch were
held. There were crowded meetings in the Public Room and
in the Market Square, where the attraction was 'ten musical
warriors on tandem bicycles'. On this, or another occasion,
in the same year, Miss Booth came to present colours and
to witness a Grand Swearing in of Troops, among which were
12 Hallelujah Lasses from the St. Neots Depot, parading under
the Blood and Fire flag. Further meetings in that year, however,
were broken up by hostile crowds, and in 1888 some men were
again before the Court for disturbing a service in the Public
Room. The men had all been before the Court recently but
the charges were dismissed because the prosecution did not
bring to the Court a certificate that the building was licensed
for religious worship.

The first Army wedding was held in the Public Room in
1888 when George Flint was married to Louisa Coleman, both
from Eynesbury. At Eynesbury, too, a large old barn in Luke
Street was being used for meetings.

Eventually money was found to build a headquarters, and
in 1891 the Citadel was built at the corner of High Street
and Church Street, where the old watchmen's hut used to stand.

X
LABOUR UNREST AND THE TRADE UNION MOVEMENT

THE DISSATISFACTION of labour with pay and conditions and the birth of the Trade Union movement had their echo in St. Neots in the second half of the 19th century. This occurred both among the mechanics and agricultural labourers, but the low wages and appalling housing conditions of the latter made them the more militant; also their masters, the farmers, seemed to be more hostile and unyielding than the business employers. There are few sources of information on this subject except in the local press, which appears to have reported fairly and objectively on events.

The first incident reported was in 1871 when 80 or 90 men from Bowers Vulcan Iron-Works on the Market Square held a meeting in the Public Room in support of the 'Nine Hour Movement'. They demanded a 54-hour week (in place of one of 60 hours), and time and a quarter for overtime. A resolution to this effect was passed and sent at once to Mr. Bower by hand. Mr. Anthony Bower came along to the meeting and conceded the demand, at which it broke up after the workers had given him three cheers.

Agitation among agricultural labourers seems to have started at Yaxley when, on 25 May 1872, 1,000 men met to be addressed by a Mr. Savage who urged them not to accept a wage of 14s. a week. The meeting was also attended by a number of farmers and their sons who tried to drown the speaker with bird-scaring clappers. This resulted in a riot with the farmers being beaten over the head with their own clappers.

A few days later, on 31 May, a similar meeting for agricultural workers was held in St. Neots Market Square. Its advertised purpose was 'To consider what steps should be adopted to induce the employers of labour in St. Neots and district to advance the present level of wages, and also to adopt means for social and moral improvement of the working men and their families'. About 800 persons were estimated to have been present at the meeting but many of these were said to have been mechanics, women and children.

The first speaker was a Mr. Lane, lately employed by the Duke of Manchester, who claimed to have started the present agitation for wage advances in Huntingdonshire. He stated that in the last 20 years the wages of mechanics had risen by 20 per cent, but those of agricultural workers by only five per cent. His object that day was to establish a branch of the Agricultural Workers Union in St. Neots district. He did not advocate strikes, and anyone who did so was an enemy of the movement, he merely wished to establish a union that would protect them against the tyranny of capital over labour. It was all very well, he said, for Ministers of the Gospel to tell them to be contented with their lot, how could a man be contented when he had not sufficient to feed himself and his family? Farmers, as a body, were implacable tyrants and their poor labourers only white slaves.

The next speaker was Mr. Bailey, of Offord, and he addressed the meeting as 'Christian fellow workers'. He had worked, he said, since the age of nine, and had not time or opportunity to educate his eight children. At the time when the sixth was born he was only earning 10s. a week. In his opinion farmers did all they could to crush their labourers.

Mr. Cooper, of Huntingdon, County President of the Union, spoke next. He said that the average wage in this country was only 11s. a week for the first six months of the year, or, if with piece work, 12s.; when harvest money was added it made an average weekly wage for the year of 13s. An estimate of expenses for a family was: rent 1s. 6d., coals 9d., shoes 9d., clothing 9d., medicines 3d. This left 9s. for food or 3d. per head per day (excluding Sundays) for a man and wife and four children. Ten years before wages were only 10s. a week, but that equalled 13s. today as food had gone up by 25 per cent.

Lane then asked if any employer of labour present would like to express his views, but there was no response. At the end of the meeting 107 men enrolled in the union.

Later in the same year the press, in a leading article, stated that the union had had some success in raising wages but that housing conditions remained deplorable. It was also having

financial difficulties, and in 1873 was sued for the value of
bread bought and booths hired at 'the great demonstration'
held at Brampton in the summer of 1872.

Another meeting was held in St. Neots Market Square on
28 June 1873, and was addressed by Lane, Richardson, and
others. This time only about 400 persons attended. The press
quoted such phrases used as, 'We will be putting a bit and
bridle on the farmer', and, 'The labourer should be paid equally
as well as the mechanics'. This, said the editor, is utterance of
such blatant rubbish as can only cause a feeling of disgust in
the minds of every intelligent person. At another meeting, on
the Square, on 12 November 1873, the slogans were 'War to
the Knife', and 'Stick to the Union'.

In 1874 came the first mention of the famous Joseph Arch,
when he was advertising locally for 1,000 labourers to emigrate.
He was born in 1826, in Warwickshire, of labouring parents
and was himself a day labourer. He was largely self-educated
and became a Methodist lay preacher. He soon acquired a
local reputation as an orator and champion of the working
classes. In the face of intolerable conditions for the agricultural workers he called a meeting which was attended by
1,000 labourers, and at which his dream of an Agricultural
Workers' Union was enthusiastically launched. In 1872 a
National Union was formed which was successful in obtaining
a general rise in wages, but this destroyed the union when
members got what they wanted. Arch was returned to Parliament for West Norfolk in 1885, after succeeding in getting
the vote for agricultural workers. On 5 May 1875 he came to
St. Neots to address a meeting on the square, when it was
estimated that 700-800 were present to listen to a speech
lasting an hour and 20 minutes. All members of the union
present wore a blue ribbon or rosette. The local press reported
his speech to fill a column.

Among other things he stated that it cost the Guardians
24s. a week to keep a man, his wife, and four children in
the workhouse, and yet employers had refused to pay 14s.
for an honest week's work. How therefore could a family
be expected to live on 12s., or even 14s. a week?

He also attacked the franchise which was attached to property and denied the vote to agricultural workers. He related

the story of a man he knew who set up as a small market
gardener, and asked his landlord for a stable and cartshed.
He then bought a jackass and this entitled him to qualify as
a voter. The jackass got him the vote! A bill to extend the
franchise would be presented to Parliament next July and
he was one of a delegation going to visit John Bright and
Professor Fawcett to press his views. In fact the agricultural
worker did not get the vote until 1884. Professor Fawcett
was a well-known and remarkable M.P., and totally blind.
He expressed views, independent of party, in favour of many
reforms, some even with a republican flavour.

It would seem that pressure from the Union was effective
in raising wages generally up to 14s. a week. This was confirmed when, in 1876, the first reported strike occurred at
Southoe. Here Mr. Bowyer, of Manor Farm, tried to reduce
the wages of his men from 14s. to 13s. a week. They all
came out on strike and were given 9s. a week strike pay by
the union. Unfortunately the result was not reported. Indeed
no further news regarding union activities appeared, and one
can only assume that, as in other parts of the country, membership fell and it became an insignificant force once its immediate
object of raising wages had been accomplished.

Meanwhile mechanics and artisans seem to have been either
reasonably content with their lot or felt economically weak
(30 unemployed were parading the streets in 1887). However
in 1892 a meeting of building workers was held in the *Cannon*
inn, New Street, to discuss the '1 o'clock Movement', and a
resolution was passed supporting the 1 o'clock closure on
Saturdays. It also asked for an increase in wages from 5d. to
5½d. an hour for carpenters, and 5½d. to 6d. for bricklayers.
It was stated that working hours were longer in St. Neots
than in other towns. Presumably the employers did not agree
to these demands, as a strike was called. However as 18 men
out of 40 refused to come out it was called off.

XI
TECHNICAL ADVANCES IN TRANSPORT
AND COMMUNICATIONS

THE GREAT ADVANCES in transport and communications
only came in the second half of the 19th century. The greatest of
these, in its impact on life in the town, was undoubtedly the
coming of the railway and the opening of St. Neots station
in 1850. Rail travel was fast and punctual but the roads still
under the semi-bankrupt turnpike trusts were poor and, not
being waterbound, were muddy in winter and dusty in summer. In the town the local authority water cart, sprinkling
water on the streets to lay the dust, was a necessary and
familiar sight well into this century.

Away from the railway connections travel was not easy,
and was little better than it had been in the early 1800s. It
still depended on the horse and there were no public services.
Only the upper middle class could afford to keep a horse or
pony of their own, other than for business; others had to
hire from the local 'job masters'. Those unable to afford horse
transport had to walk if they wished to travel, and the public
footpaths across the fields provided valuable short cuts between
villages.

The Carriers
Nearly every village had its carrier, 'who with his horse and
roomy covered cart drove to all the nearby market towns
on their market days. From the surrounding villages carriers'
carts converged on St. Neots every Thursday, putting up regularly at one of the inns where everyone knew where they
could be found. They had room for a few passengers but
mainly filled their carts with the villagers' produce and poultry
to take to the market, and returned with goods for which
they had orders.

The Bicycle

Bicycles seem to have been in use in the town from about 1870. In 1874 H. W. Pearson, from his shop in the High Street, was letting out both bicycles and velocipedes. These may have been 'boneshakers' and 'penny farthings'. By 1899 there was a thriving cycle club in the town.

The Motor Car

Probably the first motor car to be seen in the town was in 1896, and the event was thus recorded in the local press. 'A motor car, en route from Cambridge to Bedford, stopped for a short time at the Post Office [in the High Street] and a small crowd assembled. The motive power was benzine. It travelled at a good pace and appeared to be well under control, but, we are told, the smell was objectionable. How long will it be before we have to record the appearance of a horse as a strange event?

A little later in the same year another motor car was reported seen in the town. This was the property of Prince Ranjitsinhji, the famous cricketer, but lent to a Mr. Whitmore of Cambridge. The run from Cambridge to Bedford, we are told, took just two hours, using one gallon of fuel, at a cost of 8d. The weight of the vehicle was 17 cwt. and it carried four passengers. It was capable of 20 m.p.h.

There was probably no motor car owned in the town until the early 1900s. Alfred Jordan, of Huntingdon Street had the first and the author's father either the second or third. This latter was a steam car and the author can well remember riding in it to Cambridge about 1905.

The Telephone

Telegrams could probably have been sent from St. Neots Post Office in 1870, or soon after, but nothing appears in the local press about the telephone until 1892. In that year the Post Office was given the monopoly of trunk lines between towns while private companies, of which the National Telephone Company was the chief, were left to develop the local network. In 1892 that company applied to the U.D.C. for permission to erect poles in the streets, but was abruptly refused. In 1896 agents of the company were in the town trying to enlist subscribers. This was apparently unsuccessful, as the effort was repeated in 1899, when it was stated that only if enough people came in could a connection with Huntingdon be made. By the early 1900s a service was in operation and the author remembers that his father's business at Navigation Wharf was the first Eynesbury subscriber, the number being St. Neots 1Y.

XII
NAVIGATION

THERE IS little doubt that the Ouse was used for navigation as far back as Roman times, and the small Roman earthwork at Eynesbury Coneygear may well have been a trading post linked with navigation. Later the Danish invasions up the Ouse were almost certainly based on transport by water. Today it is difficult to imagine what the river would be like before the water mills were there, but probably it had a much greater variation in level. The mills, in the present form, while maintaining a level between each other, were nevertheless a definite block to navigation. When the mills were established we do not know, but there were many on the Ouse at the time of Domesday.

In spite of the difficulties caused by the mills, navigation was successfully carried on throughout the medieval period, and, for example, St. Neots Priory and all the medieval churches in the district were built of stone and timber brought by water. It must have been a long and tedious business. When a barge or boat, carrying merchandise, arrived at a water mill the goods had to be landed and carried overland to the stretch of the river above the mill and reloaded. Sometimes the boat itself was then dragged up to the next stretch. This was known as 'backing', and added greatly to the time and cost of transport.

This state of affairs became even more intolerable with the expanding trade of the post-medieval period, and early in the 17th century Arnold Spencer obtained Letters Patent from James I to construct locks from St. Ives up to Bedford, as a commercial undertaking, but not to charge above 3d. per ton at each lock on goods passing through. Starting from St. Ives, and working upstream, locks were completed as far as St. Neots by about 1620. Work then went on upstream to within four miles of Bedford. However above St. Neots the river proved difficult and expensive to maintain in a navigable condition, and became derelict during the Civil War. In fact navigation between St. Neots and Bedford did not become a reality until near the end of the 17th century. According to Thomas Baskerville's *Journals* (1681) 'boats of burden could get no further than St. Neots'.

It is probable that the new locks consisted of only one gate (as on the Nene until recent years), and we are told that the ancient enmity between millers and boatmen often resulted in delays and frustrations. The millers would often hold up water by raising their weirs and demand payment to release it to float the barges below. Nevertheless the result was a very great fillip to trade along the Ouse, and had a profound effect on the towns along its banks. This was particularly so at St. Neots which became the port for a large hinterland, which included Bedfordshire. It is known, for instance, that the Duke of Bedford used to send his wagons from Woburn to St. Neots to collect his imported wines.

Some interesting evidence of the effect that the opening of the navigation had on the town comes from depositions of witnesses, taken in 1672, in a dispute over tolls on corn sold in St. Neots market, and heard before Commissioners of the Court of Exchequer (*Special Commissions and Depositions,* P.R.O.) Some extracts from the Depositions are given below:

Robert Lettice of St. Neots, baker and maltster.
He hath known St. Neots Market for 40 years . . . hath been employed by several persons for buying and selling several thousand quarters of grain which have been exported both by water and likewise by carts . . .
[Heading name erased]
In the deponent's time the river Ouze was made navigable by Arnold Spencer, gent. deceased, not less than 60 years past. [His memory slightly at fault] The first coals, salt, and other commodities that were brought up by water to St. Neots from Lynn came up and were laid at the deponent's yard, within 60 years; but for grain there were none brought up by water to St. Neots, to the deponent's knowledge. But some years after there hath been, and still is, divers great quantities brought up by water. Before the navigation, so lately made, the town of small trade and is now much increased in trade by reason of the navigation.
Henry Goodfellow of St. Neots. 62 years old.
Hath dealt with great quantities of grain for 16 to 20 years . . . that was brought up by water and was sold in his boats or shops [corn shops] on Market or other days. . . . By reason of the navigation the town of

St. Neots is become a great town of trading . . . great quantities of grain and other commodities are imported by water from Lynn and other ports, and sold out of their warehouses, wharfs, and boats.

John Hickman of St. Ives, salter, aged 72.
Hath known and worked at St. Neots for 58 years. The Ouze began to be made navigable about 1625, by Arnold Spencer, but not (finished) until four years after. Before they were forced to carry or bring grain and other commodities in carts from St. Ives, and other places to St. Neots market, and none were brought by boat nor any grain sold on wharfs, nor any wharfs made before the navigation. The town of St. Neots was a place of small trade to what it now is. By reason of the navigation, so lately made, the town of St. Neots is advanced in trade so much for oats, coals, salt, and other commodities as are brought hither by water. But as for wheat and barley and such other commodities as were brought by horse and carts, he considers it a place of great trade and now of greater advantage.

Andrew Horner of Godmanchester, aged 72.
Hath known the navigation for 50 years, and for six years before. Many years before that they did bring all sorts of corn, as are now in boats, by backing them over at the mills, but a good part was by way of brought by carts by reason of the troublesomeness of the passage by water, by reason of backing them at the mills.

William Barwick of St. Ives, waterman, aged 69.
Hath known the navigation for 48 years since, that time there was not any corn, grain, nor hempseed, nor any other corn brought to St. Neots from St. Ives by boat but the greatest trade from bringing grain by water hath been since the draining of the fens and making the sluices. Before the navigation the town of St. Neots was an inland town and a place of small trade for such commodities as are brought up by boat. Since the making of the river navigable great quantities of corn, grain, deal boards, fir timber, iron, fish, and other commodities have been brought by boat to St. Neots.

The above extracts speak for themselves and emphasise the great changes that the navigation brought, laying, indeed, the foundations for the town of today.

A result of the business prosperity that followed was the building of merchants' houses all along the south side of the Market Square and Brook Street, with their yards and wharfs at the back along Hen Brook. Hen Brook must, at the same time, have been straightened and deepened to give it its present canal-like appearance below Eynesbury Bridge, although there is no real evidence as to when this was done. The Market Square itself, its level raised in late medieval times, was now further raised to avoid flooding, and the ditches that crossed it filled in.

It will be noted, from the above quotations, that the trade in corn was both in and out of the town, it being brought here for sale in the market and then exported, some no doubt to mills on connecting navigable waterways but most, probably, to join the great exports of corn from Lynn to Scotland, Norway and the cities of the Netherlands. These exports, helped by government bounties, continued throughout the 17th and 18th centuries, and did not cease until the early 19th. Even then 'Townborn', describing the market about 1816, says that on market days about a quarter of the space of the Market Square was filled with pitched corn. He adds that coal from Lynn was distributed over a radius of 20 miles, and that the annual revenue of the navigation company from tolls was £15,000.

The early 19th century probably saw a decline in the river traffic but it was not until the middle of the century that the fatal blow came, at least to the upper Ouse, with the building and fierce competition of the railway. The navigation interests had had it all their own way for over 200 years and had done little to improve or modernise themselves. 'Townborn' says that the then owner of the navigation, Sir Thomas Grey Cullum, refused a liberal offer from the Great Northern Railway Company, perhaps foolishly, as his share of the trade rapidly declined. A speaker at a meeting of St. Neots Local Board in 1885 said, 'the navigation is practically closed and the town at the mercy of the railway'. Major Marindin, in a report to the County Council in 1890, stated that all navigation above Tempsford ceased in 1876, and above Eaton Socon in 1878. Between St. Neots and St. Ives, he reported, the navigation will cease shortly, barges, of which only 37 remain, were only able to get up half laden, and could only complete two or three trips a month. Tolls did not exceed £250 a year.

The prospect of the disappearance of the Ouse navigation, giving a monopoly to the railways, caused great concern to business interests in the area, and in 1890 a syndicate was formed to buy, for £17,000, the navigation rights and to modernise and revive the river traffic. They proposed to cut a new canal to join Bedford with the Grand Junction Canal at Newport Pagnell, and to introduce steam tugs. The navigation was then the property of Mr. Fairey of St. Neots, who had acquired it from Mr. Kirkham, of Huntingdon Street, St. Neots, to whom he had been agent.

This scheme fell through and, in 1892, the navigation was put up for auction in London where it did not reach the reserve price, the highest bid being £5,200. In 1893 it was bought by L. T. Simpson.

It would appear that the new owner did something to improve things, as in 1895 the Ouse Transport Company were advertising for business between Lynn and Bedford, their business card giving a long list of goods they had carried by water. They also announced a weekly service between Lynn and St. Neots, leaving St. Neots each Saturday and Lynn each Wednesday. Also in July of the same year the press reported that C. G. Tebbutt had just received the largest consignment of waterborne goods in recent times, namely 20 barges of timber, ex. ship from Lynn.

What seemed like a modest revival of the navigation ended with the century. The borough of Godmanchester claimed that they had an ancient right to open the navigation sluices when their land was threatened by floods. This right was denied by Simpson who locked the gates against them. Godmanchester persuaded the County Council to take up their case and in 1899 an action was started against Simpson in the Chancery Court. The Council sought a declaration that the Ouse, from above St. Neots to St. Ives, was a public navigable river and a public highway; that Simpson was bound to maintain the locks and other works in an efficient condition, subject to boats paying tolls; and to restrain him from interfering with the navigation. Judgement was given that the Ouse between St. Neots and St. Ives and to the sea was a public navigable river and a common highway, that the locks were part of the navigation, but there was no obligation on the defendant to maintain them. This judgement, finally heard before the House of Lords, was confirmed.

There was naturally great public interest in the case locally, and at one stage a procession of pleasure boats was organised which proceeded from the town to the Paper Mill and forced its way through the navigation sluice, which had been locked. The result of all this, after both sides had spent large sums in legal costs, was perhaps inevitable. Simpson decided to cut his losses and leave the navigation to decay.

However an attempt to revive it was made in 1900. In that year a prospectus was issued by Ouse Navigation Ltd. to form a company, with a capital of £20,000, to acquire the navigation rights and itself run a service of boats on the river. It was claimed that by the use of screw-propelled barges labour could be cut down drastically and the upkeep of tow paths eliminated. Among the proposed directors were H. Cranfield of Buckden, E. A. Rose of Hartford, and C. G. Tebbutt of St. Neots. The author has no information as to why the project did not go forward; probably capital was not forthcoming. A further attempt to form a navigation company in 1907 also came to nothing.

Something should be said about the barges themselves. They were always called 'lighters', and indeed that term was used in the 17th century depositions quoted above. Pictures of the Ouse in the 18th and early 19th centuries show barges with masts and sometimes sails set (as in the frontispiece to Gorham's *History of St. Neots*). These were probably square sails on the lines of the Humber 'keels'. Latterly the lighters were about 40 feet long with a 10-foot beam, drawing a foot of water when light and three and a half feet when fully loaded with 25 tons. They were most economically worked when in 'gangs' of five or six. One of these was the 'house boat' with a cabin in which the crew slept and cooked. Often the 'gang' towed one or two smaller boats including the 'horse boat'. This had a flat top on to which the towing horse stepped at places where there was either no tow path or where it crossed to the opposite bank. Besides being trained to step on to the 'horse boat', horses, when towing, had to be trained to pause before leaping over the low field fences crossing the tow path, to allow the tow rope to become slack.

The author has talked to many people who had vivid memories of the navigation, and it was evident that the barges and the men that worked them made a strong impression on childish minds. These memories were mainly associated with Brookside, which was a public wharf used by those who had no wharves of their own. The Navigation Wharf, Eynesbury, now occupied by C. G. Tebbutt Ltd., was, until about 1850, the local depot of the navigation company. Here stores were kept and from here their own boats would travel to effect repairs to locks and tow paths. The manning of the lighters was usually a family affair, passing from one generation to the next. The Breese family of St. Ives was most often remembered as associated with the trade.

XIII
FLOODS, AND THE SPA

UNTIL THE MIDDLE of the present century floods, and flood stories, were a perennial subject of conversation and commiseration in St. Neots and Eynesbury. Almost every winter there were small floods covering the river meadows and the road to the paper mill, where the raised 'traps' enabled workers to get to the mill. Each small flood was regarded with anxiety until it had subsided.

Every three or four years or so, higher levels would occur and some of the town streets, especially parts of Brook Street, Church Street, and St. Mary's Street, Eynesbury, would be flooded. Less often still higher levels would reach the Market Square and the west end of High Street. In addition sudden violent thunderstorms in summer, accompanied by torrential rain, would quickly fill the Cambridge Street brook and overflow the road. The same conditions would make impassable the low part of Huntingdon Street, near the junction with Russell Street, and flood houses, but would quickly subside.

Houses built in parts of the town most liable to flooding were, of course, those occupied by the poorer classes, and great damage and misery was caused to people here, too poor to afford new decorations and expensive fuel to dry their houses out.

When the streets were flooded and impassable to passengers it was usual for the local authority to either organise their own, or hire, horses and carts to provide continuous free transport along the flooded streets. People arriving at their flooded homes would often step down from the cart on to the first of a line of chairs leading through the downstairs room to the stairs and dry upper storey. It was no uncommon sight to see baker's carts delivering loaves of bread on pitchforks to customers at bedroom windows. This century, when motor lorries replaced carts for these purposes, the flooding was often aggravated, as the vehicles created waves that swept into the houses doing further damage.

The causes of past flooding are easy to explain. The main reason was, of course, that much of the town is built on the flood plain of the Ouse. Floods were likely to occur after long periods of heavy rain had flooded the river meadows and before this local flooding could subside it was overtaken by a mass of water from the upper reaches of the Ouse in Bedfordshire and Buckinghamshire. This usually took about three days, and then town flooding was likely to occur.

The really big floods were the result of freak conditions, as in 1947. Then heavy snowfalls in late February had followed hard frost. Suddenly, on 11 March, came a rapid thaw, and the melted snow, unable to soak into the frozen ground, poured into the brooks and rivers causing the highest flood for over 100 years. As a result of the 1947 flood, and the great damage it did, the flood gates at the Paper Mill were rebuilt by the Great Ouse River Board. Now local flood water is able to get away before that from above arrives. However a flood of the 1823 or 1947 proportions would still probably flood the town.

The flood most talked of in the 19th century was that of 1823, the highest of the century, though Stowe in his *Annals* records a catastrophic flood at St. Neots in 1571, when boats floated over the churchyard wall. It is recorded that on 30 October 1823 there was incessant rain, with a strong NE. wind, which became a hurricane after nightfall with sheets of descending rain. On 1 November the rapidly rising water warned the inhabitants that a calamity could be expected, and by midnight the water reached its greatest height, said to be 10 feet 8 inches above normal (now recorded as 55.40 ordnance datum). Houses near the site of the Corn Exchange had three feet of water in them, and the parish church, never before known to be flooded, had two feet. Every house in the town was flooded and the water reached the bottom of Priory Hill. Ingersole, the grocer in the Market Square, lost goods valued between £800 and £1,200, and Bedells, in the High Street, £500. It lasted three days.

After this calamity no serious floods seem to have been recorded until the year 1872, when a new series started, with the High Street being flooded in that year. In 1875 a flood lasting from 15 to 22 October came, it was said, to within two feet of the 1823 flood, and was repeated in November of the same year, with 18 inches of water in the High Street. In October 1880 the river rose to over five feet above normal, and in 1883 the local press stated that there had been four severe floods in the previous six months. Town flooding occurred again in 1891.

A major flood was experienced in November 1894, with a reported height of 7 feet 1½ inches (now put at 51.85 o.d.), and said to have been the worst since 1823. All the High Street was flooded with severe losses in some shops. At the Paper Mill part of the road was swept away and a floating tree trunk jammed against the 'traps' and forced them out of line. Messrs. J. W. Addington, A. B. Brackenbury, and A. K. Bower rowed a boat from the *Half Moon* (*Bridge* hotel) to Eaton Ford, through the yard gates of Ford House, then over the river meadows to Brookside, St. Neots, and on to Mr. A. W. Atkinson's yard at 45 High Street. On the following Sunday the vicar of St. Neots preached a sermon on 'The Deluge'.

As a result of the inundation there was no water fit to drink in the town and, fearing an epidemic as had happened after former floods, the Local Board had printed and distributed to every house a leaflet advising that all drinking water be filtered and boiled. In view of the plight of the poor a committee was formed to collect subscriptions to distribute bread, and particularly coal to dry out their houses. The fire engine was used to pump out cellars and wash away sewage from the streets.

The *St. Neots Advertiser* described the scene after the water had subsided. 'After 11.00 p.m. the fall was very rapid. Of course the lower lying parts were still flooded for several days. Saturday was a fine bright day and in all directions were to be seen furniture, carpets, and other household goods put out or hung up to dry. The water had left behind a slimy mud, everything seemed damp, and even after huge fires had been in evidence there seemed a musky smell about everything for days. Many houses can hardly expect to get thoroughly dry before next summer. Almost everyone has sustained loss of some kind through the flood'.

In 1908 St. Neots and Eynesbury were again inundated in the worst flood since 1894, although the water was a foot lower on this occasion. This happened on 30 April after a heavy snowfall, followed by equally heavy rain.

Later in this century high levels, resulting in town flooding, occurred in 1918 (51.32 o.d.), 1939 (no o.d. record), 1940 (about 51.00 o.d.), and notably in March 1947 (52.33 o.d.), the highest since 1823. In this latter flood it was estimated that only about one-fifth of the flow of water was in the river bed. Almost 800 houses were flooded and over £8,000 was afterwards paid out in proved damage claims.

St. Neots Spa

The St. Neots spa derives from a spring situated somewhere near, or under, the Paper Mill, and now has its outlet on a small platform, overlooking the river downstream from the mill, and approached by a flight of steps from the road. The writer has no information as to its origin or early history. It is however supposed to be a chalybeate spring similar to, and perhaps originating from the same source as, the Hail Weston springs, used medicinally in the 16th and 17th centuries and commemorated in a poem by Michael Drayton.

The idea of popularising the St. Neots spa probably came from Mr. J. McNish who, in 1895, formed a small committee who leased the mineral spring and were reported to have dug a well 90 feet deep. At once the idea seems to have caught on in the town and everyone thought that St. Neots was going to be another Tunbridge Wells.

In the same year the spa had an official opening on Whit Monday. A procession of 30 boats were rowed from St. Neots bridge to the spa with a band on board.

Messrs. Jordan & Addington had already prepared for sale bottles of 'Neotia', and these were used in bulk as decoration for the ceremony. The pipe had been plugged and was ceremonially unplugged by Mrs. Fydell Rowley, who officially opened the spa. Its health was drunk, in spa water, from the Fellows Football Cup, newly won by the St. Neots team. In 1896 a company was formed to run the spa.

Local enthusiasm grew, and the press reported that the committee were considering building baths, and that a dog with sores had been completely cured by bathing it in spa water. Later in the same year it was reported that the Common Right Proprietors were unable to offer a site for a pump room!

However public interest soon waned, and presumably 'Neotia' did not find a local, let alone a national market. In 1900 there were complaints that the spa was in an untidy and neglected state. Even so the writer can remember that local people could be seen collecting bottles of the water, and many swore by its beneficial health properties. There used to hang on the outside wall of the Corn Exchange a framed copy of an analysis of the spa water, and what it claimed to cure or alleviate.

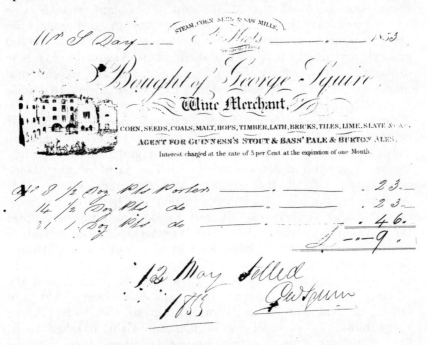

XIV
ST. NEOTS COMMONS AND
LAMMAS MEADOW

ALL COMMONS today are anachronisms, something left over
from the feudal past that today has no meaning, at least in
the agricultural sense. When commons were first created, in
the very dim past, only two parties were concerned with
them, the Lord of the Manor and the Commoners. Now a
very important third party is interested in commons, the
general public, in respect of their recreational facilities and
general amenities. It is often difficult to reconcile this new
demand with the very limited statutory use to which commons could be put, but which has often been the only
reason why they have been preserved.

Once commons played a very valuable part in the life of
nearly every parish, for every householder had, by right, a
right of common to put out a beast to graze there at certain
strictly regulated times of the year. The Lord of the Manor
owned the soil of the common and the trees, if any, that
grew on it, but the commoners owned the herbage that grew
on his soil. Neither was allowed to do anything that upset
the property of the other. The management and regulation
of the commons was usually done by the Lord of the Manor's
Court Leet, which had a jury of commoners. They decided
such things as the times and restrictions of grazing, and the
number and kinds of beasts that each commoner could turn
out. This was known as 'stinting'. Up to the 16th century
every house in a parish had a common right attached to it,
but thereafter only existing houses, or new ones built to
replace old ones, kept their rights, so that the number did
not increase.

There was also in each parish, usually, a Lammas Meadow,
often land that was low-lying and floodable and therefore
unsuitable for ploughing. Here many, or all, of the commoners
were allowed to mow, by hand, a narrow strip, or 'swarth' of

grass with which to make hay. Hay-making was assumed to be over by Lammas Day (1 August), and thereafter the Lammas Meadow was added to the common. This system of commons and Lammas land was a vital part of the Open Field System of parish agriculture almost universal and traditional in the English Midlands.

The ancient Open Field System was ended by Inclosure Acts, one for each parish, mainly, in this district, between about 1770 and 1830. Under these Acts commissioners were appointed to amalgamate the numerous tiny strips of land each farmer then had, and give him in exchange solid blocks of land in the form of farms as we now know them. In most parishes commons and Lammas land were done away with and the commoners given tiny plots of land — allotments — in exchange. To commoners who were not farmers these small plots were of little use. They were too small to plough and too large to dig, and were useless to support the cow, donkey or flocks of geese that cottagers were formerly able to pasture on the common. All they could do was to sell their allotments to the adjoining farmer who, of course, benefited greatly from the enclosure. The cottagers' feelings were expressed in the 18th-century rhyme:

The law doth punish man or woman
Who steals the goose from off the common,
But lets the greater felon loose
Who steals the common from the goose.

The St. Neots Inclosure Act 1770 was an early one and under it, very exceptionally, it was decided that the existing Islands, Hawkesden Leys and Lammas Meadow commons should remain. A similar arrangement obtained at Huntingdon and Godmanchester. Perhaps, in the case of small market towns, tradesmen and dairymen with no farm land were sufficiently influential to demand that the commons, on which to graze their horses and cows conveniently near the town, should remain. The Act of 1770 and Award of 1771 present many historical problems. Fortunately they have been the subject of considerable research by Rosa Young, a copy of whose manuscript is with the Huntingdon Record Office, and the author is grateful for much information which she has generously supplied.

It seems that all the cottagers and homesteaders who proved to have rights on the common in 1770 retained them. However, as holders of other grazing rights on the former open arable fields after harvest they were offered in compensation small allotments of land, probably between Huntingdon Street and Islands Common. The Lord of the Manor, Lord Sandwich, still remained owner of the soil of the commons, and had in addition 27 grazing rights through ownership of house properties in the town.

Common rights once attached to the Bargroves, an area of arable land south of Cambridge Road (approximately TL 200590), have no connection with the present commons. The owner, Edward Payne, illegally enclosed this area in 1607 and was ordered to pay £17 per year to the commoners as compensation. Finally in 1787 it was agreed that the money be paid to the vicar 'for an afternoon lecture during the pleasure of the inhabitants'. This is recorded on the Charity Board in St. Neots church.

In their Award of 1771 the Commissioners admit claims to 154 common rights held by 86 persons, including the 27 owned by Lord Sandwich. There is also a lengthy and important 'saving' which states that neither the Lord of the Manor nor the commoners had lost any of their former rights or privileges.

In relation to the commoners there is also reference to rights confirmed by Sir Robert Tyrwhit and Sir Henry Darcy in 1564. No copy of this seems to exist in the Public Record Office or among local records, but there was a copy with the Rowley family papers in 1958. Through the kindness of the Rowley family solicitors the author was shown a typescript copy. It referred to a dispute between the commoners and Sir Francis Williams (*alias* Cromwell), probably of Monks Hardwick. The subsequent Awards confirmed rights of common over the Islands and Hawkesden Leys commons, and to drive cattle along roads leading to them.

Some local opinion in the past has expressed the view that under the 1771 Award all manorial rights in the commons, i.e. ownership of the soil, ceased. However, the 'saving' referred to above seems to make it plain that this was not so. In fact George Fydell Rowley sold the area formerly occupied by the pound, on the common, to St. Neots Gas Company (p. 297).

Some confusion has also arisen from the fact that many people have ownership Deeds of Common Rights described as 'Freehold'. This seems to have come about since common rights began to be separated from the house properties of which they were once part. The term probably only refers to the grazing rights, and means that it is free of all quit rents and other manorial dues.

The above matter was not the only matter on which the original Award was inadequate. It gave no directions as to how the commons were to be managed, but only how they were to be stinted. This was as follows:

A commoner was entitled only to graze 'One mare or gelding, or one ox or steer or heifer, and no other kind of cattle. The Islands Common to be opened 1 May to 1 January the Islands Meadow (Lammas Meadow) 1 August to 1 April and Hawkesden Leys 1 June to 1 January. It is prohibited to put on the common any stone horse, rigel [?], glandered or mangy mare or gelding, or any mare, gelding, ox, cow, steer, heifer or calf having any infectious disorder. Provided nothing shall prevent any sucking calf from going with a cow until the age of three months, or sucking foal belonging to a mare from running with the mare until 10 October, but no longer, or prevent the owners jointly to keep one or more bull or bulls for the use and benefit of the commoners, over and above the stint'.

This was all so unsatisfactory that in the year 1774 a new Act was passed to 'explain and amend' the first Act. This resolved the difficulty of how the commons were to be managed, but said nothing of the position of the Lord of the Manor. Its main provisions were,

1. That the proprietors, or their agents, properly authorised, are required to meet in the parish church of St. Neots the first Wednesday of April each year between the hours of 12 and 2 of the clock of the same day. Those attending such meetings having a majority of common rights, providing such rights shall not be less than 10 rights, shall appoint a treasurer for the purpose of making a rate or levy, and putting the rules and order, contained in the award, and in the Act, and such rules and orders as shall be made at the said meeting, into execution.

2. The Treasurer shall continue in office for one year, and no longer, and shall be allowed such yearly salary as the majority think proper, not exceeding £5.

3. Such majority shall and may, and are hereby required, to appoint a howard or stock keeper to put the rules and orders into execution under the direction of the treasurer, and shall allow him such weekly salary as they shall think proper, not exceeding 10s.

4. Such majority, as aforesaid, are empowered to make such orders and regulations respecting stinting and stocking, and maintaining

fences, as they shall think proper, subject to the rules and orders
in this Act and the Award, and such rules and orders shall be written
in a book for the purpose and lodged with the treasurer which
shall be open for inspection by all persons interested therein, at
all reasonable times.

5. The treasurer is empowered, within 10 days of his appointment
to make a rate or levy upon the several proprietors in proportion
to their interests therein, not exceeding the sum of 3s. per right.
which shall be paid to the treasurer on, or by, 13 April in every
year. Non-payment may be recovered by distress.

6. If sufficient number of proprietors do not attend the meeting
to make a majority of rights, the treasurer and howard shall continue in office, and the rules and orders made the previous year
shall continue in full force for the ensuing year.

7. If any person shall think himself aggrieved by anything done
in persuance of this Act, he can appeal to Quarter Sessions in the
county of Huntingdon within three months of the cause of such
complaint, giving at least eight days notice in writing to the treasurer,
and within four days of giving such notice entering into recogni-
zances before a Justice of the Peace with two sufficient sureties . . .
and shall abide by the order and pay such costs as shall be awarded
at Quarter Sessions. No action or actions shall be started against any
person for anything done in persuance of the Act until 21 days'
notice be given to the treasurer.

An old minute book of the proprietors still exists, starting
with entries dated 1774. Only a few can be mentioned. There
was evidently a road over the Common in 1786 on which tolls
were charged. In 1810, during the Napoleonic Wars, it is recorded
that the Bedfordshire Militia were expected to be quartered in
the district but they were not to be allowed to parade on the
common unless compensation was paid. In 1817 some part of
the land was mole drained by means of a capstan. There are
early records of fairs being held there. In 1820 it was ordered
that all stock be kept at the south end during Holy Thursday
Fair, and the May Fair was held there on 12 May (old May Day)
1825. From the appearance of the north west end of Islands
Common it is evident that, following the permission given in
the Act, much gravel was dug there at some time. In 1877 James
Ashwell and James Ray were being employed by the Treasurer
to dig gravel for sale at 2s. 6d. a yard; they received 1s. 2d.

The willingness of the proprietors to allow sports of various
kinds to be played on the Islands Common is much to their
credit. The earliest reference found to cricket being played

there is in 1845, and it has gone on, probably without a break, until the present day. In 1881 the Cricket Club were allowed to fence their pitch, and they built a pavilion in 1882. Both football and hockey clubs used it in the last quarter of last century, the Football Club moving to Shortsands in 1899. The Golf Club first laid out a nine-hole course there about 1890, moving to Hawkesden Leys in 1908. A bathing shed, originally for men only, was put up by the U.D.C. at the north-west corner of Lammas Meadow (the Top Boardings) in 1895, but seats put on the Common by them in the same year, with the permission of the proprietors, were ordered to be removed by Mr. Rowley.

On the Lammas meadow skating was frequently enjoyed. This was made possible by the erection, at the north end of the Lammas Meadow ditch, of a brick sluice into which a wooden gate could be put to keep on the meadow water that had come there either by natural flooding or by artificially raising the river at the Paper Mill. This sluice was generously built for this purpose by Mr. Fydell Rowley.

At the Queen Victoria Jubilee celebrations in 1887 sports were held on the common with both horse and foot races.

Until 1950 there were gates at each end of the Common road, kept by old age pensioners who found shelter in small huts, one beside each gate. More details about them and their activities will be found in the description of New Street.

The long narrow pool of water and swamp that separates the north-west end of Islands Common from the osier beds has an interesting local name the 'Lagoons'. The author remembers old people calling it the 'Flagoons', which was actually nearer to its original name of 'Flagholme', which appears in the 18th century and is of Danish origin, 'holme' meaning an island.

Today we should be very grateful to the Inclosure Commissioners for preserving St. Neots common in 1770. They, of course, could not foresee the great public part that the commons have played, and will continue to play in the amenities of the town. Even from an agricultural point of view, which is what they had in mind, their judgement was sound. In 1848 common rights were selling for £38, and in 1874 for £45, although they dropped to £26 in 1897. Until recently they were sought after by graziers, and £3 to £4 was being bid for a season's grazing at the annual auction. The Island Common is an enormous asset to the town for walking and informal children's games, and has fauna and flora that are of great interest to the naturalist.

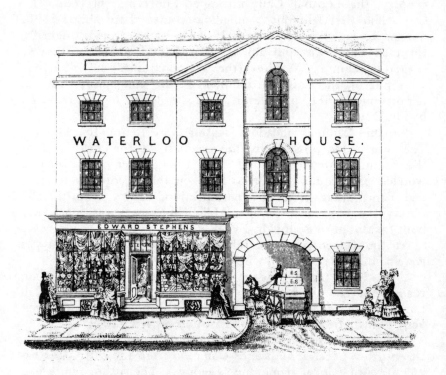

XV
MARKETS, FAIRS and FEASTS

ST. NEOTS Market Square is, without doubt, the principal feature that gives the town its character, and the one that is most remembered by passing strangers. Its large size, about 7,500 square yards, makes it one of the biggest in the country, and before the block of buildings on the east side was built it would have been nearer 10,500 square yards.

There must be some doubt as to how much St. Neots Priory contributed to the parish church, but there is no doubt of the legacy they left to the future town in the Market Square.

In the 12th century, when the monks received their charters to hold markets and fairs from Henry I and Henry II, the Priory was built on the only piece of high ground, not subject to flood, near the river, and the townspeople were living further east around the Cross, out of reach of all but the worst floods. All the land between mid-High Street and the river was then well within the flood plain of the Ouse, and subject to frequent inundations.

It must have been at this time, on gaining their charters, that a piece of riverside meadow was reserved by the monks for their market. In spite of flooding dangers its position was an advantageous one. It was on the banks of the Ouse, a navigable river connected with the Wash ports; through it ran an important east-west highway joining Cambridge and East Anglia with the Midlands; and a bridge was built by the monks, sometime in the 12th century, to carry this road over the Ouse. Furthermore only a few miles to the east was the main highway from London to the North and Scotland. Lastly it was at the Priory Gate, and so convenient to regulate and control.

The success of the market, granted for every Thursday, can be inferred from the fact that the monks enlarged it by adding land on the north side. For many years past, when shops have

Market Square, north side, 1829

Market Square, south side, 1829

Market Square, north-east corner, 1850

been rebuilt on the north side of the present Square, graves, containing human skeletons, have been found; it was always assumed that they belonged to the monks' cemetery. However, some of these graves, excavated by the author, showed that people of both sexes had been buried there. There seems no doubt that this was the town cemetery, before a separate parish church had been built, and the nave of the Priory church was being used by the parish. Some time later, probably in the 12th century when a parish church was built, the Priory precinct wall was built over this civilian cemetery leaving part of it to be added to the Market Square. Later again shop sites were let on this site, and a line of shops, known as 'Shop Row', was built against the outside of the Priory wall facing south, and corresponding to the shops as they are today.

A number of street excavations, watched by the author, have revealed what conditions were like on the Square in the Middle Ages and after. For instance a ditch, continuing from the High Street, flowed along the main road on its north side, with small foot bridges over it to approach the shops in 'Shop Row'. Another ditch, coming from the south side of the High Street, on reaching the Square turned diagonally across it to the river about half way along its west side.

Excavations on the Square itself were of great interest. They showed plainly the original turf line of the riverside meadow, but this was from two and a half feet to four feet below the present surface. Above this, from the 14th to the 17th century, the level had been artificially raised with domestic rubbish, waste soil and gravel, an astonishing performance when one considers the large area involved. The final levelling with gravel took place in the early 17th century, coinciding with the great expansion of the market following the making of navigation locks on the river. By then the level of the square was above all minor floods.

Except from the above inferences there is little information about the market in the Middle Ages. However we do know that even before the navigation was improved it did act as a magnet, drawing those engaged in trade, and their employees, from the original town centre, near the Cross, to the vicinity of the Market Square, in spite of the flood danger. Many of the houses built round the Square and along the west end of

the High Street (most of these latter have recently been pulled
down) have, behind their more recent facings, remains of timber
houses of the 15th and 16th centuries.

For the 17th century however there does survive a most interesting MS. dated 1672, which consists of the proceedings of the
Court of Exchequer in a case relating to St. Neots market tolls
(Special Commissions and Depositions. E. 134. P.R.O.). The
monks' market tolls, seized by the Crown at the Dissolution,
were then in the hands of the Lord of the Manor, and farmed
out to John Paine (or Payne) of St. Neots. He claimed toll on
all corn sold on or near the Market Square or in barge, on
Thursday or any other day of the week. The customary toll
was either in kind, a quart for every four bushels, or 4d. for
every cart load of five bushels. Godmanchester men, however,
claimed, by right of their own charters, exemption from all
tolls. From the depositions of many witnesses it is evident
that, due to the improvement in the navigation, the market
had become a great trade centre for the buying and selling
of corn, much of which was exported from the Wash ports
(see chapter on Navigation).

This weekly market for corn seems to have lasted for well
over 100 years as 'Townborn', writing of the period about
1816, remembered the Square half filled with pitched corn
in bulk. The decline must have set in as Britain gradually
became a corn importing country, the coming of the railway
in 1850 being a final blow.

By the end of the 19th century most of the local auctioneers
had acquired their own auction yards for cattle and other sales,
and the Thursday Market on the Square was reduced to a few
stalls, some occupied by local butchers and fishmongers, and
'cheapjack' stands. This century has seen a revival in the stall
trade with the advent of motorised itinerant stall-holders.

Buildings standing on the Square, or that once stood there,
must be mentioned. The most important was the Court Hall.
This was a double-cross winged timber building (see page 108)
facing the Square on the east side. Fortunately the south gable
end still survives in view, and probably much of the remainder
is incorporated in the premises of Tomson & Lendrum Ltd. All but
the south gable was destroyed in the 1820s. From the illustration
this building could well date back to the 16th, or even the late

This building, probably the *Court Hall*, was destroyed between 1820 and
1829, except for the south wing which still survives. In 1809 it is described
as 'one messuage divided into four dwellings'. On the north end is the old
Golden Ball inn, rebuilt *c.*1930. A map of St. Neots, 1770 shows this building
as slightly L shaped.

15th century, and if so would have been built by the Priory
monks for the use of their steward or bailiff who controlled
the market, collected the tolls, and used the first-floor room
to hold the Manor Court to try and sentence offenders.

Another building that once stood on the Square was the
Butter House or Butter House Chamber. It is mentioned in
documents dated 1672 and 1775, and is shown on the Inclosure
Commissioners' map of 1770. There it appears as a long narrow
building (about 150 feet long) situated along the south side of
the main road opposite the *Cross Keys* inn, with a small
detached building at its west end. During the Second World War
excavations on the Square revealed the foundations of a former
building about 19 feet N.E. of the N.E. corner of the concrete
slab on which stands the telephone booth on the centre of
the Square. The foundations contained two and five-eights inch
red bricks, probably 18th century. This must have been another
Market Hall.

The Fairs

The fairs, like the markets, were granted to the monks by Henry I and Henry II, but unfortunately the original charters granting them were destroyed in 1265, when the belfry of the Priory church collapsed. Like most fairs they were all associated with religious festivals and, before the Reformation, pilgrims would come to the Priory church to attend services. and also make purchases and enjoy themselves at the fair. Originally there were four fairs:

Ascension Day Fair, the eve, the day, and the succeeding day. Often called Holy Thursday Fair.

Corpus Christi Fair, three weeks after the above. In the Middle Ages this was the day when mystery and miracle plays were performed.

The Imprisonment of St. Peter Fair, the eve, the day, and succeeding day. This was 31 July to 2 August, and was usually called Lammas Day Fair.

The Festival of St. Neot. This must have attracted many pilgrims to the shrine of St. Neot. It was originally held on 6, 7 and 8 December, but later changed to 17 December, to coincide with St. Nicholas Day.

The first two of the above fairs have survived to the present day, but records dated 1792 and 1822 speak of five fairs, the extra one being on 3 January for horses and cattle (toll free). However Gorham says (1822) that the Lammas fair had almost died out.

The St. Neots Day Fair was still in existence in 1813 but ceased soon after that, and was replaced by a new one, the Statute Fair (usually corrupted to 'Statis' or 'Statty') held on a Thursday in late September. At this fair young men and girls from all around the district paraded to seek employers for the forthcoming year. They wore their best smocks and country clothes, and often sported ribbons which denoted the kind of job they hoped to obtain. Farmers and others looked them over and struck bargains for the year's work. This seems to have ceased by 1875.

There are few accounts of exactly what went on at the fairs. One of the few is contained in the diary of the Hon. John Byng (*Torrington Diaries, vol. IV.*). On 24 May 1794 he recorded passing 'through the great fair of St. Neots', and again on 30 May 'I took my evening ride alone, through St. Neots where continue the relics of their fair, as an elephant and the King of France guillotin'd. (Is not this a bad exhibition for the lower people?)'.

Much later the local press occasionally had a paragraph about the Statute Fair as:

1864. Sept 24th.

The Annual Statute. The number of stalls and booths was unusually large, and several 'sleight of hand' gents were present doing a flourishing trade with their charms, brooches etc. The attendant lads and lasses from the surrounding villages waiting to be hired was much above average.

1865. Sept 30th.

A large influx of lads and lasses from the surrounding villages resplendent with ribbons and gaudy coloured waistcoats.

1873. Sept. 18th.

The 'Statty Fair'. Hiring as usual with the regular carnival of lads and lasses from the country, the assemblage of shows and stalls unusually large.

1875. Holy Thursday Fair.

The largest show of horned beasts ever known in the town, but few changed hands owing to the shortage of keep. Few gingerbread stalls.

1875. Statute Fair.

No Hiring

Gingerbread cakes, known as 'gingerbread husbands' used, in the early 19th century, to be sold at Earith, Hunts., at the May Fair there. They were made in wooden moulds to represent kings and queens and gilded. Girls without sweethearts were often offered them in mockery, and they must originally have had a fertility significance. A wooden mould from St. Neots is in St. Ives museum.

Eynesbury Feast

People in Eynesbury no doubt attended the fairs at St. Neots, but they also had their own annual parish Feast, which survived well into the present century. The Feast was held on a Sunday, Monday, and Tuesday, early in September, the religious part being followed by two days' holiday. The date was that of the Nativity of the Virgin Mary, patron of Eynesbury church, fixed annually, but on the Sunday nearest to 8 September.

It would seem likely that the secular part of the Feast, with its booths and stalls, was once held near the church on what must have been the original Green, between Luke Street and Berkeley Street. G.H. remembered it being held in a field immediately south of Luke Street, before this was built on. It then moved to the Coneygear field. At the former site he remembered, about 1890, Harriss's Roundabouts, consisting of alternate horses and penny-farthing bicycles.

Some extracts from the local press give an idea of what went on at this important local holiday festival. For instance in 1871 there was the usual two-day holiday, with toy and gingerbread stalls at the feast ground. Main features were cricket and quoit matches in the Rectory meadow. In 1875 it was reported that the number of stalls was as large as ever, and that for three days everyone in Eynesbury was in holiday attire. The chief event was a cricket match between 11 members of the Star Bowkett Club (See 15 Luke Street) and 16 tailors and shoemakers (Stars versus Snips and Snobs).

In 1883 the press reported that the Feast had suffered a great decline and would soon be a thing of the past; and in 1884 that it was stated to be 'very orderly in contrast with those of 15 to 20 years ago'.

However in 1886 there seems to have been a revival as in attendance were 'Blandys Mammoth Ghost Illuminations' and a theatrical company playing *Maria Marten or Murder in the Red Barn*. It certainly did not die but probably changed its character. The writer remembers being taken there about 1905, when it was in the Coneygear field. The field was nearly filled with the stalls and booths of the usual itinerant fairground people, with swings and roundabouts, and even bears in a cage.

Harvest Festival

Perhaps because of its greater dependence on agriculture, Harvest Festival Sunday at Eynesbury seemed to be a more important occasion than at St. Neots. It often coincided with Feast Sunday. About 1870 it was the custom on that day for all farmers of the parish, with their men, to assemble at the south end of the village and march in procession to the church to attend the service.

XVI

PUBLIC ENTERTAINMENTS

AS THERE WAS no local press before the middle of the 19th century it is difficult to find out what there was in the way of public entertainments. 'T', writing of the period about 1830, says that they were very few, and only mentions Jackson's theatrical company who visited the town once every three years. They probably played in the Assembly Rooms at the Cross.

The great stimulus to public entertaiɲments was undoubtedly the building of the Public Rooms in 1845, and more particularly the Corn Exchange in 1863, where most entertainments were held after that date. There was, however, one class of travelling theatrical company that had its own tent which was erected either on the Common or in a close or paddock behind the *Cross Keys* in Priory Lane. This type of theatre was always known as the 'Gaff'. It survived until at least 1914, and possibly until about 1920. In this later period it was always associated with the name of Mr. Weight, the proprietor, and he and his shows were remembered with much affection and nostalgia. Weight's company is first mentioned in 1892.

The first mention of amateur talent is a band concert in 1876, and thereafter concerts were given, rather than drama.

It would appear that the travelling companies themselves first introduced the cinema, that was to be their downfall, as an item in their show.

The Professionals

In the 1860s the fashionable professional entertainers were apparently the 'nigger minstrels', and a company of 'Christy Minstrels' visited the town in 1865. In 1867 came the 'Great American Slave Troupe', giving plantation songs and banjo music at the Corn Exchange, with seats at 2s., 1s., and 6d.

Many of the performers were said to have been slaves before 1865, and it was reported as being one of the best companies ever to have visited the town. In 1869 another 'American Slave Troupe' arrived, and had a procession through the town with a brass band. They advertised, 'The public will notice their entry into the town in their Magnificent Band Carriage, and not confuse this Gigantic Establishment with the Miserable Specimens of Minstrelsy called Christys, which have for some time infested the country'.

In 1875 Wildman's Theatre put up a tent in a paddock near the *Cross Keys*, and played Othello, Lear and Macbeth. The year 1886 saw many performances. In September, at Eynesbury feast, a company played *Maria Marten or Murder in the Red Barn*, while in the Corn Exchange, in November, Sam. Geary's company played *My Sweetheart*, described as 'London's latest and greatest success, a Simple Story illustrating the Battle of Love between a Pure and Good Girl and a Designing and Unscrupulous Adventurer'. Seats 2s., 1s., and 6d.

Less fortunate in the same month was Bateman's Theatre that had established itself on the Common for nine weeks, playing to miserably small audiences. Finally a public subscription raised 30s., which enabled them to pay their debts and leave.

The travelling theatre seemed to reach its peak in the 1890s. In 1893 Mame Clifford took the Corn Exchange for *The Royal Spanish Serenaders*, and *A Diorama of the World*, and was followed by the Lloyd and Cooper Company in *Admiral Jack*. The diorama was a new invention, and one of the processes from which the cinema was evolved. Meanwhile Weight's theatre moved from the Common into the Corn Exchange owing to the continuous bad weather.

In 1894 Lee Southern's Dramatic Company of 13 performers, who took the Corn Exchange for three nights, had an average audience of only 15, and were stranded with no money. When their plight became known they were offered the hall free for one more night, and had a good attendance to see *Our Boys*, and departed free of debt.

In 1895 Miss Iniz Howard's Company played *Driven from Home*, and Gresham Falcon's Company *A Pair of Spectacles*, and *Private Secretary*. Also came the Comedie Anglais Company in *Silver Queen*, Mabel Luxmore's Company in *False Lights*, and the Louisiana Minstrels. Weight's theatre returned to the Common.

In 1896 Miss Iniz Howard returned with *Saved from the Sea*, Lawrence Daly's Company played *Cissy*, Mr. Rees's Company *A Grip of Iron*, and Moore and Burgess brought 40 performers in *Tableaux Vivants* and *Uncle Tom's Cabin*. Miss Iniz Howard paid a second visit, this time to play *Worlds Verdict*, while Douglas Ely's Company presented another diorama as well as playing *Merry Maids*. Perhaps saturation point had now been reached, for the London Comedy and Burlesque Company were stranded in the town, with their properties seized for debt. Subscriptions amounting to £3 7s. 6d. were raised to release them.

In 1897 Maggie Morton's Company played *Blue Beard*, Miss Iniz Howard's Company *Tommy Atkins*, Carpenter's Company *The Manxman*, and Hybert's Company the apparently never-failing *Uncle Tom's Cabin*. Innovations were the Musical Dramatic Company in *Swiss Girl*, and a show called *Waxwork Tableaux*.

In 1898 *East Lynn* was performed, and the public were told 'Not often does one have the chance to see this most beautiful play, well staged and acted ... one of the most wonderful plays ever written'. In 1899 Moore and Burgess returned, this time with 50 minstrels, and had packed audiences.

The Amateurs

The performances of amateurs, if there were any, do not seem to have been noticed by the press until 1876 when a Promenade Concert was given in the grounds of Eynesbury rectory by the St. Neots and Eynesbury Amateur Brass Band. In 1884 Miss Cosa Gregson, who was a semi-professional artist living in St. Neots, gave the first of several annual concerts in the Corn Exchange. In 1891 the St. Neots Musical Society presented *The Captives of Babylon* in the Public Rooms, and in 1893 there is a mention of the St. Neots Choral Society. In 1894 a pantomime, *Babes in the Wood* was given in the Corn Exchange, but it is not clear if by amateurs or professionals. In 1895 St. Neots Minstrels gave a concert, and in 1898 an Amateur Dramatic Entertainment included *Women's Wrongs* and *Aunt Charlotte's Maid*. Ladies were requested not to wear large hats. In 1899 the St. Neots Town Band was formed.

The Cinema

The first 'cinematograph' appeared in the Corn Exchange in 1896 as part of the repertoire of the travelling show company 'The Serenaders' who had already introduced the diorama in 1893. It was described as 'the latest sensation of the age, the only genuine machine out of London, and as now performing at the Empire at a cost of £200 a week. Living pictures that are the marvel of the 19th century'. In 1899 another company presented 'A Cinematograph of Annotated Pictures of upwards of Sixty Subjects nightly, also a Talkograph reproducing speeches, songs, etc. from life'.

The first building to be used exclusively as a cinema was at Eynesbury, where, in Osborne's Yard (see 19 St. Mary's Street) Noah Hull about 1912 erected a ramshackle wooden shed, with a tarpaulin roof, in which to show films to the public. There were a few seats and most of the audience had to stand. The projector light was an electric arc lamp from a dynamo powered by a fairground steam-engine standing in the yard. The concern was soon taken over and run by John Franks (see 7 Market Square) but ceased in 1914 when soldiers took over the yard and moved the shed to the Gun Park behind Kings Road. Within a very short time of the opening of the Eynesbury Cinema, perhaps even in the same year, an Electric Cinema was opened in the Public Rooms, St. Neots. Here a gas engine, installed in the cellar, ran a dynamo to provide the arc lamp. The film was, of course, silent, and was turned by hand, but the operator provided some sound by striking a metal sheet, flashing a light, and firing a toy cap pistol, to simulate thunder, lightning and a gun battle.

In 1915 C. A. James, landlord of the *Bridge* Hotel, bought St. Neots Corn Exchange and the Public Rooms, and turned the former into a cinema. Here, in the days of silent films, a pianist played during the whole of the showing of a film, improvising music appropriate to what was appearing on the screen.

XVII
SPORTS AND GAMES

IN CONSIDERING organised games in the 19th century one has to remember that they were necessarily mainly the prerogative of the upper, middle and professional classes, and in St. Neots those taking part were usually only business or professional men and some of the neighbouring farmers. The hours worked by those employed in shops or industry quite precluded them from joining in organised games except on the few public holidays, the first Bank Holiday being in 1873. Playing games on Sunday was, of course, completely prohibited.

It was not before the last decade of the century that there at last came some relaxation of the long weekly working hours. Indeed it was not until 1894 that the first 16 shops in the town decided to close at two instead of at five o'clock on Tuesdays, the remainder only altering to four o'clock, but coming into line in 1896. Building and factory workers, in 1892, were clamouring, unsuccessfully, for a one o'clock closure on Saturdays, but in that year only two firms, Paine & Co. and A. W. Atkinson, agreed to close at four o'clock on Saturdays.

Skating was perhaps an exception to these conditions as severe winter weather inevitably threw out of work many engaged in outside occupations.

On the few public holidays, and such special days as the Queen's Jubilees, the public joined enthusiastically in the numerous competitive sporting events organised. On 13 April 1870, for instance, a sports meeting was held on the Common, watched by six to seven thousand people.

Cricket

Cricket is probably the oldest organised game played in the town, and it has always been associated with the Common, where the naturally flat and well-drained 'Top Piece' provided an excellent ground, but there is no definite record as to when it first started there.

The first reference found by the author is in the minute book of the Common Proprietors, dated 1845. On 18 July of the same year it is recorded elsewhere that the Junior Cricket Players of St. Neots played against a similar club from Bedford on the Common, stumps being pitched at 11 a.m.

Minute books of St. Neots Cricket Club, running from 1847 to 1861, and 1879 to 1890, in the possession of Mr. Colin Lendrum, contain much interesting information. In 1847 their stock, with its value, comprised the following. A marquee £5, six bats (rehandled) 30s., four new bats 30s., old set of wickets and bails 5s. 6d., a new set of ditto 7s. 6d., two new balls 15s., two old balls 5s., chest for bats, etc., 15s. By 1858 the club had acquired, additionally, two pairs of leg guards, one pair of wicketkeeping gloves, one telegraph, and a marking board. The original annual subscription was 5s.

In 1848 they were playing teams from Huntingdon, Biggleswade, Gamlingay, Kimbolton, Caxton and Bourne, Southill, and St. Ives, hiring a 'coach and four' for away matches. In 1855 a team playing Caxton included J. and H. Alington (Little Barford) E. and L. Reynolds and R. Stanley (Little Paxton), all from local 'Squire' families, Rev. Maule (Eynesbury) and W. Cauldwell (veterinary surgeon).

It would appear that some time after 1861 the club's fortunes were at a low ebb, for in 1879, when it was reformed, it was stated that there had been no genuine club for some years past. Weighty backing for the new club was given by Messrs. Julius Alington, A. Toogood, S. Wilkerson, C. R. Wade Gery, and Rev. Budge, as vice presidents. In 1893 Lord Esmé Gordon, of Paxton Park, was president.

In 1882 a pavilion was erected, on the Common, at a cost of £118, and a club room hired at the *New Inn*. Concerts were got up to help the finances.

During the club's long history there were many attempts to get the Common Proprietors to allow the pitch to be fenced to prevent damage by their cattle. These were sometimes successful, but usually not so.

Football

Organised 'soccer' football probably hardly started before 1890 and, as with cricket, the team at first mainly consisted of young businessmen in the town. The author's father, C. G. Tebbutt, was captain for several years, including 1895, when St. Neots won the Fellows Cup. To St. Neots people the most popular and exciting game of the year was that against Huntingdon, and great was the jubilation when this rival was beaten.

Up to 1899 games were played on the Common 'Top Piece', but after that the club secured the field at Shortsands so that money could be collected.

Golf

The Golf Club was founded in 1890, a nine-hole course being laid out on the Common, and the *Cannon* inn used as headquarters. The initiative was said to have come from Dr. Good who became the first secretary. By 1897 a clubhouse had been built just off the Common, near where Priory Path enters it. The site was afterwards taken over by the Wesleyan or Council school.

Conditions on the Common were not very satisfactory, and there were complaints of long grass, frequent floods, and children playing football on the greens. In 1898 the club decided to move to Hawkesden Leys. Here another nine-hole course was laid out and a clubhouse erected.

In 1912 the club again moved to its present site near Cross Hall.

Swimming

With the proximity of the Ouse swimming must always have been popular with men and boys, although the steep and muddy banks made access difficult in many places. In 1895 the U.D.C. remedied this by erecting a bathing shed at the north-west corner of the Lammas Meadow. This place was known as the 'Top Boardings' and it is probably that there was already a wooden quay there, used for loading osiers.

Although rather far from the town this place had the advantage of avoiding some of the pollution, and was also fairly private, a necessity in view of the rather surprising Victorian habit of men bathing naked in the open. Indeed in 1895 and 1896 letters appeared in the local press, signed 'Tourist', complaining of men swimming naked from the new sheds. A great innovation, no doubt due to a demand, came in 1897, when times were set apart for the use of the sheds by women.

Later, in this century, a bathing shed was put up at Eynesbury Coneygear and the one at 'Top Boardings' moved to the south-west corner of Lammas Meadow; also attendants were appointed for the summer. It is perhaps a sign of our present 'grandmotherly' bureaucracy that these were later all done away with, on legal advice, as the U.D.C. *might* be held responsible if users were drowned or got disease while using the sheds. As a result swimming went on as before but without the convenience of sheds for changing or the safeguard of an attendant.

Rowing

No record of a rowing club has been found before 1873 when Rev. Maule (Rector of Eynesbury 1851-1890) called a meeting to consider the formation of a boat club. As a result the St. Neots Amateur Rowing Club was formed, and he was appointed president. Rev. Maule had been a notable oarsman in his younger days. While at Cambridge he had been Trinity Boat Club President, and had won the Diamond Sculls at Henley.

From that time on the club has never lacked support, and regattas became a popular annual summer event.

Skating

Once again it was the Common (the Lammas Meadow part) that provided natural facilities for this typically East Anglian sport, one of the seldom quoted benefits introduced by the Stuarts on their return from exile in the Netherlands. The skates used at St. Neots were of the 'fen' type with a wooden foot-rest and straight steel blades, turned up at the toe, a copy of the traditional Dutch type. They were secured to the boot by straps and a heel screw.

No record of skating at St. Neots has been found earlier than 1879, when races were held on the Lammas Meadow for both adults and boys of the Free School.

The winter of 1890/91 was a severe one and in December 1890 the St. Neots Skating Association was formed, and a silver cup presented by J. McNish. This is still being competed for when conditions allow. On Christmas Day races were held on the river. In January 1891, as the frost continued R. L. Toogood had a sheep of 80 lbs. weight roasted on the ice, near the Paper Mill. This was distributed free to the public, together with beer and bread. The river was said to have borne for five weeks. Among the events arranged on the ice was a Bandy Match between St. Neots and Eaton Socon. The game of Bandy was the origin of ice hockey, but played on a full-sized hockey pitch. It originated from Bury Fen, Bluntisham, where it had been played from at least as far back as 1812.

Another period of prolonged frost occurred in February 1895, said to have been equalled in severity only by that of 1860. This time Mr. Toogood provided a pig for roasting, with 15 gallons of beer.

On 26 February of this year C. G. Tebbutt carried out his record skate from Peterborough to Cambridge, a distance of 87 miles, in nine hours, 20 minutes, actual skating time being seven hours, 10 minutes.

At an unknown date, probably in the 1890s, G. Fydell Rowley had a sluice built on his property, across the Lammas Meadow ditch, at its north end. In this a wooden gate could be inserted to hold up water on the Lammas Meadow to provide ice for skating. This was managed by the Skating Association and often, when there was no actual flooding, the co-operation of the Paper Mill was sought (and never refused) to hold up the river flow there until the meadow was flooded. Members of the Association often spent much of a long dark and freezing winter night on the Meadow clearing ditches and digging grips to allow the water to flow on from the river.

Polo

A local Polo Club was formed in 1900, and used to play at Eaton Socon. It probably came to an end in 1914.

XVIII
ARCHITECTURE

IT IS UNFORTUNATE, to say the least, that in St. Neots and Eynesbury so many architecturally and historically interesting buildings, having survived to the end of the 19th century, have been destroyed in the last 20 years or so. The Royal Commission, in their *Inventory of Historical Monuments* published in 1926, listed 32 buildings in St. Neots, and 22 in Eynesbury. Of these more than a third, 13 at St. Neots and eight at Eynesbury, have since been destroyed.

In the 19th century the chief architectural changes that took place were to shops in the High Street and Market Square. These changes usually reflected the individual taste, or purse, of the shopkeeper, and were mainly to the shop fronts. This resulted in an interesting pattern, in size and design, from shop to shop which, although often changing, gave the town centre an individuality of its own, distinguishing it from other towns of similar size and importance. Unfortunately the rapid changes of the last few years have eliminated many of these smaller shops and replaced them by others of the supermarket, self-service type. These, all built to a standard type, tend to make towns all over the country look alike. Distinguishing features thus become more important and it was a sad day when such an interesting High Street building as the old Corn Exchange (used as a cinema) was pulled down in 1969.

In considering the architecture of the town in the 19th century we have to remember that it reflected the varied occupations of the inhabitants, the development of the town, and its changing social habits. Until the latter half of the century it was customary for businessmen and shopkeepers to live at their place of business or shop. There were also farmers who continued the pre-enclosure habit of having their farmhouse, with its barns and adjoining closes, in the town. This developed four main types of business and domestic architecture, that of the merchants and manufacturers, the shopkeepers, the farmers, and the servants and employees of the above groups. An important sub-group was the inns and public houses, always numerous in market towns. This mixture made St. Neots an architecturally pleasant and satisfying town in the first half of the 19th century. (See plates 4 and 5)

The influence of the merchants and manufacturers was chiefly confined to the north side of the Market Square and Brook Street, being tied to the navigational facilities of Hen Brook and the river. Here, in the 17th and 18th centuries, the merchants built houses to live in, facing the Square and with archways leading to their business premises and offices at the back. Fortunately many still remain and now form the most important architectural facade in the town.

During the 19th century, however, it became the fashion for prosperous merchants to cease living at their place of business and to take, or build, a house in the newly-developed residential areas. This resulted in the former domestic fronts to their businesses being used as offices, let to professional men, or made into shops.

The shopkeeper too, if he grew prosperous, began to follow the example of his social superiors. He now thought it rather vulgar to live over his shop and to sit out on his balcony, overlooking the Square, to watch all the excitements of Market and fair days. The development of New Street and the new Avenue Road satisfied his needs. A chief assistant, or manager, often continued to live over the shop.

It was the Inclosure Acts, when farmers got their land in one block, that gave an impetus for farmhouses to be built out in the country. Some, perhaps because of bad roads or a feeling of safety, remained in the towns for a time. There were not many farmhouses in St. Neots and Eynesbury but those that remained, especially the older ones, were of great architectural interest, preserving the form of the late medieval country house as opposed to the town house. They were timber framed and in their simplest form consisted of a hall with a cross wing at one or both ends. It is interesting that the Court Hall, that once faced the Square from the east side, was such a building (see page 108). Now only two of these survive, Hall Place in Cambridge Street, and Cressener House in Huntingdon Street. Both have been brick-cased but should be preserved.

Houses for the working classes were architecturally bad, built in the cheapest possible way for people that could afford little rent. One concentration was in the low-lying area at the north end of Huntingdon Street, known, probably derisively, as the 'Borough'. Nearby the long rows of terraced cottages in Russell Street were built about 1840 to house workers at the Paper Mill and Bedford Street factories. Most of Luke Street, Montague Square and Silver Street, Eynesbury have similar dwellings, using bricks from the local brickworks.

Less in evidence were the tiny houses built behind High Street and Market Square properties. A few were built round 'courts', but most were approached by little passages or 'jetties'. They had no outlook or space round them. Nearly every inn had two or more of these for its ostlers and grooms and the majority were occupied by employees working at the inn or shop at the front.

In the latter part of the century there was much residential development. East Street was started in 1866 and had terraced workmen's houses on one side and semi-detached better class ones on the other for foremen and managers. In the early 1880s Avenue Road was laid out and was from the first an attraction to the more prosperous shopkeeper, as was the extension of New Street.

Some of the buildings of historical and architectural interest that still survive are briefly mentioned below. It is however almost certain that there are others whose external appearance has been completely altered by a brick casing or an entirely new front. Those included in the *Inventory* of the Royal Commission will have their number added in brackets.

Medieval

This being a district with plentiful timber and no readily-available building stone it was natural that, except for such important buildings as the Priory, churches, and the bridges, all buildings would be of timber. In the two parishes the finest medieval buildings are undoubtedly the parish churches at Eynesbury (1) and St. Neots (1), representing some of the finest work of the 13th and 15th centuries.

Of the secular buildings only one remains looking anything like it originally did. This is 42 High Street (17), probably a late 15th-century merchant's house, and now tastefully restored by Messrs. Freeman Bros. Previously this was faced with 'mathematical tiles', resembling bricks, and apparently of local manufacture. They probably date from about 1800 and their use here is the only local instance known to the author. Another interesting house of the same period is 42 Market Square (12). This is an obvious 'town house' with four sharply-pointed gables facing the square. In the yard at the side is exposed its timber-framing resting on a sub wall of early bricks. The south frontage of the *Falcon* inn, Market Square (13) also appears to be of this date.

16th-17th century
It is probable that the two remaining 'farmhouse type' houses come into the early part of this group, namely Cressener House, Huntingdon Street (the present U.D.C. offices), and Hall Place, Cambridge Street (plate 12), both now brick-cased but retaining their outer form of a central hall with cross wings at each end. The south wing of the Court Hall (11), in this same form of design, is now all that remains of it on the east side of the square. The *Cross Keys* hotel (4), *Bridge* hotel (3), *Kings Head* inn (14, 15) and *Old Sun* inn (28), all have parts dating from this period.

At Eynesbury there are a number of interesting houses of this period. Farmhouses are represented by Low Farm (20), on the Little Barford road, a single cross-wing type, and by a red-brick house at the south end of Luke Street, Nos. 3 and 5 (19), built when red brick began to replace timber-framing. Another farmhouse was the Ferns, facing the Green on the east side. This was once timber-framed and thatched but has had a Queen Anne front added, and still has, in the front, the original main and attic windows with iron sashes. Opposite to each other, at the entrance to Howitts Lane, are the only two thatched cottages left in the urban district, Alma Cottage (17), and Ferns Cottage (18). These three, together with the Georgian Shirdley House, form a very pleasing part of the surroundings of the village green that should be preserved.

Eynesbury has, too, some houses of interest on the north-east side of St. Mary's Street, although several have been destroyed in recent years. They represented the homes and business premises of the small shopkeeper or self-employed tradesmen. Among them, but of rather better class, is no. 24 (5). This still has some of its original interior panelling, in the front its original windows and a very beautiful shell hood over the front door. On the opposite side of the street is the *Chequers* inn (10), some of which, probably including its open hearth, dates from the 16th century. Eynesbury Rectory (3), (now privately owned) is a fine example of such houses of the 17th century.

Outside the urban district are two interesting moated manor farmhouses. One at Monks Hardwick (1), dates from the late 16th century, and another at Eynesbury Hardwick (3), from the 17th century.

18th-19th century

It is difficult to say exactly when, in this district, red bricks went out of fashion and were succeeded by the local white or pale yellow variety, but it was probably in the second quarter of the 18th century. The red bricks may have come from brickworks on the site of the present Grafham Water but the white bricks are almost certainly from the St. Neots or Eynesbury works. (See *Proc. C.A.S.*, vol. 58 (1965) p. 146).

The obvious outstanding example of the earlier red-brick period is Brook House on Brookside, which still has its original iron garden railings, but unfortunately some windows have been replaced. Another good example is no. 24 on the south side of the Square, and of smaller houses Red House, nos. 31 and 33 Church Street. Later in date is Church House, 18 Brook Street, which with its neighbours forms a pleasant group facing the church. Another important house is the Shrubbery in Church Street which has some outstanding interior plaster work, as has 20 Market Square. Others worth mentioning are the riverside house at the Priory next to the *Bridge* hotel, no. 8 on the west side of the Square, and The Limes in Huntingdon Street.

A building of great interest, and worthy of preservation, is the old Assembly Room (plate 16), now occupied by the Co-operative Society, at the corner of High Street and Huntingdon Street. It was built by Joseph Eayre, the bellfounder, probably soon after 1750, as the *George* inn. On its upper floor is the town Assembly Room, still with its musicians' gallery and ornamental domed ceiling. Most of the original windows in the upper floors are also still intact.

Eynesbury has a fine example of the Georgian in Shirdley House, Berkley Street, and in the Red House, Montague Square.

19th century

Few middle-class houses seem to have been built in the early part of the 19th century, but of these Shortsands House, Cambridge Street is a good example, dating from about 1820. Somewhat later are the offices of Wade Gery and Brackenbury, in New Street (1846), and St. Neots Rectory (1848). Smaller houses, built over a long period to varying tastes, make New Street more pleasing than East Street which was started and virtually completed between 1866 and 1870. A later Victorian style can be seen in the more slowly-developed Avenue Road, started in the 1880s, and the Congregational chapel, built in 1888.

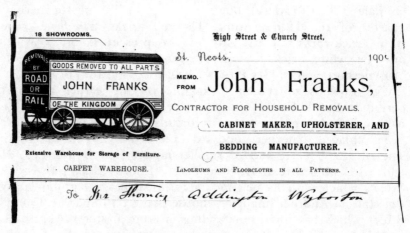

XIX

LOCAL INDUSTRY

The Priory Merchants Business and Brewery

The site of these premises in Priory Lane included, of course, much of the area once occupied by St. Neots Priory, and its river frontage must have been the monks' wharf where all the materials for building and repairing the priory were unloaded. This frontage was one of the best navigation wharfs in the town and its use for this purpose must have gone on after the Dissolution in 1539.

We do not know when the brewery and merchanting business started here, but it was probably when the navigation locks were completed up river, as far as St. Neots, in the early 17th century. From an Abstract of Title it appears that, previous to 1780, it was occupied, first by Francis Atwood and then Edward Arnold. They were probably merchants. The Anderson Estate map of 1757 shows only a dwelling house and Joseph Eayre's bell foundry, which again appears on Jeffrey's map of 1768. Eayre must have used the wharf. The existing barley kiln, a scheduled monument, almost certainly belonged to the next owners.

In 1780 the premises and house were taken by William Fowler, who was a brewers' merchant and farmer. On the east wall of the riverside warehouse, facing the yard, is a clock face, and under it a stone inscribed 'W. F. 1782'. It is recorded that he added to the existing buildings on the site, and this must be one of them. The mechanism of the clock, inside the building, also operated, by means of a rod up to the ridge of the roof, a bell to announce working times. The clock, which was taken out and acquired by Mr. Freeman of 42 High Street, in 1966, may well have been made by Joseph Eayre.

W. Fowler, who was described as a maltster, had two sons, George (1774-1811) and William (1779-1814). It would appear that William (the younger) worked with his father in the business as it was made over to him in 1800. Before that, in 1789, he acquired the adjoining bell foundry site, formerly Joseph Eayre's (see p. 133).

At the death of William Fowler the younger, in 1814, his trustees sold the business, with all its considerable property, to John Day of Bedford, who came into possession with his son John Hill Day. Included with the property was a malting and yard at the south end of New Street, probably the site of the late Police Station, which was known as Wagon Yard.

Inns and public houses in the town included in the sale were the *Queens Head* (Market Square), the *Jolly Brewers* (Cambridge Street), the *Kings Head*, the *Nags Head* (Eynesbury), the *Sun*, the *Three Tuns*, the *Blue Ball* (Huntingdon Street), the *Fox and Hounds* (Market Square), the *Fighting Cocks* (High Street), and the *Golden Ball* (Eynesbury). Out of the town were the *Angel* (formerly the *Crosshouse*) and the *Bell* and the *Dragoon*, at Brampton; the *Three Horse Shoes* (or Howitt's Cottage) at Swineshead; the *Ship* at St. Ives; the *Mermaid* and the *Wheatsheaf* at Ellington; the *Three Shuttles* at Tilbrook; the *Ringers* (formerly Lantofts) at Abbotsley; the *Crown* at Easton; the *White Lion* at Buckden; the *Fountain* and the *Black Bull* (in Silver Street, formerly Goat Lane) Bedford; the *Three Horseshoes* at Papworth Everard; the *Plough* at Great Gransden; the *White Lion* at Holme; the *Nags Head* at Chawston; the *Swan* at Eltisley; the *Bell*, the *George*, the *Chequers*, and the *Sun* at Eaton Socon; the *Cross Keys* at Sawtry; the *Crown* at Nether Dene; the *Queens Head* at Wyboston; and the *Chequers* at Little Gransden.

Thereafter for just over 100 years the business was in the hands of the Day family. John Hill Day, who presented to the town the obelisk on the Market Square, was succeeded by his son Francis (1818-63), who was for many years survived by his widow Emily Anne (1833-1910), a benefactress of St. Neots church (see the charity board). Their only son Frank (1862-1919) was unmarried and at his death the business came to an end.

By the kindness of Mr. J. S. Addington many of the early day books were salvaged and presented to the County Record Office. They give a good picture of the sort of business done by the Day family in the early 19th century. Beside the barley malting kiln they also had in 1823 a lime kiln, and were also selling coal. Beer in barrels was being exported to London. In 1824, 18 men and two boys were employed, the foreman being paid 18s. a week and the men from 8s. to 14s. Billheads of 1828 show that they were then dealing in coals, salt, slates, barrel staves (from Quebec), clunch, timber, isinglass, sperm oil, Greenland oil, and seal oil. Most of these items would have come from King's Lynn by water, and some were products of the Greenland Fishery, from that port. A connection with that trade, no doubt, was the pair of whale's jaw-bones that the writer remembers standing upright beside the entrance gate posts to the yard, and curving inward to form a sort of arch over entering traffic.

Another side line of the business was brick and pipe-making. By 1841 they had a brickyard at Hail Weston, presumably that on the west of the Great Staughton road (TL 156631). It is also uncertain when they acquired a brickyard probably then existing at Eynesbury on the east of the Little Barford road (TL 186579), but it must have been sometime between 1842 and 1860.

Very many of their customers' names appear in the books, and one item gives the names of three of their horses, 'Old Dick', 'Old Sharper' and 'Jolly', who flourished in 1830.

In the time of the last of the family, the bachelor Frank Day, little had been done to modernise the business, and things were rather easy going. Not only, as of right, were all employees entitled to their free beer, but all visiting workmen claimed the same privilege. It was said that if one went into the yard to borrow a ladder, a pint of beer was claimed, and another when it was returned!

In 1919, after the death of Frank Day, there was presumably no offer for the business, and all the property was sold in separate lots, the Priory house and yard going to Jordan & Addington, millers.

St. Neots Paper Mill (plate 32)

The site of St. Neots Paper Mill is almost certainly that of Okestubbe Mill, the medieval corn-grinding water mill belonging to St. Neots Priory. Indeed until the early 19th century it remained a flour-mill. About 1799 it was acquired by Ousley

Rowley, at the time that he was building up his St. Neots estate, and at the same time it was rebuilt, possibly by him as landlord, and let to a Mr. Hobson of Eaton Socon, who remained there until 1804.

In 1804 the mill was leased to a firm of paper-makers, consisting of Henry and Sealy Fourdrinier and John Gamble, who adapted it for the manufacture of hand-made paper. Henry Fourdrinier was a brilliant inventor who, after a careful study of all existing paper-making machines, invented one of his own that revolutionised the industry. The cost of his research and the installation of the first machines by Brian Donkins cost the firm £60,000, which was found by a mortgage to Matthew Toogood, of Rogers, Toogood & Co., bankers, Lombard Street, London.

The advantages of the new machine were so great that it was at once copied by other paper manufacturers, and in spite of costly legal action the Fourdrinier patents were found not to be water-tight. The pirate firms, not having incurred the costly initial expenses, were able to undercut prices, and in 1808 the Fourdriniers went bankrupt. Henry Fourdrinier returned to his home in the North, supported by a small pension from funds raised by an appeal in *The Times*, in recognition of industry's debt to his inventive genius.

Matthew Toogood was thus left with the lease of the mill and all its equipment, in return for his loan. He thereupon decided to move from his home at St. Albans, and to run the mill, believing correctly that he could make it pay. He came to live at Heddings Manor, Little Paxton, a house now long since pulled down, that stood in Paxton Park, between Paxton Park House, now also gone, and the river, and where John Gamble lived.

He knew little or nothing about paper-making but by engaging first-class paper-makers and introducing sound business methods soon made the venture a thriving success. The mill at that time was of course run entirely by water power. It was during his time here that the great flood of 1823 occurred when the river was 11 feet above normal level and the machine rooms five feet under water. Four men were imprisoned for four days in the mill before rescue was possible. Matthew Toogood died in 1830 and was buried at Little Paxton. He was said to have had

24 children, those concerned with the mill being Edward (1801-85), Frederick (1807-60), and Alfred (1828-88).

After the death of Matthew Toogood the mill was taken over by Edward and Frederick, trading as Toogood Bros. Edward was remembered as an exceptionally good business-man, well versed in all aspects of the paper-making trade. He was sometimes said to spend a busy day at the mill, sleep in the office for a few hours, then make his way to the Great North Road to catch the midnight coach for London. His business there completed he would return again at midnight to snatch a little sleep at the office before starting another full day's work at the mill. About 1840 he bought Sawston Paper Mill, near Cambridge, for his son Hamer. He lived for a short time at Cedar House, Cambridge Street, before moving to Paxton Hill House where he died. There is a story of his reaction to some members of his family who, against his orders, spent too much of their time in the *Windmill* inn, that once stood next to the windmill on Paxton Hill, at the corner of the Toseland road. He bought the house and immediately had it pulled down. He retired from business in 1883.

Frederick Toogood does not seem to have made as much impression on the public mind as his brother. About 1838 he built 'Riversfield' at Little Paxton near the mill, living there until about 1856, when he retired from business and moved to London.

The third brother Alfred had left the district to manage Arborfield Paper Mill in Berkshire. When this mill was destroyed by fire in 1861 he bought Helpston Paper Mill, near Peterborough, and, on his brother Frederick's retirement, he joined Edward at St. Neots, moving into Riversfield. He carried on alone after Edward's retirement in 1883, until deciding to sell the business in 1887.

During the management of the mill by the three brothers considerable improvements were made. These included the addition of steam power units in 1851 and again in 1861. This made the mill independent, when the need arose, of the uncertain water power.

The effect on the town of 60 years of Toogood prosperity had been an important factor in its growth and well being. The mill employed a large labour force, which included women as rag-pickers, and often a night shift was worked. There was also a small élite of skilled paper-makers of which Joseph Wright, the St. Neots historian, was one. Many of the houses in the area of Bedford Street, Russell Street and Huntingdon Street were occupied by mill workers. It is not known when the raised footway, called locally the 'traps', was first put up at the mill, but its chief use was to enable mill workers to get to work when the frequent winter floods made the road impassable. It is not known how much use was made of the navigation by the mill, but it is perhaps significant that the first steam unit was not put in until after St. Neots railway station was opened.

One can imagine the consternation felt in the town in 1887 when the mill was closed with little likelihood of being reopened. This coincided with the decline in the Vulcan Iron Works and there was much unemployment and distress among the poor. What followed throws an important and interesting light on the characters and emotions of the local business heads, supposed, in the Victorian age, to be governed only by the doctrines of 'supply and demand' and 'laissez faire' in their business life.

Early in 1888, after six months' closure, the St. Neots Paper Mill Co. Ltd. was formed for altruistic reasons, on the initiative of John McNish, (of Paine & Co.). The first directors were J. McNish, Joseph Wilcox, W. Emery, James Paine, and W. Bowyer, all with no remuneration. C. R. Wade Gery was appointed secretary and F. Slade manager. Capital of £30,000 was raised in £5 shares and J. McNish elected chairman. Although an experienced paper-maker had been appointed as manager he did not stay long, and others followed. All were handicapped by old and out-of-date machinery with which no profit or progress could be made.

A change for the better did not come until 1893 when Mr. Bricknell was appointed manager and Mr. C. Horsburgh as chief engineer. Between them they introduced many improvements and, in 1903, turbines by Turnbull of Glasgow and a new steam engine were added, although some of the original machinery by Donkin continued in use.

In 1912, when 200 people were employed at the mill, it was almost completely destroyed by fire, with the exception of the rag sorting house on the other side of the navigation lock. Rebuilding started immediately, this time in brick, in place of the old wooden building covered by feather edge boarding. The company now had a 'Sentinal' steam wagon and this was used to bring a million bricks from Warboys, at the rate of two loads a day. By the team work of Bricknell and Horsburgh the plan of a new and modern paper mill was drawn up and carried out, although still making part use of water power. A new era of prosperity began.

In 1913 the mill was producing the finest grades of bank, writing, ledger, drawing, chart, cartridge, typing, loan, and envelope papers, and cream and tinted typing and envelope papers. Their stock watermarks were 'St. Neots Mill Fine', 'St. Neots Air Dried Vellum', 'Wylverly Parchment', 'Ouse Vale Extra Strong', 'Merculon Extra', 'Quality Ledger', 'Hereward Ledger', 'Hereward Extra Strong', 'Paxton Extra Strong 1799', 'Paxton Air Dried Vellum', 'Paxton Fine', 'Paxton Ledger 1799', and 'Elldon Linen Bond'.

In the years of depression after 1920 the fortunes of the mill once again declined and when it was closed down in 1939 it seemed unlikely that paper making would ever be done there again. However, after the outbreak of war the well-known paper-makers, Wiggins Teape Ltd., having to evacuate their Dover mill owing to the danger from German long-range guns at Calais, were glad to avail themselves of it. They brought with them some of their skilled paper-makers who were accommodated in houses built for the Land Settlement Association at Wyboston. After the war was over there was a busy trade in paper for India, Ceylon, and the Far East, to fill former Japanese markets, but after turning over to the manufacture of nylon the mill closed again in 1947 or 1948. In 1950 however the lease was sold to Samuel Jones Ltd. and paper and allied manufactures were resumed. Under their management the mill completed its 150 years of paper-making.

Joseph Eayre and the Bell Foundry

More research than the writer has had time for might discover new facts about Joseph Eayre, his antecedents, and what sort of man he really was. It is tantalising that we know so little about this remarkable man. It is even not known why he came to St. Neots where he rapidly achieved fame and fortune, chiefly as a bell founder, and to a lesser degree as a clock- and watch-maker.

No published material that the writer has seen gives the date of his birth, but it was probably about the end· of the first decade of the 18th century, and for some unknown reason, like his brother, he was not baptised until 1731, when adult. This happened at Kettering, his home town. His father was almost certainly Thomas Eayre (d. 1716), a clock-maker, but it is uncertain if he made bells. When of age he went to work for his elder brother Thomas (1691-1758, baptised 1711) at Kettering, and also in the firm was a John Eayre, who may have been another brother or an uncle. This firm were clock-makers and also bell founders of high repute, but whether they started this or carried on the bell founding from their father is apparently not known.

In 1735 Joseph decided, for an unknown reason, to leave Kettering and start up a new business for himself at St. Neots. A possible reason for choosing St. Neots was the marriage of Joseph's sister to someone of the name of Arnold, whose son Edward was afterwards taken into the business. It is not known for certain if these Arnolds lived in St. Neots but there was a Francis Arnold, builder, living there who was a trustee under Joseph's will. He died in 1770, but was not the father of Edward Arnold. It was a local family name occurring in St. Neots since the 16th century.

Besides having money it seems likely that Joseph Eayre had some local influence as he was able to acquire one of the best business sites in the town, at the Priory, with room for his foundry and workshops, as well as an excellent navigation wharf. A year after starting up he returned to Kettering to marry Sarah Soames of that town. No doubt to their sorrow they had no children, and she died three years before her husband in 1769.

The actual site of the foundry, in which church bells were cast, was somewhere on the present Priory Lane roadway, in front of the entrance to the old brewery premises. Its exterior appearance was said to have been the shape of a church bell. During his 37 years at St. Neots, Joseph Eayre became one of the best known of his trade in the Eastern Counties and he cast bells for churches over a wide area, in many cases recasting the metal from old bells to make the new, in improved shapes and alloys. Much local information about his work can be found in Owen's *Church Bells of Huntingdonshire*, but it should be recorded here that originally all the eight St. Neots bells were his work, the seven smaller ones being cast in 1753 and the 'great bell', 14 feet in circumference, and weighing 3,051 lbs., in 1764. This latter, however, had to be recast in 1832, and all were again recast by

Messrs. Taylor of Loughborough, the present day successor to his firm, in 1919.

Owing to his fame as a bell founder his clock- and watch-making has been almost forgotten. Indeed the writer has only come across three examples of his clocks and a record of one of his watches. One clock the writer is very lucky to possess. It is a small grandfather, standing about six feet high, and with a brass face signed 'Joseph Eayre, St. Neots'. Clock experts have expressed surprise that its date cannot be earlier than 1735, pointing out that it is a single-hand 30-hour clock, wound by pulling up the weights, and is mounted on a frame with brass corner pillars, similar to the 17th century bracket clocks.

The only reference, known to the writer, of his watch-making, comes from a rather strange source. The Cambridge Chronicle, of a date in 1769, reported that three footpads set on John Banks of Hail Weston, near Cross Hall, and stole from him, among other things, 'a silver watch, maker's name Joseph Eayre St. Neots, with two very strong cases, a very dirty name plate, but movement very good'.

However further proof of Eayre's interest in clocks has only recently come to light in the diaries of Rev. William Stukeley, the well-known 18th-century antiquary. (See Milburn, 'Some Horological Extracts from Stukeley's Diaries', *Proceedings of the Horological Society*, no. 4, vol. 6 (1969).) Stukeley was the rector of a church in Stamford, and appears to have met Eayre there. A diary entry reads; '3 Jul. 1741. Mr. Eayre of St. Neots visited me, an excellent mechanic, clockmaker, bellfounder etc. . .'. We discussed much on improvements in mechanics'. This was probably the first time the two had met, and Eayre had come to Stamford to discuss repairs to the Rector's church steeple, possibly in relation to bell hanging. Judging from the diary most of their time together was spent in talking about automata and bells. Eayre explained some of his ideas for improvements in bells and the diary entry includes a sketch, showing a bell in cross section, to illustrate these. Thereafter he became a firm friend of Stukeley and often figured in the diary over the next 10 years.

Their mutual interest in clocks, and clock experiments, remained constant, as the following diary extract shows. '10 April 1752. My frd. Mr. Eayre of St. Neots is making a spring clock with horizontal wheels, that will goe half a year: wh. is to be put into a vacuum or exhausted receiver. This will not be subject to the variations of the external air, and will last a west india voyage or more: and will show the longitude. Mr. Eayre has made a clock with a pendulum 40 feet long enclosed in a wall to keep it from the influence of the external air. He finds by it, that our equation tables are not exact, and this must be owing to the mutation of the earth's axis'.

The house where Joseph lived was in Huntingdon Street, just south of the Wesleyan Chapel (plate 18). It was pulled down in 1960, and part of the Co-operative Society shop is now built over the site. It is not known when he took this house, or whether he lived there all the 37 years he was in St. Neots. It is certain that it was originally a Tudor-type wooden-framed house that had had a mid-18th century red-brick front added, and that the stone set in the top of the middle window of the first floor, facing the street, with the inscription 'J.E. 1754.', probably dated this event. The writer was able to salvage this stone from the building rubble when the house was demolished. Shortly afterwards a young American attaché named Eayre, and a descendant of a branch of the family that had emigrated in the 18th century, called on the writer to learn something of his family in the town. He was delighted to be presented with the stone which he said would be set up in a place of honour in his brother's engineering factory. In the roadway, in front of this house, Joseph Eayre was said to have built a large underground well or cistern of brick, to supply a public pump for the benefit of the nearby cottages, there being no other public pump anywhere near. This was exposed and destroyed during street trenching in the 1950s.

A number of items of interest can be found in the church-wardens' minutes and accounts. In 1737 there occurs the first of these, when Eayre was paid £3 15s. for repairing the church clock. In 1754 a subscription list was opened to provide new fire engines. Joseph Eayre subscribed £5 5s., a sum only exceeded by Lord Sandwich (20 guineas) and Geo. Reynolds, of the Little Paxton squires family, (10 guineas), and equalled by three wealthy St. Neots families (Williams, Bailey, and Hatley). There may have been a business reason for this for, although nothing was done until 1758, he was given an order for one of the new fire engines, at a cost of £40.

In 1753 the following appears:

Several of the Principal Inhabitants, desireous of having a compleat peel of 8 bells in the steeple of the Parish church of St. Neots, have raised by voluntary subscriptions the sum of £200 plus £33 agreed by the inhabitants of the parish to be raised by a Churchwardens Rate, and the old bells now hanging will be sufficient to compleat same. Joseph Eayre, in consideration of £81 7s., already paid to him by Jeremiah Davies, who in consideration of which agrees with Loftus Hatley, Stephen Scarbrow, and Jeremiah Davies that Joseph Eayre shall take down the old bells and recast them with the addition of 26 hundred weight of new bell metal, into 8 bells, and the same 8 bells shall be tuneable and toneable, and good in all respects as any bells in England, and of the same weight, in the opinion of 2 competent judges in bells, the one to be nominated by Joseph Eayre and the other by any 5 or more of the Principal Inhabitants and subscribers, and to erect and maintain for one year, and then pay him the sum of £33. Later £218 13s. to be paid. If 2 judges disagree they to appoint and agree on a 3rd. whose decision shall be final'.

During his 37 years at St. Neots it is obvious that Joseph Eayre made a lot of money and used some of it buying and developing property in the town. At his death he owned not only his home in Huntingdon Street, but all the property between it and the High Street corner, and along the High Street nearly as far as the Congregational chapel. On the corner he had built the *George* inn, facing the High Street. This he obviously intended to be the principal inn in the town, and on its first floor was the town's Assembly Room. This venture would seem not to have been a success as, at the time of his death in 1772, the inn was already divided into tenements, although the Assembly Room remained in use for its original purpose until the middle of the 19th century. It fortunately remains preserved in the present Co-operative Society shop. Shortly before his death he bought the site of the old Place House, in Church Street, together with all its extensive grounds, occupying most of the east side of Church Street and with a frontage on Cambridge Street. The original Place House had been recently pulled down. He had other unspecified property in St. Neots, Eaton Socon, and Eynesbury. Cash legacies in his will amounted to £1,650. These included £100 to St. Neots church, the interest to be distributed among the poor in the first week of the Christmas holidays each year.

After the death of Joseph Eayre, in 1772, the business was taken over by his nephew Edward Arnold, who is always described as a clock-maker, and who perhaps specialised on that side of his uncle's

business. There are a number of his long-case clocks in private
hands in the district, including a fine example at Little Barford
House. To run the bell-casting side he went into partnership with
his uncle's former foreman, Thomas Osborne of Downham Market,
who was probably his own cousin. This arrangement did not last
long and Osborne left, returning to his home town to set up on
his own.

He then engaged a new foreman, Islip Edwards, under whom
worked an apprentice Robert Taylor. In 1784 Arnold started a
new foundry at Leicester, and very shortly after, probably in
1786, he left St. Neots, turning the business over to Taylor, but
retaining ownership of the premises.

Robert Taylor, who has been described as 'the first of a series
of bell founders who have raised their art to the highest perfection',
would seem to have soon been in trouble because of a romantic
attachment to 'the girl next door' in the person of Elizabeth
Fowler (d. 1805) daughter of Wm. Fowler of the Priory Brewery
next to the foundry, whom he married in 1789. While there is no
direct evidence that the Fowlers disapproved of the marriage,
there is a tradition that they did, and it is significant that in the
same year they bought the foundry site from Arnold, and Taylor
was turned out. He then moved to premises, not now certainly
identified, in Cambridge Street. It would seem very likely that
they were either in the yard behind no. 14, on the south side of
the street, or behind no. 23, on the north side, there being, in
both places, blacksmith and engineering workshops there in the
19th century. While at St. Neots Taylor cast at least 29 bells for
Huntingdonshire churches before his Cambridge Street premises
were destroyed by fire in 1821. After the fire he decided not to
rebuild but to move, with his two sons, to Oxford.

Here the business was carried on later by William (b. 1795) and
John (b. 1797) Taylor (sons of Robert), with a branch at Bideford.
By 1839 these had been given up and the main factory was at
Loughborough, where the firm still flourishes.

Thomas Osborne, on setting up as a bell founder at Downham
Market, took as partner his grandson, Wm. Dodson. He carried on
the business after his grandfather's death and, in 1882, recast the
St. Neots 'Great Bell', originally cast by Joseph Eayre, then found
to be cracked. It was sent to Downham Market and returned by
water, as was another for Eaton Socon church in the same year.

Paine & Co. Ltd.

James Paine (1789-1855) was the son of Jabez Paine (d. 1846) a farmer of Wilshampstead, Bedford, who moved from there to Eltisley and then to Manor Farm, Great Paxton in 1800. These were prosperous times for farmers and Toseland Hall and farm were added to the family possessions, besides a farm house and 16 acres at Eynesbury (Low Farm?). James, on his marriage to Elizabeth Main of Kingston Wood in 1815, took over the management of the Great Paxton Farm but moved next year to Toseland Hall. His brother Joseph took over Manor Farm, Great Paxton later, in 1834.

At Toseland Hall were born James's four sons, William (1816-96), Jabez (1821-93), James Junr. (1825-96) and David, also two daughters, Ann (who married J. S. Geard) and Mary (who married a Mr. Lyon).

In 1831 or 1832 James decided to enter trade as a merchant and to this end acquired from the trustees of Wm. Foster's estate a merchantile property known as the 'wharf premises' on the south side of St. Neots Market Square. This property consisted of the present composite group of buildings nos. 32 to 36 now owned by Paine & Co. Ltd. bearing the date 1831. They may have been built by Wm. Foster as they appear very much as they are now in a drawing dated 1829. Foster was a relative of the Paines, and there was a Wm. Paine Foster in 1863. William Foster, besides being a merchant, had been a banker and the west side of this building (now the Local Office) was occupied by his bank. Here in 1829 occurred the famous St. Neots bank robbery. Under the archway was the *Bull* inn and a yard and buildings extending back to the Hen Brook wharf. East of the archway the frontage was let as a shop to Ebenezer Geard, linen and woollen draper. The John Stammers Geard who married Ann Paine may well have been his son.

The red-brick Georgian house (no. 38) east of the above group had been the residence of Wm. Foster. It was to here that James Paine moved and where he was followed by his son William.

It is not recorded exactly how Wm. Foster used the yards but he would almost certainly have brewed beer there and stocked the numerous kinds of imported goods coming up the river as were later kept by James Paine.

On starting the merchant's business James Paine immediately took his son William, then aged 16, into partnership and called the firm James Paine and Son. In the west yard was established the Stone Flour Mill and in the yard of his house the brewery and office (counting house). Extra room was soon gained here by purchasing the back part and wharf of no. 40 next door, from Mr. Wm. Newman, cooper and ironmonger, who had a shop facing the Square.

In 1841 James junr. joined the firm and the name was altered to James Paine & Sons.

James Paine's private Cash Account book dating from 1843 is in the possession of the present company, and the author is greatly indebted to the directors for its loan to him. It shows that besides the milling, brewing and merchanting business he was also farming at Great Paxton and running brick kilns there, and had other brick kilns at Riseley and Gamlingay. The Great Paxton kilns were at Low Farm and the brickpit along River Lane opposite. He also had a maltings at Eynesbury in St. Mary's Street (present nos. 12 and 14, Kayser Bondor Factory) and the Eynesbury Farm.

His personal expenditure shows a generous support of the nonconformist Old Meeting (Congregational) and the British School established in the old Independent chapel behind no. 20 in the High Street.

To drive the stone mill there was installed in 1840 a beam steam engine which was actually in use until 1935, when it was replaced by electricity. It is now preserved in the Milan Science Museum, to whom it was presented by the firm.

Among the properties held by the firm in 1855, at the death of James Paine, were: the *Hand in Hand* inn, Toseland, (bought 1829), the *Golden Crown*, Great Barford, (bought 1836), a house and shop at Eaton Ford, (bought 1838), a site in Russell Street on which was built *The Boat* (name changed to *Lord John Russell* in 1871), the Riseley brick kilns bought 1848 (formerly hired), *The Plough*, Abbotsley, (bought 1848), a farmhouse and 16 acres and a malting at Eynesbury, (inherited from his father), *The Kings Head* and nos. 5, 7, 9, 11 and 13 South Street, corn shops in the Bell Yard, the *New Inn*, Girtford, (bought 1838), and an inn at Keysoe.

Under James Paine's will his fortune was left to be divided equally among his six children, subject to an annuity to his wife. However, he left his share of the business to be run, until 1864, by his four sons as trustees of his partnership in James Paine & Sons, and to apply his share of the profits to the payment of his debts and legacies. This arrangement actually went on until 1865.

It seems likely that the two remaining partners William and James did not get on well together. In the next year after their father died James junr. married Miss Oliver (her father had a furniture and upholstery business in the High Street where the Corn Exchange was afterwards built) and went to live at Elm Lodge, Potton Road, Eynesbury, near the site of Eynesbury brickyards, which he probably started. A condition of the dissolution of partnership was that James took the Riseley brick kilns, and the Eynesbury malting, as well as capital to start the Eynesbury brickyard.

After 1865, with the main firm now in his own hands, William Paine started a rapid expansion of the business. His chief venture was the purchase, from Thos. Smith, of a flour mill in Nutters Lane (Bedford Street) in 1865. This mill had originally been built by John Medlock after the steam mill in New Street was burnt down in 1846; and it had afterwards belonged to Joshua Malden, and then Thos. Smith. He at once spent £200 on improvements and another £100 on a sawmill which was attached. He also bought back from his brother, for £170, the Riseley kilns and hired the Eynesbury malting. Trade bill-heads of this period show that besides the products of the brewing and flour mill he was dealing in the following; malt, hops, coal, malt calms, linseed cake, slates, bricks, tiles, building stone, salt, tar, hair, whiting, ladder and scaffold poles, glass, chimney pots, fireclay, staves, lath (single and double fir), cement (portland and roman), lime (burnt, slack and clunch), deals and battens (Petersburg, Wyberg and Memel).

To cope with his timber business he hired from his father-in-law, Wm. Abbott of Berkeley House, Eynesbury, a yard and wharf at Eynesbury on the east side of Eynesbury bridge and attached to the *Dog and Duck* inn. On this he put a sawmill shed, no doubt for a pit saw as there is no mention of an engine.

By 1869 he had bought the St. Neots *Railway Tavern* and there is in the stock list a curious item: 'a raft on the brook'.

The Riseley kilns were given up by 1870 and the Eynesbury malting (bought from his brother) proving inadequate, a malting attached to the *New* inn, High Street, was hired.

New capital was badly needed to finance and improve all these properties and in 1872 he took a partner. He was Wm. Osborne Atkinson who, as a circular issued at the time states, 'having been engaged in the Corn Trade will more especially confine his attention to that part of the business . . . Mr. Wm. Bennett will continue to supervise the Building Dept. and his office will be at the Saw Mill. Mr. John Sibley will remain at the Counting House as Ledger Clerk and Cashier. My intention is to supervise the entire business'. The name of the firm was now changed to Paine & Atkinson.

In 1874 a new malting in Nutters Lane (Bedford Street) was built and equipped at a cost of £2,400 and as a result the old Eynesbury malting was sold to Geo. Taylor of the *Chequers* inn, Eynesbury, for use as a mineral water factory.

Meanwhile, in 1873, a John McNish, son of a Manchester architect (or builder) married Wm. Paine's eldest daughter Alice Mary, and in the same year entered the firm, to which he brought some capital, to develop the insurance agency that they held.

Four years later, in 1877, W. O. Atkinson dissolved the partnership to take over a Birmingham brewery, and John McNish became a full partner. In the same year his brother Alexander Copland McNish married Wm. Paine's remaining daughter Rosa, and also entered the firm, which now became Paine & Co.

In 1880 the Nutters Lane flour mill was pulled down and a new mill built in the same site. It is probable that this also covered the site of the saw mill which disappears from the stock at the same time, and was not renewed. The steam engine, used in the saw mill, was sold to Daintree & Jewson, timber merchants of Navigation Wharf, Eynesbury, as was the Dog and Duck timber yard opposite their own premises. The engine ran continuously at these premises until superseded by a diesel engine in 1931. It is probable that the builder's merchants' business had been given up some years before.

In 1882 Wm. Paine retired after fifty years in business and went to live at Neotsbury, Hastings, leaving the business to be carried on by John and Alexander McNish as partners. All employees were invited to a Jubilee Dinner (cost £20 16s.). Wm. Paine died at Hastings in 1896.

The partnership of the McNish brothers lasted until 1896 when Alexander left the firm. The firm was then launched as a public limited liability company as Paine & Co. Ltd. with John McNish and his son Wellwood as directors.

In 1903 a fire destroyed the Bedford Street Nutters Mill, damage being estimated at £15,000. It was rebuilt and stands today but with later additions.

In 1905 the brewery and Stone Flour Mill on the Market Square were destroyed by fire. It was fortunate that at the time Elgoods Mill in the SW. corner of the Market Square was vacant and on the market. It was at once purchased and milling started within a few days, the former premises being all rebuilt as a brewery.

About 1900 the production of Malt Extract was developed and a world-wide export trade followed. This was first carried on in the Bedford Street malting, but after the First World War further premises were necessary, and the derelict factory premises in Brook Street—once Bower's Gas Meter Works—were bought and equipped. These premises were badly damaged by fire in 1947 and, after rebuilding, again burnt in 1955. Since then they remained derelict for many years and the business was transferred back to Bedford Street.

John McNish died in 1913, aged 62, and Wellwood McNish became chairman of the company until his death in 1955.

It seems beyond doubt that when James Paine started the business in St. Neots he moved into the Fosters' house (no. 38) on the Market Square and was followed there by Wm. Paine, until his retirement in 1882. He was followed by Alexander McNish who in 1889 moved to Cressener House, Huntingdon Street. From here he moved in 1893 to Shortsands House, Cambridge Street where he remained until he left the town in 1896.

John McNish on his marriage went to live at the White House, Huntingdon Street (afterwards called Wisteria House, and now pulled down—the site occupied by a garage). He moved to the Limes, next door, about 1882, and followed his brother at Shortsands in 1896.

From 1889 to 1897 the Market Square house was let to P. C. Tomson, editor of *St. Neots Advertiser* and after that was occupied by John Sibley, chief clerk and afterwards director of the firm. He had entered their employment in 1862 and his family remained here until 1951.

C. G. Tebbutt Ltd.

The origin of this firm really stemmed from the variety of merchanting trades carried on by Wm. Paine (see above), one of which was importing timber from abroad, and stocking materials for the building trade. His yard had been in Bedford Street, and there was also a saw mill attached, but it was afterwards moved to the *Dog and Duck* inn yard, Eynesbury, near Eynesbury bridge.

The Jewsons of Earith, Hunts., were family friends of the Paines, and also in the timber business, so it was natural that young George Jewson should come as an apprentice to St. Neots before going to Norwich, where he set up the important, and still existing, business there. Local relatives of the Jewsons were the Daintrees who wished to give up farming and enter trade. At the same time Wm. Paine decided to concentrate on his brewing and milling and sell his timber and building material business. It was arranged in 1879, probably through the Jewsons, and with money borrowed from them, that Charles Daintree should purchase this business and take as partner the experienced Fred Jewson of Earith. This was to last only until Charles Daintree junr. had completed his apprenticeship with the Jewson firm at Norwich.

The new firm, Daintree & Jewson, found the *Dog and Duck* premises too small for their needs and so first hired, and then bought for £700, the Navigation Wharf across the street. This had been the wharf and depot of the Ouse Navigation Co. until the decline in navigation after the railway was opened in 1850. There were a few storage sheds on the site and a lime kiln. They at once built further sheds, and a new saw mill, with an engine and boiler house, which still survive. For power they installed a steam engine, originally from Paine's Bedford Street mill, and reputed to date from about 1850. It was still running quite efficiently up to 1931, and was then only replaced by a diesel engine owing to high fuel costs. Bill headings dated 1881 read:

DAINTREE & JEWSON
Deal Timber and Slate Merchants,
Dealers in Lime, Lath, Chimney Pots, Stone, Whiting, Hair, Sewerage Pipes, Cement etc. Proprietors of the New Sawing, Planing, and Moulding Mills.

On the return from Norwich of Charles Daintree junr. the partnership with Fred Jewson was dissolved and the firm becam ˙ Daintree & Son. However it did not prosper, perhaps on acc of the inexperience of the principals, or because of the agricultural depression, then at its height. As a result the Daintree family had to leave Morton House Shortsands, and lived for a time in the house next to the Navigation Yard. Finally the whole family emigrated to Australia, leaving the business and premises in the hands of Jewson Bros. of Norwich.

In 1887 Richard Jewson, then aged 20, and the youngest of J. W. Jewson's 13 children, came over from Norwich to try to put the business on its feet again. His hard work and business acumen enabled him to do this, and later led him to become the highly-successful chairman of his large and important East Anglian company.

Meanwhile another young member of an old Huntingdonshire family was learning the timber trade. The families of Tebbutt at Bluntisham and Jewson at Earith had been friends for many years and Charles Goodman (1860-1944), son of Charles Prentice Tebbutt of Bluntisham, had reluctantly given up his wish to become a farmer, owing to its extremely poor prospects. At the age of 20 he went to Norwich to learn the timber trade with the Jewson firm. He was there from January 1881 to February 1882, working the same hours as the men in the yard, 6.30 in the morning until six at night, and during the latter part of his time acting as yard foreman. On public holidays he would get up at dawn and ride his 'penny farthing' bicycle home to Bluntisham. On 24 January 1881 he won the Norfolk Amateur Skating Championship on Wroxham Broad, over a course of one mile with one turn, in three minutes, 50 and one fifth seconds.

On returning home from Norwich he spent three years successfully breaking in horses by a humane and scientific method. No doubt from his love of horses and their welfare came his invention and patenting of 'Tebbutt's Patent Stable Brick', a blue Staffordshire brick with a surface of eight round and flattened knobs, for use in stables and cattle yards. They provided a non-slip surface, were dry for the animal's feet, and easy to clean. For this invention he was awarded a silver medal at the National Inventions Exhibition in 1885, and in the same year opened an office in London for their sale. They were well received and met with a ready sale into the next century. Notable orders were for the Sandringham stables of the Prince of Wales, and St. Ives and Northampton cattle markets. In 1887 he sailed for America, visiting friends at New York and

Philadelphia, and trying, without success, to interest agents there in the stable bricks.

In 1889 he bought from Jewson & Son the yard, stock and goodwill of their business at Navigation Wharf, coming to live first as a lodger at 26 St. Mary's Street, Eynesbury, and later at 'The Ferns', Eynesbury Green, which he purchased.

From the first he worked at the business, making it a success, and at the same time threw himself into the sporting life of the district. Of all sports it was at speed ice-skating that he excelled, and a succession of hard winters gave him every scope. In the winter of 1890/91 he took a team to play Bandy (the origin of ice hockey, and originating at Bluntisham and Earith) to Holland, thus introducing the game to Europe, and in the same winter skated over 80 miles of the course of the Ouse, between Pavenham, Beds., and Denver Sluice. In 1892 he won the Littleport Amateur Skating Cup, and in 1895 lost, by only four-fifths of a second, to S. E. Tebbit, in the English Amateur Championship held at Swavesey Cambs., his last race. In the same year he accomplished what is claimed to be the longest fen skate in one day, from Peterborough to Cambridge, covering 87 miles.

Details of his skating career can be found in *Skating*, (Badminton Library), in which he contributed articles on 'Speed Skating' and 'Bandy'.

Nearer home he captained the St. Neots Cricket Club team that won the Smith Barry Cup in 1896, was captain of St. Neots Hockey Club from 1898 to 1903, and captained St. Neots Football Club for a number of years. He was moderately good at tennis and golf and enjoyed shooting. His love of horses took him into the hunting field and even to compete successfully at Brampton Races, but did not stop him acquiring one of the first motor cars in St. Neots, driven by steam.

He married Katharine Mary Warren of St. Ives in 1899, and the writer and his sister and brothers were all born at 'The Ferns'. After the death of his father in 1909, he moved, in 1910, to Bluntisham to live in the family home there, coming over to St. Neots several times a week, and spending the rest of his time on his duties as county councillor and Justice of the Peace.

In the First World War timber importing almost ceased but the demand for timber for the war effort was great. In response the Felmongers Yard, on the St. Neots side of Eynesbury bridge, was acquired, and fitted up with a rack bench driven by a portable steam engine to convert home-grown trees to timber. This trade was not given up until 1922, when the old factory buildings on this site were utilised for joinery and portable building manufacture.

In 1935 the firm became a private company, with C. G. Tebbutt and his two sons C. F. and P. D. Tebbutt as co-directors. In 1938 the company bought from J. R. H. Bedford the old-established merchants' business of A. W. Atkinson & Co., who dealt in timber, builders' materials and coal, and moved their office to that of this firm at 45 High Street, St. Neots. This office was given up in favour of a new building near Eynesbury Bridge in 1966, and the High Street yard sold.

In the Second World War the firm once again turned to the home-grown timber trade, setting up a mill in the yard behind their High Street Office. This was given up in 1965 when the whole mill was destroyed by fire.

During the War, in 1944, C. G. Tebbutt died at Bluntisham at the age of 84.

In 1949 a booklet was published entitled *Diamond Jubilee of C. G. Tebbutt Ltd., 1889-1949*, written by the author, and giving a rather fuller account of the history of the business.

George Bower and the Vulcan Ironworks

George Bower (1826-1911) was almost certainly the most remarkable business man ever to live in the town, and also the one who had the most influence on its prosperity and development in the second half of the 19th century.

He was born at Caister in Lincolnshire, and in 1850 married Sarah Spencer of Higham Ferrars. In the same year, perhaps influenced by the opening of the railway, he bought the ironmonger's business and shop of John Carrington at 22 Market Square on the south side. He and his wife started their married life in the house attached to the shop.

However his active brain found little stimulus in retailing ironmongery, and almost at once an engineering business was being developed in the back premises. In fact, in 1858, he gave up the ironmonger's shop, which was taken over by Walter Lanning, but retained the yard. In a few years no. 24, next door, was also acquired, and the whole became the Vulcan Iron Works. Increased affluence soon enabled him to move his home to 'The Shrubbery' in Church Street.

In the first five or six years his products were varied and included all types of agricultural machinery, including Ransom ploughs, and apparatus for the then expanding gas industry in the form of gas lighting and heating plants. Finding it difficult to obtain the castings he needed locally he built his own foundry on the same premises.

Very soon he began to concentrate on the manufacture of gas plants and to patent a number of improvements on existing types. As early as 1852 he was advertising a small patent gas-producing apparatus for as little as 10 lights, and a Patent Gas Cooker in two sizes. Size 0 was designed for mechanics and priced at £2 10s., while family size 2 would roast at the same time a large piece of beef and a couple of fowls, besides having an additional hot closet. In this year too he established an ironmongery warehouse at Kimbolton.

In 1853 he began to develop a coal gas apparatus for up to 5,000 lights, which he had patented in 1850. As a result, in 1854, he received the contract to light the towns of Quornden and Mountsorrel in Leicestershire, and built the Kimbolton gasworks. These town lighting contracts were the first of a list that was eventually to exceed 1,000. Another venture in the same year was a contract to make and supply a type of patent portable building which was shipped out to Australia for use in the gold-fields.

A notable patent, taken out in 1856, was for a 'gas regulator', which stabilised the gas pressure irrespective of how many lights were being used. In this year too he began to manufacture gas meters, and premises on the west side of Eynesbury bridge, given up by George Squire, were acquired and adapted for this purpose.

Thereafter business prospered exceedingly and orders for gas plants were received from all over the country and many places abroad, including the palace of the Viceroy of Egypt. At the height of his prosperity about 150 men were working at the Vulcan Iron Works, some of these travelling abroad to erect plants. In addition a new foundry for heavy castings was opened at West Hartlepool.

This growth of industrialism brought results very familiar today. In 1871, inspired by the popular 'Nine Hour Movement', 80 or 90 of his men met in the Public Room to demand a 54-hour week, in place of the 60 hours they then worked, and time and a quarter pay for overtime. The meeting agreed to wait while their leader, Mr. Scott, went with a delegation to interview Mr. Bower. The demand was conceded and the meeting finished with three cheers for Mr. Bower and Mr. Scott.

In 1874 Bower had either bad luck on a stupendous scale or badly overreached himself. His large and lucrative trade with Brazil probably tempted him unwisely to become financially involved with the formation of Rio Grande Da Sul Steamship Co. Ltd., with a capital of £150,000, of which he was a director and chairman. They contracted to build four steamers and transport 37,000 settlers to Brazil. The *Conde d'Eu, Donna Isabella, Rio Grande Da Sul,* and *Porto Alegre* were each to carry 300 steerage and 24 first-class passengers besides cargo.

In 1876 he was forced to file his petition in bankruptcy. What actually went wrong is not explained in the contemporary press, but there was said to have been a shipwreck, a defaulting insurance company, and a South American revolution followed by a repudiation of debts. Losses were also incurred on contracts with Russia.

George Bower estimated his losses, in that year, to exceed £100,000, and promised, if allowed to continue in business, to repay all his debts in full. To this the creditors agreed and business was resumed aided by more patents from his inventive brain.

In 1883 he combined a patent process of his own with one taken with Barff, to perfect the 'Bower-Barff Process', a method of protecting iron and steel surfaces with a coating of magnetic oxide. This was a notable advance, and separate companies were formed to develop it in Great Britain, the Continent, and America. The local press, of that year, reported that men from St. Neots were sent to America to build a furnace at Brooklyn, and were there pronounced the finest workmen they had ever seen, in spite of the fact that the man trained to start the furnace could neither read nor write.

In 1887 he formed a new company, Bower's Gas Lamps Ltd., with a capital of £30,000, to exploit another new invention. In the same year, however, creditors, who had not been paid their debts in full, again petitioned for bankruptcy. At a meeting of creditors George Bower disclosed a deficiency of £38,000. He declared that in the 11 years before 1876 he had made £100,000, but had lost £139,000 in that year. He blamed his present default on general business depression and proposed a scheme to pay off all his debts. The creditors, by a majority, agreed to allow him to carry on for a further two years.

Contracts were still coming in from all over Europe and South America, and in 1888 he contracted to light the town of Mackay in Queensland, Australia.

Creditors, however, were still not being paid as promised, and in 1895 there was a complaint that he was still living in a large house in the same style as he had 25 years before, with several servants, a butler, and several gardeners. Also that his engineering works now only employed 10 or 11 men. However he seemed to be successful in keeping his creditors at bay and continued to live at the Shrubbery until the day of his death. Even in 1899 a new gas plant was patented.

In his later years he was fortunate in having the help and co-operation of his son, Anthony Spencer Bower, himself an outstanding engineer, but from his earliest days in business he made it a rule to prepare all his own plans, designs, and specifications, and manufacture all the parts he needed in his own factory.

Something must be said of his interest in the life of the town, which started when he was appointed Town Commissioner in 1857. When this authority came to an end in 1878 and the Local Board was set up, he pressed, unsuccessfully, for it to include Eaton Socon. He was elected to the new body and became its first chairman, being subsequently re-elected for 12 years. His views were always progressive and he strongly advocated, against a majority opinion, a public water supply and improved sewerage.

The Conservatives considered him their leader in the town and he founded, initially for his own workmen, a Working Men's Club, which developed into the present Constitutional Club in New Street. At the Queen's Jubilee every child in St. Neots and Eynesbury received a medal from him. St. Neots church benefited greatly from his generosity, and he was a regular worshipper there.

One of his outstanding acts of enterprise was the purchase of land on the east side of Huntingdon Street, putting in roads and sewers to form Avenue Road and East Street, and making building plots available there.

To his friends he was a well-read, witty and charming companion, with an exceptional memory and keen sense of humour, and always an incurable optimist. Of his children Anthony Spencer Bower was an outstanding engineer, and George Spencer Bower K.C. became a well-known barrister and author.

XX
THE ROWLEY FAMILY AND PRIORY HILL

Although taking little part in local affairs, other than those of the Church and the Bench, the Rowley family, as squires of the parish, exercised a great influence on the town and its development for nearly 150 years.

Of the first four generations that lived at Priory Hill few were loved and most feared but respected. They were all wealthy and accumulated more wealth by marriage and shrewd investment. They were not, however, noticeably generous, except to the church. None were spendthrifts, and indeed a mean and miserly streak was a family characteristic. One can only speculate about the effect on subsequent generations of the genes of Anne King, wife of Ousley the founder of the family at St. Neots, with her dwarfish, almost deformed body, and possibly dwarfish mind, herself the daughter of the miserly and eccentric attorney William King. George Dawson Rowley, the distinguished amateur scientist, seems to have been a break in the pattern but after him it resumed as before.

Their influence on the town is still apparent. They undoubtedly used their money successfully to force the railway away from the town centre, in their desire to prevent the line approaching their house and park. What appears to be more sinister was an apparent policy, followed by each generation, of buying up, when it came into the market, all land east of the town. The final result was that they owned all the land to the east of the town, circling it from the Paper Mill to the B 1046 Abbotsley road. Once acquired no land was ever sold, which effectively prevented any large-scale development of the town eastward, the only direction in which it could expand. We shall probably never know if this policy was merely one to enlarge the sporting estate, to prevent the town getting bigger, or to enable some future member of the family to hold the town to ransom. This stranglehold was not broken until

1919, when, under the threat of the new powers of compulsory purchase, land to build the Cromwell Gardens Estate was taken by the Urban District Council.

Another form of local control came with the purchase from the Earl of Sandwich of St. Neots Manor, which included possession of the Market Square and its tolls. Sufficient common rights on St. Neots Common were acquired to control voting at meetings of the Proprietors. The purchase, in 1864, of the advowson of St. Neots church, gave the family the right to choose the vicar and so to decide if the services should be 'high' or 'low'. They were always 'low'.

Finally, on the credit side, the landscaping of many acres round Priory Hill House with its park trees, avenues, tree belts and spinneys, has provided, in this century, an attractive setting for new schools, playing fields, and a public park for the town.

It would be unfair not to record that the family considered that their public duties lay mainly at county level. The office of Justice of the Peace was automatically conferred on each head of the family, several members served long terms as chairmen of Quarter Sessions and, in the case of G. F. Rowley, as chairman of the County Council.

Ousley Rowley (1755-1824) was the son of George Rowley (1731-1798), a member of a Shropshire family that had come to live at Godmanchester about 1750. Ousley seems to have lived at Huntingdon and his decision to leave there and found a family seat at St. Neots was probably influenced by the fact of his marriage to Anne King (1752-1835), heiress and only child of the eccentric and miserly attorney William King of the house now known as the Limes, Huntingdon Street, then the farmhouse of Priory Farm, now Priory Park. Anne King was described by her contemporaries as dwarfish and even slightly deformed, and even with 'her weight of gold' as a dowry was long in finding a suitable husband. Her father, who died in 1814, not only owned Priory Farm but much other land in the parish, and at his death his fortune of £30,000 went to his daughter.

Ousley started acquiring property in St. Neots in 1793, laying out his park on the former Priory Farm and building a rather austere house in 1798 (plate 11). An avenue of trees was planted along the approach road (Priory Hill) and an underground ice-house dug in the park just west of the house. When this became ruinous it gave rise to stories that it was the exit of an underground tunnel from St. Neots Priory to Priory Hill. Among property acquired at this time was Monks Hardwick Farm and probably the freehold of St. Neots mill (now the Paper Mill). For some unknown reason Monks Hardwick was sold in 1812 and not recovered by the family until 1859.

No surviving records depict Ousley Rowley as a likeable or popular figure. Joseph Wright wrote down some stories about him told by his mother, who described him as a 'hearty blackguard'. His plebeian neighbours at Huntingdon were said to have been so overjoyed at his departure that they 'tin kettled and hooted him out of the town' when he left. She remembered him as of medium height, stoutish build and with a quick temper. This latter trait she illustrated by a scene in Mill Meadow, when a violent thunderstorm broke while hay-making was being completed. To the fury of the squire the hay-makers ran for shelter, and he galloped his horse furiously round the field in rage, trying, with every insult and obscenity, to force them back into the rain to continue getting in the hay.

As the squire he was automatically appointed a Justice of the Peace, and was said to have served as chairman of Quarter Sessions for 25 years, and was twice Mayor of Huntingdon. It should be recorded that when the equally culpable St. Neots Poor Law Overseers 'sold' Ebenezer Shaw, aged nine years, (no doubt an orphan) to John Fowlson of Heanor, Derby, framework-knitter, for child factory labour, in 1801, he was willing to sign the deed committing him to an apprenticeship of 11 years. The signature of a J.P. was required as it was supposed to be a protection against exploitation.

His eldest son was David, who died unmarried in London, aged 65, in 1855, and it was his second son, George William, who succeeded to the St. Neots property.

George William Rowley (1796-1878) was trained in the law and was said to have been tall and handsome with a distinguished appearance. He was pressed from all sides to follow his father in accepting the chairmanship of Quarter Sessions, but continued ill health forced him to decline. His obituary reads 'The deceased was born and educated amidst the wars of Napoleon, and the tendency of Mr. Rowley's mind, both in matters social and political, was strongly tinged with the tone of thought that prevailed at that period and during the Regency. He was a Tory and a Churchman of the most pronounced type . . . It might be said of him that he held to certain constitutional and political dogmas with as much tenacity as if they were religious truths, and during the Premiership of Sir Robert Peel he shared to the utmost the antipathies of the Protectionist Party against that states-man . . . He fought many a battle, through a long series of years, in support of the maintenance of Church Rates, with as unflinching a determination as if he was defending a Catholic verity . . . He had qualities which would have insured success in any department of life, and which, had he followed a Parliamentary career, would have lead him to distinction. He never knew when he was beaten. . . His love of retirement formed a portion of his natural character, and he enjoyed, above all things, the seclusion of his family place'.

He married Jane Catharine Maine (1801-86), a descendant of the ancient Scottish family of Kers of Cassford, Earls of Roxburghe. She continued to live at Priory Hill after his death, and in 1880 bought Tithe Farm to add to the family estate. Their three sons were George Dawson, John Ousley (1825-43), and Charles Percival.

He was chairman of St. Neots Bench and High Sheriff in 1854, and was remembered as travelling in some state in a yellow four-wheeled coach, hung on leather springs, and attended by a coach-man and footman in livery.

His death caused a stir in the neighbourhood as it occurred only a few hours before that of his eldest son, George Dawson, at Brighton and was followed by a double funeral.

George Dawson Rowley (1822-78) was undoubtedly the most gifted and versatile member of the family, and became widely known as a scientist and antiquarian. He was educated at Eton and Trinity College, Cambridge where he took his B.A. and M.A. degrees. His early life was spent at Priory Hill and soon after leaving college in 1849 he married Caroline Frances (1821-99) only daughter of Archdeacon Lindsay. Thereafter he devoted his life to scientific, antiquarian, and literary pursuits, of which orni-thology was perhaps his special interest. His *Ornithological Miscellany* was published in parts and is now a rare and valuable work. He also contributed to *Ibis* and *The Field*. His collection of bird skins came from all over the world, and were so well preserved and stored that a few years ago, when they must have been about a hundred years old, they were found to be still in good condition.

Some skins of now extinct New Zealand birds were then gladly accepted by the British Museum.

The most famous part of his collection related to the Great Auk, of which he had stuffed specimens and eggs. These were sold by the family in 1934, the Great Auks realising £500 each and the six eggs a total of £1,375.

He also collected fossils from the local brick-pits and described them in scientific journals.

Local and family history were of great interest to him. He is said to have prepared, in MS., a history of the Rowley family, and to have been engaged on a history of the county of Huntingdon when he died. None of these MSS. has, as far as the writer knows, ever come to light since. He has, however, seen a Scrap Book, kept by G. D. Rowley and his wife, which contained many interesting anecdotes and items of local folklore.

He was also greatly interested in St. Neots Church, and with his brother Charles Percival contributed generously to its restoration and adornment.

He succeeded to the estates of his wife's uncle, S. R. Fydell Esq., in 1868. These included property at Boston, Lincolnshire, and Morcott Hall, Rutland, where he then mainly lived. He died in 1878, at Chichester House, Brighton, on the same day that his father died at Priory Hill, but some hours after, and was succeeded by his only son George Fydell.

Many people now living will remember G. F. Rowley, (1851-1933) familiarly known as 'Old Rowley', in his old age. He presented a bent, rather short, bandy-legged figure, with a stubby beard, and shabbily dressed in a hard-wearing cloth jacket, breeches and soft leather leggings. He always carried a stout stick to help his pronounced limp.

Like others of his family, after going to Eton he was trained in the law, perhaps with the idea of fitting him for his assured place in the magistracy of his county. This no doubt stood him in good stead later as chairman of Quarter Sessions and his local Bench. He was also J.P. for Lincolnshire and Rutland, where he inherited Morocott Hall, and was High Sheriff for the latter county in 1891.

As a young man he developed political ambitions and managed to get himself adopted as a Parliamentary candidate in the Boston, Lincolnshire, division. This was probably done through the influence of his mother's family, who had large property interests there. However, after the election, which he presumably won, there was an Election Petition presented bringing charges against him of bribery, which included the distribution of £1,500 in gold sovereigns. As a result he fled to France and his agent was sentenced to a term of imprisonment. There is little doubt that, although technically responsible, he was the innocent dupe of his unscrupulous agent, and had no idea of what was going on.

After spending three or four years abroad it was intimated to him that if he now returned home no charges against him would be preferred. This he did, but with, of course, all possibility of a political career ruined. As a result of this bitter disappointment he is never remembered as again taking any active part in politics. Many years later he was persuaded to make an exception and take the chair at a meeting in St. Neots in support of the Conservative cause. At this meeting he was heckled by 'Jobber' Sharman, the Eynesbury butcher, with the provocative question, 'Why did you run away to France?' He never attended another political meeting.

He did however take the part his family had always done in local affairs at county level, acting as chairman of Quarter Sessions from 1905 to 1933, and as chairman of the County Council from 1916 to 1933. He was also chairman of St. Neots Bench from 1893-1933, which included the time, in the first quarter of this century, when Buckden became nationally notorious for its regularly manned 'police trap' where motorists were timed and, if found to be exceeding the speed limit of 20 m.p.h., were heavily fined at St. Neots court. There was much public criticism of this which reflected on the chairman, who was known to be 'anti-motorist'. Indeed he could be severe in his sentences, but no one ever questioned his fair and impartial judgment in the finding or rejection of guilt.

An example of his sense of fairness occurred when in 1893, while he was away from home, one of his keepers named Perkins brutally assaulted a local man named Townsend, caught poaching on his estate. Cross-summonses were granted and the cases heard by his fellow magistrates, who dismissed all the cases. This caused such strong feeling in the town that the keeper had to have the protection of five policemen to get him from the Court to his house. Hearing about the case, on his return, G. F. Rowley at once dismissed the keeper and sent Townsend £5.

It was indeed true that as he grew old he developed many prejudices against the rapidly-changing world, showing particular dislike of the motor car. Guests invited to Priory Hill, for house parties or shooting, were expected to use horse transport or the railway, and were unlikely to be asked again if they arrived in a motor car.

His old and shabby clothes were a local by-word, and they, combined with his love of walking, produced many stories of strangers mistaking him for a tramp, although he was the richest man in the parish. He would often go by train to Huntingdon, to attend meetings, and walk back to Priory Hill. On one such occasion a drover, driving cattle towards St. Neots, asked his assistance to deliver his herd to 'Old Rowleys' farm. When between them they had got them all safely into the field the drover offered his helper 6d. for a drink. As they walked back together, the drover was astonished to see him turn into the front drive of Priory Hill.

On another occasion one of his own labourers had to cross the rain-swollen Gallow Brook, with no bridge at hand. Fydell Rowley happened to be there and ordered him to mount his back. He then waded across the stream, up to his waist in water, and delivered him dry on the other side, saying 'I am going home and can change, you have to stay out all day'.

Over long periods he was at variance with St. Neots Urban District Council over public footpaths crossing his property, and much bitterness was engendered by his determination, if possible, to exclude the public from long established rights of way. In this he was fortunately unsuccessful. In 1896 he wrote to the Council demanding the removal of seats which he said they had put, illegally, on the Common.

His interest in the Common was great and he used to take the chair at meetings of the Proprietors. However he never claimed rights there as Lord of the Manor, and indeed paid the Proprietors a shooting rent for Hawkesden Leys.

Like all his family he was deeply interested in St. Neots church, the living of which he owned, and he was generous both to the needs of the vicar and the building.

He seems to have died with a deep distrust of everything in what had become to him an incongruous world, and it is said that after his death the key to his safe was found tied to a string round his body.

In 1884 he married Alice Nina, eldest daughter of Sir Vincent Corbett, and they had two sons, Ousley and Richard, the former being the last member of the family to live regularly at Priory Hill.

Mrs. Fydell Rowley was a popular figure in the town, taking an active part in local good works, such as the Nursing Association. She survived her husband for some years but kept up the tradition of being driven into the town in a trap by her coachman in livery coat and cockaded top hat.

Priory Hill House and Park were bought by the St. Neots Urban District Council in 1964, and the house pulled down.

GAZETTEER

Author's note: This gazetteer was mainly completed by 1966 and many changes since that date have not been included.

CHURCH STREET

1505: Saynt Maristrete.
1721: Bridge Street (The short length between the church and Eynesbury bridge).
1788: Great St. Mary's Street.
Early 19th century: Church End. (The part near the church).
1843: St. Mary's Street or Church Street.
1878: The Local Board named it officially Church Street.

The East side from Eynesbury Bridge

No. 47. Present offices of C. G. Tebbutt Ltd. This is the site of a waterside inn doing trade with those engaged in the navigation. There were steps down to the Brook and a ring in the wall to moor boats. The first certain reference is for 1757 when it was called the *Bull's Head* but in some later records there may be confusion with the *Bull* in the Market Square. In 1830 Jos. Foskett was landlord and in 1877 Saml. Ray, when there was complaint of gambling and drunkenness. Sometime after 1830 its name was changed to the *Bear*. In 1888 the landlord was S. W. Hawkesford a basket-maker who worked in part of the Fellmongers Yard premises at the back. His son was also a basket-maker (see Brook Street). At some time this rather low-built house, with attics in the roof, had been extended towards Hen Brook to provide a large room on the ground floor. G. H. remembered that dancing used to take place here with the landlord Hartop playing the fiddle. As closing time at Eynesbury was 10 p.m. and at St. Neots at 11 p.m., customers from over the bridge would troop in here at 10 p.m. The licence was given up when E. H. Williams was landlord in 1908; the annual trade was then 29 and a half barrels of beer and 12 gallons of spirits.

Next to the *Bear* was an **old cottage** occupying the frontage as far as the gateway to Fellmongers Yard.

No. 43. The Fellmongers yard. This yard and premises, now used by C. G. Tebbutt Ltd. as a joinery workshop and store, was used, at least as far back as the beginning of last century, for fell-mongering. The older buildings of brick with iron window frames are typical of the Industrial Revolution.

The first records show them in use by the Fairey family, pro-bably the same that lived at 11 Market Square. There was a Jas. Fairey fellmonger, in 1816, and Ann Fairey fellmonger, Church End, in 1830 and 1839. John Fairey, fellmonger, leather-dresser, parchment-maker, and wool-dealer was here in 1854 and 1862, but in 1870 he had died and his son, aged 17, was drowned.

In 1873 the business was in the hands of Fred Whitley, soon joined by Jas. and Wm. Whitley. They added new buildings which were destroyed by fire in 1874, and in the same year the firm was prosecuted for persistent and offensive nuisance. Further trouble followed. In 1878 there were complaints of a smoke nui-sance and pollution of the Brook. In the same year their chief clerk absconded with £20 and fled to America. Next year, how-ever, he returned, was arrested at Liverpool and brought before St. Neots court. Later in that year the firm, whose headquarters were at Bradford, Yorks. were declared bankrupt with liabilities of £21,000.

In 1885 Jas. Osborn, engineer, millwright, and brassfounder, started business here, but in 1888 moved to the yard at 19 St. Mary's Street, Eynesbury.

From at least 1858 part of the premises had been used by Saml. Richardson basket-maker, probably a descendant of Henry Richardson basket-maker, who came to St. Neots from Dunton, Beds. in 1770. A Thos. Richardson was here in 1890 and 1895 and later Len. Richardson, who moved the business to Eaton Socon. While he was here he lived at 4 St. Mary's Street, Eynesbury. For the Richardson family worked S. W. Hawksford landlord of the *Bear* inn (see above) followed by his son 'Sammy' (see Brook Street).

Early this century the property was unoccupied and in 1914 soldiers of the Fife and Forfar regiment were billeted there for a time. In 1915/16 the yard was hired by C. G. Tebbutt who installed a circular rack-saw bench, driven by a portable steam engine, to convert home grown timber during the war period and for a few years after.

Nos. 37, 38, 39. Terrace of brick cottages.

The Corner. In road improvements to widen the corner, the corner house was pulled down about 1910. There had been a shop attached to the house and G. H. knew it as 'Wenham's Corner'. In 1858 a Mrs. Brown was here, and in 1870 W. Lugsden. From 1871 to 1877 there was W. B. Lawfield, draper, grocer, and wine merchant, who left to go to Thrapston. He was followed by W. H. Brown, and in 1880 by G. Wenham who advertised as 'The Huntingdonshire Stores'. W. J. Graves was there in 1890, and in 1892 R. Freeman left here for the Cross. He was followed by the last shopkeeper, F. (or J.) Cook.

No. 35. The *Woolpack* inn. The present house was built about 1925-30 and replaced an old house (R. Hist. Mon. Comm., No. 25). Foundations had to be very deeply dug to reach solid ground through black mud, an indication of made up ground or an old channel of the Brook. From this came Roman pottery. In 1860 it had two cottages in the yard. Landlords include: 1850, 1858 Geo. Pye; 1870, 1878 Geo. Luff; Jas. Lawson (died 1885); 1898 Lawson.

Nos. 31, 33, Red House. This house in red brick in the Georgian style would appear (from a MS. in the Norris Library) to have been built in 1795, and the present name goes back at least as far as 1885. At various times last century it was, as now, divided into two dwellings.

The site was formerly occupied by a public house called the *Three Blackbirds* of which there are a number of records between 1720 and 1790, and which, in 1723 was owned by E. Gurry. It was part of Robt. Pullen's property in 1768.

It is possible that the present house was built by John Denniss, joiner, who was living here in 1809, and was followed by Wm. Denniss builder and carpenter, (1797-1873). His wife (1798-1888) sold the business to T. Cox, and, in 1879, the house to a Mr. Brown.

From about 1830 to 1847 Dr. John Jewell Evans lived here before moving to Brook House (see below).

In 1885 Mr. and Mrs. Coleman moved from Brookside into part of the premises. She set up a dressmaking business employing seven or eight girls as apprentices and, as was then the custom, paying only a nominal wage and working 8 a.m. to 8 p.m. on weekdays and 8 a.m. to 4 p.m. on Saturday. Mr. Coleman was a parchment and cloth label cutter. He bought scraps and offcuts from Harvey's parchment factory at Eynesbury and sold his labels to the export trade for conditions where paper was too perishable. John Coleman died in 1894 and Mrs. Coleman advertised her business for sale in the same year.

No. 29. The Vicarage. This was built in 1848/9 to replace the old vicarage (St. Mary's Cottage in Church Street next to the 'Shrubbery') and was enlarged by Rev. Vaughan (vicar 1854-65). Part of the additions may have been extra stabling for Neville Day, who kept his horses here. Later Rev. Mead (vicar 1875-1902) kept his own horses here.

Site of Hall Place. Rev. Cole, who visited St. Neots in 1754 (Add. MS 5837 f.127) recorded in his diary, 'Mr. Pullen had an exceeding good house, now in the Cotten family, which stands to the east end of the churchyard. Mrs. Markham and her sister Watkins, and their priest, Father Charles Bedingfield a Recollect Friar [a reformed order of Franciscans] . . . about a year or two ago rented Mr. Pullen's house'.

In 1770 the Cottens sold the whole site to John Broughton of Kettering, who is described as carpenter, and who may have bought it for the materials after demolition. At any rate in the same year he sold the site to Joseph Eayre, the bellfounder, who may have had ideas of building here, but died in 1772. In 1773 the site is described as 'where a capital messuage lately stood'. In 1791 Joseph Eayre's trustees sold the site of the house and part of the grounds to Dr. Alvey of Old Hall, Cambridge Street (now Hall Place). It seems to have remained attached to Old Hall until the insolvency of Samuel Day in 1881, which was probably the time when it was bought by Geo. Bowyer, of the Shrubbery, Church Street, to which house it remained attached until well into this century.

Since the first discoveries made by the author in 1929, this site, in the angle of Duck Lane and Green End Brook, has become famous as the type site where late Saxon pottery, now known as St. Neots ware, was first recognised for what it was, and a number of small pit huts excavated. (*Proc. Camb. Antiq. Soc.,* Vol. XXXIII (1933), 133-151). In 1961, after planning permission for building development had been given, a large scale excavation was undertaken here by P. V. Addyman, F.S.A., on behalf of the Ministry of Public Buildings and Works, and evidence of large wooden houses of the late Saxon period were found, as well as Roman, medieval and post-medieval occupation. (see *Proceedings of Cambridge Antiquarian Soc.*, Vol. 44 (1973), 45-99, and *Post-Medieval Soc.*, Vol. 6 (1972), 69-106.

Grounds enclosed by high red-brick wall with ornamental iron gate. (Plate 12) This was the site of the mansion of Hall Place of the Pulleyns, which was built just inside the present iron gates and was said to have been rebuilt in 1712. It was rediscovered during the excavations in 1961. It was found to have a square plan measuring 51 ft by 53 ft with four rooms at entrance level. Just behind and partly under it to the east a fishpond 12 ft deep and 15 ft across had been filled in, probably about 1600.

This was probably the principal house in the town in the 18th century and, with the exception of the church, is the only building shown pictorially on Jeffery's map of 1768.

It seems possible that it was built by the Pulleyn family as there was a Robt. Pulleyn of St. Neots, steward to the Earl of Sandwich, in 1678, who died in 1710. His son Robt. Pulleyn, attorney, is named among the church records in 1737. This latter was the last Pulleyn in the town. He died in 1741, leaving his property to his relative John Hart Cotton. No Cottons appear to have lived here but they kept the house and let it. In 1742 there was found in the house, under what circumstances is not known, a 13th-century Limoges enamel shrine or reliquary which was taken possession of by Sir John Cotton, later passing to Dr. Stukeley the antiquary. At his sale in 1776 it was bought by Gustavus Brandar, and again came up for auction, at Sothebys, in July 1930 when it was bought for £4,800. Its present whereabouts is not known but a coloured illustration hangs in the Norris Museum, St. Ives. (see also: *Dr. Stukeley's Diaries*, III, 504; *Surtees Soc. Pub.* 76, 215; *Philos. Soc. Trans.* No. 490). One can only surmise that this rich shrine may have been originally in St. Neots Priory church.

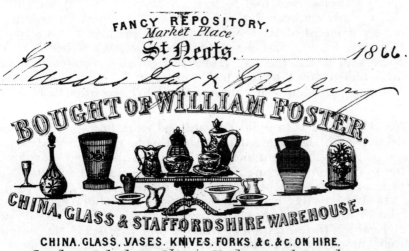

The parish workhouse. At the north end of the high red brick wall is a contemporary entrance, inside which a modern one has been built, and which must once have led to the Hall Place stables and grooms' quarters. This was the site of the parish workhouse, but there is some doubt as to when it was established here. Wrycroft's *Almanac* 1902 states categorically that the first workhouse was at the common gate in New Street (we have found no confirmation of this) and moved to Church Street in 1768 on land rented or leased from Stephen Scarbrow of Old Hall (now Hall Place), Cambridge Street. He had acquired it after the death of the last Pulleyn and it comprised the stable block, adapted for use as a workhouse.

There is, however, a reference, in the churchwardens' accounts, to rent paid in 1730 to Mr. Pulleyn for the workhouse. There is no doubt, however, that in 1788 the trustees of Stephen Scarbrow sold the site to the parish for £200 and that it then comprised the workhouse and a yard and garden.

In 1831 a resolution of the vestry meeting ordered that a fire engine shed be put up on the same site. It was to measure 18 ft by 24 ft with three pairs of doors to hold three engines and five buckets, the cost not to exceed £30.

When the Union Workhouse was built in Eaton Socon in 1843 the whole site, which was stated to contain a hospital, almshouse and workhouse, was sold to Samuel Day of Old Hall for £625. He probably considered it an eyesore to his property as he immediately demolished the buildings and sold the land to his relative Wm. Day of the Shrubbery, Church Street, as a walled garden. Some remains of the old stables and groom's cottages survived until pulled down by Hunts Motors Ltd. in 1963. They were alongside an additional entrance to Hall Place from Cambridge Street.

No. 17. House with builder's yard and workshop. From its connection with the high red-brick wall this house is obviously contemporary with the entrance way described above and must have been built for someone serving, in some way, the Hall Place mansion. It has now been a builder's premises for over 100 years.

In 1854 it was occupied by Basford and Osborne, builders, who dissolved their partnership the next year leaving the house and yard in the possession of Wm. Osborne (1810-93). He became well known for high-class work, restoring many churches in the district and building many houses, including Little Barford House for Julius Alington. Among his workmen was Geo. Wrycroft, foreman, bricklayer, founder of the late Huntingdon Street firm of the same name, and foreman carpenter Francis Wellham, father

of Frank Wellham, who also built up a large and prosperous building business (in Eaton Socon). The scale of Osborne's work is
shown in the record of a dinner he gave to his 34 men at the
Plough, Cambridge Street, in 1864.

In 1894 the premises were taken by Wm. Wade, builder, and
after being used as a furniture store (1914–18) were taken by
A. W. Childs, builder, in 1925, followed by his son, the present
occupier, after his death in 1948.

No. 15. House with business premises behind, pulled down 1960.
(*Hist. Mon. Comm.*, no. 27) In this house lived Thos. Ganderson,
blacksmith (1819–96), with his smithy at the back. The yard was
shared with Jas. Wade, stonemason. After 1896 the business was
carried on by his son William ('Little Billie') Ganderson, into this
century.

Nos. 13, 11. Timber-framed houses, pulled down in 1961.

Nos. 9, 7, 5. Terrace of three cottages built by John Franks (see
High Street) with a panel inscribed 'Franksville Terrace 1906'.

Previously the site was occupied by four old whitewashed 'stud
and mud' cottages belonging to the Waresley Poor Charity, who
sold them to Franks in 1899 for £300. The cottage next to the
Wheatsheaf inn was also a small shop in 1858, kept by Thos.
Wrycroft.

The *Wheatsheaf* inn. The present house was built about 1905 to
replace an old low-roomed house that probably dated back to the
early 16th century. The earliest reference found to this house was
in 1738, and in 1788, when Saml. Warwick was the victualler, it
was described as 'an ancient messuage called the Wheatsheaf with
a brewhouse in Gt. St. Mary's Street', and it had a common right
attached. Other landlords include: 1809 Saml. Rycroft; 1823 Thos.
Rycroft; 1830 Jas. Savage; 1835–45 Mrs. Savage; 1850–70 Wm.
Lucas; 1870 Mr. Hensman (carpenter and undertaker). 1877 Jos.
Gilbert; in 1877 A. W. Gilbert left for the *Wrestlers* (South Street);
1890 Isaac Hitch; 1899 Mrs. Hitch, after her husband lost both
legs in an accident.

Nos. 1, 2. Corner house and shop at junction of Cambridge Street.
Pulled down 1964 and replaced by a block of shops with flats
above.

In 1809 this was occupied by Jas. Barringer (probably baker)
in 1824 by John Barringer, baker, and from 1830–77 by Joseph
Barringer, baker. His wife and daughter also kept here a school
for girls and small boys. Joseph Barringer's hobby was his hot-
house in which he had a grape vine of which he was inordinately

proud, and from which he made wine. Indeed, he advertised himself as 'Bread and Biscuits. Champagne Manufacturer. Ladies School'. It is recorded that on one occasion Queen Victoria was due to pass through St. Neots by train. Disappointed at learning that the train would not stop at St. Neots station he travelled to Peterborough with a prize bunch of his grapes to present to Her Majesty. At Peterborough he persuaded the officials to allow him to approach the royal carriage and the Queen graciously accepted the grapes which he handed to her on his best silver dish. As he waited on the platform with bowed head the train drew out of the station. He never saw his silver dish again.

In 1877, probably after her husband's death, Mrs. Barringer sold the school to Mrs. Julia Crofts, a widow of Rev. H. O. Crofts (once President of the Methodist New Connection Conference). She died in 1895 and in 1896 the premises were opened by Mr. A. C. Claxton as the *Spa* Hotel, which became the headquarters of St. Neots pigeon racing club.

In 1905 Lord Roberts happened to be passing through the town and called in at the *Spa* Hotel for refreshment. On seeing a picture of himself, cut from a newspaper, hanging on the wall, he asked the landlady who it was. She did not recognise the man who was then the hero of the Boer War and replied 'that is our dear old Bobs'. He was so delighted that he later sent her a framed portrait of himself.

By 1913 the hotel had been given up and R. Freeman, grocer, moved here from corner premises at the other side of the Cross (at the east end of High Street) which he sold to the Co-operative Society. He built a new shop on this corner. He was followed by his son William who gave up about 1960.

In 1964 the demolition and clearance of the house and shop on this site gave an opportunity for excavation on an archaeologically important area in the centre of the town. This was undertaken by G. T. Rudd and the author, with the co-operation of the developers. In spite of much disturbance by cellars in the centre of the site it proved a microcosm of history of the town.

The primary feature was a deep defensive ditch which ran roughly parallel with, but finally disappeared under Cambridge Street. At the corner it swept round at right angles to follow Church Street. Sections were cut across it in several places, including the site of the demolished cottages nos. 13 and 11 where it appeared to have had a causeway across it. It had been dug down to some seven feet below the present surface and was about five feet wide. At the bottom there were signs of stakes supporting a wattle lining and on the inside postholes probably representing revetment of a bank of earth or timber fence. This ditch had been deliberately filled in, probably, from evidence of pottery in the filling, in the 12th or early 13th century, and it seems likely that it was the defensive ditch enclosing the late Saxon settlement found a little to the south west (see above).

Over the ditch filling buildings had almost at once been erected, the most notable, on the side facing Church Street, being one containing two small iron-smelting furnaces and a melting furnace for copper alloys. Coin and pottery evidence dated these to the 13th century.

On the side facing Cambridge Street a series of successive house building could be traced, with a return along Church Street. The first, immediately above the ditch filling, was 13th century, and pulled down in the 16th or 17th century. The second building, again timber-framed, was probably that rebuilt in 1913. (*Medieval Arch.*, vol. X, (1966), p. 158).

WEST SIDE OF CHURCH STREET

The corner building, now Salvation Army Citadel, see High Street.

Small shop, now a greengrocer's. In 1854 this was kept by Catherine Crick, stay-maker (there was a Jas. Crick, stay-maker in the High Street in 1830). In 1888 Ellen Mercer Chaloner started a 'Fancy Repository' here, and was succeeded by Miss Maud Gore in 1893.

Entrance gateway to Britain Ltd., High Street. This formerly led to stables where delivery carts and horses were kept to serve Carpenter's shop on the the High Street corner.

St. Mary's Cottage. (*Hist. Mon. Comm.*, no. 26), pulled down 1969. This was originally the St. Neots vicarage, the last vicar to occupy it being Rev. Appleton (Vicar, 1837–48). When sold in 1856 it was described as 'Small genteel residence with real iron fence in front, entrance hall, dining room, drawing room, four bedrooms, detached scullery, with sink and pump. 10 foot carriageway to the north, formerly the vicarage, Chaise house, . . . cellar, . . . part of laundry yard, hen house, dung pit, and cinder place. Frontage 58 feet, depth 128 feet'.

After the sale it was occupied by Miss Raynes with whom lodged C. R. Wade Gery and his sister, until his marriage, when he moved to Cedar House, Cambridge Street. Geo. Bower also lived here for a short time before buying the Shrubbery next door.

The Shrubbery. This fine and sumptuous 18th-century house was obviously built by a prominent and wealthy citizen of that time. It is built of the local grey brick which came into fashion about the middle of the century and the interior has some beautiful wood and plaster work. It is curious that the surrounding wall is of red brick, as is that of Hall Place opposite, and may have belonged to an earlier house.

The earliest owners traced are the Reynolds family, members of which had at one time Brook House (Brook Street) and Little Paxton Hall as their main seat. This house seems to have been used as a dower house. The rate book shows a Walter and a John Reynolds having property in the town in 1686, and a Mrs. Reynolds in 1722. A Geo. Reynolds was almost certainly living here in 1757 (perhaps Rev. Geo. Reynolds who died 1769) and he may well have built the house. (See memorials to the Reynolds family in Little Paxton church.)

A study of the deeds, by the late owners, Dr. and Mrs. Povey, showed that Geo. Reynolds gave the property to his daughter Clemence on her marriage to Rev. Anthony Reynolds in 1768. Their son Lawrence (1771–1839) was given the property as part of a marriage settlement when he married Mary Cole (died 1839) in 1802. On the death of his uncle Richard in 1814, they apparently moved to Little Paxton and sold the house to Wm. Day, attorney. In this transaction it is first called the Shrubbery. Wm. Day probably lived here until his death in 1885, using it also as his office, with his father Geo. Day. I was reminded that as an old man he was pushed round the town in a bath chair, by his gardener, Piggott, and on fine days taken to his favourite spot, the field on which Avenue Road was afterwards built. In 1856 his trustees let it to Geo. Spencer Bower of Vulcan Iron Works (see Market Square) and finally sold it to him in 1865. He lived here until his death in 1911. Possibly in his time, but more likely during the ownership of Wm. Day, there was added most of the extensive garden land opposite enclosed by the high brick wall, and once the grounds of old Hall Place. Here were laid out tennis lawns, greenhouses and orchards.

At the death of G. S. Bower the property was bought by Dr. E. H. Harrisson who moved here from the Priory and became well known as doctor to the St. Neots quads.

Stocks and Whipping Post. These stood in a small square recess in the churchyard in the angle formed by the pavement and the churchyard path leading to the vicarage on the north side of the church. Different capping on the churchyard wall shows where it was extended to cross the gap. They were dismantled about 1850. J. W. told the author that the last two men to be flogged here were named Billing of St. Neots and Hunt of Eaton Socon; and the last man to be put in stocks was Jeremy Jupp of Toseland. This would be about 1824. His mother remembered seeing a woman whipped there. In the churchwardens accounts there are several references to payments for whipping, e.g. 1686 'whipping a boy 4d.', 1701 'whipping a man 4d.', 1710 'whipping 2 boys 8d.', 1712 'whipping a boy 6d.'.

The frontage of the road from the corner to Eynesbury bridge was occupied by three cottages that were pulled down about 1935 when Paine & Co.'s malt extract factory was developed.

CEMETERY LANE

18th century: Little Bridge Street. Beyond the bridge, 17th-20th centuries: Duck Lane; 1848: Brick Kiln Lane, Beyond the railway it becomes a public footpath to Caldecot.

Six Cottages in a terrace used to stand on the south side, next to Red House; they were pulled down in the 1930s, after being derelict for some time. They used to be badly affected by floods. They were owned, and probably built, by one of the Denniss family, builders, of Red House.

The Bridge. This crosses the Green End or Fox Brook, a tributary of Hen Brook. In 1883 the local board discussed who was responsible for its upkeep. On enquiry Saml. Day (then living at Stamford) replied that he built the bridge (to replace an older one) to reach his field, now sold to the Burial Board as a cemetery, and the bridge was included in the sale.

In 1886 the Local Board decided to replace the 'dipping place' by the bridge by a pump.

The Cemetery. A burial board was set up in 1879, and Trap Close was bought from Saml. Day at £300 an acre. John Peck was appointed the first ground keeper. Thereafter there arose much controversy between nonconformity and the established Church as to whether all, or half, and if half which half, of the ground should be consecrated. The Church faction objected to nonconformists being buried in consecrated ground.

The Pest House. Opposite the old cemetery gates a public footpath runs north to Cambridge Street. About 335 yards along it, on the east side, stood the pest house to which people with infectious diseases were taken to be isolated. It is marked on

Jefferys' map of 1768. No record has been found as to when it was pulled down but there is a reference in the local newspaper of 1887 to a Robt. Linford born in the pest house in 1804. A field of about four acres on the south side of Duck Lane, and about 250 yards from the old cemetery, was called in 1899 'Pest Pit Close'. This may indicate a burial site of plague victims.

Brick kiln House or the Brickills. This house and buildings is on the north-west side of the short lane (Dark Lane) that led from Duck Lane across the Hen Brook to Howitts Lane, Eynesbury. It was almost certainly connected with the brickyard that was once situated near by. On the opposite side of the lane, within the angle of the bend, an unnaturally steep bank must be the site of the clay pit and over the field broken bricks are scattered. They are of the local grey or yellow variety.

The St. Neots Award map shows this land belonging to Stephen Gorham (see 22 Market Square) in 1770, and on it long narrow buildings that suggest a brickworks. G. J. Gorham, son of the above, had a brickworks in 1809 in St. Neots (there was no other in the parish) producing 500,000 bricks annually, valued at 2s. 6d. per 100, undoubtedly on this site. It is not known when production stopped. In 1892 the site is called the 'old Brickilns'.

BROOK STREET

Before being officially named in 1878 the west end was usually called Brookside and the east end Church End. In Pigot's *Directory* of 1830 it is treated as a part of the present Church Street and called St. Mary's Street.

The Corner with Church Street. This was formerly occupied by a butcher's shop and premises, the shop facing Brook Street with the slaughter-house at the back along Church Street. This latter had slatted 'hit and miss' windows and small boys would sometimes peer through them to see animals being slaughtered.

Here we had the earliest members of the oldest family business, that of the Bartletts, still extant in St. Neots (now in Huntingdon Street).

There was a William Bartlett, butcher in 1792, almost certainly here, and quite certainly in 1809 and 1823, and the same, or a son of the same name, in 1830 and 1836; at the latter date there was also a Geo. Bartlett living next door. Soon after this the Bartlett family moved to South Street, and in 1872 this shop was occupied by a Mr. Topham, butcher (1812–83), who, it was stated, had been there many years. Topham's widow sold the property in 1883 to Charles Clarke of Eynesbury for £375, and it was then let to Jonathan Blott, butcher, who remained until 1893. He was followed by Fred Kendal, 1893–1899. In 1902 Geo. Frost had it, in 1908 J. Whitlock, in 1910 G. Sharp, and 1911–13 B. Eggleston. The last butcher was probably a Mr. Hopperton and it was permanently disused by 1918.

Nos. 20, 22. House, now made into two flats, with yard and factory premises behind. This house is really part of the large business premises behind which was once a wharf on the navigable Hen Brook. In the earliest reference found to the site, in 1754, all this area, including that occupied by Church House, belonged to the Rawlings family, merchants and watermen, with houses in which lived William and John, or Jonathan, Rawlings; probably the same family of St. Ives who operated the last barges coming to St. Neots at the end of the 19th century.

In 1769 John Rawlings sold the site to James Squire (1740–1825) landlord of the *Swan* inn, a little further along the street, where he had followed his father John Squire (1708–60) as innkeeper. We do not know how or why he was suddenly able to launch out as a merchant but obviously he was a man of enterprise and determination. On starting his new business as a corn, coal, and timber merchant he seems to have left the *Swan* in the hands of his son William (1768–1837) and built, or rebuilt the present house for his own use. It appears that the venture prospered for he also became a partner in the London to Oundle coach, his share obliging him to provide horses for the stage from Stratton Bottom, Biggleswade to St. Neots. At Stratton the stables were attached to a farm where he had set up his son John Burder Squire (1763-1841). He had altogether six sons and three daughters. He is described as having a dark swarthy complexion and was nicknamed 'Old Mahogany'.

On his father's death in 1825 J. B. Squire left Stratton and took over the merchant's business in Brook Street living in his father's house there. The family had now moved into upper middle class society. He himself had married in 1780 Suzanna Peppercorn of Monks Hardwick, and his sister Henrietta was the wife of Rev. Bewsher, vicar of St. Neots. He seems to have maintained a good business, taking his youngest son George into the business while his eldest son, John Burder the second, farmed at Basmead and Cross Hall.

George Squire took over the business, probably on his father's retirement, a little before his death. In 1838 he bought from William Peppercorn, attorney, the fine Georgian Church House, next door to his yard, probably leaving his parents in their old home at the yard (his mother lived until 1848). The old saying 'shirt sleeves to shirt sleeves in three generations' seem to have applied here, and one has the impression that George Squire had not the grit and business ability of his father and grandfather, and that the business was not prospering. Disaster came swiftly in 1855, when gas fitters were repairing some pipes in his warehouse. They had naturally turned off the gas at the meter and were amazed to see lights still burning in his office. These, they found, were supplied by a pipe inserted to by-pass the meter. The police were informed and George Squire was arrested and eventually tried at Assizes. He employed a high-class barrister who secured his acquittal, but on what public opinion considered a technicality. He felt completely disgraced and decided to leave the town. His business and stock were sold and he moved to London, where he died in 1882. The sale advertisement mentions machinery for flour-milling and timber-sawing, and corn and spirit stores.

The premises were apparently unused until 1859 when they were taken by John Powers, who advertised as a miller and merchant at Brookside Steam Mills. He did not stay long after 1862.

The next occupier was G. S. Bowers of the Vulcan Iron Works, Market Square, who probably did some rebuilding. The premises became known as the Meter Works, where he made meters for his gas-producing plants. However, he probably made other plant here as there was a memory of heavy plant being taken from here down the brook on a raft to be unloaded and assembled experimentally on the last meadow before reaching the river. The factory was given up when the firm finally went into liquidation, about 1885.

From about 1900 to 1907 it was used by a company making 'Maltcon' dried vegetable cubes. In 1914 it was empty and was at once requisitioned for the troops stationed in St. Neots. Soon after the end of the war Paine & Co. Ltd. equipped the factory for making malt extract. It was however severely damaged by fire in 1947, rebuilt, and abandoned after another fire in 1955.

During the time Bower used the factory, his foreman occupied the house. The last foreman was E. C. ('Teddy') Ireland, the founder of the present business in New Street. He stayed on in the house (he was there in 1894) and started business on his own by letting out bicycles.

No. 18 Church House. A very complete history of this fine Georgian house exists in deeds dating from 1766, in possession of the owner, Mr. Norman Tebbutt. At that date there were two dwellings on the site. A house in the occupation of William and Jonathan Rawlings, watermen, and formerly Dianah Abbott, which Wm. Rawlings sold in 1766 to John Waller of St. Neots, gentleman (see also Huntingdon Street) for £52. Also a cottage immediately west of the above with a garden between it and the brook. Attached to it also was a pew in the former gallery in St. Neots church. This cottage was sold in 1768 by Henry Williams victualler to Abraham Triston citizen and liveryman of London and a peruke-maker of St. Dunstans West, and formerly of St. Neots, for £45.

In 1770 John Waller sold his house to A. Triston for £45, thus giving him both properties. It would seem probable that he now pulled down the two houses and built a new house, perhaps to retire to in his birthplace after making his fortune in London: Unfortunately nothing further has come to light about his career. However by 1809 he had died and his nephew and heir, John Triston, sold the property to Thomas Chandler, tailor of St. Neots, for £240.

He seems to have bought the property for his son Peter to use, at least in part, as a workshop. In his memoirs 'T' recalls 'Peter Chandler who conducted a drapery business and hat manufactory in premises facing the south side of the churchyard in the retired neighbourhood of Brookside. He was an active man of business and a zealous Wesleyan'.

The next change came in 1826/7 when Peter Chandler sold the property to William Alexander Peppercorn, (died 1833) acting for Wm. Peppercorn, then a minor. Here Wm. Peppercorn established his office as an attorney, and in 1835 enhanced its value by buying the three tenements to the west for £157. These he immediately resold to Robt. Rich but retained a 10 foot right of way along the west side of the property.

It is not certain if Wm. Peppercorn ever lived here or only used the house as offices. He was then very young and probably unmarried, and he may have intended to live here sometime in the future but never did. 'T' says 'At his (Peter Chandler's) death or removal, the property was bought by Mr. Wm. Peppercorn who cleared away his residence and business premises from the site and erected commodious offices in making his debut as an attorney at law'. So it may well be that he built the present house or at least put on the front. At any rate in 1830 it seemed that only a part was being used as offices and the rest let as a ladies' boarding school to a woman named Foundy Madox who had had a remarkable career, preserved in the churchwardens' records when she applied to become a legal inhabitant of the town in 1802. She was born in 1772, daughter of George and Sarah Madox, in the very rural surroundings of Southoe. About 1782 the family had left for Eynesbury when her father, a master-carpenter, hired a house, shop and farm at £30 a year. It seems probable that they did badly here, for three years later they moved to St. Neots, hiring a house at £2 2s. and a shop at £1 1s. a year. It would seem that Foundy had to leave home to seek work for in 1787, at the age of 15, she engaged herself in service, by the month, as servant to a Mr. Pipps, engineer and surveyor in the service of the government of Sierra Leone. After a voyage, which included being detained in the Channel for three months by contrary winds, she arrived at Sierra Leone. Here her master soon died and she became housekeeper at Government House. This must have been at the founding of the colony for freed slaves. After three years in the colony, then notorious as the white man's grave, she returned to settle in St. Neots. There is unfortunately no news of her activities between the ages of 18, when she returned from Africa, and 58 when she had this girls' school in St. Neots.

While practising here Wm. Peppercorn took a partner, O. R. Wilkinson, and they acted as clerk to the Poor Law Guardians, with the office here. In 1838 they decided to move to a more central position at the Cross, where the firm still remains (Wilkinson and Butler), and the property was sold to George Squire for £800 (see above). As he went to live there the school must already have ceased or been turned out.

Geo. Squire and his wife lived here until 1855/6 when his business was sold and he left for London. He retained possession of the house, letting it to a series of tenants.

From 1870 to 1875 it was let to Rev. Gunn. He was a Scot who had been minister of the St. Neots Congregational church, but had resigned after a disagreement. He started a boys' school here which he called 'Church House School'. This was the first time it was given the name 'Church House'. Fees were 25 to 28 guineas a term for boarders and four to six guineas for day-boys.

In 1882, when Geo. Squire died it was occupied by Thos. Hind, builder, who left for Eaton Ford in 1883.

In 1884 Amelia Caroline, widow of Geo. Squire, sold the house to Dr. James Morley Chadwick L.R.C.P. for £400, he being already the tenant. He came here from Manchester, and, in those days of strict religious allegiance, was considered the 'Dissenter's doctor'.

In 1895 he was succeeded by Dr. Campbell Grey, as a tenant, who moved to New Street in 1898.

In 1910 John Perry Burr, veterinary surgeon, bought the property from Dr. Chadwick for £550, having come here as a tenant two years before, from the Market Square, on his marriage. He remained until 1929 and was followed by veterinary surgeons, Bishop Young, Elam, Tovey and N.F. Tebbutt (1960).

No. 16. House. This site was formerly occupied by three cottages, owned in 1775 by John Upchurch of St. Neots, cordwainer, and in 1783 by Jas. Upchurch, cordwainer who willed it to his wife Mary. She died in 1835 and the property then went to Ann Smith a sister of Jas. Upchurch. In 1835 she sold the cottages, then occupied by Eliza. Goss, Jas. Bull, and Wm. Norman to Wm. Peppercorn. He only bought the property to secure a right of way on the west side of his next door property, and immediately resold the remainder of the site to a builder, Robert Rich. Rich probably pulled down the old cottages and built himself the present house. Rich was born between 1790 and 1800 and died in the workhouse in 1874. He was parish clerk for 30 years but sometime after 1862 had a violent disagreement with the vicar, resigned, and joined the Wesleyans. It is probable that his son Robert (1830–80), likewise a builder, also lived here. Other members of the family in the building trade, in 1823, were Jas. and Wm. Rich. A. Tuckfield, painter and plumber was here 1890-1908.

In 1908 a very remarkable man, Samuel Walter Hawkesford* (1874-1966) came to live here. He was a basket and hamper-maker, following his father in the same trade at the *Bear* inn in Church Street, where both worked for Richardsons in the Felmonger's Yard. In Brook Street he set up on his own and was the last of his trade in the town. His first association with the church was at the age of 10 when he became a chorister, and in 1897 at the age of 23 he became parish clerk and verger, offices he held until 1961, surely a record of faithful service. Besides these duties he was a bell-ringer and, until it was stopped in 1939, never missed ringing the one o'clock 'dinner bell'. During his clerkship he never missed a Sunday service. His small but intensely active figure was an inseparable part of all church activities for over 60 years, and his kindly sense of humour and independent character made him beloved by all.

No. 14. House. It is possible that this house was built by one of the Squire family. In 1835 it was owned and occupied by Mrs. Henrietta Bewsher (born 1792) daughter of Jas. (Old Mahogany) Squire (see above) and widow of Rev. Wm. Bewsher, a former

* See plate 22

vicar of St. Neots. After her death her son Wm. Noble Bewsher, (1796–1883) a retired London business man, and a bachelor or widower, came to live here. After his death there was a local scandal when his will, in favour of an illegitimate son by his housekeeper, was disputed in the courts, but upheld.

Nos. 12, 10, 8, 6, 4 and 2. A terrace of poor slum-type cottages, built about 1900 to replace four older cottages. They were condemned and demolished recently.

Boathouse. At the west end of the above terrace was a small triangle of land containing a boathouse belonging to Brook House opposite. The remainder of the south side of Brook Street (known locally as Brookside) runs immediately alongside Hen Brook, with a low wall between it and the stream. This was used in the last century as a wharf and the wall had openings with steps down to the water for the convenience of both navigation and people wishing to dip water. This wharf was used by those who had no private waterside of their own. There were memories of sand being shovelled by hand and thrown over the wall on to the street, to be collected later by carts from Eynesbury brick-yard. Here too came sacks of china clay to be fetched with a hand truck by Joseph Sleigh, clay pipe maker of Russell Street. The greatest trade done here was probably in corn and meal which was stored in the 'corn shops', separate first floor storage barns with doors opening on to the street. Some of these still exist along the west side of South Street and most of the inn yards nearby had some for letting.

About 1887 the brook wall was raised after complaints that owing to the road level being raised the wall was now only two feet high and a number of children had fallen into the brook.

Gill's Bridge. Built originally by Chas. Gill about 1900 to give access to his holiday centre and boat-hiring business on the far side of Hen Brook at its junction with the river (see Chas. Gill, South Street).

NORTH SIDE OF BROOK STREET

The Churchyard. Pictures of the early 19th century show sheep grazing in the churchyard and a path leading from opposite Church House to the south door.

No. 23. House next to the churchyard, pulled down 1960. This was an old timber-framed house cased with brick with a garden bordering the west side of the churchyard and on part of which the churchroom was built in 1902. One of the men working on this building was A. W. Rowlatt* and he noticed a heap of old scrap iron lying in the garden that R. Chasty, who lived in the house, had bought from E. D. Fisher & Sons, Market Square, his employers. Among this he noticed an old tinker's anvil, but the whole lot was quickly taken away from sale by Mr. Chasty.

In 1887 this was known as 'Squire House', and had been occupied by one of the Squire family. It may have been by Peter Squire (1777–1841), one of the numerous sons of James (Old Mahogany) Squire (see 20 and 22 Brook Street) followed by his son James (c. 1812–81), or James ('One Armed') Squire (1804–87) a son of William the son of 'Old Mahogany' who had been left at the *Swan* inn when his father became a merchant.

In 1887 the house was taken by Robt. Chasty, plumber, and his wife Emma, a dressmaker. They had previously lived in East Street in 1871 and in Windmill Row (1877). Mrs. Chasty employed a staff of girl dressmaking apprentices, who worked the long hours almost without pay as was the custom of the day. The Chastys were here well into this century.

Walnut Tree Square. No information has come to light as to the origin of this little square which was formed by Brook House on the west, Squire House on the east, and several cottages on the north. It was probably developed by the Squire family and once had a walnut tree in the centre.

In houses facing the square lived two Squire families, one in Squire House and the other on the north side, it is not quite certain which one was in which. They were Jas. Squire, born deformed and always known as 'One Armed', and Peter Squire, his uncle. A perpetual feud existed between these two families and among other things in dispute was the ownership of the walnut tree. One night, in a fit of exasperation it is said, Peter Squire went out and cut the tree down.

Another feature of the square was a large boulder stone which was put there, to quote *St. Neots Chronicle* of 1883 'more than 90 years ago to mark the boundary of property owned by Jas. Squire and to protect the fence from the wheels of vehicles. It weighed several cwts. and was thrown into the Brook. Mr. Squire offers a reward of £2 to discover the persons responsible'. The culprits were not found and Mr. Squire (probably 'One Armed') had the stone raised and restored to its old position. After his death it was removed to the *Royal Oak* yard in the High Street to serve as a mounting block, but was later moved again by the Local

* See Plate 23

Board and placed on the west grass verge of the Little Barford Road to mark the urban district boundary, where it still is.

From the north-west corner of the square was a private footpath leading to the High Street, for the use of the occupiers of four cottages on the square (on the north side) and a carriage way for Brook House. This would be valuable when Brook Street was flooded, as it often was. Children from Eynesbury used to use this path when attending the British School in the old chapel at the back of 20 High Street.

Brook House. (*Hist. Mon. Comm.*, no. 24). This fine house, dated to about 1700, is one of the most architecturally important in the town, and its iron railings were saved from requisition in the Second World War due to their age and merit.

It is not certainly known who built it, but most probably a member of the Reynolds family of Little Paxton Hall. In 1743 it formed part of the estate of 'the late Mrs. Reynolds', and sometime during that century the family disposed of it. In 1775 it was probably occupied by a Mr. Longland. In 1809 Eliza Duce, who was both owner and occupier, let an attached malting to Wm. Foster, brewer, of 38 Market Square. About 1820 a Capt. Hedding was in occupation, and in 1830 possibly Mrs. Ann Manning. In 1836 Neville Day, attorney, was owner and occupier, and had stables built at the Vicarage for his horses. John Holland was here 1842-7 before going to Monks Hardwick. He was probably followed directly by Dr. John Jewel Evans (1805–92) (see Red House, Church Street and 20 Market Square) who remained here until his death. During part of this time Dr. Evans used it as a home for old or invalid ladies. It also housed his collection of natural history, geological and archaeological specimens, with which St. Neots Museum was founded in the Corn Exchange when he presented them to the Literary Institute in 1887. He had come from Cornwall, where his father was Rector of St. Keverne, to St. Neots in 1830, taking the practice of Dr. Adams at 20 Market Square. In 1834 he had become bankrupt, but recovered his fortune. We should be grateful to this outstanding man who recovered and saved some valuable local archaeological material now in the Norris Museum, St. Ives. Besides his interests in natural science and archaeology, he was a notable wood carver and fisherman. He retired from his practice in 1879 in favour of Dr. Good (see 20 Market Square).

In 1892 the house was bought by Arthur W. Atkinson, merchant of High Street for £800, and he lived here until his death in 1918.

No. 11. Cottage. Probably at one time part of the *Swan* inn.

Nos. 7, 9. Cottages that were, until 1913, the *Swan* inn. This is probably an old timber house cased in brick. It was a waterside inn catering for carters and bargemen employed on the Brookside wharf. Until recently 'Pony and Trap for hire' could be faintly seen painted on the front. From here the Squire family, who later occupied so much of Brook Street, seem to have originated. The earliest landlord discovered was John Squire (1708–60), who was followed by his son James ('Old Mahogany') (1740–1825) who left about 1773 to become a merchant at 22, 23 Brook Street. In his place he left his son William (1768–1837) as innkeeper. Others that followed were; 1823 Wm. Allen, 1836 Geo. Hunns, 1839 C. Fisher, 1850 John Neal (also a fishmonger), 1854 Robt. Wilson (also collector of the market tolls, died 1897), 1870 Robt. Gaunt, 1873 sold at Wm. Bowyer's sale to Mr. Young for £530, about 1885 'Teddy' Wilson, 1889, 1895 Mrs. Eliza Wilson (who also had boats and canoes to let), 1908, 1912 Mrs. Woodcock. In 1913 the licence renewal was refused.

No. 7. House pulled down and site added to Ibbett's yard. This house was occupied in 1858 by Jas. Nichols, but soon after the Forscutt family came here, members of which were, at different periods, dressmakers, dyers, and shoemakers. There was a Wm. Forscutt (1814–75) dyer and probably brother to John Forscutt (1815-72) dyer and scourer of High Street. At the death of William his widow advertised that she was carrying on dyeing, scouring and hot-pressing, by a capable employee. In 1867 a Miss Forscutt started a dressmaking business here, and in 1890 and up to about 1914 Misses Ruth and Martha Forscutt, daughters of William, were running the business with a number of girl apprentices. The dyeing had now been given up but another Forscutt had a small bootmaker's shop in the front.

Ibbett's yard, with blacksmith's and engineering workshops, formerly Bell yard. This is a very old blacksmith's business said to go back to the 17th century and formerly attached to the *Bell* inn in South Street whose landlord was the smith. It also formed a common back entrance to 11 and 13 South Street, and even had a doorway to the King's Head yard. Along its east side, above the blacksmith's shop, was a row of 10 corn shops used for storing corn in connection with the navigation by barge at Brookside wharf. They still exist almost intact. In 1881 they were sold for £78.

In 1823 and 1830 John Dixie was blacksmith here and also landlord of the *Bell*, and in 1850 Mrs. Dixie was still managing both trades. In 1851, however, she sold the blacksmith business to Thomas Ibbett.

Thomas was born in St. Neots about 1832 but had been apprenticed to an Alconbury Weston blacksmith, named Rowlatt. Hours were 6 a.m. to 7 p.m. on weekdays finishing an hour earlier on Saturday. He would walk home after work on Saturdays returning after attending chapel on Sunday. On completing his apprenticeship he worked under contract on the railway, then being built through St. Neots. For this he got 17s. to 18s. a week and was allowed to charge the masons a fee for sharpening their tools.

After St. Neots station was opened in 1850 he bought Mrs. Dixie's business, and in 1873 the goodwill of Wm. Taylor, blacksmith of Eynesbury Bridge. Of his four sons Arthur (1866-1939) became a blacksmith and succeeded his father after his death about 1904. He introduced an engineering side to the business, such as the repair of steam engines and millwrighting. To the end of his life he worked at the forge stopping at intervals to pick up a glowing coal with the tongs which was then dropped into the bowl of his pipe to rekindle it. After his death in 1939 he was followed by his son Cyril, also a skilled engineer, who not only developed the business in the sale and repair of agricultural machinery but made and marketed a number of successful inventions. The fourth generation is represented by his son Valentine who assists him.

House, now used as offices by A. Ibbett & Son. This was formerly the *Bushel and Strike* inn. It is one of the rare houses with two upper floors and was for many years a common lodging house where tramps, Italian organ-grinders, and other pedestrian travellers could hire a bed for as little as 2d. a night. It had an ill reputation and the police were frequently called to stop drunken brawls and even knife fights. It was no doubt named in reference to the corn trade, the principal traffic on the nearby waterway. Up to about 1914 it still had its picturesque signboard. This depicted a wooden bushel measure on which rested the strike stick; on the floor a cat stalked some mice feeding on spilt grains of corn. In the last 20 years of the century Charles 'Darky' Adams was landlord, a half-caste who also had a horse and cart and hawked coal. The house was probably built on part of the site of the parish almshouses.

A cottage next to the above used to be a small sweet shop. It appears to be timber framed with wattle and daub now cased with brick. It may quite likely be part of the parish almshouses. An almshouse is referred to in 1485 (Rentals and Surveys). A title abstract of 1693 describes a small property lying between

1. Aerial photograph of the area c. 1950, showing Eynesbury in foreground.

2. St. Neots Church

3. Market Square, north side, about 1910, showing Fox and Hounds inn
and Half Moon Hotel (now Bridge Hotel). Note cobbled pedestrian crossing.

4. St. Neots Market Square, drawn by John Sunman Austin, 1853.

5. St. Neots Market Square, drawn by E. H. Buckler.

6. St. Neots river bridge, 1911, with Mr. E. G. Rowell, tailor, New Street, on his water cycle.

7. St. Neots Bridge, west side, *c.*1780

8. The Public Rooms with public landing stage and bridge, 1962.

9. The Public Rooms, 1962.

10. Shortsands House, Green End, Cambridge Street.

11. Priory Hill House, built *c.* 1790. Now demolished.

12. Hall Place, Cambridge Street.

13. Gates of original Hall Place, Church Street.

14. House at corner of Huntingdon Street and East Street, 1964

15. House on south side of Market Square (view about 1913), birthplace of Rev. Cornelius Gorham, local historian.

16. The former George Inn and Assembly Rooms (now the Co-op) at The Cross, 1961.

17. High Street, south side, c. 1900, showing Royal Oak (centre) and Kurr, Pork Butcher (right).

18. House, Huntingdon Street (between Wesleyan Chapel and Co-op shop at corner of High Street). Traditionally the home of Joseph Eayre, bellfounder. Pulled down 1961.

19. Residence of Dr. Rix (1803-1878) 21, Market Square (north side). View pre-1900.

20. Toll Gate Cottage at Wintringham, 1935

TOLLS PAYABLE at this GATE.

s. D

For every Horse, Mule, Ass or other Cattle drawing any Coach,
Chariot, Landau, Sociable, Chaise, Curricle, Phaeton, or Hearse, — 8
For every Horse, Mare, Gelding, Mule or Ass drawing any two
wheeled Chaise, Chair, Gig or any Taxed Cart . . . . — 9
For every Waggon, Wain, Cart or other such Carriage with six 1. 2.8
or nine Inch Bellies drawn by 7 or 8 Horses, or other Beasts of draught
by 5 or 6 D.º . . . . 2. —
by 4 D.º 1. 4
by 3 D.º . . . . 1. —
by 2 D.º . . . . — 8
by 1 D.º . . . . — 4

For every Waggon, Wain, Cart or other such Carriage with Wheels of the breadth of four
inches and a half and less than 6 inches drawn by 4 Horses, Oxen or other Beasts of 1. 8
draught including the additional Toll authorized by the General
Turnpike Act of 37 Geo. 4.º Cap. 126.
by 3 D.º including D.º 1. 5
by 2 D.º including D.º . — 10
by 1 D.º including D.º . — 5

For every Waggon, Wain, Cart or other such Carriage with Wheels of less breadth
than four inches and a half drawn by 4 Horses, Oxen or other Beasts of draught 2. 0
including the additional Toll authorized by 3.º Geo. 4.º Cap. 126.
by 3 D.º including D.º . 1. 6
by 2 D.º including D.º . 1. —
by 1 D.º including D.º . — 6

For every Horse, Mare, Gelding, Mule or Ass laden or unladen and not drawing . . — 1
For every Drove of Oxen or neat Cattle . . . Per Score . . . 1. 8
And so in proportion for any greater or less number.
For every Drove of Calves, Hogs, Sheep or Lambs . . Per Score . . 1. 05
And so in proportion for any greater or less number.

SAINT NEOTS and ELTISLEY GATES are Ticket Bars
to each other. COTON is not a Ticket Bar.

21. Toll Board from the Wintringham toll-gate, on
the St. Neots — Cambridge turnpike road.

22. Samuel Hawkesford of Brookside, 1936. Verger and basket-maker.

23. A. W. Rowlett (Doctor) 1867-1946. Herbalist, antique dealer, roadman, finder of Bunyan's Anvil (plate 24).

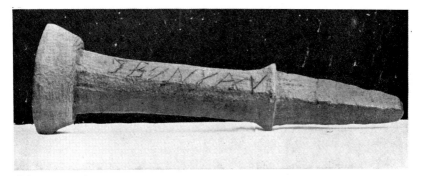

24. Bunyan's Anvil.

25. The Thrush, houseboat, St. Neots.

26. Limoges enamel reliquary found in old Hall Place, Church Street, 1742.

27. Huntingdon Street, north end, about 1910, showing Globe inn.

28. Cottages east side of Huntingdon Street, between East Street and Avenue Road, 1938.

29. Charles Percival Rowley of
Priory Hill and Wintringham Hall
(1827-1904).

30. Joseph Wilcox of High Street
(1816-1894).

31. Rev. F. Newman, Pastor of the Gospel Hall, New Street, 1867-1902 or later.

32. Paper Mill previous to the fire of 1912, river in flood showing use of the wooden 'traps' for pedestrians (now replaced by concrete ones).

the *Bell* inn and the almshouses, which then had two tenants and so were presumably two in number. The churchwardens spent money on repairs to almshouses in 1688.

The corner house. In 1858, this was a small shop kept by Geo. King. In 1888 it was kept by Chas. Bazeley (1825–96) corn chandler, a relic of the waterborne corn trade up the Hen Brook. He also had a refreshment room where market dinners could be had on Thursdays for 1s., cups of coffee were 1d. with an extra ½d. if a bun was added. After his death the business was taken over by Geo. Britten who advertised himself as 'corn chandler dealer in hay, straw, and offal, and serving dinners daily, and well aired beds'. By 1908, however, he had moved the whole business to 3 High Street.

SOUTH STREET

Formerly known as Bell Lane.

Showroom of A. Ibbett & Son., formerly the *Bell* inn. The first reference to this inn is found in the churchwarden's accounts dated 1752; its trade would be with the watermen and corn traders of the area and it gave its name to the street. In 1801 the landlord was Wm. Nightingale and from at least 1823 to 1836 was John Dixie, who was also a blacksmith with his premises in the yard at the back (see Brook Street above). In 1850 it was being kept by Mrs. Dixie, but the blacksmith's business was separated and sold to Thomas Ibbett in 1854. This long association with the Dixie family no doubt prompted its nickname the 'Bell and Dickie' (or 'Dicksie'). Wm. Wells was landlord in 1854 and Geo. Wells in 1858. From about 1860-1879 it was kept by Lavender Ashwell who also had a fishmonger's shop here, with a market stall on Thursdays. In 1888 J. W. Richardson was the landlord, changing the shop to a greengrocer's, and there is some evidence that the name was changed temporarily to the *White Horse*. Sometime between 1895 and 1898 it was taken on his marriage by Chas. Wren, a fishmonger from Biggleswade. He developed the fish business, selling cooked fish and chips, hawking fish round the neighbouring villages by horse and cart, and setting up stalls at St. Neots, St. Ives and Bedford markets. A prospering business enabled him to move to 38 High Street, still occupied by the same firm, between 1904 and 1907. In 1907, when the licence for the *Bell* was surrendered, E. Norman, a butcher, was landlord and kept the shop.

House, now pulled down, and the site now occupied by A. Ibbett & Son's showroom, was the home of Thomas and later Arthur Ibbett.

No. 13. Baker's shop, bakehouse and dwelling house, at present owned by W. S. Shepherd. This old baker's business was run in 1838 by Jas. C. Shepherd (1810–46) and after his early death by his widow. On her remarriage to a Mr. Tilcock in 1851, she sold the business and premises to John Hinde Ekins (1813–96). He knew nothing of baking and had been an employer of Ingersole, grocers of 28 Market Square, also, as a side line, contracting privately to light and supply oil for the town street lamps. He was paid 13s. 6d. for each lamp, and 27s. for four large ones, for the winter season. On taking the baking business he employed a journeyman baker for the first three months, thereafter doing the work himself, and built up a prosperous business. Besides making bread and confectionery he was remembered for his home-cured ham at 5d. per quarter pound, and dinners on market days. He retired leaving the business to his son John who predeceased him, aged 46, in 1892. His widow carried on for some years and was followed by Ernest Whiting, and in 1902 by W. V. Hyde, from a Shefford baking family. He left for Great Gransden in 1918, where the firm still is, and in 1921 the business was returned to its original name by W. S. Shepherd.

No. 11. Shop, dwelling house with premises at the back. These were the premises of the firm of McLauchlan & Vinsen, high-class coachbuilders, who were probably there before 1850. Latterly the business was run by Jonathan McLauchlan and his son Robert, and was sold to Saml. Preston, in the same trade in Bedford, probably when Robert died in 1885. The shop window was used to display finished vehicles.

In 1896 the premises were up for sale and were taken by Charles Gill (1863–1953), one of the town's most remarkable inhabitants. He was born at Princes Risborough and apprenticed to a turner and chair-maker at High Wycombe. He left, however, and came to Little Barford when his father was appointed head gardener to Mr. Alington in 1885. About 1892 or 1893, probably on getting married, he moved to Eynesbury, setting up as a furniture repairer in Jarvis's Yard (behind the terrace 48–60 Berkeley Street) and working part-time for John Beagary, furniture dealer at 7 Market Square. In 1897 he moved to these premises and after a few years started to make houseboats to put on the river for letting to visitors. This was an extraordinary and daring venture considering that he had no experience of boat building. To develop the business he hired, in 1900, part of Eynesbury rectory glebe at the corner where Hen Brook joins the river, and built a footbridge over the brook at the west end of Brook Street. The first houseboat, *Ouse Lily*, was launched in 1901, to be followed by *Sunflower, Iris, Thrush, White Wings* and *Swan. Iris* was built on the hull of an old barge houseboat but all the others he built in his workshop during the winter. In the spring they were taken to pieces and reassembled and launched at 'Houseboat Corner'. In addition to these he built over 50 rowing boats, punts, and canoes, for sale or hire. The houseboats were all moored in the vicinity of 'Houseboat Corner'. On shore he built three 'pavilions' and various sheds and stores all fantastically adorned with turrets and sham gothic features in cork. On summer evenings he arranged riverside concerts by local amateurs by the light of chinese lanterns. For many years a model houseboat was displayed in a glass case on King's Cross station and houseboat holidays on the Ouse became very popular with London people. In *Homeland Handbooks* (1905) is advertised '*Ouse Lily* and *Sunflower*, with pianos, will sleep 8 persons, £5 week July and August, £4 10s. June and September. *Thrush* will sleep 2 persons, £2 5s. week. 120 visitors last year'.*

His difficulties may be imagined when it is realised that every winter his site would be flooded, often to the depth of several feet, and thus all his stock and boats had to be made very secure. The houseboats themselves were nearly all made of second-hand timber (he could afford no other) and needed constant repair to overcome leaks. During all these activities he kept on with his furniture repairing, restoring antiques with unique skill and craftsmanship. Often he would buy at sales badly damaged articles, take them to pieces and make one or two perfect examples out of several, making it impossible to tell that repairs had been done.

Another of his skills was wood carving, and in the 1920s he was teaching a class in this subject. One of his most apt pupils was Mrs. Fydell Rowley of Priory Hill, some of whose work is in St. Neots church, while Eynesbury church has some of Gill's own. He was a prolific worker in oak, and there must be very many examples of his work still in the district.

In 1922 he sold his boat business to Capt. Adcock, a retired sea captain, and moved to the south end of the Old Falcon building in the Market Square, then a separate house, and a few years later to 3 Huntingdon Street, once the home of Joseph Eayre the bellfounder. Part of this he made into a workshop where he still worked at his trade until his death, at the age of 90, in 1953.

No. 10. Now part of Trustee Savings Bank site. This was a small shop, probably occupied in 1850 by Saml. Sly and in 1858 by Wm. Shaw. In 1870, James Gray, watch and clockmaker, came

* See Plate 25

here but moved to the south corner of the east side of the Market Square in 1872. In 1890 it was a barber's shop, kept by John Holden, who had a striped barber's pole as a sign outside.

No. 9. Now part of the site of the Trustee Savings Bank. This small house and shop, before its destruction to build the bank, was (*Hist. Mon. Comm.*, no. 15) one of the oldest houses in the town and almost certainly medieval. It was timber-framed and had a jettied first floor. When it was pulled down, in 1953, a wooden window was found embedded in the south wall. It had narrow lights with gothic heads and fittings for sliding shutters without glass. It was preserved and is reset in the east wall of the timber-framed house on the south side of High Street (no. 42). Much of last century this was occupied as a butcher's shop and premises by the Bartlett family, apparently coming here from the corner of Brook Street and Church Street about 1838. Known to have been butchers here were Wm. Bartlett (1780–1855), John Bartlett (1789–1855), James Bartlett (1831–95), and Chas. Bartlett (1860–1896). The latter died of blood poisoning from a cut finger.

It would seem that in 1854 the family also had shops in Brook Street and Huntingdon Street, and Bernard Bartlett, still occupier of the latter, told the author that he had been told by his grandfather that Bartletts had been butchers in St. Neots for 300 years and 'before the Earls of Sandwich came to Huntingdon'.

Nos. 7, 5. Forscutt, boot and china shop. (*Hist. Mon. Comm.*, no. 14). This appears to be a jettied house, like the one that used to be next door, and has a moulded beam exposed inside. The front has now been cased in. There is a reference to the *Wrestlers*, in Market Street in 1485 (Rentals and Surveys). In the 18th century this was the *Wrestler and Crown* inn. Thos. Burridge was landlord in 1710, Jas. York in 1792, and Geo. Atkinson in 1890, when it had nine grain shops. About 1830 J. H. Day, brewer of the Priory Brewery, to whom it belonged, built the present *Wrestlers* in New Street transferring the licence, and dropping the latter part of the name.

It was now acquired by Jas. Paine, brewer, and added to his adjoining property, the *King's Head*. By 1854 it had become separated again, and was occupied by Wm. Lovell, tailor, who died in 1880. His occupancy no doubt accounts for the 'tailor's oven' still existing, used to heat, or keep hot, pressing irons. Lovell left, or retired, in 1868, and was followed by Alfred Forscutt who started a boot shop here, which has now been running for 100 years. About the end of the century he was succeeded by his son William who added the china shop and a photographic sideline. He was followed by his brother Charles and he by his son Herbert, father of the present proprietor.

King's Head **inn.** The first mention found of this old and important inn refers to 1710 when it was sold by Robt. Fox to Wm. Chapman the innholder, and is described as 'formerly called by the sign of the Wyldman, now or late the King's Head, formerly in the tenure of Robt. Small, then John Hubbard then Robt. Fox'.

In 1733 there is again a reference to its former name *The Wildman* which evidently died hard. Tenants before that date had been Robt. Sewell, John Hulbert, John Gale, and John Flanders. In 1745 Richard Emery had it at a rent of £10 a year. In 1809 it belonged to Fowlers, the Priory brewers and had nine cornshops. Landlords were, 1809 Wm. Reedman, 1830 Ann Garner, 1839 Rich. Burgin, who was also a carpenter and builder, 1850 Thos. Arnold, a former coach driver. In this year it was put up for sale and is described as, 'One of the best inns in the town, with commercial rooms, several parlours, scullery, kitchens, ample cellarage, tap room, club room, numerous bedrooms, stabling for 50 horses with loft above, corn shops, coach houses. Could be converted into a brewery'. Other landlords were: 1854 Thos. Harkness, who came from the *Queen's Head*, 1865-1878 Thomas 'Gentleman' White, formerly chief clerk to Elgoods, millers Market Square. He started a corn-dealer's business here, and retired to 24 Berkeley Street, Eynesbury. In 1878 Thomas Gregson came here from the High Street. He gave up the corn business but carried on his own trade as a tailor. 1892 Chas. Long (1847-92), 1893 Mrs. Long, 1899, A. I. McLaren, 1905 T. W. Conyers, a billiards professional.

No. 3. Now called Staffordshire House. This property appears to have once been part of the *King's Head*. At the back on the first floor is a large long room which may have been the club room referred to as part of the inn in 1850 (see above). In 1858 this property was already separate and occupied by Geo. Simpson (1815-72), who had been established since 1840. He described his trade as 'plumber, painter, writing, graining, and gilding', and probably moved here from New Street. In 1870 Misses Simpson, presumably his daughters, started a shop here for 'Berlin Wool and Fancy Trade'. They retired in 1875, probably selling the business to Mrs. Keeling who started a similar shop at the corner of New Street and Market Square. Meanwhile W. G. Simpson carried on his father's business, letting the front shop as an office of John Dew Fairey, late managing clerk to Geo. Day in Huntingdon Street, who set up here as estate agent. He acted as agent to Mr. Kirkham, owner of the Ouse Navigation. In 1894 this office, or possibly a small building opposite, was used by Saml. Day, solicitor, and was also the County Court office.

The large upstairs room, mentioned above, was used as a billiard room attached to the Literary Institute premises in the Corn Exchange next door, and also by St. Neots Social Club. In 1896 however it was vacated by those organisations and became head-quarters of the Liberal Club, moved from the south-east end of High Street. An opening tea was provided for 150 in the Corn Exchange. The Liberals stayed here until 1910 when they moved again to the south-west corner of the Market Square. When the first Boy Scout troop was formed they used this room as their headquarters. The remaining part of South Street was the west wall of the Pavilion Cinema, formerly the Corn Exchange, facing the High Street (pulled down 1969). Before this was built, in 1863, there had been a private house occupied by Thos. Lewis (1800-81) blacksmith, who had his workshop opposite, on the site of the present Midland Bank.

From Hen Brook to the south east corner of the Market Square the west side of South Street consisted of warehouses and corn shops used for corn storage in connection with the navigation on Hen Brook. A few of these still remain, and most, if not all, were part of the back premises of the *Queen's Head* inn at the corner.

MARKET SQUARE

In the 17th century the south side of the square was called 'Market Street' and in the latter part of last century the eastern end 'Market Place'.

No. 46. now a shop, formerly the *Queen's Head* inn, at the corner of South Street and Market Square. This used to be one of the large and important inns and had an imposing sign with a half length portrait of a queen, hung on an ornamental iron bracket. It owned all the property behind it, down to the brook. The first mention of this inn is found in the churchwardens' accounts for 1772 when Nailorer Squire was landlord. In 1800 it was bought by John Day of the Priory brewery. John King was then landlord, followed by Thos. Boscutt, who was there from 1809 to 1823, and Mary Boscutt in 1830. About 1848 it was rebuilt. Thos. Harkness was landlord and he moved to the *King's Head* in 1850, being replaced by Wm. Franklin (1816-55), followed by his wife until at least 1862. Then came Jas. Emery 1866, John Morris 1869, W. Cross, C. Leng (left 1877), S. R. Bull (late hairdresser, High Street) 1890. From then on there was a quick succession of land-lords and in 1897 the house was sold to Eaton Socon Brewery.

When the licence was given up in 1908 a statement to the Bench stated that there had been seven tenants since 1902. It was selling annually 73 barrels of beer and 90 gallons of spirits.

No. 45. At present a shop (*Hist. Mons. Comm.*, no. 12). This is part of a group of architecturally important buildings that must be Tudor in date. In the course of alterations in 1963 the ceiling of the present ground-floor showroom was taken down, exposing a fine moulded beam supporting flat floor joists of the first floor. It was also evident that the first floor had been jettied out over the passageway leading to the brook.

In 1809 there was a 10-quarter malting here, and in 1820 it was occupied by Chas. Banks, merchant, with no doubt a wharf on the brook. In 1848, however, it was used as a private house by Robt. Edwards. In 1848 Valentine Barford started an ironmongery business here, followed, in the same trade, by Wm. Pentelow in 1876. He had also a shop at Huntingdon and used the yard opposite (now the Eastern Electricity Board offices) to store and display agricultural implements. About 1910 Pentelow sold the St. Neots shop to his manager there, Robt. Browing. Its nearly 100 years of use as an ironmongers ceased soon after the death of Robt. Browing in the 1950s. Old stock found in the shop at this time included breast ploughs and pattens.

No. 42 (*Hist. Mon. Comm.*, no. 12). Now divided into two properties including a small shop: an architecturally important timber-framed Tudor building with four sharp-pointed gables facing the Square, probably the only examples in St. Neots of 'town' houses of that period. The house on the east can be seen to have its wooden frame set on a low wall of 15th- or 16th-century bricks. There is a suggestion that it was once the *Falcon* inn, but at least from the beginning of last century there was a shop on the frontage and a bakehouse in the yard.

The front shop was kept as a grocer's for over 100 years, being recorded, in 1792, 1823 and 1839, as kept by John Stead. John and Mary Stead, probably children of the above, had it in 1848 and 1860, John being a deacon of New St. Baptist Chapel. They were followed about 1870 by Geo. Flanders, who claimed in an advertisement in 1886 that the business was then 100 years old. He retired about 1908, and was followed by Edward Samuel Flinders, who retired between 1920 and 1930, bringing the long-established business to an end.

The bakery in the yard was not so long lasting. In 1809 it was being run by Francis Hare (1766–1827), and after his death by Ann Hare, probably his widow. From 1839 to 1858 it was run by Mary Hare, of unknown relationship to the above. She was followed by Peter Whittet. On his death in 1887 his son Alfred moved to no. 33, on the opposite side of the Square.

No. 40. Shop and dwelling house. It once had a wharf on the brook, which was sold separately to Jas. Paine by Wm. Newman. In 1775 and 1792 there was a Thos. Robinson, ironmonger, here, and in 1809 his widow Mary. In 1820 it is again Thos. Robinson, perhaps their son. From 1830 to 1855 it was occupied by Wm. Newman, ironmonger and cooper, and also surveyor to the Great North Road Turnpike Trust. By 1855 it had become the private residence of Robt. Handford postmaster, and also the Post Office. Handford was also, in 1852, headmaster of the British School in the High Street. The Post Office remained here until 1860, when it was removed to separate premises on the east side of the Square. To Handford the post office was a part-time job. Every day he personally delivered all the letters in St. Neots, Eynesbury and Eaton Socon, before taking up his duties as headmaster of the British School.

From about 1865–1870 a watchmaker's and jeweller's shop was started here by W. J. T. Mole, followed, in 1871, by a draper's and milliner's shop kept by J. Jones, who called it 'London House'. However he went bankrupt in 1874 and was succeeded by Wm. G. Chambers, another watchmaker, who called it 'Vulcan House', and had moved here from the east side of the square. It was almost certainly here that occurred the tragic episode which resulted in the sudden death of Wm. Peck of Shirdley House, Eynesbury at the age of 31 in 1871. He called to sell some scrap silver to Chambers, and to clinch the deal Chambers poured him out what he thought was a glass of beer, but which was really cleaning liquid containing cyanide. W. Chambers retired and died in 1892 and was followed by E. A. Denner, and in the new century by F. J. Thomas, both watchmakers.

The yard had at some stage been let separately from the frontage. In 1874 F. J. Wood set up as a coal merchant here, followed in the same trade, in 1875, by John Brown junr., probably son of the New Street auctioneer. He again sold his business to Geo. Taylor, landlord of the *Half Moon* Hotel (now *Bridge* Hotel) it being run under the name of Taylor & Parker.

No. 38. Private house and office, now used as an accountant's office. This is an old merchant's house, although Miss Sibley told the author that her father had gleaned from the deeds that it was once an inn called *The Admiral's Hat*. In 1775 it was occupied by a Mr. Vickary, and in 1801 was transferred from I. C. Sharp to Wm. Foster senr. who was a merchant, brewer and banker. In the yard was not only a wharf, but a brewery and 22 corn shops, and besides these Foster hired a malting attached to Brook House, Brook Street. His bank premises, where a famous robbery took place in 1829, were a little further west at no. 32. Wm. Foster must have died about 1832 for in that year his trustees sold the business and premises to James Paine (1789–1855) probably a relative of Foster's, who had farmed at Great Paxton and Toseland Manor, and decided, in partnership with his son William, to start up in business, as Paine & Son (see separate account of this firm).

Jas. Paine moved into this house, had an office in the yard, and probably lived here until his death in 1855, after which it was occupied by his son William, until his retirement. Alexander McNish, who married Wm. Paine's third daughter and was a member of the firm, probably lived here from 1877 to 1889 when he moved to Cressener House, Huntingdon Street. It was then let to P. C. Tomson, editor of the *St. Neots Advertiser*, until 1897. In 1898 John Sibley, then chief clerk to Paine & Co., moved here from Eynesbury, his family remaining here until 1951.

No. 36. Now Paine & Co. general office. Part of the property belonging to Foster and later Paine, but let as a shop. In 1775 it was occupied by a Mrs. Hull, and in 1820 by Ebenezer Geard, woollen and linen draper, son of Rev. John Geard of Hitchin. In 1839 Mrs. Salome Geard, perhaps his widow, was here. In 1844 and 1848 E. Geard and Son, and in 1850 Thos. Geard, followed by his widow. A Thos. S. Geard, son of one of the above, and described as an Australian merchant, married Ann, daughter of Jas. Paine, from next door. He borrowed money from his father-in-law, who deducted it from his daughter's legacy. In 1855 Mrs. Geard either died or retired and the shop was let to Edward Stevens, draper and silk mercer, who named it 'Waterloo House'. He may have been related to either John or Joseph Stevens who were wool-staplers at 20, Market Square in 1820. In 1878 he sold the business to Walter Blott, and retired to Wyboston, where he built North House. Blott left and moved to Bedford in 1878.

In 1890 the post office moved here from the south east end of the High Street, W. H. Summers being postmaster. It remained here until the present New Street premises were built and ready in 1913. Mr. Frank Britain then used the premises as a furniture shop until he was called up for the army about 1916.

No. 34. The *Bull* inn. Now up the yard, but once had frontage on the Square. This is an old house and may be the *Bulle* referred to in the Close Rolls in 1471, when the landlords were William and Alice Kynge. It was sometimes referred to as the *Black Bull*. In 1791, when James Smith was landlord, it had attached three common rights and nine acres of meadow in Eaton Socon. In 1809 Thos. Brewster was landlord and had stabling for six horses. In 1823 T. Pope was landlord and in his day it was the headquarters of the Old Club (benefit club). On the annual club day a procession of some 500 people would start from here, with a band, to walk to the church. After a service they returned to the *Bull* to a dinner under a booth covering the whole of the yard.

Other landlords were, 1836, 1848 Anthony Reeves, 1857, 1868 Robt. Wilson, 1890-94 T. Morris, 1894-96 W. Reed, 1897-8 J. F. Stocker.

No. 32. Now Paine & Co., local office. In 1775 this was occupied by Thos. Wells, and in 1809 probably by John Paxton. After Wm. Foster acquired the property he made this part into a bank, and it was here that the famous bank robbery took place on 9 July 1829. Two men entered the bank during the two clerks' 30-45 minute tea break, soon after they left the building. They opened the locked doors with false keys and got away with one £500 Bank of England note, 200 £10 notes, 2,000 Country Bank notes, 2,000 sovereigns, and other monies to a total of £8,000. One of the robbers, Thos. Hollingshed, was afterwards arrested and at Huntingdon Assizes was sentenced to transportation for life. He had acquired considerable property from bank robberies without being detected. He was seen to alight from the Stamford Coach at Eaton Socon and leave by a footpath for St. Neots. The £500 note had been paid into the bank that day by Saml. Sprigg to buy business premises at 23 Market Square, and was recovered as the thieves were unable to change it.

In 1832, when the property was sold to James Paine the bank had been given up and for a time the premises appear to have been added to the *Bull* inn as a frontage on the Square. In 1855 it was occupied by a Mr. Mole. This may have been W. T. Mole, here temporarily before going to no. 30, or W. J. T. Mole, watchmaker, who was here before moving to no. 40. About 1856 it was in the hands of Geo. Osborne, tailor and draper, who remained until 1874. From then on at least until 1877 W. T. & F. Ward, in the same trade, had it, as well as another shop in Bedford.

By 1890 it had become a branch office of W. Cranfield, solicitors, of St. Ives, and later named Cranfield & Wheeler. At the house lived their articled clerk Thos. Spencer, who afterwards qualified, became a partner, and ran the St. Neots office. Sometime before

1909 T. Spencer and his office moved to 18 Market Square. The premises then again became a draper's shop kept by Horace Clarabut, who had moved from 62 High Street, and later went on to Bedford.

No. 30. Present chemist's shop, formerly the *Bear* inn. This is a house dating back at least to the 17th century and a print of the Market Square in 1790 shows it without the present Georgian front, with a pantile roof, and a pictorial sign hung on an ornamental iron bracket. The first mention found of 'the *Beare*' is in a church rate of about 1670. In 1752 the landlord was Thos. Pheasant and the owner Loftus Hatley, probably of Cressener House, Huntingdon Street. In 1775 it was occupied (and possibly owned) by John Musgrave or Musgrove. In 1809 Michael Goodliffe was landlord and it had two grain shops. Other landlords were, 1820-23 Wm. Cooper, 1823-39 John Fountain, who was also a hairdresser and perfumer and who died in 1855. He was possibly followed by John White, who was in turn followed in 1848 by Henry Waller, a former landlord of the *Cock* at Eaton Socon, in 1853 by H. Nottingham and in 1854 by Thos. Street.

In 1855 the inn was converted to a shop of Wm. Tingey Mole (1816-85), chemist and ginger beer manufacturer, not to be confused with W. J. T. Mole the jeweller. He retired and died at Hemel Hempstead. Following Mole in 1879 came a chemist who was to remain here for over 50 years and to become an almost legendary character, James ('Jimmie') Wise.

In the way of all chemists of his time he was half doctor, and prescribed for numerous ailments when asked by people unable to afford a doctor. He was chiefly noted for his caustic wit and forthright remarks, especially to his assistants in the presence of customers, knowing they dare not answer back. Across the Square opposite was the shop of his business rival Mellor and later Dukes, and every customer entering that shop was watched and noted. If the customer was unable to obtain what he needed at the rival shop and came over to see if 'Jimmie' Wise had it he would be greeted with sarcasm or irony. Indeed to avoid unpleasantness customers had to stick to one shop or the other. One famous story illustrating this concerned the Rev. Caine, vicar of Great Paxton, who came into Wise's shop for a quantity of sulphur to smoke out his bees. When told the price he remarked that he had been charged less at the rival shop across the way. 'And if you go to hell you could get it for nothing', retorted Jimmie, to the delight of a shop full of people and to the discomfiture of the vicar. Those who remember him as a rather sour and blasphemous octoge-

narian will be surprised to learn that in 1897, when presiding at
St. Neots Cycle Club annual dinner, he was given a presentation,
subscribed for by the shop assistants and apprentices of the town,
in recognition of his successful efforts to secure early closing on
Tuesdays. He died in 1932 and the business has been carried on
to the present day, first under his assistant E. S. Calcutt, followed
by his son, J. E. Calcutt.

No. 28. Now a showroom for E. D. Fisher & Son, with a private
house at the back and a yard and premises running down to the
brook. This was business premises with a wharf, warehouses, and
a shop at the front. It was for many years occupied by the
Ingersole family, and there were other Ingersoles next door, no
doubt related but not necessarily connected in business. Here in
1775 lived a 'Mr. Ingersole', and in 1792 either John or William
Ingersole (one of these being next door) grocer and corn chandler
lived here. In 1809 and 1820 it was Thos. Ingersole, grocer, corn-
dealer, wine merchant, and linseed cake dealer. He was said to
have suffered £800-£1,200 damage in the great flood of 1823. In
1848 and 1850 there was still an Ingersole here, possibly Joseph,
described as grocer, cheesemonger, and wholesale grocer. It was
stated that there were four generations of Ingersoles here from
1825 to 1851, and the business had, at one time, a turnover of
£8,000 a month.

It is probable, however, that the Ingersole connection ceased in
1848, for a billhead of that date advertises James Crawley (late
Ingersole), grocer, tea dealer, wax and sperm candles, and hop
merchant. From 1850 to about 1863 it was occupied by a wholesale and retail grocer named Schlemoker, and a photograph of
this date shows a double row of windows on the first floor above
the archway and a plate-glass window to the shop. In 1863 it
was occupied by Cowley & Son, wine and spirit merchants and
auctioneers. A contemporary photograph shows the shop front
now bricked in and the appearance of a private house. In 1868
Crowley & Son moved to Bedford, selling their wine and spirit
business to Wm. Atkinson of 45 High Street. Another photograph
of about 1874 shows the name E. Wood (or possibly Elwood),
London House, over the premises.

In 1877 Sharp & Maddison started a mineral water factory in
the yard, and probably at the same time one partner, James
('Jimmy') Sharp, set up as a dentist in the house at the front.
Sharp had been an apprentice to H. Spring, chemist, surgeon
dentist, and mineral water manufacturer, at 23 Market Square.
After setting up on his own, in 1814, Sharp had first practised

for a short time, on the east side of the square, and in 1875 in New Street, before coming here. The partnership with Maddison was soon dissolved, and Sharp ran both enterprises. He was a bluff laconic character, and a friend of the redoubtable 'Jimmie' Wise of next door. Many stories are told of the practical jokes one played on the other. They usually involved the discomfiture of a third innocent party. Typical of these was of the countryman, arriving late at night with violent toothache, and asking 'Jimmie' Wise the way to the dentist. He was shown the door and told to knock and bang on it with all his strength as Sharp 'was almost stone deaf'. Jimmie waited just inside his doorway to hear the explosion that occurred when the door was opened. About 1914 'Jimmy' retired and was followed by his son, Jimmy Sharp junr., a qualified dentist, who, about 1930 removed his house and surgery to 8 Market Square.

No. 26. Another commercial business premises with access to Hen Brook at the back. In 1775 it seems to have been owned by a Mr. Hatley, and in 1820 by John Ingersole (died 1856). He is described as a merchant, and in 1848 as a former partner in the St. Neots Bank. He seems to have retired about 1840 and sold the business to Thos. Smith Darnell, senr., from Hail Weston.

In 1855 it was the post office, and then a private house occupied by a Mrs. Atkinson.

In 1866 Henry Dixon Fisher (1831–93), a native of Lincolnshire, set up here as an ironmonger. He had previously had a shop on the north-west corner of the Square (the site is now Barclays Bank) where he had probably bought the ironmongery business of Thos. Dudley in 1855. In 1866 he came to these premises at the same time buying the stock and business of Walter Lanning of 22 Market Square. He had been a town commissioner from 1873 to 1876, and retired and died a bachelor at Ivy House, Eaton Ford. He was followed by his brother E. D. Fisher who died in 1895, and he in turn by his sons Fred and Sidney, another son managing a similar shop in Biggleswade, under the name E. D. Fisher & Sons.

No. 24. A red-brick house probably of the early 17th century, with extensive back premises that extended westward along the Brook behind other neighbouring properties.

In 1775 they belonged to Mr. Archdeacon, and in 1795 Henrietta Wiles may have lived here. In that year she was fined £5 for letting out posthorses without a licence. Wm. Wiles, brewer and corn merchant, possibly son of the above, occupied the business premises from at least 1790 to 1830. In 1809 he was not living in the house and it may have been occupied by Wm. Alex. Peppercorn, father of Wm. Peppercorn the attorney, who was at that time renting a house from Wm. Wiles. From 1839 to about 1855 the business was run by Stephen Wiles, presumably son of the above, and in that year was advertised to let as 'a large dwelling house, large yard, malting, granary, brewhouse, lately S. Wiles'. There had been a number of members of the Wiles family living in or around St. Neots. Thos. Wiles and Silvester Wiles were farmers there in 1792, and there is a memorial to the former in the Strict Baptist cemetery (he died in 1804 or 1834 aged 75). Before 1796 the *White Horse* inn, Eaton Socon, belonged to the Wiles family. About 1855 the premises were taken by Geo. Bower, ironfounder, and adapted as a factory to manufacture gas-producing plant, and the house turned into offices. The story of this remarkable man and his enterprises in the town are told under a separate heading, but he occupied the premises until about 1885 as the Vulcan Iron Works.

In or about 1887 the house was taken once again as a private residence, by Geo. Taylor, on his retirement from the *Chequers* inn, Eynesbury (see *Half Moon* Hotel, Market Square) and after his death his widow lived there until her death in 1919. Sometime soon after coming there he let the yard to Jordan & Addington, millers. They had offices and restricted premises in New Street, which they moved here on the death of Mrs. Taylor. They remained here until they concentrated all their business at Eaton Socon mill in 1965.

No. 22. House (now garage) (plate 15) with premises that formerly ran down to the Brook. This house was the birthplace of the St. Neots historian Geo. Cornelius Gorham (1787-1857) who wrote *The History and Antiquities of Eynesbury and St. Neots in Huntingdonshire and of St. Neot's in Cornwall*, first published in 1820. He has recorded in a MS., now in the Norris Library, St. Ives, that he found title deeds for this property going back to '1 Edward VI', when it was the *Antelope* inn. At that date it was sold by Rich. Slade, Robt. Hatley, Philip Hatley, executors of the late Wm. Hatley of Southoe, to Robt. Goode and Joan his wife, who still owned it in 1570. This shows one interesting origin of inn signs as the crest of the Hatley family was an antelope. In 1586 it was occupied, probably on lease, by Hugh Newman, and in 1600 granted by Thos. Salter to Robt. Goode and Mary his wife, on their marriage. In 1630 Robt. and Mary Goode, and Thomas their son, conveyed it to Thos. Hallam, Citizen and Salter of London, whose widow Margaret owned it in 1648. In 1671 it was conveyed to Wm. Woodstock and later to his son Edmund. In 1696 it was conveyed to Jas. Taylor and in 1698 sold by him to Henry Gorham, grocer. This started an association of the house and business premises with the Gorham family which was to last for 127 years. John Gorham (1635/6-1725) a mercer, had come to St. Neots from Glapthorne, Northamptonshire. He had five children of which John (1671-1704) and Henry (died 1737) were grocers at St. Neots but appear to have left no heirs. In 1698 Henry bought the old *Antelope* premises, but in 1706 he sold them again to Stephen Bainton of Priory Farm (see Huntingdon Street) who leased them back to him for 11 years. The next owner to appear is another brother Jonathan Gorham (1685-1753), who had married Stephen Bainton's daughter Elizabeth, and may have had the property back from his father-in-law as part of a marriage settlement.

Jonathan and Elizabeth had three children. Jonathan (1714-94) a surgeon and bachelor, living at 11 Market Square; Stephen (1721-89) who married Martha Wye, co-heiress with her sisters Rebecca and Elizabeth, the last of a well-known St. Neots family, and John (born 1727) who emigrated to America in 1774 and was never heard of again.

Jonathan senr. died in 1753 and was buried in the Wye family vault in the Jesus chapel of St. Neots church. His widow Elizabeth, then described as a grocer and tallow chandler, at once gave the business to her two sons Stephen and John. The latter seems to have dropped out at once, and, as described above, emigrated in 1774. Stephen was evidently a man of enterprise and business capacity. He enlarged the scope of the family business, calling himself a merchant, and almost certainly started the Duck Lane brickworks (Grid ref. TL. 190594). Here he produced the white or yellow bricks which became fashionable following the period of red brick building in the 17th and early 18th centuries. Many of the present houses on this side of the Square are built or cased with these bricks. At his death in 1789 he left a fortune of £30,000 to his only surviving son George James (1752-1840) who had entered his father's counting house at the age of fifteen. On his marriage to Mary Greame Folkthorpe of Hesington, York, he was given Ford House, Eaton Socon, where they went to live in 1783 but returned to 22 Market Square the following year. Here their 12 children were born, including George Cornelius (1787-1857) later to become clerk in holy orders, a Fellow of Queen's College, Cambridge and author of the first and chief history of St. Neots and Eynesbury.

Geo. James Gorham, father of the historian, was probably not as competent a business man as his father but it was not unusual in his age that he should wish to employ some of his fortune in banking. This he did in 1807, in partnership with Francis Rix and John Ingersole (of 26 Market Square) forming the St. Neots Bank, probably on premises now 16 Market Square and later the Liberal Club. In 1824 or 1825 the bank failed and was found to be insolvent involving the private fortunes of all the partners. The Gorham family claimed that Francis Rix was incompetent in business and that John Ingersole was the tool of his unprincipled and speculating son John, who was permitted to play with the capital of the bank.

At the sacrifice of all his private estates Geo. Gorham discharged the bank's liabilities and his own debts and retired to Ford House, Eaton Socon, which was his wife's property, living there on her small private income until his death.

The next recorded occupant of the premises was Joseph Carrington, who came here from the north-west corner of the Square between 1836 and 1839. He was a wealthy man and although called an ironmonger probably used the back premises for engineering, (see below). In 1850 he sold the business and property to George Bower, (see separate item) on his first coming to the town, who lived in the house until 1856.

In 1858, while retaining most of the yard, Bower transferred the retail ironmonger's business to Walter Lanning, who had come to St. Neots from Ironbridge, Coalbrookdale, Shropshire. He gave up in 1866 selling the stock and goodwill to H. D. Fisher, who in that year had started business at no. 26 (see above). In 1912 the premises were occupied by Compton & Sons, cycle makers, and it became one of the first garages doing motor repairs in the town.

No. 20. Present 'Pompadour'. Another original merchant's house and premises. In 1762 and 1767 it was occupied by John Baily, merchant, who also had the yard behind no. 18, and probably by Mr. Knightley, merchant, in 1775.

In 1809 Saml. Stevens, woolfactor, had it, and the front room, or parlour, was used as a bank by the bankers, Rix, Gorham & Ingersole, (see above). 'T' recalls that in the early 1820s a Mr. Bunn was manager of the bank. By 1820 the wool business was in the hands of John and Joseph Stevens, possibly nephews of Samuel. A memorial on the New Street Baptist chapel records the death in 1831 of a John Stevens, son of John Stevens late of Willingham, Cambridgeshire.

About this time the house was taken by Dr. Jonathan Adams, who died in 1830. He began as the first of a series of doctors who occupied this house, with one short break, for at least 130 years.

In 1830/31, Dr. J. J. Evans came here, moving to Brook House in 1847. From then until 1848 Mrs. Ann Raynes had a 'Ladies Seminary, girls' day and boarding school' here.

The next occupant was Dr. Wm. Sole, F.R.C.S., who seems to have moved here from elsewhere in the town. He died in 1855 aged 52, and was buried at Caldecot, Cambs., his widow surviving him by 47 years.

He was followed by Dr. Saml. Wright M.R.C.S.E., L.S.A. (Univ. Coll.) F.L.S. (1828-83). He was a worshipper at the 'Old Meeting', High Street and was described as the 'dissenter's doctor'. He was much loved and respected and when he died, at the age of 55, it was said that the town had never seen such a numerously-attended funeral.

He was succeeded by Dr. F. T. Good (1855-94). He had come to the town as an assistant to Dr. Evans at Brook House, and after a few months purchased his practice. At the death of Dr. Wright he bought his practice also, and moved into this house, where he lived until his death at the age of 39. His widow and three small daughters went to live at 61 Huntingdon Street where she out-lived him by 43 years. He was one of the founders of St. Neots Golf Club. It was during his time here that there arose the saying that on this side of the Market Square there was 'a Good doctor, a Sharp dentist, and a Wise chemist'. In 1894 Dr. E. J. Cross came here from Wareham, Hants., liking the town from having frequently acted as a locum here. He came from a Norfolk family living near Cromer and was a fine horseman, riding both to hounds and to reach his country patients in bad weather. About 1920 he retired to Berkeley House, Eynesbury, selling his practice to Dr. Craven Veitch. Dr. Veitch died in 1960, bringing to an end the long sequence of doctors in the house. The house itself has inside some richly-decorated fireplaces and plaster ceilings and cornices.

No. 18. This house, now divided into several flats, forms one side of the archway leading into the business premises known as Elgoods Mill. A large yard runs back to a frontage on Hen Brook at its junction with the river, and at the corner is the circular base of a lime kiln.

In 1702 the premises belonged to Wm. Goodfellow and were let to Eliza. Maddy. In 1762 John Bailey, who lived at no. 20, was the owner and the entrance was through an archway forming part of the *Saracen's Head* inn (no. 16). The yard seems to have been let to a number of tenants; Thos. Throughgood and Thos. Alsop the younger, then Henry Oliver and John Pedley, and in 1762 Joseph Oliver, John Milware and Henry Musgrove. It is recorded that in 1775 'Mr. Bailey had a house, yard, kiln, and counting house' there.

Probably soon after this last date the property was acquired by the Rix family as general merchants, bankers, and local agents for the owners of the Ouse Navigation. These in 1816 were Palmer & Franklyn, John Palmer being a nephew of Francis Rix. The Rix family probably lived at no. 16, then a private house, and between 1809 and 1830 the house at no. 18 was occupied by Dr. Robert Sabine, surgeon. In 1848 Rix & Darnell sold the business and premises to Thos. Elgood & Sons. They already had Eaton Socon Mill and were corn, coal, timber and general merchants, but did not take over the Ouse Navigation agency, which went to Geo. Day of Huntingdon Street. Thos. Elgood (1796–1874) and his wife Mary (1811–81) are buried in the Baptist cemetery, New Street. It is probable that they lived in the house, and may have been followed by their son John, who died in 1892. Some time after this the business was given up and the premises were empty in 1905 when they were taken over by Paine & Co. after their disastrous fire, and they have remained in possession.

Sometime soon after 1905 the house was let to Thos. Spencer, solicitor, as a partner in the firm of Cranfield & Wheeler, afterwards Wheeler & Spencer. He moved from 32 Market Square and lived here for the rest of his life. He was a remarkable character, coming from a large family brought up by a widowed mother in poor circumstances. He was almost entirely self-educated and had become qualified against great odds as an articled clerk in the office of Cranfield & Wheeler at St. Ives. He was at one time a member of St. Neots U.D.C. and later, for many years, their clerk. His only hobby was reading literature, his knowledge of the best authors was encyclopaedic and he had a vast library.

No. 16. House, now part of the Liberal Club. In 1702, and at least until 1762 this was the *Saracen's Head* inn, at the latter date owned by Wm. Bidwell. Part of the inn consisted of an archway giving access to its yard, with a room over the archway. This was also a right of way to a merchant's yard and wharf. In 1763 it was owned by Wm. Ridwell or Bidwell, clerk, but by 1814 Francis Rix had acquired at least part of the property and it was here that was established the bank of Rix, Gorham & Ingersole, which went bankrupt about 1824 (see no. 22 above).

After the sale of the Rix business to the Elgoods in 1848 some of the family may have come to live in the house, but the bank room, at the front, was used as a branch of the London & County Bank under Mr. R. S. Davison, manager, and open on Thursdays only. Later this became the London, County & Westminster Bank and moved, in 1908, to its present site at 37 High Street.

In 1910 it was acquired as a Liberal Club, in place of the former premises in South Street, and opened by Lord Lucas. It was fitted with billiard, card, and reading rooms, and a flat for the caretaker. From 1942 to 1945 it was the A.R.P. headquarters for the St. Neots urban and rural areas.

River Terrace. This terrace of 12 houses was probably built by Thos. Elgood soon after he bought the adjoining premises in 1848; indeed they probably form part of the same site. The first mention found of them was in 1854. The boathouse with a room above, at the end of, and joined to, the terrace, was certainly built by Mr. Elgood, and the whole terrace was owned by S. Elgood in 1892.

At no. 2, in 1873, F. Hall, surgeon-dentist, attended on Wednesday and Thursday, and at no. 5 Miss Dent had a 'Preparatory School for young ladies and gentlemen', but next year went into partnership with Rev. Gunn in his school at Church House, Brook Street.

At a number unknown Miss Jarvis had a 'High Grade School' in 1887 and 1888. At another lived Medbury Joyce, architect (1812 to after 1892). He was born in St. Neots and brought up as a builder but emigrated to America in 1833. He returned however, a few years later, on the death of his brother, to carry on his business as auctioneer. He also practised as an architect and probably designed the Public Rooms (pulled down 1963) and Wade Gery & Brackenbury's office in New Street. About 1863 he left St. Neots to practise as a timber surveyor in London. From 1886 to 1892 he contributed a number of articles to the *St. Neots Advertiser* describing the life, people, and events of the town as he remembered them 50 years or so before, under the pen name 'Townborn'. They are intensely interesting and much of what he wrote has been used in the present narrative.

MARKET SQUARE, WEST SIDE

A watercolour in the Norris Library, St. Ives, dated 1780 depicts St. Neots bridge from downstream, and through one of the arches it can be seen that the river bank behind this side of the Square is piled to form a quay but is free of buildings except for a warehouse on the Public Rooms site, and another perhaps behind the *Old Falcon*; a small artificial inlet runs from the river beside the former.

During the bridge rebuilding in 1962 postholes dug in the river
bed for the temporary bridge (upstream) produced many skulls
of cattle, all split down the centre, together with pottery of the
16th and 17th centuries. As other bones were absent it would
seem likely that slaughter-houses were then situated along this
side of the Square.

The *Old Falcon*. (*Hist. Mon. Comm.*, no. 13). The south end of
the front block probably dates from late in the 15th century,
and late in the 17th century a back wing was added extending
towards the west, and the building was at the same time extended
towards the north, probably incorporating some earlier work. In
modern times the west wing has been heightened, additions have
been made at the back, and the front refaced with brick. This
inn was probably a posting house and, like many other inns in
the town, had a small cottage in the yard. It went into a decline
in the early 19th century and let off its valuable frontage, facing
the market, to tenants, the cottage in the yard becoming a public
house.

The first mention of this inn relates to 1693, and in 1753 Mary
Stacie, spinster of Hackney, sold it to John Bailey (see above). In
1792 Thos. Small was the landlord, and in 1814 Suzanna Small.
There was then attached to the property a 'swath' (a half rood)
in the Common Meadow. In 1809 it had stables and a yard with
nine grain shops assessed at £36 (compared with £40 for the *Cross
Keys*). The first meeting of the St. Neots Commissioners was held
here in 1819.

Wm. Thornton was the landlord in 1823 when it was termed
a posting house and in 1830, under Geo. Briggs, the 'Perseverance'
coaches called each afternoon, from and to Boston at 1.30 and
2.30. Michael Thornton was landlord in 1836, and John W. Brown
in 1862.

Meanwhile the frontage south of the archway had been turned
into two shops or business premises. At the corner, in 1854 came
Henry Ekins (1830-1916), tailor and draper who remained here
until he retired about 1906. Two of his sons, Samuel Thomas,
and Sidney Victor, became auctioneers and founded the present
New Street firm. Henry Ekins was followed by E. Blandford, tailor,
and in 1922 Chas. Gill came to live here.

The other shop was taken in 1848 by Wm. Lee, plumber and
glazier. Either he or his son, with the same name, moved to 44
High Street, sometime soon after 1864.

That part of the inn north of the archway was taken, about 1826,
by a veterinary surgeon, Thos. Levi Wilmer Caudwell (1803-77).

He was a well-known character in his day, well summed up, when he died, in a refreshingly frank obituary in *St. Neots Advertiser.* Part is worth quoting '. . . an ardent disciple of rod and gun. He lacked perhaps the air of refinement which professionals of the present day look upon as an indispensible requisite. Somewhat plain and blunt in his conversation and at times made use of language more forcible than polite. To those who were unacquainted with his peculiarities, his eccentric behaviour frequently engendered a spirit of dislike, but those who knew him best were aware that under the rough exterior there was a genuine element of good feeling, and a kind-hearted but unostentatious generosity'. His son, Wm. Hill Caudwell (1824-57) M.R.C.V.S., was taken into partnership by his father, under the title W. Caudwell & Son. He continued after his father's death but on account of failing health sold the practice in 1885. G.H. remembered that in his time there was a window facing the Square containing large bottles full of coloured liquid, as in a chemist's shop. He was followed by Clement Burston, M.R.C.V.S., who sold his practice to J. P. Burr, the latter moving to Church House, Brook Street, about 1908. It was not until 1938 that the whole house was once more turned into a hotel by Miss Betty Jewson.

No. 8. Present dentist's surgery of G. H. Lees. A former house on this site was, sometime just before 1681, in the possession of John Abbott, shopkeeper. By 1693, it had been divided into several tenancies and was sold by Henry Fox, ironmonger, to Thos. Atwood gentleman. It was then described as a house with shop, warehouse, and lime kiln.

The present house may have been built by the Reynolds family of Little Paxton and the Shrubbery, Church Street (it was owned by a P. Reynolds in 1836), or by a Dr. Geo. Reynolds, who lived somewhere in the town in 1753 and 1800. In 1809 and 1823 it was probably occupied by Octavius Marmaduke Saunders, surgeon. His tombstone is in the churchyard where his age at death is given as 50; other particulars are now illegible. Mrs. Saunders was here in 1836. In 1848 the house was occupied by John Savill, (otherwise spelt Savile and Saville). He was a draper with his shop next door, and he left here about 1850. He probably died in 1883 when an annuity from the Paine family ceased.

In 1855, and until at least 1873, Philip and Cornelius Chapman, widower and bachelor son, lived here. They were remembered as slightly eccentric retired businessmen with money, mainly invested in railway stock. They made frequent visits to the railway station to observe how business was doing! They were followed by Geo.

Beagarie (died 1898), who had the grocer's shop next door. He had two sons, Frederic James, who followed him in the business, and John who went into furniture and upholstery. There was a bitter feud between the brothers, who even as adults never spoke to one another. This was said, perhaps romantically, to have been because both wanted to marry the same girl. Frederic probably lived here, after his father died, until his own death in 1917.

No. 6. Corner shop at the foot of the bridge. In 1792 a shop on this site was kept by Joseph Saville, draper (died 1836) who no doubt lived over the shop. He was followed by his only son John who went to live next door at no. 8. He does not seem to have prospered and the business closed in 1851, the stock being sold and the premises pulled down. There seems to be no record of what happened until 1865 when it was occupied by Geo. Beagary, (see no. 8 above), described as grocer, Italian warehouseman, and wine and spirit merchant. Under his management it became the most high-class grocer in the town. He was followed by his son Frederic, who sold the business to F. Cobb about 1906. In 1895 the shop was receiving consignments of sugar here by barge.

At the back of the shop was a small cottage, occupied, in 1848, by Miss Francis Ladds, dressmaker.

The St. Neots Public Rooms (plates 8, 9). Before the rooms were built this was a commercial site with a wharf on the river. When they were pulled down, in 1963, the author found that part of the floor of the cellar was of well-worn cobbles and the flat sides of cut limestone blocks, some moulded, probably from the Priory. Crossing the building from north to south at 42 feet from the east end and under the cellar floor was an 18-inch red-brick wall foundation, probably of about 1700.

In 1819 the Town Commissioners pulled down a shop and house here, belonging to Richard Slade, to improve the approach to the bridge, and about 1820 Joseph Northern had a stonemason's yard and wharf here.

The Public Rooms were built in, or just before, 1845 as a private investment by Wm. Medland of New Street. They were intended to replace the old Assembly Rooms at the corner of High Street and Huntingdon Street, (the present Co-operative Society shop) inconveniently situated on the second floor.

They were first called the 'New Rooms' or 'New Public Rooms' and later the 'Public Rooms'. The building consisted of a large and lofty hall with two small rooms at the west end. At the east end was a wide gallery approached by steps from the hall, and a further room to the east of this. Under the whole length was a cellar, let, in later times at least, to the next-door grocers. The original heating was by two large open fireplaces in the south wall. The whole long rectangular building was built of local yellow brick with a slate roof.

Almost immediately it was finished it was used as a Corn Exchange on Market Day, and as the County Court, and the Town Commissioners met here, abandoning the room they had built in New Street. Most public functions, balls, shows, and sales were held here until 1863, when the Corn Exchange was built, and thereafter business was shared to the detriment of this hall.

About 1910, when roller-skating became all the rage, Ireland Bros. opened a roller-skating rink here, and for a time it was very popular. In 1912, or just before, it was opened as an 'Electric Cinema'. A gas engine was installed in the cellar to run a dynamo which provided an arc lamp to project the then silent films. The film was of course turned by hand, and the operator himself added some sound effects by striking a metal sheet (thunder), flashing a light (lightning), and firing toy pistol caps (shooting). The ownership of the property had passed from Wm. Medland, probably at his death in 1872, to Geo. Beagary, of the next-door grocer's shop. He had it until his death in 1898. About 1915 it came into the possession of Mr. James (see *Bridge* Hotel), who had bought the Corn Exchange for a cinema. He put in a new sprung maple ballroom floor following a fire in the cellar in 1930.

About 1940 it became known that the property was for sale and likely to be purchased to become a boot-repairing factory. Since the Corn Exchange was no longer available this was now the only available hall in the town for large public meetings, dances, or theatricals. The author felt strongly that in those dreary days of wartime the young people of the district, and the many soldiers stationed in the area, should not lose this last remaining place of entertainment. Following the receipt of good advice and encouragement from Mr. L. Abraham, solicitor, a small private company was formed to buy the property. With no promise of any dividend, money was quickly raised from a number of public-minded citizens and the property bought.

At once an Entertainment Committee was formed, of which Miss Dorothy Wrycroft was the leading spirit, to run dances and put on concerts and variety shows by all the local talent available. Any profits were used to decorate and improve the Rooms. Outside lettings provided a small dividend for the shareholders. Entertainments and dances were held throughout the War and for a time the hall had a daytime use as a much-needed lunch restaurant.

By 1959 its use declined as large halls became available at Longsands School and at St. Neots Paper Mill, and the property was sold to St. Neots U.D.C. to be demolished in 1963 to make way for a temporary bridge during rebuilding of St. Neots bridge.

Public access to the river. A public pedestrian access of ancient origin existed between the Public Rooms site and the bridge, with steps leading to the river. Although used for landing from boats its chief use must have been for dipping water from the river before a public supply was available.

St. Neots Bridge. The site of this crossing of the Ouse and its significance has already been discussed in a previous chapter. It is quite certain that an important road from East Anglia to the Midlands crossed the river at this spot, and that the St. Neots monks built a bridge and causeway of which the earliest existing mention is in 1180. This was undoubtedly a wooden bridge probably resting on stone piers.

In 1906 the author's father, taking advantage of the river being emptied, walked across under the bridge and saw, and sketched, the foundations of five piers of an earlier bridge under the arches. They were of Barnack stone with a rubble core, approximately six feet wide, and with cut-waters on the downstream side. Remains of three could be seen under the centre arch with a passage of 25 feet between them. These were no doubt the piers of the medieval bridge which would support balks of timber on which would be laid the decking of the wooden bridge roadway. That whatever parapet there was at the sides was not very adequate, can be surmised from the record of the death, in 1180, of William de Ferrers, Earl of Derby and Lord of the Manor of Eynesbury. Being a sufferer from gout he was being driven over the bridge in some sort of carriage when the horse got out of control and he was thrown over the edge of the bridge.

The necessarily recurring repairs to wooden bridges are recorded for the years 1293, 1388, and 1588. In 1542 there was an enquiry as to who should pay for repairs now that the Priory had been dissolved and the inhabitants of the town disclaimed all responsibility. In 1606 there seems to have been a major repair with timber specially felled in Bedfordshire. In spite of this last expense, in 1616 and 1617 between £1,000 and £2,000 was spent and this may well have been the time that the stone bridge was built. It is perhaps significant that it was at about this time that the navigation by locks reached up to St. Neots from the sea, and the old bridge may have been an obstruction to navigation.

During the Civil War, Parliament, in 1645, made the Ouse a
defence line against the King's army. For this purpose the bridges
at Huntingdon, St. Ives and St. Neots had an arch removed and
replaced by a drawbridge. The date 1647, out on the downstream
side of one of the causeway arches, may have recorded its replacement. The stone was unfortunately lost in the recent rebuilding.
In 1885 the bridge was widened by corbelling out on cantilevers.
Although this was a joint venture of Huntingdonshire and Bedfordshire, the east half was done in stone and the west in brick!

About 1960 the stone bridge was declared to be unsafe, and
after several years of restricted traffic was demolished in 1963,
and the present replacement built.

Gorham and other writers have suggested that the stone bridge
was built with stone taken from the Priory. However, on its destruction it was found that almost all the stone was new, only a
negligible amount being re-used.

Bridge **Hotel site.** The south side of this site and part of the back,
a property of the Earl of Sandwich, and often described as at the
'bridge foot', was occupied by a shop. In 1809 Wm. Andrews had
a house and shop here, but by 1819 it had been taken by John
Brown, butcher, who lived here and bought his premises in 1848
for £400. He died in 1885 and was followed, some time before his
death, by his son James (Jim) who died in 1899. Under his
management it came to be regarded as the leading butcher's shop
in the town. A.C. recalls that on Saturday mornings all the prominent farmers from round the district would gather here to buy
their Sunday joint and hold what became known as the 'Farmers'
Parliament'. At Christmas 'Jim' Brown would hire the Public Rooms
to display, for sale, choice joints and birds from prize-winners in
the Christmas auction sales. He employed three or four men driving
butchers' carts to sell meat in the surrounding rural area. He was
also a farmer and became a wealthy man, living at Church House,
Eynesbury. After his death he was followed by his son Harry
who in a few years moved to 21 Market Square, selling the bridge
premises to the owner of the hotel next door.

The *Half Moon* **inn.** (*Bridge* **Hotel**). (*Hist. Mon. Comm.*, no. 3).
This was the original name of the present *Bridge* Hotel which
dates back at least to the 16th century, but has been considerably
altered. On the outside of the south wall, site of the old butcher's
shop, is reset a late 17th-century plaster panel with an ornamental
pattern, and inside is exposed some late Elizabethan plaster with
painted decoration.

An early reference to this inn is in the Huntingdon Assize Rolls of 1668 when Obedia Gee was landlord. At this time it probably comprised the whole of the block, as the present hotel does, later going into decline and selling off part of the frontage as a shop. It is remembered late last century as a small inn with a three-quarter-size billiard table, some boats to let, and two or three bedrooms where visiting anglers stayed. The success of Charles Gill's houseboats in popularising the town as a holiday resort no doubt prompted the owners, Day & Son, about 1912, to rebuild it as a riverside hotel, and, perhaps rather unfortunately, change its ancient name.

Landlords were: 1809 Thos. Handley, 1823 Jos. Foskett, who by 1830 had moved to the *Bull's Head*, 1836 (about) to 1850 Mrs. Harriet Palmer. At this time it was the terminus for a fort-nightly carrier from Northampton, bringing goods from the Midlands. In 1850-72 Christopher Cox, master waterman, traded here as Cox & Son, watermen, and had barges for hire and ran weekly 'fly boats' to Bedford, Huntingdon, Wisbech, Lynn, etc. He had a wharf on the opposite side of the river. A Thos. Cox, waterman, of Eaton Socon, who also used this wharf, was probably his son. He died at the *Wheatsheaf* inn, Tempsford, aged 63 in 1885. The landlord in 1873-80 was Geo. Taylor. His career is a Victorian success story. He arrived in St. Neots in 1870 with no money and carrying all his belongings on his back. He was given work at Bower's Vulcan Ironworks and persuaded the landlord of the *Fox & Hounds* to trust him for a week's lodging. Within three years he had married his landlord's daughter and taken the *Half Moon*. Here he increased its business and developed the boating and fishing facilities. In 1875 he bought the mineral water business of Herbert & Emery at Eaton Socon, and in 1877 he bought, from John Brown junr., a coal business at 40 Market Square and transferred it to the Malting Yard, Eynesbury. In 1880 he left, after buying the *Chequers* inn, Eynesbury for £700, and moving there. In 1887 he retired to 24 Market Square.

Other landlords were: in 1887 Wm. Hide, who was also manager of Day & Sons Brewery, who owned the house; in 1889 'Jolly' Nash; in 1905, 1908 F. H. Beeson; in 1909, 1911 G. F. Stone; in 1913, 1914 G. A. James, owner of the Corn Exchange and Public Rooms and first landlord of the newly-named *Bridge* Hotel.

Public Passage to the River. This ancient right of way, called in 1757 the 'Watering Place', and in 1899 the 'Priory Wash Bank', was for long in dispute between the owners or tenants of the adjoin-ing inn and the public. In 1899 it was claimed by the owners, who asked the Urban District Council to remove a public convenience they had built there. On taking legal advice they agreed that Day & Son, owners of the inn, owned the soil subject to a public right of way over it, and removed the convenience. Again in the 1920s tenants of the hotel attempted to bar the public and the U.D.C. were again persuaded to establish the public rights, one hopes for good.

NORTH SIDE OF MARKET SQUARE

This side of the square has continued the medieval tradition of being the shopping side. This was perhaps because the medieval shop usually had its craftsmen working in the shop, or just behind it, producing the goods to be sold. With little or no artificial light or heat it was necessary to get as much sun as possible into the building. The original shops were built right up against the Priory wall, some possibly lean-tos against the wall. Excavations under and just behind the present shops have often disturbed burials of both men and women, apparently outside the Priory wall. It seems likely that when the first parish church was built, about 1214, and the civil population no longer used the Priory church and its graveyard, the Priory wall was set further back. This would have given greater space to the market into which part of the old churchyard was thrown, and shops built over it.

In 1505 this was called Shopperowes, and all the occupiers paid rent to the Priory. In 1757 it was called Shop Row or Market Street, and in 1776 Market Row.

Corner premises at present Barclays Bank. From the sale catalogue of the Earl of Sandwich's property, auctioned in 1848, it is clear that there were three dwelling-houses on this site. Of the two nearest the corner, one had a shop occupied by a Mr. Slade, confectioner, who afterwards became landlord of the *Star* inn, High Street. In the other lived Mr. Watchorn, clerk or manager to Day & Son at the Priory Brewery. Later came Wm. Hide in a similar post, before going to the *Half Moon* opposite.

The third house was occupied, in 1770, by Thos. Gurry, ironmonger, who was still in business in 1809. St. Neots churchwardens' records show that he was appointed headborough in 1777 and constable in 1778. He seems to have been followed, in 1810, by John Carrington, ironmonger, (1789-1852) who came from Biggleswade at the age of 21. He was appointed a Town Commissioner in 1829, and remained one until his death. He never married and retired in 1850 to the riverside house in Priory Lane.

He was buried at Biggleswade and was reputed to have left
£60,000.

After J. Carrington left these premises they were taken by Thos.
Dudley, ironmonger, who married Emma Wiles, daughter of Jabez
Thorns of the *White Horse* inn, Eaton Socon, probably between
1836 and 1839. He sold his business to Henry Dixon Fisher,
ironmonger, in 1855, who remained here until he moved to the
south side of the Square in 1866 (see no. 26).

Next door, to the east of the above properties, was the home and
business premises of the Emery family for well over 100 years.
A Wm. Emery was living here in 1775 and he was probably the
father of Richard Emery (1742-1801) who started a bookseller's
business here, and may also have been a hairdresser. He was succeeded, after his death, by his son William who published Gorham's
History of Eynesbury and St. Neots in 1820. He also became
manager of a branch of the Huntingdon bank of Rust & Veasey,
which was established on part of his premises. By 1848 the business was known as Emery & Son, so William had probably by
then taken his son Frederick into partnership. In 1854 Frederick
Emery (1812-75) (his father had died or retired) is described as
a printer and stationer, and manager of the Veasey, Desborough, &
Vessey branch bank. The Austin lithograph (see plate 4) of St.
Neots Market Square dated 1853 shows here a two-storey house
with a row of four windows to each storey. On the ground floor
are two shop windows divided by a door. The one to the west has
a sign 'Emery' and the other 'Bank'.

In 1870 Frederick took his son William into partnership, and in
1872 the bookselling part of the business was sold to R. R. Keeling
and moved to the corner of New Street. The bank now probably
took over the whole of the premises, and Wm. Emery remained as
manager until his retirement in 1898. He then left the family
home and bought Eynesbury House, where he lived until his death
in 1915.

About this time this local bank had been amalgamated with
Barclays Bank, and these premises, together with all those to the
west up.to the corner, were acquired and pulled down and the
present bank, with manager's house, built. The date 1901 is on
the brickwork at the front. The new manager was Saml. Armstrong
who remained for over 20 years.

Many burials from the Priory graveyard were found during the
rebuilding.

No. 7. At present a cafe. In 1775 probably occupied by John
Smith, and in 1830 probably by Miss Eliza. Smith. In 1848 this

was a house and shop kept by Mrs. Bax, draper, who had put in
the first plate-glass window in the town. In 1853 it was occupied
by Wm. Ennals, (1829–54), chemist, who is buried in the Old
Meeting graveyard High Street. After his death it was taken by
Wm. Dring, chemist, who retired in 1874 and died in 1905. His
son W. E. Dring qualified as a surgeon.

He was followed by J. B. Parnell, chemist, who also extracted
teeth. He named the shop 'Medical Hall', a name still found over
chemists' shops in Wales and Ireland. After a few years he sold the
business to Isaac Matthews, chemist, who, about 1880, moved
his business to 21 Market Square. In 1887 the shop was taken by
John Franks, furniture dealer from Wyboston. This remarkable
man is said to have started business as a pedlar, carrying a basket
of goods for sale round the villages on foot. In 1884 he was at
Wyboston advertising as a furniture dealer and having tents to
hire out. From this shop he developed a very successful business
and was able, in 1890, to buy, pull down and rebuild a large
area of old property at the east end of the High Street, no. 62
etc. He died a wealthy man.

He was followed here, in 1893, by John Beagarie, antique furniture dealer and bookseller, who added these premises to those he
already owned next door. He was the son of Geo. Beagarie of the
grocer's shop at the foot of the bridge (see above). Part of his
business and hobby was the collection of books and pictures relating to the local history of St. Neots, and when he retired to live
at Hitchin he sold his library of local books to Col. L. Tebbutt
of Cambridge, who later presented it to Huntingdonshire County
Library. The firm became Beagarie & Young about 1910.

No. 9. Present Arcade, west side. In the course of building the
Arcade, in 1954, remains of the Priory church walls and some
burials were found. In 1775 a house and shop here was occupied
by a Mr. Joice, and in 1809 by Thos. Ward, probably a saddler.
In 1820 a Mr. Ward, saddler was here, and a Geo. Ward, saddler,
from at least 1823 to 1853. From about 1860 there was Wm.
Whitehead, saddler (1836–91). The business was then sold to Walter
Elliot but the premises were bought and occupied by John Beagarie,
and added to those next door.

The history of the premises next to the above is difficult to
disentangle, and it seems probable that in the 18th century it
may have been two properties. In 1775 a Wm. Summers was
here, and for some time, and certainly in 1794, Jonathan Gorham,
surgeon (1714–94) a bachelor and great uncle of Rev. G. C. Gorham,
the St. Neots historian.

By 1792 the property, or part of it, seems to have been occupied by the Fairey family. In 1792 there was Samuel Fairey the elder, weaver, who was a trustee of the Particular Baptist Chapel, and his son Samuel the younger (1872-1822), also a trustee of the chapel and who appears to have died before his father. They are described as drapers, but in addition to the shop they had a rope-walk behind and were sack and twine factors. Saml. Fairey the younger may also have had the fellmonger's business at 43 Church Street. His wife Ann (1787-1851), who is also buried in the Particular Baptist cemetery, may have been the Ann Fairey who owned the fellmonger's business in 1830 and 1839, but perhaps it is more likely that this was another branch of the family.

Another Samuel, probably son of Samuel the younger and Ann, and described as a linen weaver, was here in 1830, and in 1854 Chas. Fairey draper and milliner. After his death in 1863 his widow carried on the business until 1873 when with all her family she emigrated to St. John's, New Brunswick, where she died in 1892.

John Beagarie, who bought the premises, later added to them those to the west. In 1897 however he sold this property to Tom Armstrong, later a partner in Smith & Armstrong of Huntingdon, who opened it as a draper's under the name of 'Bon Marche'. He moved from here to 37 Market Square early this century and was followed by Marie & Francis, milliners.

The *Cross Keys* Hotel. (*Hist. Mon. Comm.*, no. 4). This old inn, probably dating from the early 17th century, is partly of brick and partly plastered timber framing on a half E-shaped plan with wings extending towards the north. In the 18th century the front was faced in brick. It has for long been one of the principal inns of the town. There seems little doubt too that it was here that the ill-fated Earl of Holland was staying on the night of 9 July 1648, and was captured by the Parliamentary forces who, in the early hours of the following morning, broke through the Royalist defences on the bridge to fight and win the 'Battle of St. Neots' on the Market Square.

Before the coming of the railways this was a coaching inn, and in 1830 there was calling there:

The Royal Mail, London to Glasgow at midnight, return at 2.30 a.m.
Post Coaches, Oxford to Cambridge at 5 p.m. Monday, Wednesday and Friday.
> Return at 9 a.m. Tuesday, Thurday, and Saturday.
> To London every day at 11 a.m.
> To Oundle at 2.30 p.m. Tuesday, Thursday, Saturday.
> To Stamford at 2.30 p.m. every day.

'T' describes a typical Christmas season scene about 1827, when 'the Old Boston Coach changed horses at the *Cross Keys*. Carrying a breakdown load of three tons of Christmas fare; turkeys, geese, and game; piled to a great height and suspended from temporary rails so that no portion of the coach was visible except the wheels. Six horses brought it to the *Keys* with a like number of postillions, and it could not mount the bridge until Arnold the landlord had received the assistance of the porters—the Luffs and Wm. Thorley' (presumably to push).

In 1792 the inn was kept by Joseph Howitt, who was also the local postmaster. In 1809 the landlord was Thos. Norrington, who also farmed 56 acres and had the Market House in Priory Lane. In 1820 it was kept by Mrs. Ann Arnold, followed by Mr. Arnold, perhaps her son. In 1848 and 1850 there was Michael Thornton, also a farmer. In his time it was put up for sale by the Earl of Sandwich, with a reserve of £2,000, and withdrawn at £1,850. Thornton was followed by Daniel Taylor (1808–55), and at his death by John and Suzanna Taylor. He died about 1874 and she in 1879. They were succeeded, in 1876, by Edward or Edmund Cranstone (1828/9-1882/3) and after his death by his widow Elizabeth. She, after a time, retired and was followed by her daughter, Miss E. H. Cranstone, who remained here well into this century. In 1896 she bought the property for £4,000 from Lord Sandwich.

After the opening of the railway station the *Cross Keys* maintained a horse omnibus which met every train. At the end of the century they had both a one-horse and a two-horse 'bus to meet trains, carrying passengers and their luggage as well as parcels to the stations and returning with arriving passengers and parcels for delivery all over the town. They also kept a 'fly' for persons wanting transport to the surrounding district, and carriages to hire for weddings and funerals. Commercial travellers staying at the hotel could hire a man with a truck to take round the boxes and cases containing their samples.

The back part of the *Cross Keys* property, extending to Back Lane, undoubtedly covers the site of the east end of the Priory church, and burials have been found here when the ground has been disturbed.

No. 15. Now a confectioner's shop. (*Hist. Mon. Comm.*, no. 5). Almost completely rebuilt in 1960. There still remains, however, a stone-walled cellar, in the west wall of which is reset a length of 15th-century stone panelling, or arcading, with cinquefoil heads and sunk spandrels. Unfortunately the cellar was filled with rubble at the time of the recent rebuilding.

In 1757 this was the *White Lion* inn, not to be confused with another *White Lion* in Huntingdon Street. In 1775 it belonged to a Mr. Rutter, and in 1792 the landlord was Thos. Atkinson, victualler, and in 1809 Thos. Arnold, who may have moved to the *Cross Keys* next door. Sometime soon after this date it must have ceased to be an inn, and by 1820 it was in the hands of Thos. Lovell, currier and bootmaker. He may have had a son, also Thos., as there was one of that name, a currier and tanner in New Street in 1854.

Sometime before 1848 the premises had been turned into a shop and were occupied by Samuel Newman, grocer, tea dealer, and tallow chandler (1797–1865). The Newmans were an old St. Neots shopkeeping family dating back at least to the 17th century, when they issued tokens inscribed 'Thomas Newman. In St. Neots. His Halfpenny. 1667'. In 1675, at Huntingdon Quarter Sessions, Thos. Newman charged his step-father Wm. Smith with theft. He was alleged to have taken, 'woollen cloth, broad and narrow, and stuffs, Holland, both plain and stuffed, ribbons, stockings, gloves, Gallones, ferritt ribbons, lockeraine and cambrick; which he sold to Thos. Middwinter of Longlaine, London, broker'.

Samuel Newman was followed by his son Charles, who was here until about 1912. The shop was noted for its excellent cheese and home-cured bacon. Charles Newman also had premises in Luke Street, Eynesbury, consisting of a large barn where rods (osiers) were peeled and stored to supply the basket-making trade.

Present Boots Ltd., chemists, formerly two shops nos. 17 and 19, with a common lean-to tiled roof coming down to below the first-floor window level and covering the doorways and shop bay windows. During the building of the present chemist's shop both male and female burials were found, no doubt from the town cemetery before there was a parish church. Also found were coins of Alexander III of Scotland (1269–85), Edward III, Richard II, and a French jetton.

No. 17. Here for a number of years, up to 1783, lived Wm. Le Tans'ur (1699/1700–1783), a minor composer, poet, and music teacher. He was born at Dunchurch, Warwick., and in 1730 married Eliza. Bulter of Ewell, Surrey (she died, aged 58, at Ware in 1767). He seems to have lived an itinerant life, his published works being dated from Barnes, Surrey 1737, Stamford 1756 and 1759, Boston 1761, Cambridge 1776, and he is also known to have lived at Leicester, Ware, Witham and Market Harborough. He is stated to have spent the last 40 years of his life chiefly at St. Neots, as a stationer, bookseller, bookbinder and teacher of music. In a poem entitled 'The Booksellers Shop' he describes some of the things he sold,

> Books and Paper, Ink of every Sort,
> Prints and Sea Charts, guides from Port to Port,
> Most curious Toys, Corn-Tables and of Tide,
> With Music Books and Instruments beside,
> Turlington's Balsam, Scotch and Female pills.
> Norton's rare Drops, Eliziers for all Ills,
> Fine Telescopes . . .

He seems to have pronounced his name to rhyme with 'answer', and spelt it variously as Tanser, Tansur, Tans'ur, and latterly he signed himself as 'William Le Tans'ur Senior Musico Theorico'. This title he explains, in his *New Musical Grammar and Dictionary* (1746 and 1756) refers to 'a person who studies the Science of Music in general and private, writes Treatises and Comments thereon and endevours to explain all Critical and obscure Passages therein, both Ancient and Modern, as well as to give instruction by Practice etc.'

His published works include *South Anatomised*, 1724, *A Compleat Melody*, 1724, *Melody of the Heart*, 1730, *The New Royal Melody Compleat, Sacred Mirth*, 1739, (which contains a portrait of the author) *Heaven and Earth*, 1740, *Poetical Meditations*, 1740, *The Excellence of Divine Music, The Psalm Singers Jewel*, 1760, *The Elements of Music*, 1770, 1772, *Melodia Sacra*, 1771, 1772, *The Life of Holy David a Poem*, 1772, *The Christian Warrior*, and *The Beauties of Poetry*, 1776.

He had a son, probably also William, who was at one time a chorister at Trinity College, Cambridge. He joined his father as a music teacher, and is said to have been still living in 1811. A daughter, Christiana, contributed verses to the *British Magazine* of April 1760, on the subject of a prolific garden pea that provided green peas for Christmas Day 1758.

He was buried in St. Neots churchyard, and a flat stone, now largely illegible, can be seen on entering the east gate, just inside on the right, south-east of the chancel. It is inscribed 'Will. Le Tansur Sen. Musico Theorico. Died Oct. 7. 1783 aged 85. Born Dunchurch Warwickshire'.

In 1848 these premises were occupied by John Clarke, watchmaker, and in 1850 by Peter Chandler, (1829–97), bootmaker, who may have been a son of Peter Chandler of Brook Street (see no. 18). He retired and sold his business to Amies & Tyler, bootmakers, who were here in 1870. They moved to the east end of the Square about 1880, and were followed by Chas. 'Jockey'

William Tans'ur

Wright, who already had a shop next door, and the two shops were amalgamated.

No. 19. In 1820 and 1830 this shop was occupied by John Barker, fruiterer and toy dealer, who in 1850 was postmaster. His son, Wm. Barker, (1816–90) was for 17 years an assistant to Wm. Islip, draper, of 39 Market Square. In 1850 he emigrated to Australia, living at, and possibly founding, Mount Barker, where he died, one of its most respected citizens. About 1830 John Dunkley, cabinet-maker, came here and built a workshop in the yard. He emigrated to the Cape of Good Hope in 1850.

In 1850 the shop was taken by Chas. 'Jockey' Wright, hair-dresser, who had been an apprentice to J. Elgar at 30 High Street. Here he not only did hairdressing but started a Fancy Shop. About 1880 he took the next door shop and added it to this one. He died about 1903 and was followed in the business by his son and two daughters, all unmarried and slightly eccentric. The son inheri-ted the nickname 'Jockey', although he often protested that he had never ridden a horse in his life. The shop stocked a great variety of goods, including fishing tackle, fireworks, toys, and Valentines; everything, it used to be said, except white elephants. About 1930 when paying a local builder for some repairs and decoration to the shop he settled the bill in gold sovereigns, at par, much to the delight of the builder, as at that time they were worth about 35s. each.

No. 21. Present butcher's shop. In 1809 this was a doctor's house occupied by Dr. Ward, who in 1827 sold his practice to Dr. Joseph Rix and moved to Huntingdon*. Joseph Rix (1803-78) was born at Hayward Hall, Diss, Norfolk, and educated at Christ's Hospital. He became L.S.A., in 1825, and M.R.C.S., in 1827, F.R.C.S., in 1844, and M.D., in 1860. In 1874 he retired, selling his practice to Dr. Turner who went to live in Priory Lane. The author has found no evidence of any relationship with the merchant family of Rix on the south side of the Square. There is a memorial window to him in St. Neots church.

It is, however, as a local historian that he will be remembered. He published supplementary notes to Gorham's *History of Eynes-bury and St. Neots*, and collected many printed and MS. items relating to the town. His interleaved copy of Gorham's work was used to paste in, and preserve, these additions. He was elected a Fellow of the Society of Antiquaries of London, and was their local secretary for Huntingdonshire in 1869. He was a frequent contributor to *Notes and Queries*. After the death of Dr. Rix the premises were turned into a chemist's shop by Isaac Matthews, who moved here from 7 Market Square. In 1903 he sold the pro-perty to John Beagarie for £680, who used the first floor as a furniture store and let the ground floor and shop to the butcher Harry Brown (from the bridge shop) for a few years. The shop then went to Jas. Smith, butcher, as a branch of his George Street,

* See plate 19

Huntingdon, business was there in 1909. In 1911 it was taken by Wm. Eayres, butcher.

No. 23. Present office of Ekins, Witherow & Handley auctioneers and land agents. This is a strikingly tall but narrow building with two upper floors and an attic. It was already in this form in 1829. About 1820 it seems to have been a small shop, kept by a brother and sister named Robins, and in 1823 by Geo. Robinson grocer. About 1829 the property was bought by Samuel Sprigg (1808–59) and converted into a chemist's shop. Cash to pay for the property was paid by Sprigg into Fosters Bank (see 38 Market Square) on 9 July 1829, the day that the bank was robbed. However, the greater part consisted of a £500 note which the thieves did not dare to change, and was recovered.

He was followed by his son Harry Sprigg, (1835-73) who besides being a chemist advertised himself as a surgeon dentist, and as such attended, on specified days, at Ramsey, Biggleswade, Potton, Sandy, Baldock, and Kimbolton. He also called himself a Photographic Chemist and was a keen amateur photographer, one of the first in the town. He had besides a mineral water business. It was stated, in 1896, that one of his former assistants, G. S. Boutall, then owned 14 chemists' shops in London.

Another of his apprentices was James Sharp senr., who learnt both dentistry and the mineral water business and later set up for himself at 28 Market Square. In 1873 Sprigg sold his chemist business to J. G. Mellor and went to live in New Street, still practising his dentistry. He died the same year at the age of 38. His eldest son, Frank Samuel, died, aged 27, at Hay, New South Wales, in 1892.

Mellor only remained here until 1879 when he moved to 39 Market Square. The shop was then taken by Edward Soloman, draper, a former assistant of Thos. Goodgames at 37 Market Square, who stayed less than a year. The next occupier was Mrs. Heptzibah Bax, widow of Rev. R. Bax of the New Street Baptist Chapel, who died in 1878. She kept a 'Berlin Wool and Fancy Repository' and was there until 1899, followed by Miss Gambrell in the same trade.

Nos. 25 and 27. Present Cadge, clothier. This site had formerly two shops (of which one was *Hist. Mon. Comm.*, no. 6). They were probably combined into a single shop about 1879. During rebuilding in 1958 a group of four wine bottles (dated 1660-1710) were found 18 inches below the Victorian ground floor. They were upside down, unbroken, with their corks intact and still containing liquid which was very foul smelling. One was given to the Rothschild Wine Museum in France.

No. 25. In 1820 there was a chemist's shop here kept by a Mr. Smith, but by 1839 it was occupied by Franklin & Son. They were described as 'Straw and Tuscan Manufacturers'. In 1850 it was Sophia Franklin 'Straw Bonnet Manufacturer', and in 1854 Jos. Franklin 'Farmer and Strawplait Dealer'. He was a small farmer and his wife had a dressmaking and millinery business. In 1874 the shop was advertised to let and the Franklins retired to live in Russell Street. He died in 1888.

No. 27. In 1809 this shop was occupied by Robert Pattison, ironmonger and brazier, and he was probably assisted, and perhaps followed, by his son, also Robert (1807-38). In 1848 it was a butcher's shop kept by Charles 'Wido' Clark, who left, in 1879, for Eaton Socon, and died in 1887. His wife lived to the age of 109.

Nos. 25, 27. Edmund Wilson, clothier, had taken part of the premises in 1877, and in 1879 he combined them to make one shop. He was there until the end of the century, and was followed by J. H. Thittle, and in about 1914 by R. E. Cadge, all in the same business.

No. 29. Present rebuilt butcher's shop with offices above. In 1820 the occupier here was Mr. Gurry, maker of furniture and turnery, and in 1823 Ebenezer Gurry chairmaker. In 1830 there was Saml. Gurry 'turnery, chair maker, and straw hat maker'. In 1836 there was a bakehouse here as well and the Gurrys remained at least until 1839.

By about 1850 the shop was occupied by Wm. Shaw (1809-94) cutler and scissor grinder who came from Mildenhall, Suffolk, and first started at 36 High Street. He used to sit at work just inside the shop window in full view of passers-by. He attended regularly at the Baptist Chapel, New Street, and was greatly respected in the town. Mrs. Shaw carried on the business for sometime after his death.

About 1894 part of this property was taken by J. P. Burr, veterinary surgeon, who had succeeded M. Riddlington of New Street. He also hired part of the stabling at the *Angel* inn next door. In 1908-10 he moved to Church House, Brook Street.

No. 31. Part of the site at present occupied by Woolworth Ltd. This, before it was pulled down in 1935, was the *Angel* inn, (*Hist. Mon. Comm.*, no. 7). Although an old inn it had been much altered and had an unimposing outside appearance, with the gateway to the Square blocked up. Inside, over a fireplace on the first floor, was an early 17th century plaster panel modelled with four amorini (illus. in *Hist. Mon. Comm.*, plate 119). This was removed and reset in the *Golden Ball* inn opposite. These plaster panels were probably done by itinerant Italian craftsmen, and one from the same mould was done in a farmhouse in Adams Lane, Great Paxton, and is now reset at the Ferns, Eynesbury Green.

In the Earl of Sandwich's sale in 1848, it was described as having a parlour, tap room, five sleeping rooms, kitchen, cellar, and good stabling. It was sold for £900.

It was remembered, at the end of the century, as a rather rough house with plenty of fighting on Saturday night. It was the usual rendezvous of the 'Duloe Gang' who generally proved more than a match for the town customers.

In 1792 the landlord was Thos. Wiles victualler, and in 1809 John Freshwater. In 1820 the house was kept by a well-known and popular figure, Geo. Maile (1790–1874). He brewed his own beer and sold three or four barrels (of 36 gallons) a week. He was also a shoemaker. A song was composed, sung to a topical tune, of which the first two lines ran:

> Here lives George Maile
> Who keeps pegging away and drawing of ale.

He was followed, after his death, by Wm. Chambers, who let out a pony and trap, but left in 1880 to take over the *Fox and Hounds*. Geo. Waite (1852-89) was here in 1886 but left in 1888. He seems to have been followed by Henry Waite, and in 1892 by A. Scard. Thereafter followed a series of landlords who seldom stayed more than a year or so.

No. 33. Part of the Woolworth site. These premises seem to have been divided into two separate properties, made into one about 1860. It is probable that the one to the east was once part of the *Angel* inn.

No. 33A. (*Hist. Mon Comm.*, no. 8). In 1848 these premises were occupied by Joseph Marshall confectioner, and in 1854 he was succeeded by J. Hine, in the same trade.

No. 33B. In 1839 these premises were occupied by Wm. Sharp, chemist, there was also a Mr. Sharp here in 1848, and a Wm. Cratefield Sharp, chemist, in 1850.

No. 33. The two above combined. In 1860 this was the shop and premises of Wm. Whittett, baker and confectioner, succeeded by James Whittett (1824-93). In 1895 the business was taken over by Alfred Whittett. He does not appear to have been a near relative, but the son of Peter Whittett, baker, of 42 Market Square. He remained here until he retired about 1925 to live in part of Hall Place, Huntingdon Street.

Present shop, part of Woolworths. In 1820 a shop here was occupied by Joan Pattison, ironmonger, and in 1823 and 1830 by Robt. Pattison (probably 1807–38). At the Earl of Sandwich's sale in 1848 the premises were bought, for £350, by W. Edward Mackaness, who came here after moving from 32 Market Square. He was a signwriter, painting inn signs, and to him we owe the only known sketch of the Court Hall on the north side of the Market Square done in 1820. He died 1869 leaving two sons Charles and Edward. Edward junr. (1812–94) set up in the same trade in Kimbolton about 1842, but moved to Biggleswade in 1846. Charles remained at St. Neots but was joined by his brother at his father's death. Edward seems to have taken charge of the business on his return. Like his father he was a signwriter and was long remembered for his talented work on inn signs, some of which lasted long after his death. For example the *Village Blacksmith* at Eynesbury was said to have been a speaking likeness of Wm. Taylor, blacksmith of Eynesbury Bridge. He also painted a number of watercolours of local scenes. Besides his artistic work he was a keen cricketer and devout Wesleyan.

After the death of Edward Mackaness in 1894, the business, which had employed a number of men, ceased and the premises were let to Sharp & Son, in the same trade. They only operated for one year, however, and after a year's occupation by Chas. Gill, who moved from here to South Street in 1897, they were taken by Mr. Murkitt as a bicycle shop, formerly at 38 High Street. This firm developed into the present motor engineers at Bedford and Huntingdon.

About 1902 came another change when Chas. Gambrell came here from Kimbolton. His father was a blacksmith there and he started making bicycles as a sideline. His 'Kim' bicycle became a popular local model and he decided to move to St. Neots to concentrate on its manufacture. Here he not only made the bicycles but stove-enamelled them. In 1902 he was advertising the manufacturing of motor cycles, and his premises as a garage. He was here until about 1910. About 1917 Compton & Son, motor engineers, came here from 22 Market Square.

In 1961 the back part of these premises were pulled down and rebuilt. They consisted of old buildings of timber-faced construction of 15th- to 16th-century date. Over a fireplace was an indecipherable black-letter inscription, and there was a baker's oven. Below ground level were a number of filled-in pits and shallow ditches containing pottery of the late 15th to 17th centuries. Under these were graves with burials of persons of both sexes, with 12th-century pottery in the fillings. A large amount of carved medieval stone-work from the destruction of the Priory was found, and a stone-lined well.

No. 35. A small shop, now a tobacconist's. Except for a short interval this was a hairdresser's shop for nearly 100 years. In 1820 and 1830 it was kept by Joseph Richard Goodliff, hairdresser and perfumier, and in 1848 by a Mr. Wright, hairdresser. By 1860 it had passed to Edmund Berrill, hairdresser, and by 1872 a 'bazaar' had been added. By 1872 the business was being run by Mrs. Berrill, and in 1879 she gave up the hairdressing side and ran a servants' registry office here.

In 1883 the shop was occupied by Stephen Bull, hairdresser, and in 1890 by H. Potter, followed very shortly after by Mr. Flanders, hairdresser and tobacconist, who remained for many years.

No. 37. This was formerly the site of two shops, made into one probably about 1840.

No. 37A to the west. In 1809 and 1823 this was the watch and clockmaker's shop of Wm. Paxton, who was possibly the son of John Paxton, watchmaker, mentioned in 1792. William Paxton was also the postmaster and the post office was here. There is, however, some possibility of confusion as in 1830 there was another John Paxton, also a clockmaker and also postmaster, and a Wm. Paxton, clockmaker, who had a shop on the east side of the Square. In 1830, at the post office on the Square, letters from London and the south arrived by the Glasgow mail coach every morning at 2 a.m., and were despatched south every night at midnight. From Bedford, Buckingham and Northampton they arrived by horse post every evening at seven, and were despatched every morning at seven. From Huntingdon, Cambridge, Norfolk, Suffolk, and Essex, they arrived by horse post at 6.30 a.m. and were despatched at 7.30 p.m. From Kimbolton they arrived by horse post at 7 p.m. and were despatched at 7 p.m.

No. 37B. In 1820 these premises were occupied by Wm. Bell, woollen warehouseman, and in 1823 by Alex. Bell, draper. There were corn shops at the back. In 1836 the shop was taken by John Hipwell Goodgames, draper, who had formerly been on the east side of the Square. He was able to buy, and add to the shop, the property next door to the west, and took a partner, the new shop trading as Goodgames & Shrosberry. They also had a branch at Potton and Mr. Shrosberry took this when the partnership was dissolved. When his son Thomas came of age John Goodgames took him into partnership and he himself soon retired to live at Berkeley House, Eynesbury. However, Thomas was at the age of 32 in 1879 killed by a fall from his horse. His father then sold the business to Thos. C. Fison. He and his son had made the shop the leading draper's and milliner's in the district. He was a much respected figure in the town, a town commissioner, and one of the promoters of St. Neots Gas Co. in 1845. He died at a great age in 1896.

In 1898 the business was sold to W. F. Potts of Hitchin, and in 1899 to R. Cutlack, and very soon after to Thos. Armstrong, who had it for many years. He came from an old local farming family and his brother was the first manager of Barclays Bank (see also 9 Market Square).

No. 39. Present Turners Ltd., chemists. In 1809 and 1820 these were the premises of Wm. Abbott, cabinet-maker and auctioneer, and in 1823 of Wm. & Jas. Abbott, auctioneers. This was possibly the Wm. Abbott, also described as an architect and surveyor, who became a rich man and lived at Berkeley House, Eynesbury, or perhaps more probably his father who was also named William.

In 1830 and 1848 this was the premises of Wm. Islip, (died at Denton, Norfolk, 1878) described as a linen and woollen draper, and dealer in broadcloth.

From about 1855, and up to 1879, it was a china, glass, and fancy shop, kept by Wm. Foster. In 1879 J. G. Mellor, chemist, moved here from 23 Market Square. He remained until 1890 when he bought a manufacturing chemist's business at Warwick, leaving his former apprentice, H. J. Dukes, as manager. In 1898 H. J. Dukes took over the business into which he introduced his two sons Tom and Harry, who succeeded him until the business was sold by them in 1963.

No. 41. Present off-licence Wine and Spirit shop. (*Hist. Mon. Comm.*, no. 10). This was the former *Fox and Hounds* inn, probably built about 1700, and turned into a shop in 1963.

Landlords included: 1775, 1792, 1809, Wm. Palmer victualler; 1814, Sarah Palmer, 1820-48 Christopher Cox who was also a waterman and barge-owner, and in 1848 left here to take over the *Half Moon* inn, Market Square. He was followed by Stephen Illsley, and in 1854 by Joseph Illsley (possibly Joseph Mins Illsley 1805-56) who had been landlord of the *Three Tuns*, High Street. He was followed by Wm. Ely (1814-71) and his wife who retired in 1880. Next there was Wm. Chambers (1836-85) followed by

Martha Chambers who left in 1888. Her son William did horse clipping and ringing in stables at the back. They were succeeded by Ed. Feazey and in 1899 by John Newman.

There were fairly extensive premises at the back of the inn with public accesss to them along Fox and Hounds Lane, which runs through to Back Lane along the east side of this property and still retains its old cobbled surface.

In the *Fox and Hounds* yard were several small cottages and formerly some small industrial premises. In 1809 there was the inn brewhouse here as well as a cooper's workshop, and in 1814 there is a record of two cottages and a comb shop. In 1867 rods (osiers) were peeled here for basket-making. The most interesting building here was the Baptist chapel, used by a breakaway sect from the Baptists (see chapter on Nonconformity). The building used was probably the present wooden loft approached by an outside staircase, although the author has been told that they used a building behind no. 43 across the lane. Because of the site of their Meeting House (in the *Fox and Hounds* yard) the attenders were nicknamed locally the 'Tally-ho Baptists', and that name survived well into this century. The only further record found of this chapel was in an obituary of John Freeman, who died, aged 86, in 1890. He remembered attending worship there as a lad when the 'celebrated John Stevens' was the pastor.

No. 43. Present Claytons, saddlers, fancy, and sports shop. This has been a saddler's shop for probably 200 years. In 1775 it was owned by a Mrs. Cook, and in 1792 and 1809 by John Cook, saddler. In 1820, 1823, 1830 (saddler and tawer), and 1839 it was still John Cook. In 1854 there was a Thos. Cook, who died in 1871. He was followed by Henry Hind Bowtell (1839–76) saddler and jobmaster. After his death the business was taken over by his son Alfred Harry Bowtell. He had obviously great business ability and became a wealthy man and a well-known and colourful local character, familiarly known as 'Bucky'. Besides running this business he became a bookmaker and later owned and trained racehorses of his own. From winnings on his horse 'Hacklers Pride' he built himself a house in Huntingdon Street (next to the County Library on the south), calling it by the same name. In 1892, as jobmaster, he advertised for hire: 'Fly with 1 horse or a pair, Waggonette with a pair, 1 horse or a cob, Horse and Dog Cart, Cob and Dog Cart, Pony and Rustic Cart, Horse, Cob, and Pony to ride, Broughams for Weddings and Funerals'. In 1897 he bought the *New* inn in the High Street, and the same year started a 'Break' service to Bedford every Saturday. In 1912 he sold the saddler's business and these premises to Clayton & Son, saddlers of Huntingdon, with whom it has remained.

The corner block of property, now Barretts, with a frontage on both the Market Square and New Street. This block, extending as far up New Street as Back Lane, was once part of the extensive property belonging to the Earl of Sandwich in the town.

In 1823 all, or much of it, was occupied by John Medlock (1787-1874), miller and millwright, then or later in partnership with his son Henry Arthur. He lived in a house at the west end of the property, facing the Square, and had his mill at the back, with an entrance into Back Lane. In 1841 he, in conjunction with the Town Commissioners, had bought this property, the commissioners retaining only a site on which to build their New Rooms in New Street, (now the offices of Wade Gery & Brackenbury). In 1846 the mill was burnt down and he proposed replacing it with one powered by steam. This caused great indignation and concern to all the occupiers of neighbouring properties, including the Town Commissioners, who had just built their New Rooms next door. Mr. Medlock was persuaded to build his new steam mill in Nutters Lane (Bedford Street), after being compensated by £50 from the commissioners' funds and £70 from neighbours' subscriptions.

Besides the Medlock's house there were, on the north side, two shops, including the corner shop which had also a window facing New Street. At some time, perhaps about 1850, a further shop was added to the block in New Street.

When John Medlock died in 1874 it is probable that his son had predeceased him as the property was all left to his widowed daughter, Mrs. Anne Withers. She lived in the family home until her death, at the age of 95, in 1908. She was remembered as a rather eccentric old lady who felt that her father's property had been left to her as a trust, and was not to be altered. Tenants were quite unable to persuade her to improve or modernise the shops, or allow them to do so. It was said that one tenant (Mr. Keeling) was given notice for making an unauthorised alteration. No tenancy was given for longer than a year and all rents had to be paid in gold on the day they were due.

The shop between the corner shop and the Medlock's house. In 1820 this was a hairdresser's, kept by Samuel Mees (there was a brazier of the same name in the town in 1792). In 1867 and 1870 it was occupied by James Gotton, milliner, and in 1875 by D. Swann, draper, who called it 'Victoria House'. In 1876 Walter Blott, draper, moved here from 25 High Street. He also

had another shop on the Square at no. 36. In 1880 he complained
about the droves of ponies standing for sale, on market days, on
the pavement outside his shop. He left in 1883 and was followed
by Edmund Ibbett, draper, who renamed the shop 'Perseverance
House'. He also hired the New Street shop, separated from the
other by the corner shop. This he used as a boot shop, communi-
cation between the two being by means of speaking tube. There
was a plug at each end of the tube in the form of a whistle, and
to 'get through' one withdrew the plug and blew into the tube
to sound the whistle at the other end. This novelty was vastly
intriguing to the children of that time.

Edmund Ibbett left for Kimbolton in 1892, and was followed
by A. D. Davison, draper and milliner, and later by Thomas Barnes,
greengrocer and fruiterer.

The corner shop. This is traditionally said to have been the site
of an inn, but in 1820 there was a chemist's shop here kept by
a Mr. Andrews. In 1848 it was occupied by F. Topham, bookseller and printer, who was afterwards the publisher of the *St.
Neots Chronicle*. He moved from here to 15 High Street about
1855. After this it was probably taken by John Neal, fishmonger,
and then Amies & Tyler, bootmakers, who left in 1871. In 1872
R. R. Keeling, bookseller, came here after buying Wm. Emery's
business on the Square (now Barclays Bank). Mrs. Keeling started
also a 'Fancy and Baby Linen' shop, perhaps in the New Street
window.

In 1887 the Keelings left for 35 High Street, and the shop was
advertised to let as 'a corner shop suitable for booksellers, two
plate glass windows, door at angle to two streets, and a balcony
over'.

In 1888 the shop was taken by Arthur Edward Barrett, clothier
and outfitter, who came from Gloucestershire. He revived the old
name of the next-door shop 'Victoria House'. In 1893 he died at
the age of 28 leaving the business to be carried on by his widow,
who later married her chief assistant, Charles Huckle.

The lock-up shop in New Street. In 1865 and 1870 it was occupied
by Rich. Sherman, butcher, and was unlet in 1873 and 1874.
Wm. Day, grocer, was here in 1875, and Edmund Ibbett had it as
a boot shop when occupying his other shop in the block.

**The block of buildings on the Square between the Square and
South Street, north.**

Present Midland Bank, opened 1936, and offices to the west. In
1848 there was one small shop here, the rest of the property as

far as the end of the block being occupied by a blacksmith's shop and yard and a pig market with numerous auctioning pens.

In 1775 the blacksmith was Thos. Lewis, there was a Mr. Lewis here in 1792, and Richard Lewis in 1809. In 1820 and 1831 it was John Lewis, and in 1832 Thos. Lewis (1800–81). He retired in 1874 and was succeeded by his son-in-law Jabez Jeffreys, who was also landlord of the *Falcon* inn, New Street, and a blacksmith's shop was started at the rear of the inn. The 1854 directory gives his address at New Street and it is probable that both premises were used at the same time. The Lewis home, in 1848, was a house in South Street immediately north of the *King's Head*, which was probably pulled down when the Corn Exchange was built in 1862.

It is not known when the blacksmith's business was given up here but towards the end of the century it was used exclusively as an auction yard and by the ironmonger's shop opposite (45 Market Square) for storage and display of agricultural implements for sale. Here in 1890 Saml. Thos. Ekins (1866–95) first started his auctioneering business on his own premises, previously using the *New* inn yard and the Market Square, and built up a fine business before his early death. He was followed by his younger brother, S. V. Ekins, who moved to New Street about 1902.

In 1897 the St. Neots Urban District Council built a small office on this site, where the Midland Bank now is, for the use of its part-time surveyor, A. T. Blood. This was thus the first U.D.C. office, and, in 1899, the St. Neots Water Co. moved their office here from Bedford Street. The site of the present Eastern Electricity Board office and showroom was used as an ironmonger's store until the present building was built.

The *Golden Ball* inn. Before rebuilding, in 1935, this was a timber-framed single cross wing house, probably of the 16th or 17th century, although not included in the *Hist. Mon. Comm.* report. It may well, at some time, have formed part of the Court Hall, next to it. Austin's 1853 engraving and other early pictures of the Square show this inn with a free-standing sign post with a pictorial sign, at the north-west corner. In the inn is reset a plaster panel from the now demolished *Angel* inn. Landlords of the *Golden Ball* were, in 1809, James Arnold, who was also a butcher, and in 1820 Wm. Simpson, who came here from the *Royal Oak* in the High Street. He was still there in 1823, but in 1839 Wm. Jordan was landlord, and in 1848 he bought the inn from the Earl of Sandwich for £1,200. He may have come here from the *Rose and Crown*, Eaton Ford where a Wm. Jordan was landlord in 1830. He was also for

many years the collector of market tolls, paying an annual sum
to the Lord of the Manor for the privilege. He was probably
followed after his death by his widow, but in 1864 the landlord was B. R. Yates, in 1875 W. R. Ennals, in 1883 J. R.
Richards, in 1887 H. Bannister, and in 1888 Geo. Bradford,
who remained at least until the end of the century. It was recalled
that this inn used to do a prosperous trade during the time
of the Vulcan Iron Works, it being the rendezvous of the men
working there.

During the building of the Midland Bank, in 1935, a north-
south trench was dug, parallel with South Street and 21 feet west
of the South Street frontage of the bank. The trench started at
the road edge on the north side of the bank, and under the pavement southwards, at a depth of two feet, were the remains of a
series of parallel oak sleeper beams lying east and west about 10
feet apart. These were possibly part of a medieval building. At
the south end of the trench, 30 feet from the road, was a shallow
pit in which were 15th-century shoes.

The east end of the Market Square. It is fortunate that there still
exists an old undated engraving, and a more detailed pencil drawing
of this end of the Square by W. E. Mackaness dated 1820. From
this latter it can be seen that with the exception of the *Golden
Ball*, the whole of the west face of the block is occupied by a
large composite timber-framed building. This consists of a central
hall with gabled cross wings at each end, the hall only having a
jettied or overhung upper storey. It seems likely that this building
must be dated to the late 15th or early 16th century. From its
position, overlooking and dominating the Market Square, and its
obvious importance, it must be the Court Hall. From here the
Prior, as Lord of the Manor, would administer the town's affairs
through his Manor Courts, control the markets and fairs, and hold
Courts of Justice to try minor offences. After the Dissolution it
would be used by the secular Lords of the Manor through their
stewards. The court room would be on the first floor of the central hall where the pictures show four narrow windows overlooking
the market.

From Mackaness's drawing it can be seen that a number of
architectural changes had taken place. A central ornamental gable
had been added to frame a clock, probably in the 17th century.
The roof of the central block is slightly higher than that of the
wings, which suggests a re-roofing at some time. In the 18th century the lower floor had been let as shops and venetian and other
types of windows added.

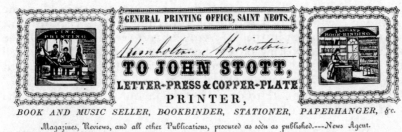

The deeds of the property (kindly lent by Mr. C. Lendrum)
only date back to about 1800, but from an Abstract with them
it seems that in 1707 the building was already divided into four
tenements or dwellings in the occupation of Thos. Edis, John
Paxton, Sarah Reynolds and — Aspland.

The north and central face of the Court Hall was pulled down
between 1820 and 1828, probably by James Hatfield, and replaced
with the present façade. It is almost certain, however, that some
of the back of the present premises of Tomson and Lendrum are
part of the old building. The south gable still remains as the only
part of the Court Hall still visible.

The four former premises, from the north, next to the *Golden
Ball* **inn.**

A. In 1820 this was occupied by Thos. King, shoemaker. In 1828
James Hatfield, who originated in Spalding, Lincs., came here from
15 High Street. He was a printer and bookseller and advertised a
Circulating Library, and it is almost certain that he demolished
the front of the old Court Hall and built the present façade.
In 1835 he left for Huntingdon where, in 1854, he published the
History and Gazetteer of Huntingdonshire, a work of great interest
and value to local historians.

He was followed by his apprentice John Stott (1813–81). He
was probably the son, or grandson, of David Stott of St. Neots
(1741–1816), buried in St. Neots churchyard. He was for a short
time in partnership with his brother or father, David. Like most
of his trade at that time, he was also a paperhanger, as well as a

printer and bookseller. In 1848 he emigrated to Australia where he died, having sold the business to his nephew and apprentice. This was David R. Tomson who thus, in 1848, first gave his name to the present firm. The author owes much to a reminiscence written much later in the *St. Neots Advertiser*, describing all the business houses existing on the Square on the day he first opened his shop. He lived on until the early years of this century, but retired, in 1887, in favour of his son Percy Calder Tomson (1867–1958), who himself retired in 1946 in favour of his stepson, the present managing director.

B. In 1707 this shop was occupied by Thos. Edis, and by another Thos. Edis in 1792, and also in 1809, when a barber's shop had been added. Mrs. Edis had it in 1820, and about 1828 it was rebuilt. It was then taken by J. H. Goodgames, draper, who moved to 37 Market Square in 1836.

In 1839 it was the office of Wm. Medland, auctioneer, surveyor, and estate agent, and included a branch of the bank of Wells & Co., Biggleswade. Medland was a wealthy man, doing business over a wide area, and owning much property. He lived in New Street at the house now the Constitutional Club, and died in 1872. In 1874 the premises were used by James Sharp, 'Mechanical and Practical Dentist', who in 1875 moved from here to New Street, and after to 28 Market Square. Mr. Maddison, auctioneer, was here in 1896 and 1899, and it was probably at this time that it was added to P. C. Tomson's premises.

C. In 1820 this property was occupied by Dr. Adams, but in the 1828 rebuilding it was converted into a shop with an office above. In 1848 the shop was used by Wm. Tingey Mole, chemist, who, in 1855, moved to 30 Market Square when the *Bear* ceased to be an inn. At the time he was there the upstairs office was used, on market days, by Mr. Beedham, solicitor of Kimbolton; a business taken over, much later, by Wade Gery & Brackenbury of New Street.

About 1858, or soon after, the post office was established here under Robert Hanford, who moved with it from 40 Market Square, and in 1863 there was also a savings bank attached. In 1862 Edward Squire became postmaster here, but in 1876 he moved the post office to 63 High Street.

In 1876 it became a bootshop first under Amies & Tyler, and then in 1879, under J. B. Turner. In 1888 T. Ellwood had a bootshop here before moving to 37 High Street in 1890.

He was followed by Chas. Galpin with a fish and poultry shop, and about 1902 by H. R. Chick, tailor from New Street. In 1908 and 1914 London Central Meat Co. had a shop here before it was taken by P. C. Tomson and added to his premises.

D. This south corner of the block still has the gable of the Court Hall. (*Hist. Mon. Comm.*, no. 11). In 1820 this property was occupied by Wm. Newman, cooper and ironmonger, who was here at least until 1830. He was followed by Wm. Paxton, watchmaker, (1785–1867) who was here until about 1866.

This Wm. Paxton seems to have been the last of several generations of clock- and watchmakers of that name in the town. Their grandfather clocks are still not uncommon in the district. There was a Wm. Paxton at 37 Market Square in 1820, and a John Paxton possibly there in 1830. The Paxtons seemed to use no other christian names than John and William and it is difficult to sort them out. From tombs in St. Neots churchyard and other evidence there is: John Paxton 1757–1832, Wm. Paxton 1785–1867, his son John 1837–69, and a John making clocks and watches about 1770.

In 1866 the shop was taken by W. Chambers, watchmaker, who in 1870 moved to 26 Market Square. In 1872 James Gray, watchmaker, was here, and about 1885 L. Marshall had a hairdresser's shop and fancy bazaar.

In 1888 came George Sawford, hairdresser, from an apprenticeship at Carters in the Strand, London. He was a lovable but excitable and flamboyant Cockney character whose words and deeds long remained a part of local folklore. One story concerned a long drawn out feud with his neighbour, H. R. Chick, the tailor. When this appeared to have died down Chick ventured into the barber's shop for a shave. When the sheet was firmly fastened round his neck 'Georgie' poured out a torrent of abuse and denunciation on the subject of his neighbourly conduct. When the wretched Chick tried to answer, he got more and more excited, brandishing his cut-throat razor so that Chick feared for his life. The phrase used by Georgie that delighted the waiting customers, and was still remembered 50 years afterwards, was 'Chick or no Chick, off comes your blooming chivvey'. Georgie Sawford was not only famous for his barber's shop dialogue, he was a talented music-hall artist whose services were always in great demand at local concerts and entertainments.

THE PRIORY

The Market House. This was next to the present *Bridge* Hotel, north of the public passage to the river, and the present building there must be part of it. It was almost certainly the site of the

Priory Mill in the 16th century. Its purpose is not quite clear but in 1848, when it was sold for £145 to J. H. Day of the Priory Brewery, it had corn shops and was hired by Wm. Jordan, farmer of the market tolls. It was therefore probably used to store market stalls and corn arriving before market day. Attached to it at that time was a garden on the north side, now belonging to the next house. This may at one time have been a wharf for the Market House.

House. Now for nearly 100 years occupied by one of the town's doctors. This house is built within the precincts of the Priory and set in the garden wall is an inscribed stone indicating the site of the Priory gatehouse, which survived until 1814.

It would seem that a former house here was attached to Joseph Eayre's bell foundry which was sited just beyond the house on what is now the roadway. It seems likely that Joseph Eayre once lived here, but there is no evidence of this. In 1809 it belonged to the Earl of Sandwich and was occupied by Wm. Towndrow. It was then called the Old Priory House, and had a shop in front. Soon after this it seems to have been bought by the Fowlers of the Priory Brewery, who probably pulled it down and built the present house. They probably did not include it in their sale of the brewery in 1814 as there were Fowlers living here in 1820. In 1843 a Mr. Habershon, a noted architect in his day, was living here. He had an articled pupil, named Wicks, who later wrote a standard Victorian work, *The Spires and Towers of England.*

In 1850 John Carrington, ironmonger, came to live here on his retirement, but died two years later. His shop was on the near corner of the Square (see above).

In 1855 the house was occupied both as a residence and office by Wm. R. Ennals, who was a wine merchant, auctioneer, appraiser, selecting agent for Australian emigrants, clerk to the Guardians, registrar of B.M.D. for the Kimbolton district, and had a servant agency. Later the firm became Ennals & Son, and in 1874 Ennals & Parnell, a partnership dissolved the next year. W. R. Ennals died in 1880 and was followed by Dr. John Turner, who bought the practice of Dr. Joseph Rix at 21 Market Square on his retirement in 1874. He died about 1890, but his widow lived here until her death in 1895. The practice however had been sold to a Dr. Arthur Cromach who finally came to live here. He was followed by Dr. Ernest Harrisson, who left to live at the Shrubbery, Church Street about 1912. He was followed by Dr. Bowe, formerly living at Denmark House, 44 New Street, who bought the house for £750 at Day & Sons sale in 1919. He was here until he retired in 1932.

The Priory House and Brewery. This house was obviously built at two periods, the older part being at the back. It seems likely that the older part was built by the Fowlers, who acquired the brewery in 1780, pulling down a 17th- or early 18th-century house matching factory buildings to the north, and that the front was added by the Days, who came here in 1814. Attached to the house was a cottage for a groom. The garden, which until 1963 extended as far as Priory Path, covered part of the site of the Priory buildings including the refectory, kitchen, and part of the western range and cloisters. At some time it had been enlarged, to the east, by diverting Priory Path further east. In 1700 the path was still in its original position so it is probable that either the Fowlers or the Days, having built their mansion, wanted a larger garden round it and disliked a public path so near it.

At the sale of the property in 1919 one of the doors was taken off and sold as a separate lot, and its present whereabouts is not known. It is however illustrated by an engraving in Gorham's *History of Eynesbury and St. Neots*, and by a photograph in the *Trans. Cambs. & Hunts. Arch. Soc.*, vol. V, part 4.

The extensive brewery buildings must have been built and added to over a long period, from the late 16th or early 17th century onwards, some for use in a general merchant's business in conjunction with the navigation. There is now no trace of the lime kiln that was in use at the beginning of the 19th century, but fortunately the fine and picturesque barley malting kiln still survives, and its tapering circular tower is a notable landmark as one approaches the town across the Common. This kiln is shown on Jeffrey's map of 1768. No doubt many of the yellow-brick buildings were put up by the Fowlers, and the large riverside warehouse across the yard west of the house has a stone, set in the wall under the clock, inscribed W.F. 1782. The clock itself, which was sold to Mr. Freeman, watchmaker, of 42 High Street in 1966, was of 18th-century date, and may well have been made by Joseph Eayre, who then had his workshops next door. From the clock a wire ran up a rafter of the building to a bell on the ridge outside. The clock could be set to ring the bell at the time for stopping work. This was in use in recent years. (See the chapter on St. Neots firms for an account of the business carried on here.)

THE HIGH STREET

This was always the most important street in the town and it developed westward from the Cross during the Middle Ages. Like most medieval streets it had a ditch running along each side, as

recent street excavations have shown. An interesting reminiscence
was recorded in 1899. Mr. Lovitt, senr., recalled his grandfather
telling him that he remembered a brook running along the north
side of High Street, with planks across it at intervals. to reach the
houses. This could be in the period 1760-80.

Property deeds of the 17th century often refer to 'High Street
or Sheep Street', and there can be little doubt that the street,
abnormally wide for a medieval street, was once used on market
and fair days as an extension of the Market Square and was
particularly used for sheep sales.

At the east end of High Street is the Cross. This is obviously
the centre or focal point of the original street plan of the town,
and there is a strong tradition that a stone cross once stood here.
Gorham also records a further tradition that the Cross marked the
spot where the bones of St. Neot rested for one night before
being brought to rest in the Saxon monastery. The Cross was
apparently here in the 16th century, when the Priory rent roll of
1505 describes a property as 'at the corner of Cambridge St. near
the High Cross'.

HIGH STREET, NORTH SIDE

No. 1. Present Freeman, Hardy & Willis Ltd. For 100 years this
was the site of a watchmaker's shop in the hands of one family,
all ardent supporters of New Street Baptist chapel. In 1792 the
shop was kept by Jas. Kirby (1759–1829), who was one of the
trustees of the New Street chapel, and is buried in the cemetery.
He was also the first surveyor, part-time, to the St. Neots commissioners. At that time the house and shop had attached an acre
of land at the back. His son Richard, also described as an auctioneer,
succeeded his father as surveyor to the commissioners, but proved
unsatisfactory and was replaced in 1832. In 1850 a James Kirby,
probably the eldest son, was at the shop, and in 1854 James
and John Kirby. In 1866 part of the premises was used as a
Savings Bank. A James Kirby, late of St. Neots, died at Leicester
in 1894, aged 73, and the last of the family at the shop seems to
have been Alfred Stephen Kirby. In 1888 the family connection
ended and the business was taken by Wright & Sale, becoming
A. G. Sale in 1890.

The present owners, Freeman, Hardy & Willis probably came
here in 1893, or soon after, but at first only occupied part of
the premises, and, of course, rebuilt the old gabled shop.

No. 3. Present Liptons Ltd. Dr. Sole lived here for a time when
he left 20 Market Square, but in 1854 it was the house and pre-

mises of Jas. Cooper, bootmaker and leather cutter, who had once been a partner of Thos. Lovell of 15 Market Square. He retired in 1884 and died in 1901. He was a prominent Wesleyan and one of the founders of Wesleyan School. He was remembered as always walking about with his head down and eyes on the ground, studying people's shoes!

The next occupant of the shop was Albert Wm. Barker, (1850–1919) draper, milliner, and hatter, who also had a furniture shop on the opposite side of the street. He was here until early this century and was followed by J. J. Foulger, in the same trade. In about 1908 the premises were taken by G. Britten, formerly at the corner of Brook Street and South Street. He turned the shop into catering and refreshment rooms, and advertised it as a Temperance Hotel.

No. 5. Before rebuilding, 16th- or 17th-century timber-framed building. In 1839 it was occupied by Daniel Allen, baker and green-grocer, and in 1880–90 by Geo. Allen. Soon afterwards it was added to the shop next door by W. Norris.

No. 7. Another timber-framed building pulled down in 1962. Under it were pits and ditches containing pottery and shoes of about 1500. About 1850 this was the shop of Wm. Norris, (1815–87) tailor and outfitter, advertising 'Harvest gloves for hand reaping'. After his death his widow carried on the shop, and was followed by their grandson, G. L. Downs, in the early years of this century.

No. 9. Present International Stores. In 1823 this was the shop of Samuel Bedells, grocer, tea-dealer and tallow-chandler. Tallow candles were undoubtedly made on the premises, as Day & Sons were selling him fat for candles in 1824. It is recorded that he suffered £500 damage in the great flood of 1823. About 1860 the shop was being run by Ebenezer Bedells (1828-81), his son. A pictorial billhead of that period shows what is substantially the present building, with windows containing chests of tea, and tall, conical sugar loafs. Ladies in crinolines and gentlemen in top hats and frock coats promenade along the pavement. It was recalled that this shop was noted for its speciality Leicestershire cheeses, bought at Leicester Cheese Fair. A less favourable reputation was from the strong-smelling tallow candle manufacture at the back. Every Friday butchers brought in their waste, and it was rendered down to make rush lights and '¼d. dips', the only lighting used by the poor. A sideline was maggots sold to anglers. After the death of her husband Mrs. Mary Bedells carried on the business until the first years of this century.

The shop was then taken by the Central Supply Stores, one of the first multiple shops in the town, who only stayed until about 1909.

No. 11. Little information has been collected about this shop. In 1775 it belonged to John Oliver, and before 1864 to a Mr. Warner. In 1864 it was taken by J. Paris, cabinet-maker, and about 1872 probably by J. Wilcox next door, and turned into a boot shop, attached to No. 13.

No. 13. In 1775 this property was owned by French Flanders, and early last century by W. Barker, tailor and clothier, who emigrated to Australia. The business was then taken over by his great friend Joseph Wilcox, (1816–94)* through whom he joined the Independent (Congregational) Chapel, and gained an interest and link with Australia. Wilcox was born at Boxhill, Surrey, to a Church of England family originating from St. Neots, where his grandfather had been a currier. His early life was one of great struggle through lack of capital, even with the help of his friend W. Barker. His subsequent career and rise to fortune was remarkable in view of the fact that he had 13 children, of which 10 survived him. He was particularly generous toward the Congregational chapel, and the present building was only able to be built because he defrayed much of the cost.

It is likely that the greater part of his fortune was gained in his business connections with Australia, through the co-operation of his equally remarkable second son George. George Wilcox (born 1838) was first employed at James Paine's office on the Market Square at the age of 12, and afterwards served a five-year apprenticeship with S. Bedells, grocer, of 9 High Street and a year with a Leicester grocer. In 1857, at the age of 19, he sailed in the 'Royal Charter' to Australia and, possibly under the wing of W. Barker, got a job as a clerk at £1 a week. In 1858 he joined a small grocery business which a year later amalgamated with an old established drapery shop. This, in partnership with his father, he took over under the name of J. & W. Wilcox, although his father never visited Australia. In 1863 he returned to England and married Anne Fuller of Manor Farm, St. Neots. Altogether he made 13 voyages between England and Australia, and was joined at Adelaide by his brother Joseph. His knowledge of the goods needed in the new colony enabled him, with the assistance of his father, to build up a large import business, as well as to arrange the export of wool, hides and frozen meat to England.

* See Plate 30

In 1899 he was the largest exporter of frozen lamb in Australia. He also practised farming, and in 1908 owned the Koonamore sheep station with 40,000 sheep.

Joseph Wilcox at his death left a fortune of £39,000. He had retired from his shop in 1887, and it was taken by W. Seward, and became the high-class tailor's shop of the town. He retired about 1920 to live at Great Barford.

No. 15. J. Stanford, printer and bookbinder, was here from 1821 to 1826, and left to go to Stagsden. Among material he printed was *Songs to be sung at His Majesties Coronation July 18th, 1821*.

He was followed by James Hadfield, printer, who came here from Spalding, and moved in 1828 to the east side of the Market Square. He was followed by the Tophams, printers, booksellers, paper-hangers, and tea and coffee retailers. It is possible that there was a Frederick Topham, who died at Woodbury, Tempsford in 1855, followed by his son Joseph. Certainly it was Joseph Topham who was here in 1844. It was he who started the first St. Neots newspaper, the *St. Neots Advertiser*, which ran from November 1853 to June 1855. It was then followed by, and incorporated with, the *Illustrated St. Neots Chronicle and Pictorial Weekly News*. This only ran to 21 numbers, and was followed by the *St. Neots Chronicle*. In 1872 D. R. Tomson, of the Market Square, bought the business, selling it a few days later, but retaining the copyright of the *St. Neots Advertiser*. One of Topham's reporters was Somers Vine, afterwards secretary to the Lord Mayor of London, and later knighted. The next successors were Evans & Wells, printers. This firm consisted of Zachariah Wells, a former reporter to Topham and grandfather to L. Evans, builder, 17 Cambridge Street. Zachariah Wells had been a printer's apprentice to D. R. Tomson. They carried on the publication of the *St. Neots Chronicle*, until 1886, when the copyright was sold to the *Hunts. County News*, and they soon after dissolved their partnership. This was probably in 1892. After this Wells took his son Frank into partnership, with a printing works in New Street, he himself living at 64 Berkeley Street, Eynesbury. The High Street premises were given up about 1911, being taken by Eastmans Ltd., butchers, and the New Street ones some time later.

No. 17. In 1775 this house and shop, with a cottage up the yard, was occupied by James Smith, and in 1809 by James or Job Smith, butcher, who had a slaughterhouse here. Before 1850 it was a clothier's shop kept by Ingle Bros. These two brothers were remembered for their prowess as speed skaters when races were held on the Common Meadow. They were followed, in 1850, by

Wm. Slade, who had a boot shop. He died in 1880, the shop being carried on by his widow. In 1887 it was taken by R. Pentelow, bootmaker, followed in 1888 by J. & A. Bull, in 1891 by Miss H. Porter, and in 1893 by E. Tuckfield, all in the same trade. In 1885 the shop was taken by Wm. Edwards, bootmaker, who moved here from 27 St. Mary's Street, Eynesbury, and was still here in 1914.

In the Yard was the *Star* inn and four cottages. This was kept by Geo. Slade in 1836, and later by Wm. Slade, together with the front shop. The licence was given up in 1885.

In one of the cottages, in 1848, was a Mr. Frankin, straw-plait dealer, and in another, in 1883, was Chas. Wooten, cobbler. Through this yard is a private right of way for the occupiers of the house in New Street, now the Constitutional Club, to reach the High Street.

No. 21. Now Lloyds Bank. This site, together with no. 23, is almost certainly that described by 'T', and referring to about 1820. 'C. Pamplin had in the High Street a comfortable old house, demolished by the late Mr. Lovell, who, in its place, put sundry shops. It had in its rear a home close on a portion of which Mr. Tomson's house [Vernon House, New Street] was built'. It would seem that this was one of the 'farm house' type of houses in the town, probably timber-framed. In 1809 Mr. Pamplin is described as having a dwelling house, brewhouse, croft, large garden, and about one acre. The house and home close is plainly shown on the map of 1770, and in 1775 was owned by a Mr. Robinson, who also had a malting there.

Mr. Pamplin was here in 1830, but by 1848 the site was owned by Thos. Lovell, (see 15 Market Square) and it seems to have had two small shops. In 1850 one was occupied by Thos. Gregson, tailor and clothier, who left in 1878 to become landlord of the *King's Head* in South Street, but carried on his tailor's business here. His daughter, Cosa Gregson, was a professional musician, well-known locally as a music teacher and singer at local concerts. The second shop was occupied, in 1854, by Thos. or Geo. Ubsdell, draper. The latter may have been the son of the former. He, or they, were followed, in 1872, by Walter Blott, draper, who moved to 36 Market Square in 1878. By 1887 the two shops had been pulled down and rebuilt as one shop for the Consumers Tea Co., the first 'company' shop in the town. They were here for at least 25 years.

No. 23. This was part of the site developed by T. Lovell (see no. 21). About 1855 it was occupied by Joseph Edey (1815–77), as a bootshop, and by his wife, a dressmaker and milliner. In 1871 the dressmaking was being done by the Misses Edey, before they moved, in 1876, to the south side of High Street, near the Cross. They were followed in the same business by Mrs. Sharp, and in 1877 by James Bettles, watchmaker and jeweller, who came here after 30 years in the trade in London. In 1888 he advertised ladies' silver brooches with a view of the new Congregational church depicted on them.

He was followed, about 1894, by E. Ellwood, watchmaker, jeweller and umbrella-maker, who moved here from somewhere on the Market Square. He was followed, in 1897, by A. G. Barritt, watchmaker and jeweller, who remained for over 30 years.

No. 25. In 1804 this shop was kept by Miss Smith, milliner, and in 1849 by Geo. S. Allen, draper and dealer in hand-made lace. In 1873, when he took his son into partnership, he advertised in *St. Neots Chronicle*, 'Mr. Hill will attend at Mr. G. S. Allen's shop to buy white pillow lace, no Yacks will be bought'.

In 1874 the business was bought by D. Swan, and in 1876 by Walter Blott, who had another shop at the corner of Market Square and New Street.

In 1877 John Dalzell junr., grocer, came here from 56 High Street, after dissolving partnership with his father, and remained until 1895. In 1895 the premises were taken by the International Tea Co., and partly rebuilt. They remained until moving to 9 High Street about 1914.

No. 27. The *Three Tuns* inn. This was one of the houses sold by Fowlers, the Priory brewers, to J. H. Day in 1804. It was then described as being formerly the *Bird in Hand*, and having attached to it, to the west, five tenements. These were probably the five cottages formerly in the yard at the back. In 1775 the landlord was Susan Summers, and in 1800 and 1809 Wm. Summers, who had, in the yard, a glazier's shop and a thatched rope-walk. He was followed by Wm. Lovell, and in 1830 it was John Lovell. In 1839 the landlord was Joseph Illsley, who by 1859 had moved to the *Fox and Hounds*, Market Square (there is a tomb in the churchyard to Joseph Minns Illsley, died 1856 aged 51).

Later landlords were: 1850 Robt. Whitty, 1854 Geo. or Thos. Gay, 1890 Robt. Edey, 1892 Robt. Bradley Ekins (1823-92), also W. Hunt, who advertised market dinners, 1894 Mrs. Hunt, 1895 Mrs. Morris, 1896 Tom. Morris, and 1908 and 1912 T. R. Putt.

No. 31. Present Plum's Cafe. The founder of this old-established business, Thomas Plum, is said to have been the son of a French refugee from the Revolution who settled in London, changing his name from Plume to Plum. His son John, it is said, was bound apprentice to a pastrycook in London, and when his time was served they started up in business at St. Neots, but on the south side of the High Street nearly opposite the present shop. The family always asserted that the business was started here in 1814, but this is difficult to reconcile with the facts that in 1814 Thos. Plum (1772–1828) would be 42 and his son John (1802–79) twelve. Perhaps Thomas was a French pastrycook and John was sent to London after he was established here.

John Plum was joined in the business, and succeeded by his son Thomas (1826–1915), and he by his son Walter Joseph (1872–1944), after which the family connection with the business ended.

Over the century the business gained a high reputation for its products and catering. By 1880 they had dining rooms and were dealers in game and poultry, as well as wines and spirits, and at the end of the century they opened a shop at Huntingdon. Thos. Plum the second was an expert rifle shot, competing at Bisley, and winning outright seven silver cups, one for each of his four sons and three daughters. He was also an active member of the volunteer Duke of Manchester's Light Horse, acting as Quartermaster Sergeant for 20 years. Great indignation was caused locally in 1880, when, being required to retire on grounds of age, he was prosecuted for refusing to give up his sword, to which he would have been entitled had he been allowed to serve a few more weeks. The prosecution was eventually withdrawn.

No. 33. In 1775 and 1809 this property was occupied by John Smith, farmer, and had attached 41 acres of land. In 1850 and 1854 it was the shop of John George, butcher. In 1876 James Moore, draper, built a new shop here, and later took his son Charles into partnership, remaining until about 1925. The father was nicknamed 'General' and the son 'Gunner'.

No. 35. Present R. Hall, stationer. This was the site of the *Pigeon*, or *Three Pigeons* inn, kept in 1775 and 1809 by John Hunt, and having a brewhouse attached. In 1823 Jas. Warren was landlord and in 1830 and 1854 Thos. Chapman (died 1880), also described as a brewer and maltster (see also Cambridge Street malting). In 1855 it is recorded that the two town fire hooks (23 feet long) were kept here. The hooks were used to drag off the thatch from burning cottages.

In 1865 Thos. Sporn had it. By 1868 the licence had been given up, and a shop built on the frontage at a cost of £314, probably by James Moore of next door.

About 1887 the shop was taken by Robt. R. Keeling, stationer and bookseller, who moved from the corner of New Street and Market Square. He was still here in 1900. In 1910 there was T. Robins, stationer, and in 1912 David Wrycroft, stationer and bookseller. The latter was a collector and dealer in printed and MS. items of local history, much of which is now in the Norris Library, St. Ives.

No. 37. Present Westminster Bank. There is the distinct possibility that this was the site of a goldsmith's shop in the 14th century. In 1389 Richard Stalworthy, apprentice to Walter Paunfield, goldsmith of St. Neots, was granted a pardon for his crime of leaving before his time was served. About 1962 service trenches dug along the north side of High Street coincided with the medieval open ditch that formerly ran there. In the black silt accumulated at the bottom of this ditch, and associated with 14th-century pottery, the author found a short length of gold foil, cut from the edge of a sheet. Was the loss of this, in sweeping out the shop, the reason why the apprentice dare not face his master, and ran away?

About 1885 there were two shops on this site, occupied by Samuel Ebbutt, tailor and Chas. Franklin, shoemaker. In 1869 Geo. Peacock, whip and thong-maker, was in one of these. In adjacent buildings the Congregational Sunday School was first held, when it was started in 1798.

About 1886 the whole site was bought by Thomas Ellwood, boot-upper manufacturer, currier, and leather merchant. He also added part of the property to the east, the other part going to the Congregational chapel. The old buildings were pulled down and a new factory and warehouse built to enlarge his business, which he moved from the east side of the Market Square.

This building is the same as that housing the present bank, and the monogram T.E. 1890 can still be seen on the side facing the High Street. A currier's business in March, Cambs., was also owned by T. Ellwood.

In 1908 the property was acquired by the London County & Westminster Bank, who moved here from 16 Market Square.

Private Footpath to the Old Meeting Chapel. This path was variously known as Chapel Path or Moore's Path (being a right of way to no. 33). Before the present Congregational chapel and Westminster Bank were built the path entered the High Street under an archway between buildings. At its north end it connects with another private right of way through to New Street. In times of severe flood this path would be opened for public use to enable pedestrians to get from New Street to High Street, when Huntingdon Street, the Market Square and the west end of High Street were under water.

The Old Meeting or Independent Chapel and graveyard. This red-brick chapel seems to have been built about 1718. It was rather ruthlessly restored in 1875 when the old gallery, box-like pews, and pulpit were removed, a new gallery built and pitch pine pews put in. Gas was substituted for the former oil lamps, and a new organ costing £175 installed by Trustam & Sons of Bedford. Altogether £300–£400 was spent. A Sunday School room, in white brick, was added, perhaps about mid-century. After building the new chapel it was used as a Sunday School only, but during the week was used for meetings of many kinds. Early in the present century a private day school (which the author attended) was held here. It is recorded that in the great flood of 1823 there were 18 inches of water in the chapel. In 1968 the building was almost entirely destroyed by fire, and it was pulled down in 1970.

The present Congregational Chapel. The site for this was formerly occupied, on the frontage, by two, or possibly three shops. In one of these, in 1855, was Chas. Jackson, tailor, well-known at local entertainments as a comedian and impersonator; in another the sweet shop of 'Marm' Robinson.

The Congregational chapel was built and opened in 1888, at a cost of £2,500, foundation stones having been laid by James Paine and Joseph Wilcox, who contributed most of the money.

Present block of shops and flats east of the Congregational chapel. In 1855 all this property belonged to Geo. May, baker and confectioner, part occupied by himself and part let. In addition to three shops and houses on the frontage there were five cottages in the yard at the back, described as the 'Lodging House Estate'.

Nearest the chapel was Geo. May (probably 1837–1914), next Mrs. Allen, dressmaker, succeeded by Mrs. Impey, greengrocer and sweet shop, and later Geo. Simons, saddler and harness-maker (died 1932). The third shop was occupied in the 1890s by J. Jones, bootmaker, followed in the new century by E. Haynes, bootmaker. Meanwhile some part of the property was, in 1870, used by W. G. Packinson, M.R.C.V.S., veterinary inspector to St. Neots district, and in 1877 by E. M. Ridlington, M.R.C.V.S., before moving to New Street. In 1917, at the death of another Geo. May, the whole property was bought by C. B. Neaverson, and part was used for his butcher's business.

No. 45. This house and shop, with an archway leading to an extensive yard at the back, was at some time faced with brick, but con-

tains within it a timber-framed house with a roof of different pitch.
It was once an inn, and deeds of 1844 refer to it as 'formerly an inn
called *The Dolphin*, and since then *The Crooked Billet*, and now
in the occupation of Wm. Atkinson'.

It was here that Wm. Atkinson (1783-1847), lived and founded
his business, at the age of 61, in 1844. He had been chief clerk to
Rix & Darnell of 18 Market Square. In a leaflet, dated 9 October
1844, he states 'Wm. Atkinson takes this opportunity of informing
his Friends and the Public, that in consequence of Messrs. Rix and
Darnel declining business as Merchants on 31st December next, he
intents to commence at that time, on his own account in the
SPIRIT TRADE and as GENERAL MERCHANTS, on his premises
in the HIGH STREET; and trusts, by his experience in the business (having been with them for 40 years), and keeping good
articles, to merit a share of their Patronage and Support'.

Although dying so soon he left a promising business to his two
sons as partners, William and Frederic, the latter living at this
address. In 1863 Frederic died, at the age of 43, as a result of a
fall from his horse, and is buried in the Baptist cemetery, New
Street. William then moved to the High Street house. In 1868
he bought the wine and spirit business of W. A. Cowley of 28
Market Square, and sometime, probably by 1865, had started a
brickworks at Potton Road, Eynesbury. He died, at the age of
58, in 1873, leaving the business in the hands of his son Arthur
W. Atkinson (1853-1918), then only twenty.

Arthur moved to Brook House, Brook Street, on the death
of Dr. Evans in 1892, and after his death the business was carried
on by his son-in-law, J. R. H. Bedford, who discontinued the brickworks about 1920, but carried on the business of timber and
builders' merchant and wine and spirit merchant. The former part
of the business, and the premises, were sold to C. G. Tebbutt Ltd.
in 1938 and vacated by them in 1966.

No. 47. Present J. Rayns Smith Ltd., wholesale and retail butchers
and pork pie manufacturers. In 1854 this was the site of a shop
kept by Joseph Cox, shoemaker, who also had a china and glass
shop here. He made a Deed of Assignment to his creditors in
1855. In 1876 John Edmund Bingham, cooper, was here. In his
workshop he made all kinds of wooden vessels, bushel measures,
wooden bowls and scoops. He was the son of John Gorham
Bingham (1803-79) of Windmill Row and later Eynesbury (10
Berkeley Street), and it would appear that this shop was a branch
of the Eynesbury business. In 1877, however, the .Eynesbury
premises were sold and the business transferred here.

After the death of J. E. Bingham, in 1879, this shop was kept
by a James Bingham, cooper. He was also a plumber and ironmonger and contractor for fêtes, flower shows, and garden parties.
In 1895 he set up a branch shop at 27 St. Mary's Street, Eynesbury.
The frontage here also included a baker's shop, with a bakehouse
in the yard at the back. In 1832 this was opened by Jeremiah Moss
(1801–89), who had emigrated to America and returned. About
1850 he moved to Russell Street. In 1860 John Andrews, baker
and confectioner, came here from 11 Cambridge Street. T. Andrews,
probably a son, was here in 1912.

In 1930 the premises were sold to A. W. Atkinson Ltd., for use
as an office, and about 1936 resold to J. R. Smith Ltd., to enlarge
their butchers' shop next door.

**The east side of no 47, including the bay window, with gateway
on its east side.** About 1850 this was the *Anchor* inn kept by Thos.
Edey, who was also a butcher. In 1873, at the sale of Wm. Bowyer's
property, it was sold for £210. In 1874, the licence having been
extinguished, it had become an ironmonger's shop kept by H. W.
Pearson, who also advertised 'velocipedes and bicycles for hire'.
Later it was kept by John Pearson, who rebuilt the shop in 1899
and was here until at least 1905.

About 1876, Edmund Pearson, brother of John, set up in the
yard as a coachbuilder, after 18 years' working experience with
Mulliner & Wilson of Northampton. From here he moved to
the Washbank, Eynesbury, and then, in 1887, to the corner of
Huntingdon Street and Avenue Road.

In 1910 John Raynes Smith came here and opened a pork
butcher's shop from which he built up a large and profitable
business as a wholesale and retail butcher and pork pie manufacturer, sending his pies, for the quality of which he became
nationally known, all over the country.

He first started in a little shop at 10 Cambridge Street,
which his wife kept, he himself buying and killing pigs in
a slaughterhouse at the back of the *Rose and Crown* inn (no.
10) opposite, and is said to have borrowed money from the
landlady to buy his first pig. Sometime between 1905 and
1910 he bought the shop and bankrupt pork butcher's business
of S. Wright at 6 Huntingdon Street. With this he acquired
the secret formula for making what he advertised as 'Sly's
Famous Sausages'. For over 50 years the Sly family had been
making sausages, first at Eynesbury (see 48-60 Berkeley Street)
and then on the south side of St. Neots High Street (between
nos. 44 and 56).

No. 49. Present offices of J. R. Smith Ltd. This is the site of one of the old inns of the town, and used to have a full rigged ship depicted on a hanging sign. There is an unchecked reference to *The Shyppe* at St. Neots in 1540, when Richard Brown was landlord, followed by his kinswoman Elizabeth Bentley, and an even earlier one in 1486 (Rentals and Surveys). In 1726 and 1738 the Great North Road Turnpike Trust held meetings here, and there must have been a large room as 52 trustees were present on one occasion. In 1850 and 1890 Jas. Boutell, tailor, was landlord, in 1896 S. Markham, and in 1905 and 1914 W. Peacock. As with most inns, there were cottages in the yard, in this case two. About 1855 John Nottingham, tailor, lived in one of these; he had a club foot and was remembered as having the contract for making the charity suits, in green cloth, for the boys at the Church School nicknamed 'green linnets'.

The other cottage was occupied by John Congo, a negro, well known for his great strength. He worked for Geo. Squire, the Brook Street merchant, and it was said that he could carry two sacks of wheat at a time, equalling 38 stone. He was almost certainly the only non-white in the town and had arrived with an unpronounceable name. Someone had immediately nicknamed him 'Congo', and this thereafter became his name and that of his children.

Present Co-operative Society supermarket. This site had formerly been a range of small shops, pulled down in 1961. Starting from the west:

A. 1823, 1850, Wm. Wiles, shoemaker. 1855 Jos. Wiles, shoemaker. 1864 Josiah Wiles, glass and china shop. 1867, Wagstaff & Turner ditto. 1874 Thos. Paris, barber and tobacconist. He moved here from elsewhere in the town, coming from London in 1867, and was still here in 1914. He had a barber's pole over the shop.

B. In 1855 this shop was occupied by Thos. Newman, cooper. About 1879 the shop was taken by David Smith, greengrocer and fruiterer. He and his wife moved in within a few hours of their wedding, getting the shop ready to open the next day. He was the son of Robt. Smith, chimney-sweep of the south side of High Street. Here in the small house attached to the shop were born their 18 children, of which 12 sons and four daughters lived to become adults. In 1913 he moved to the east side of Huntingdon Street, and was followed by Ernest Harvey, in the same trade, who remained until 1926.

C. This small shop, about 1885, was kept as a fancy shop by a Mrs. Guthrie. She was followed by Edward Haynes, bootmaker. He had a notice displayed in his window which read 'The Devil ruins your Souls, but Ted Haynes mends them'! He was followed by Ernest Chambers, bootmaker, about 1914, and later the shop was added to that next door by Ernest Harvey.

D. The last shop in the row was occupied, about 1855, by Wm. Richards, shoemaker. In 1885 it was taken by Geo. Pack, harness-maker and saddler, who had worked for A. Bowtell of 43 Market Square, for 13 years. He died in 1912.

The present Co-operative Society shop at the corner of High Street and Huntingdon Street.* This building, both historically and architecturally, is one of the most interesting in the town. It was built, probably just after the middle of the 18th century, no doubt as a speculation, by Joseph Eayre, the bellfounder, to become the principal inn in the town. To this end it contained on the second floor an Assembly Room, which still remains with its musicians' gallery at the east end and domed ceiling centre with ornamental plaster work to take a chandelier.

To effect his development J. Eayre bought all the corner property as far along High Street as no. 45, and along Huntingdon Street as far as the *Sun* inn yard. This area was at that time occupied by two properties and four messuages. They included a bakehouse in the occupation of John Bull (probably part of no. 47 High Street), a messuage in occupation of Henry Musgrave (probably also part of no. 47); a barn in occupation of James Bruce, and a dovehouse and garden in occupation of John Bull.

The inn was called *The George*, and appears to have been a financial failure, as an inn, during Joseph Eayre's lifetime. In 1773, a year after he died, it is described by his executors as 'a messuage, lately built by Joseph Eayre as an inn, but now made into seven tenements occupied by John Needham, Maxey King, Rich. Dawson, John Bradley, John Marlow, and Rich. Chattriss'. In 1802, when part of the site on the north was sold to the Methodists, it was described as 'commonly called the George yard'.

Although the building soon ceased to be an inn, the Assembly Room continued to be used, indeed it was the only room of its kind in the town until the Public Rooms were built in 1845. Robson's 1839 *Directory* lists 'Assembly Rooms High St.' under Public establishments, and here all balls, routs, and public meetings would be held. Indeed the author's grandfather addressed a poli-

* See Plate 16

tical meeting here about the middle of the century. The Congregational Chapel Sunday School was also once held here. There is a firm tradition in the town that Wesley preached here on one of his visits to St. Neots. The first of these was on 19 January 1776, when his diary records 'preached in a large room to a numerous congregation'. Other visits were again in 1776, 1778 (twice), 1782, and 1788. A barn in East Street and another in Cambridge Street, also claimed to be his preaching places, do not seem to fit his own description of his 1776 visit.

The building itself has obviously been reconstructed at some time as the west side of the back is built of red brick, and the rest, as far as is visible, in local brick. Some windows on the east side have original sashes with three panes across and four down, and thick sash bars. Furthermore there is no parapet on the roof. All this seems to point to the first half of the 18th century, and one wonders if Joseph Eayre reconstructed rather than built anew. Trade card pictures of the 19th century show a carriage archway on to the High Street just west of the centre of the frontage.

About 1800 the building was bought by Thos. Carpenter (1770-1833) grocer, he himself occupying 'a shop, and house with two parlours and chambers over'. He took his son, William (1807-62) into partnership, and was succeeded by him. He is buried in the Baptist cemetery, New Street.

William was followed by his son, Langley Carpenter (1836-89). By this time the business was one of the leading grocers in the town, advertising as wholesale and family grocers, tea dealers, provision, wine, spirit, ale and porter merchants. A barn opposite, on the side of the present Salvation Army Citadel, was used as an extra store and stables for two horses and delivery carts. As early as 1871 the shop was advertising tinned meat, 7lb. tins of beef and mutton at 3s. 6d. each.

Langley Carpenter was regarded as a dashing wealthy young man, and at one time caused a minor sensation by driving a pair of pure cream ponies. He was appointed a Town Commissioner in 1871. He retired in 1885, and the business was put up for sale in the Assembly Room. The shop and business was then taken by Joseph Henry Kinsley, being known, until 1889, as Kinsley & Carpenter.

In 1892 Kinsley sold the business to Richard Freeman, who moved here from Church Street. He sold the premises to the St. Neots Co-operative Society in 1913. Their principal shop had previously been at the corner of Huntingdon Street and Avenue Road. At the same time R. Freeman moved his grocer's shop to the diagonally opposite corner of the cross.

HIGH STREET, SOUTH SIDE

No. 64. The present Salvation Army Citadel. Before the present building there was an old barn here, with whitewashed stud and mud walls. It was used by L. Carpenter, of the grocer's shop opposite, as a store and stables for his two horses and delivery carts with an entrance in Church Street. In 1886 the Local Board served a notice on the owner that it was a dangerous building, and in 1888 the site was sold for £140, with a condition to pull down the building.

Previous to this part of the buildings had been used as the town night watchmen's hut. From here the watchmen patrolled the streets during the night, calling the hours. They were on duty at St. Neots from 10 p.m. to 5 a.m. and cried the hours of 11 p.m., 1 a.m., and 3 a.m. Each man carried a staff, handcuffs, and keys of the lockup (at 14 High Street). County police were appointed in 1849 and 'watching' ceased about 1856. The Salvation Army Citadel was built on the site in 1891.

No. 62. Present National Health Service office. There was formerly a private house here, probably the family home of the well-to-do Musgrove family. It was described as having seven bedrooms, dining and drawing rooms, entrance hall and cellar. Later it became the home of Miss Harriet Cole (1800–76), who is buried in the Congregational Old Meeting cemetery.

At her death it was bought by Edward Squire, postmaster, who then moved here from the east side of the Market Square, making this the town post office for 14 years. Edward Squire, a relation of the Brook Street Squires, was a well-known character, took part in many local affairs, and was a member of the Local Board. A.C. remembers him as having a somewhat irascible, overbearing and autocratic manner, and a strong objection to persons smoking in the post office. On one occasion a gentleman riding by on horseback dismounted and entered the post office smoking a cigar. Mr. Squire immediately exclaimed 'no smoking in here, put that cigar out'. The gentleman took no notice but handed him his card. It was the Duke of Norfolk, Post Master General in Gladstone's government. He was staying at Kimbolton Castle, and following his habit of visiting local post offices to see how they were operating. The postmaster was never able to live this one down!

G.H. recalled that from here, every night at 8 p.m., 'Billy' Worboys left with the mail cart for Cambridge, returning each morning at 8 a.m., with the Eastern Counties mail. This he did seven days a week, all the year round, and in all weathers, perched up unprotected from weather, on the box. The letters were carried in a locked box painted bright red. Another cart took parcels to Henlow. Many stories were told of hold-ups by highwaymen and upsets in snowdrifts.

In 1887, a year before he retired at the age of 71, Edward Squire gave a dinner to his staff of 23. He had then been post master for 25 years, and he recalled that in his predecessor's time men on horseback, with satchels on their backs, delivered all the letters in the rural area. Now, he said, 17,000 letters pass through St. Neots post office each week.

Mrs. K. Smith of Eaton Socon told the author that her grandfather was a postman who rode each day to Kimbolton. On one occasion his horse took fright on St. Neots bridge and jumped the then low parapet into the river. In the fall he became separated from the horse, but was rescued, and the horse swam ashore.

In 1890 the post office moved to 36 Market Square, and the premises were bought by John Franks for £580. He moved his furniture business here from 7 Market Square calling it 'The Domestic Stores'. He also later bought the old property to the west, converting it into a large shop, and for a time occupied both properties. However in 1898 this property was either let or sold to Frank Russell Stevens, draper, who was followed early in the new century by Horace Clarabut, draper. He moved to 32 Market Square in 1909, and the shop was once again taken over by J. Franks. About 1918 the property was bought by St. Neots U.D.C. for use as a meeting room and offices.

Nos. 60, 58. Present Brittains Ltd. Before the acquisition of this property by J. Franks, about 1893, the site was occupied by about five small houses, most of them used as shops, often just using the front room, with no special shop window. Starting at the east:

A. In 1882 this house was bought by Geo. Bower, of the Vulcan Iron Works. At his expense it was converted for use as a Working Men's club. The frontage however was detached and let as a shop, which in 1883 was occupied by a Mr. Burdin, fishmonger and poulterer. The club ran very successfully for a number of years, and at the annual meeting in 1894 the chairman, Mr. G. Bower, suggested that as the great majority of members were Conservatives, it should become a Conservative or Constitutional Club, possibly on new premises. In 1895 a Constitutional Club was formed to amalgamate with the Working Men's club, and premises were bought in New Street where the club is still housed.

B. The next shop was an old butcher's premises occupied in 1745 by Wenham Smith, followed by his son, Roger, who was there until 1781, and he by his son James who was there in 1840. In 1854 it was occupied by Samuel Barnes, butcher and farmer, who was followed by his son Thomas, who was here in 1868. In 1868 Thos. Rolph, butcher, was here. About 1871 Robert Bonham, butcher, came here, in partnership with his brother, moving to 56 High Street in 1884. They were followed by Geo. 'Ferrety' Sharman, fishmonger, who cured kippers and bloaters on the premises. In 1893 he left for 10 St. Mary's Street, Eynesbury.

C. This shop, in 1872, was occupied by Alfred Carr, fishmonger. G.H. recalled that he used to walk round the town and neighbouring villages, with a 'skip' (basket) carried on his back, selling herrings, bloaters and rabbits. Often he had these strung on a stick, one on each shoulder, and would call in the streets 'Rabbit and Herring-O'. So penetrating was his voice that it was said that he could be heard in Eynesbury when calling in Wyboston! He was a notorious poacher and rough character. In 1876 he was convicted of poaching with a running dog, and stealing sheep skins. In 1883 he was again in trouble for stealing cigars from the *Bear* inn, Church Street, and in the same year given 18 months' imprisonment for assaulting a gamekeeper at Weald.

All the above properties were bought by J. Franks and pulled down to build his new shop, which he opened in 1897. In 1918 the shop and business was bought by a Grantham firm named Hall, and, about 1922, by Frank Brittain, who moved here from 25 High Street.

No. 56. Present shop W. Bonham & Sons, butchers. Early in the century this was the butcher's shop of Jesse Chessum (1790-1864), pork butcher and mealman, who had his slaughter-house in the *Royal Oak* inn yard. 'T' refers to him, about 1825, as hiring 'Professor' King, the Town Crier, to advertise his 'spare ribs, loin bones and pork steaks'.

He was followed, about 1876, by Dalzell & Son, grocers. In 1877 father and son dissolved the partnership, John Dalzell senr. (1809-80) remaining here, and his son John setting up a rival shop at 25 High Street. J. Dalzell senr. also had a shop at the corner of Huntingdon Street and Russell Street. He was one of the pioneers of the Early Closing Movement, and in 1870 announced his intention to close his shop every evening at 7 p.m. except on Saturdays.

In 1884 the shop was taken by Robert Bonham (1839–1900), who moved from a few doors further east.

Nos. 54–46. A range of newly-built shops and flats, built about 1954, and replacing a row of old houses, shops, a 'yard' and an inn. They included the *Dew-Drop* inn (*Hist. Mon. Comm.*, no. 19). This old inn with its rather curious punning name dated back to the 17th century, at least, and had a cottage in the yard at the back. Landlords included: 1870, Jas. Gray; 1888, Mrs. Walters; 1893, Thos. Caress; 1895, Alfred Churchyard and Rebecca Jones; 1898, Wm. Clerk and Arthur Mears; 1899, W. F. Lummock.

Next was a small shop kept by Mrs. Mary Sly (1794/6–1869), sausage-maker and pork butcher, who came here about the middle of the century, from one of the terrace 48–70 Berkeley Street, Eynesbury, and using the bakehouse in the yard at the back. Her husband was probably Saml. Sly (1788–1850), a thatcher. As a widow she carried on the business with the help of her daughter, Mary Anne Sly (1831–90). It is not clear when the Sly secret home-made sausage recipe began to achieve a more than local fame, but certainly in the last quarter of the century they were known over a wide area for excellence of quality and flavour, and in or over the shop was displayed 'Patronised by H.M. Attorney General' (Sir John Karslake). After the death of Mary Anne Sly, the business was carried on by Lucy Sly (1817-93), and then the recipe was inherited by a nephew-in-law, S. Wright, pork butcher of Huntingdon Street. In a few years he failed in business and sold the famous recipe to J. R. Smith, then developing his successful St. Neots business.

Next in a cottage lived Robt. Smith, chimney-sweep and soot merchant, who moved here in 1887 from a cottage in the yard of the Wesleyan chapel, Huntingdon Street. He was probably a descendant of Robt. Smith, chimney-sweep, who came from Hemingford Grey to live at St. Neots in 1757.

Next was a glass and china shop kept by Geo. Ebbutt, (1809-77) who was also a painter and glazier. He was followed by his son E. B. Ebbutt. The next occupier of the shop was H. Pearson, watchmaker and jeweller, who married the widow of E. B. Ebbutt. He succeeded his father as a verger, sexton and sidesman at the parish church. In 1897, however, he was convicted of stealing money from the collection and dismissed. He was said often to slip out of church by the south chapel door, during the sermon, to get a drink at the *Woolpack*. His wife had contracts for bead work, and in 1890 was advertising for bead workers.

No. 44. Present 'Tobacco Box'. (Part remaining of *Hist. Mon. Comm.*, no. 18). In 1858 and 1864 it was the shop of Saml. Day, grocer. In 1880-90 it was kept by Arthur Lee, tobacconist, also plumber and glazier, and probably son of Wm. Lee of part of the *Old Falcon*, Market Square.

Lees Yard. A court of three or four miserable two-room cottages at the back of the above, pulled down in 1962. About 1860-70 it was known as Day's Yard, and Chas. Tokens, the last survivor of the town watchmen, lived here.

No. 42. Present Freeman Bros., watchmakers and jewellers. (*Hist. Mon. Comm.*, no. 17). As restored by Freeman Bros., this is now the most interesting medieval-type house in the town, and possibly dates back to the late 15th century. When it was restored in 1958 the apparent brick-faced front was found to contain a timber-framed and jettied upper storey covered by 'Mathematical tiles' to simulate bricks. Wheatsheaf-design carving on the jetty and brackets are similar to those on a restored house east of the church at Southoe. From the strength and arrangement of the oak timbers at the west end it would appear likely that the house once extended further west, and may have had an archway under it through which ran Church Walk. The medieval wood window, set in the east wall, came from the medieval house at 9 South Street, pulled down in 1953.

In 1803 this property was bought by some St. Neots inhabitants for the use of the Charity School, the headmaster living in this house, and a schoolhouse built on land at the back. This latter was replaced in 1883 by the recently abandoned Church School buildings (see chapters on Schools).

Church Walk or Path. Before 1890 this was always called Church Lane. As now, there were a number of small cottages built along the west side as far as the churchyard. A.C. remembered that about 1860-70 the occupants in order were as follows. In the second cottage was 'Dutchman' Silby, who had a costermonger's cart drawn by a donkey, named 'Lady Flycatcher'. With this he toured the countryside selling Yarmouth bloaters and rabbits, and collecting rabbit skins, rags, bones, and other junk, which he disposed of at Cliff & Carter, scrap merchants, 24 High Street.

Next came 'Jonny' Wooten. He owned a box mangle, and on Tuesdays housewives would come with baskets of linen to be mangled at the rate of 2d. a basket. He also had a hand water cart, consisting of a large barrel, painted red, lying on its side in a frame, mounted on a pair of wheels and with shaft handles.

Water was drawn from a spigot at the back. Before the Public Rooms were built he would fill his barrel by means of a pail alongside the bridge, afterwards from Hen Brook in Cemetery Lane. This he took round the town, selling the soft water for washing purposes at 1d. a 'gate', a 'gate' being two pails full. He wore a fustian suit and a peaked cloth cap. Wet weather with everyone's water-butt full meant lean times for Jonny, but in long dry spells he was in great demand, due to the extreme hardness of well water in the town. Described as 'a happy and contented, if poor, man' he was not spared by the press, who apparently did not think it bad taste to write the following satirical account of his wedding to Miss Mary Ann Daysley on 16 May 1870.

Marriage in High Life

Immense numbers of people assembled in the High Street and Church Lane to witness the wedding procession of Jonny Wooten, a noted inhabitant of the town, fallen victim to the snares of Cupid for the second time in a chequered life. The happy pair left John's residence, Watercart Villa, at 10 a.m., escorted by two policemen. Both bride and bridegroom were faultlessly attired, the former carrying a magnificent bouquet of wall flowers and cowslips. The Church was crowded in every part where a glimpse of the ceremony could be obtained. John caused a titter at its close by tugging his venerable white forelock to worthies nearby. As they emerged from the sacred edifice bells set up a merry peal, their joyous clamour being supplemented by boisterous cheers from the spectators.

On arrival home the newly-married pair, with their friends, partook of a sumptuous dejeuner of bread, cheese, and tea. The free hearted host apologised for the absence of more substantial viands, from the fact of his having depended upon the promises of certain individuals, who at the last moment have been unaccountably seized with loss of memory.

A booth was erected in the yard of an adjoining inn, during the afternoon, and dancing was kept up to a late hour, the whole being wound up by the loving couple's window getting smashed'.

It is sad to have to record that on March 1871 the Town Crier was announcing that Jonny would not be responsible for his wife's debts.

In the next house was 'Crump' Lovitt, driver of the Kimbolton Mail. He left each day at 8 p.m., arriving back at 4 a.m. next day. The rest of the day he spent as assistant to a fishmonger. Next to him was Mr. Davison, cabinet-maker and upholsterer. Then came Thos. Clarke, a travelling butcher who was called to farms and cottages in the district to kill, and help prepare, pigs for the owners. In the next house lived John Dalzell senr., whose shop was at 56 High Street.

Present shop at the north-west corner of Church Walk. This was previously the site of two small houses.

A. The home and business premises of the Snowdon family, rope-makers, of which there seems to have been at least three generations, and probably preceded here by Eliza. Gray, ropemaker (1830). John Snowdon was here in 1854, Edward in 1860-70, and John 1885-90. They had a ropewalk in Priory Road near the Wesleyan School, but the last Snowdon became a merchant, selling the products of his son's factory at Peterborough, and left the town in 1898.

B. Here lived Chas. Richardson (1824-1903), Town Crier. When performing his duties he wore a top hat, and of course carried his bell. Besides making public announcements he could be hired to advertise such events as auction sales and even shopkeepers' goods.

He had succeeded, in the office, John Robinson, and before him, about mid-century, was Thos. 'Professor' King. About 1820 there was a John King, Crier, possibly the former's father.

About 1898 the two premises were pulled down and a new shop built for Robert Scott & Co., clothiers, who were here until about 1910. They were followed by Machin's Music shop.

The *Royal Oak* Hotel. The present hotel was probably built in 1885 by R. Sherman, to replace a much smaller inn, of which the earliest reference found was in 1809. Before the rebuilding it had a shop window on the west side, used as a wine shop and off-licence.

Landlords included: 1809 Wm. Simpson, 1823, 1830 Chas. Warner, 1850, 1858 Ebenezer King, 1864 Thos. Chapman, who left in 1875, followed by Richard (Dickie) Sherman (1837-1924), who probably built the present hotel. He was followed by W. R. Ennals (1840-98), and after his death by his wife. In 1907 there was A. H. Bond, then T. Rouse, and 1910-14, H. L. Whitehead, who emigrated to Australia.

The *Royal Oak* Yard. In this yard were six cottages as well as a butcher's stables and slaughter-house, belonging to the Chessum family; indeed it was often called Chessum's Yard. They were here from at least 1830 to 1876, and had their shop at 56 High Street.

The next two shops, nos. 38 and 36, occupy the site of three shops bought by Chas. Wren, about 1904-7, and pulled down. Each was a dwelling house, that next to the *Royal Oak* having, on the frontage, only a door and window, and the other two, a door with a window on each side.

A. Here was Wm. Shaw (1809-94), cutler and scissor-grinder. He came here from Mildenhall, Suffolk, and later moved to 29 Market

Square. Afterwards it was opened as a bicycle shop by Mr. Murkitt, who later moved to 33 Market Square, and thus founded the present motor engineers at Bedford and Huntingdon.

B. At the end of the century this shop was occupied by R. Pinnock, watchmaker.

C. In 1850 and about 1870, this was a toy shop, kept by Job Smith, who was also a tailor. On Thursdays he minded a confectionary stall on the market for Plum's shop (31 High Street).

About 1877 a remarkable immigrant to the town set up business here as a pork butcher. This was John Kurr, a German who had previously traded under the name of G. Rothernel. He soon made a name for himself for his pork products, and became widely known. An expanding business and careful saving earned him enough money to invest in building seven houses in Avenue Road. He was followed, in 1900, by E. E. Mortimer, and in the same year by W. Corby, both in the same trade. The latter remained until 1908. Behind the property was Kidman's Yard.

This was one of the 'yards' in the town which were really small square courtyards of tiny cottages lying behind a rather larger house on the frontage in which the owner lived, or had lived, and who usually gave his name to the yard. The entrance was often under an archway, and in the yard would be a communal pump. They usually became slum property, and even in the 19th century the owners were being continually urged by the health authorities to improve conditions.

This yard was probably owned by several generations of Kidmans, as it had this name about 1820, and between 1871 and 1888 there was a Wm. Kidman, baker and muffin-maker, who probably lived here. 'T', remembering back to about 1820, states that in this yard lived Nanny Izzard, the reputed Great Paxton witch, who came here after being driven away from that village by persecution. Apparently she did not entirely escape it here, as he said that he had often seen her cruelly treated. A number of Great Paxton inhabitants were sent to prison for violent assaults on her. One or more of her supposed charms was in the Cotswold Witch Museum at Bourton-on-the-Water. Even in the time of the author's childhood children were told that if they went to Potton Corner (Grid. ref. TL. 204558) at midnight they would see Nanny Izzard riding on a broomstick.

After the three old shops and Kidman's Yard were pulled down they were rebuilt, as two shops, by the owner, Chas. Wren, fishmonger. He had come to the town from Biggleswade in 1895-8, and opened a small shop in South Street, attached to the *Bell* inn, of which he was landlord. From here he developed a prosperous business from stalls in the surrounding markets.

No. 8. Present H. Mortimer, butcher. This new shop was opened as a pork butcher's, by C. Wren, in 1909, under the management of C. B. Neaverson (1889-1967) of Peakirk, who later was in business on his own account at 40 and 41 High Street for 45 years. In 1911 the shop was taken by J. S. Mortimer, butcher, who came here from 11 St. Mary's Street, Eynesbury, and had moved there from Shefford in 1904.

No. 36. This new shop was first opened by C. Wren, and has remained in the family ever since.

No. 32. At the west corner of Windmill Row. This was an ironmonger's shop for nearly 150 years. Beside the shop there was the owner's six-room dwelling-house, yard, warehouses, blacksmith's shop, and two cottages. Part of the above was behind the next property to the west, later incorporated. In 1830 it was the business of John Claxton, who was here until 1859. In that year it was taken over by Philip R. Wallis, who was also a Town Commissioner. On 1 January 1870 it was transferred to John Lynn, who died in 1911. He fought a bitter fight with the Local Board on the issue of the rights of shopkeepers to display goods for sale on the pavement outside their shops. Finally, in 1890 he was prosecuted for obstructing the highway. He vigorously defended the action, citing many other shopkeepers who habitually did the same. A subscription was raised among shopkeepers to pay his defence costs, but he was eventually convicted and fined 6d. Although it did not appear to have been used by the defence, one wonders if High Street shopkeepers did not have traditional rights on what was once an extension of the market area.

John Lynn was followed by his son Howard (*c.*1880-1964), who modernised the business, but it came to an end, two years after his death, under his son John.

No. 30. Now added to No. 32, above, but formerly a separate shop. In 1839 this was the premises of John Elger, hairdresser and perfumier, who was here until he retired about 1880 (he died in 1897). He also sold toys, kept a Servants' Registry Office, and let a room to a visiting dentist. At the back of the shop on the ground floor was a large room fitted out as a Billiard Saloon, that could be hired, and had an unobtrusive entrance from Windmill Row. It was considered slightly disreputable and was used by young Victorian 'bloods' on Sunday. After Elger retired it was taken over by John Lynn, to add to his shop next door.

No. 28. This shop, kept in the 1870s by Jabez Whiting, was especially remembered, by those who knew it as children, for the remarkable variety of goods sold. The chief stock consisted of haberdashery, hosiery, hats, cheap jewellery, and second-hand clothing. Much advertised was 'Tippers Mystery', a panacea medicine for all the ills of horses, cattle, sheep, pigs, and poultry. Special items were bird cages and mousetraps made by Mr. Whiting. His super mousetrap had six entry holes, and when the trap was sprung a metal spike went neatly through the head of the mouse. He died about 1893, and his widow carried on the shop until her death in 1897.

The old shop was then pulled down, and a new shop built by the owner, Geo. Abraham. The design was much admired at the time, and it was considered an architectural ornament to the High Street. It was let to F. G. Riseley, draper, who moved here from New Street (next to the Police Station) in 1899, and named it Manchester House. After his death his family, all keen supporters of the Congregational chapel, carried on the business until 1957.

No. 28. The Yard. Here, between 1894 and 1897, Edward (Teddy) Ireland, founder of the present New Street firm, started his motor business. He had been a foreman at G. Bower's Vulcan Iron Works, and when they finally closed down was living at 22 Brook Street. Here he started letting out and repairing bicycles, and then moved to these premises in High Street with a shop at no. 24. From making bicycles, (his model was called 'Defiance', and said to cost £20), he went on to making motor-car engines and chassis. In 1905 he was advertising Pratts and Carless petrol, and in 1907 was agent for Panhards, Stars, Darracques, Renaults, and De Dion motor cars. The firm moved to New Street about 1917.

No. 26. This was formerly two properties, one of which was a private house. The other was a greengrocer's shop, kept, in 1890, by Frank E. Brightman, and early this century by C. J. Ibbett.

No. 24. In 1864 a business was started here by Cliff & Carter, general merchants, marine stores, and scrap merchants. The manager and partner was Wm. Carter, from Peterborough, who had married his employer's daughter, and been made a partner. The partnership was dissolved in 1875, and the business name changed to Wm. Carter. At that date he took over the frontage shop of 20 High Street, having, from the beginning, hired the yard at the back, and left these premises. He was a highly-respected man, a keen cricketer, and original member of the Local Board.

The next occupant of the front shop was probably E. W. Frost, hairdresser, followed, in 1880, by Mr. Forscutt, boot and shoe-maker, and later by Edward Ireland, who used it as a bicycle shop.

No. 22. This was once an inn, *The Cock*, or alternatively *The Fighting Cocks*, and the present brick face conceals an early timber-framed building. During alterations, made in the 1920s, a 17th-century rapier blade stamped 'Solengen', was found concealed in a wall.

In 1809 the landlord was Rich. Franklin, who followed Thos. Hall. In 1814 it was divided into two tenements. The property is described then as having an orchard, and as extending from the street on the north to the brook on the south. It was in the occupa-tion of Thos. Jaques and Sam. Berrell. In 1833 it was in the occupation of James Bull and John Carr. In 1850 a Jas. Bull, boot-maker was still there, and in 1857 it was J. & A. Bull, bootmakers.

In 1858 the premises were in use by I. S. Hall & Son, corn chandlers, followed in the same trade by James B. Tyler, in 1870. He was followed by Thos. Wady, who was here in 1873 and 1881, and came from Brampton. In 1883 W. Bennett, baker and corn chandler, was here. In 1885 came Walter Edward Davies, tailor and later foreman to T. C. Fyson, of 37 Market Square. He also started a restaurant on the premises, and frequently worded part of his advertisement in the local weekly press in Welsh. He was here in 1899, and was followed by Geo. Abraham, butcher.

No. 20. These large premises, with a wide frontage on the street, and extensive warehouse and yard space at the back, had, at dif-ferent times, two separate occupants on the frontage and another at the back. There was also, until it was extinguished in 1963, a private right of way for pedestrians and vehicles through to the High Street, for the occupants of Brook House, in Brook Street, and for pedestrians only from four cottages in Walnut Tree Square. By 1809, part of the frontage was owned by Wm. Fox, who had a bookseller's shop here, and the yard was let by him to Thos. Wells of Bedford, basket and rush mat maker. Wells got his supplies from the Flagholm osier beds, north of the Common, which he hired from the Earl of Sandwich.

In 1823 Thos. Wells was still using at least part of the yard, and the frontage (or part of it) was a grocer's shop, kept by Adam Bailey from Diddington, who had bought the whole property, the yard being known as Bailey's Yard. About 1833 Adam Bailey seems to have given up the shop, but retained the property. The frontage was definitely now in two parts. One was a fishmonger's shop, and the other became a beer-house called *The Horse and Dray*, to which was probably attached a brewhouse in the yard. The beerhouse was still there in 1858, when Wm. Greaves was landlord.

In 1856 Elizabeth and John Bailey, children of Adam Bailey, re-established their family grocery business in what must have been the fishmonger's shop, but in 1863 the Baileys sold their property to James Warren, shoemaker, who let the yard to Cliff & Carter, scrap merchants, of 24 High Street.

In 1867 a fire destroyed the old brewhouse and part of the stock. In 1875, when Cliff & Carter dissolved partnership, Wm. Carter bought the whole property and the frontage was rebuilt as a hardware shop. In 1888 part of the yard was being used as a slaughter-house by G. Moss Abraham. This business was taken over by Frederick Chas. Larkinson of Biggleswade in 1907, adding wholesale grocery to his trade, and was run by members of the family until 1963. It was here, in 1905, that the famous 'Bunyan's Anvil' was discovered among scrap iron by a labourer A. W. Rowlett, nicknamed 'Doctor' on account of his sideline as a herbalist. Another of Rowlett's sidelines was dealing in antiques and he had previously spotted the anvil among a load of scrap iron in the yard of a house in Brook St. (see no. 23). It had probably originated from the ironmonger's business at 26 Market Square (see *Bedfordshire Times* 26 Dec. 1924). Rowlett sold the anvil to John Beagarie (see no. 7, Market Square) who was said to have later made a large sum from its sale. Many people believed it to have been a fake made by Rowlett, but this seems unlikely. The object itself is a tinker's anvil and is crudely inscribed on three of its sides as follows: 'J. BUNYAN', 'HELSTOW', '1647'.*

The Chapel in the Yard. In 1827 there was a split in the Independents (Congregational), using the Old Meeting, High Street, and Stephen Dobson the minister, with a part of the congregation, separated and formed a new sect. They bought space in this yard and built a chapel here, Dobson becoming its minister in 1831. However in a few years the chapel closed, and in 1844 a committee, formed from the Baptists, Wesleyans, and Independents, opened a British School here. This carried on until 1862, children from Eynesbury using the private path from Brook Street.

The building, pulled down about 1968 after long use as a warehouse, measured, outside, 40 feet by 32 feet. Inside it was planned somewhat like the Old Meeting. The pulpit was at the

* See plate 24

west end and along the east end was a gallery with a staircase at each end.

The *New Inn* **Hotel.** This old inn, once a posting house, had extensive premises at the back which included stabling, a malting, seven grain shops, and a large yard. In 1870-72 Owen Saunders advertised clipping and singeing horses in the yard, in 1880 Alfred Jordan hired the malting and took orders for malting barley, and in 1890 S. V. Ekins held here his first publicly-advertised sale of 'a choice herd of dairy cows'.

Landlords were: 1792 Wm. Adkin, 1809 Mary Adkin, 1823, 1839 John Adkin, who was also a turner and chair-maker. 1850, 1862 Thos. Franklin, 1872 Mrs. Emery. In 1876, she transferred to her son Chas. Emery (1855-84); 1885 Geo. Bradshaw. In 1892 the posting business was sold to Alfred Boutall (see 43 Market Square). In 1893 the landlord was J. W. Ince, in 1895 D. Hancock, in 1897 Alfred Boutall, in 1902 Alfred Hartop. In 1908 much of the inn was rebuilt.

Next to the inn on the west, and now a hairdressing saloon, was the *New Inn* Tap, and ostlers' house. Here, in the 19th century, working men, who were not welcomed in the inn, were served with beer. It was a hairdresser's shop in 1911, kept by A. E. Wiles.

No. 14. At present two properties (*Hunts. Post* office, and the 'Salad Bowl'). This was the site of the parish lock-up or cage, which was in use until the police station was built in New Street about 1863. It was then turned into a fire-engine house, and the ·manual fire-engine was kept there. For the previous 20 years it had been housed in part of the Town Commissioners' New Rooms in New Street. In 1888 the Local Board built·a new engine house in the *Dog and Duck* yard, at Eynesbury, and sold these premises to Geo. Moss Abraham for £160. He built a new butcher's shop, using part of the yard of 20 High Street as a slaughterhouse, and was here until at least 1914.

Nos. 12, 10. At present two shops. In 1809 Eliza. King had a shop here described as 'next the prison'. In 1830 the site was occupied by the Oliver family, who in 1848 bought it from the Earl of Sandwich, as part of the whole corner block to South Street. There was a Silvester Olyver in St. Neots in 1568, a Matthew Oliver in 1685, and a Henry Oliver in 1752, both the latter being churchwardens. On this part of that site was a house and butcher's shop, occupied by Joseph Oliver, with a wide entrance on the east leading to a yard at the back, common to this and the corner property. He was still here in 1851.

In 1870 Thos. Ekins, cabinet-maker, was here and in 1883 it was a furniture and upholstery shop kept by Ekins & Son. About 1889 the firm was Ekins & Barker, and in 1890 A. W. Barker, who also had a draper's shop opposite at no. 3. In 1889 some upper rooms in this property, to which there was access by a stair from the High Street, were used as club rooms by the 'St. Neots Liberal and Radical Association', newly refounded from the original association formed in 1884. G.H. recalled an election time when election 'ladders' were put up here, on the High Street frontage. The election results were then spread over a week or so, and Gladstone and Salisbury gradually and excitingly climbed up their opposing ladders.

In 1896 the Liberal Club moved round the corner into South Street, and the premises were taken by James Phillips, photographer, who moved here from Cambridge Street, where his business premises were a wooden hut on the site of the present Cambridge Gardens estate. Part of the frontage was used for a short time by a Mr. Smith, grocer, before Phillips occupied the whole. In 1910 E. Albone (1883-1968) came as manager to Phillips, and took over the business in 1920, and at the same time the frontage was made into two shops.

The Corn Exchange or Pavilion Cinema, (pulled down in 1970). Before the late building was built in 1863, this corner site had, facing the High Street, an old timber-framed double cross winged house, probably of the 16th century or earlier, and to which had been added a separate house on the east, with a common yard at the back. This was probably the family home of the Oliver family, who lived in the town in the 16th century (see above). Until sold in 1848 the house itself belonged to the Earl of Sandwich, which probably means that it had been Priory property. Occupying such an important position in the town it could well have been built for an important Priory lay official, or wealthy merchant.

Living here in 1823 and 1830 was Joseph Oliver, linen and woollen draper, and lace dealer. In 1848, when the property was sold by the Earl of Sandwich, a Joseph Oliver, almost certainly son of the above, bought the corner house for £600, and the adjoining one, where his son Joseph junr. had a butcher's business, for £350. He is described as a cabinet-maker, upholsterer, and furniture dealer. He died in 1855, and was stated to have been 40 years in the business. In the same year his son Frederic died aged 35. He was also an upholsterer, and no doubt intended to carry on the business. Altogether he had nine children, one married James Paine junr. in 1856, and another Elizabeth (1829-1912),

kept Prospect House School, 34 New Street, originally built by
her father for her sister Anne, who married a Mr. Adkins. A son,
Francis, seems to have taken on the business after 1855, and until
1862, when the whole site was sold.

In 1862 the old Oliver house on the corner, together with the
house of Lewis the blacksmith, next to it in South Street, was
bought and pulled down by the newly-formed Corn Exchange
Co. The company had been formed to build a Corn Exchange in
St. Neots, and the money was subscribed by local businessmen in
exchange for £10 shares.

Designs for the building were prepared by Bellamy & Hardy,
architects, of Lincoln. They provided for a large room on the
ground floor where, on market day, millers and merchants had
portable desks and stands, and farmers met to sell their produce,
buy seed and manures, and talk with fellow farmers. The room
was also designed to be used for public and private balls and
dances, concerts and plays, both by local and professional companies. Subsequently auction sales and sittings of the County Court
were held here, and it was stated to seat 700. The upper floor was
approached by a flight of winding stone stairs, and consisted of a
large room which was at once furnished by the Literary Institute
as a reading room, where books, newspapers, and magazines were
available to subscribing members.

The contract for the building was given to Mr. Wildman, of the
Washbank, Eynesbury, for £4,000 and he is said to have gone
bankrupt in fulfilling it. In 1876 the newly-formed Local Board
held their meetings in the reading room. In 1887 Dr. J. J. Evans,
of Brook House, Brook Street, offered to the Local Board his
lifelong collection of natural history and other specimens. This
they refused on the grounds of a lack of statutory powers, but
it was eventually accepted by the Literary Institute after an offer
had been made for it by Huntingdon Literary Institute, and opened
as part of the 1887 Jubilee celebration. The collection was displayed
on all the wall space not occupied by books, and overflowed on to
the staircase. It included 240 cases of stuffed birds, 15 stuffed
monkeys, and two stuffed crocodiles. Besides these there were
glass cases with mineralogical and geological specimens, and archaeological finds from Eynesbury and, the Avenue Road
Saxon cemetery. The author remembers, as a small boy, a rather
gruesome human skeleton, mounted standing upright, that one
met on the wall of the staircase.

For 25 years the establishment was a success, five per cent was
paid on the shares, and in 1889 they were selling at 15s. premium.
After 1890, however, profits declined and in 1892, although a divi-

dend of four per cent was paid, shares were being sold at £3, a drop from £10 15s. in 1889. It is said that they finally were only worth 2s. 6d.

The museum too was initially very popular. In its first half year it was visited by 5,197 people, and by 1889 the total had risen to 7,488. In 1893, however, the Literary Institute was appealing for funds to support the museum, and obviously finding it a burden on its resources. The Institute struggled on to the early years of this century, until declining membership obliged it to close in 1910. The Urban District Council then took over the museum, but, having no place to display it, the cases were put into store, and, after being moved several times, many disintegrated and the glass was broken. Labels also became detached from specimens. Finally the author was able to arrange for some of the rarest and finest of the stuffed bird cases to go to the British Museum (Natural History), and a few of the others, together with all the local archaeological specimens, to the Norris Museum, St. Ives. Stuffed animals are now, fortunately, out of fashion, but some of the cases, done by a local taxidermist, W. Chamberlain of Russell Street, were works of art of the highest order.

Part of the 1887 Jubilee celebrations was the collection, by Geo. Flawn, of £64 to provide a public clock, to be placed on the Corn Exchange, by Jennens & Son of Clerkenwell. Gas burners were provided to illuminate it at night, automatically controlled by the clock. The hours were struck by a bell, with an F sharp note, placed in the turret of the main building. It was ceremonially unveiled by Geo. Flawn, standing on a ladder, with the Rushden Town Band in attendance. Besides other local events, such as amateur concerts, balls (it had a fine polished maple floor), flower shows and auction sales, many touring theatre companies played in the hall. *Maria Marten* and *East Lynn* always drew crowds at 1s. for seats and 6d. standing room.

In 1900 the company was still paying three and three quarter per cent, but in 1915 they sold the building to C. A. James, landlord of the *Bridge* Hotel, who opened it as a cinema. The main hall was however unaltered, and could still be hired for its traditional purposes, and was used as a Corn Exchange on Thursdays. In 1929 a fire destroyed much of the interior, and the ornamental turret fell. It was then rebuilt as the Pavilion Cinema, with a gallery, and could no longer be used for most of its former functions. The cinema itself closed in 1968.

WINDMILL ROW

This long but narrow street on the south side of the High Street reaches nearly back to Brook Street, but there does not ever seem to have been a right of way through. There seems little doubt that it was a development of James Tristham (or Trustham), a retired miller, who invested his savings in building the property, keeping one house for himself. He had owned, and worked, the windmill that once stood on Paxton Hill, (near the site of the present R.D.C. reservoir), and was not demolished until 1870. He also owned the Little Paxton windmill which stood beside the hauling way just south of the paper mill lock. Mill Cottage still stands at the site. James Tristham, however, retired early in the 19th century, appropriately naming his new development Windmill Row. He was alive in 1835, when he sold some of the property there. In 1962 a trench was dug along the north end of the Row to replace a damaged gas main. In the course of this a lead 'Bulla' (Papal Bull) of Innocent III (1243-57) was found (see *Serafina* vol. 1, p. 29, no. 1, plates 1-6). It is now in the Norris Museum, St. Ives.

From the beginning the Row seems to have been the abode of small tradesmen, whose actual houses cannot now be identified, and probably also had a beerhouse.

Among those who lived there were: Matthew Bingham (1807-70), a black- and white-smith. He became bankrupt but was discharged in 1865 followed by John Bingham, cooper. There was more than one of this name, but this was probably J. G. Bingham, (1803-79) who moved to 10 Berkeley Street, Eynesbury, and then to 47 High Street. Next came Samuel Charlton, builder. He bought his property from Jas. Tristham in 1835. There were Charlton & Son here, in 1850; John Jackson, beer retailer was here in 1839, and Thos. Jackson, bricklayer in 1854. Fredk. Bull, carpenter, in 1854; Fredk. North, bootmaker, in 1854; Robt. Paris, butcher, in 1854; Wm. Jas. Chessum, carpenter, in 1850; Miss Mary Scarbrow (1784-1855). She was apparently the last survivor in the town of the once wealthy and important local family of Hall Place, Cambridge Street. Thos. Hind (1827-72), builder, followed. He was probably followed by his son of the same name who moved to Walnut Tree Square in 1894. Next came C. Gray, ropemaker, who had his rope walk in New Street and was the son of F. Gray. (There was a James Gray, ropemaker, in the town in 1792). There was a Geo. Slade (1776-1855), tailor, and A. M. Townsend, dressmaker, who was here in 1878, 1888. Hales Laundry once occupied the end of the Row. It was started by Mrs. Hale, a widow, from Prospect Row, Cambridge Street, who moved here about 1908. The laundry was given up about 1958.

CAMBRIDGE STREET

This was one of the medieval town streets, and almost certainly the name then only applied to it as far as Popes Bridge (corrupted to Post Bridge), where it crosses the Fox Brook. Beyond this was Green End. In the first half of the 19th century there were no buildings east of where Shady Path crosses it, until one reached the neighbourhood of *The Bulls Head* inn at Green End. Almost all the 19th-century development east of Manor Farm followed from the opening of the railway, or its building, about 1850. In 1898 the Local Board decided that Cambridge Street ended at the railway bridge.

SOUTH SIDE FROM THE CROSS

Corner property with Church Street, see Church Street.

Nos. 4-12. A terrace of small houses and shops, probably all built by R. Freeman of the corner shop, to replace a row of old white-washed 'stud and mud' cottages. In no. 10 J. R. Smith first opened a pork butcher's shop (see High Street).

No. 14. Private house, built about 1908 to replace an old timber-framed house, with a yard and business premises at the back. In 1792 and 1809 this was probably the house and business of Bingley Perkins, millwright. In 1843 it was in the possession of Robt. Westley, and in 1830 and 1858, Geo. Peach, either in the same trade or more probably blacksmiths. In the 1860s it was the black-smith's shop of Thomas Hill, son of a blacksmith father, Thos. Hill (1788-1883), who had another smithy in a yard on the opposite side of the street, and a branch business at Great Paxton. These were the leading blacksmiths in the town and had a large business. Thos. Hill was followed by his son, David Fraser Hill, who died, aged 31, in 1898, and was followed by his widow Harriet. In 1900 the business was bought by C. Cooper, who rebuilt the old house and retired in 1923. He was followed by Fields & Pateman, motor engineers and carting contractors, who moved to Huntingdon Street in 1928.

No. 18. Now part of Hunts. Motors Ltd., works and showroom, formerly a house with a shop window, and nursery garden behind. On the street frontage, east of the house, was a red brick wall, similar to that on the east side of Church Street, and there is little doubt that it once belonged to the original Hall Place in Church Street. It must indeed have been the back entrance to that mansion. In 1963 some 18th-century buildings, that had once been stables and grooms' quarters, were pulled down. These were behind the above house, some way back from the street, facing east, and no doubt built along the carriage way to the mansion.

It seems that soon after the old Hall Place mansion was pulled down, about 1770, this area was taken over as a market or nursery garden by members of the Franklin family. In 1790 there was a Fanny Franklin and her sons Richard and John, both gardeners. After her death they became partners. In the churchyard there are tombstones to a John Franklin (1763-1849), and another John Franklin (1786-1851). In 1899 the *St. Neots Advertiser* published an epitaph, then obliterated, but copied in 1841 from near the belfry door:

> Ann Franklin slumbers here
> To wait the morn when Christ appears
> One thousand seven hundred and ninety nine
> She died, her soul and body resigned.
> On her birthday was twenty nine
> She hopes to meet with Christ in Heaven.

'T' recalled (1820-30) that Richard Franklin would take two cartloads of vegetables, each week, to supply Cambridge colleges and market. C. J. Lee, a grandson of Richard Franklin, writing to *St. Neots Advertiser* in 1899, from Santa Barbara, California, recalled his grandfather's house in Cambridge Street, with its high red-brick wall and garden, in 1825. He mentions that he also had a garden on the east side of Huntingdon Street, north of Pipers Path and another north of Bedford Street.

In the 1809 Valuation is a Richard Franklin, landlord of the *Fighting Cock* inn (22 High Street), who had Poors Close of two acres, 'his own garden well stocked with fruit', and three gardens (four acres) rented from Dr. Alvey of Old Hall (now Hall Place). In 1854 a Mrs. Franklin of 'near the Cross, Cambridge Street', was a dealer in pillow lace.

About 1854 the property was taken over by Wood & Ingram, a firm of nursery gardeners from Huntingdon established there since the middle of the 18th century. Their manager occupied the house, and the business was finally closed in 1957. A pond at the end of the gardens was the scene of a tragedy which horrified the town in 1871. In it Mrs. Barlow, wife of the manager, drowned herself together with her four children.

Present site of remainder of Hunts. Motor Ltd., garage. Here was formerly a row of old cottages, and to the east stables, coach house, grooms' quarters, and carriage yard belonging to Old Hall (Hall Place), next door.

Present Hall Place (now divided into two houses) formerly, and up to about 1900, known as Old Hall, after which it was given the name of the mansion in Church Street, pulled down about 1770.

The house is now completely cased in white brick from the local brickyards, probably done in the 18th or early 19th centuries. From its shape however it is obviously a timber-framed double cross wing house of the country or farmhouse type, and probably dating back to the 16th century.

Its early history has not been traced, but in 1770 it was owned and occupied by Stephen Scarbrow, attorney, who died in 1781 and is buried, with his wife Anne (nee Sutton, from Old Warden) Beds.), in the North Chapel of the church. Formerly it had been part of the estate of Rev. Wm. Gretton, and seems to have come to Stephen Scarbrow by a marriage settlement of 1764. It is likely that his father was also named Stephen as he had a sister named Elizabeth, and it was an Elizabeth Scarbrow, daughter of a Stephen Scarbrow, who, in 1771, married the notorious John Bellingham (see below) and went to live at the corner of Huntingdon and Cambridge Streets.

Stephen Scarbrow junr. and Ann had four children, of which Ann married Edward Billett of Eynesbury (see 24 St. Mary's Street, Eynesbury). After the death of Stephen Scarbrow senr., in 1781, his trustees let the house; first to Thos. Johnson, and then Thos. Morris, but in 1787 Stephen Billett of Eynesbury bought the property from the trustees for his son and daughter-in-law Ann. They were not to enjoy the new house for long, as Edward died in 1790, and the house was again to let.

In the same year it was taken by Dr. Samuel Alvey (1762-1826), one of the most remarkable men living in the town at that time. At the same time he bought a considerable quantity of land at the back of the house, including the site of the original Hall Place, for £620, and in 1812 he bought the house itself for £3,000. He had taken a degree at Edinburgh in 1788, and it is not known why he chose to come to St. Neots.

An interesting account of one of his activities was contributed by Dr. R. Rook of Cambridge to *Medical History* (vol. IV, no. 3, 1960, and vol. V, no. 4, 1960). This describes a MS. 'Transactions of a Local Medical and Surgical Society, 1793-1801'. This society covered the county of Huntingdonshire, and parts of Bedfordshire, Cambridgeshire, Northamptonshire, and Lincolnshire. Dr. Alvey seems to have been the leading spirit in it and was probably the founder. At the first meeting he was elected to the chair as perpetual president. Meetings were held half yearly at Peterborough,

Bourn, Stamford, and Stilton, in rotation; and the date fixed as
near as possible to full moon for the convenience of travelling.
Members pledged to consult with each other when second
opinions were asked for. At meetings members read papers
describing specially interesting cases and the treatment they
had given. New members, after being proposed, had to read
a paper for discussion before being ballotted on, at the next
meeting.

Of Dr. Alvey's work and reputation in the district we have only
the evidence of a memorial tablet in the South Chapel of the
church which records: 'Dr. Samuel Alvey, died 1826 aged 64, and
Sarah his widow died 1837 aged 77. Long will be cherished the
recollection of his skill as a physician, his kindness as a friend,
his virtue as a man, and his piety as a christian. By his death the
public, and particularly the poor, for whom with unwearied
benevolence he, for nearly 40 years, devoted one day in the week,
have sustained an irreparable loss'. The above obituary suggests
that he was living and working in the town some time before
taking this house in 1791.

Sarah Alvey lived in the house until her death in 1837, and in
her will it was left to her husband's godson, Samuel Day, son of
Wm. Day of the Shrubbery, Church Street. The bequest was subject to the payment of £1,200 to her son. The son is not
named and it is possible that he was by a former marriage,
she being slightly older than her husband. Samuel Day was,
by all accounts, an engaging young man and treated by Dr.
Alvey as a son.

Samuel Day (1817-93) moved into the house in 1837 to practise his profession as a solicitor and attorney, succeeding to his
father's practice, and had his office there. He was made a town
commissioner and registrar of the St. Neots County Court and
later elected to the Local Board. His practice flourished and he
took as partner his nephew C. R. Wade-Gery, who came to live
at Cedar House, nearly opposite.

In the late 1870s things began to go wrong for him financially.
One cause was said to have been the lending of large sums to fen
farmers, many of whom went bankrupt when hit by the agricultural depression. C. R. Wade-Gery dissolved their partnership in
1880, just before he was finally declared bankrupt in 1881. All
his property was taken over by his creditors and sold, and he
died in Kensington in 1893. In 1882 the house was occupied by
the Rev. L'Strange Ewen, who retired here from Offord Darcy,
and died in 1889 aged 57. The property was then put up for sale,
and was described thus:

OLD HALL

Old fashioned county house, with ornamental garden, magnificent lawn, extensive kitchen gardens, well planted with fruit trees. Paddock of rich old pasture land. Gardeners cottage, stabling, coach house and outbuildings. Total of nine acres. The brick and tile residence comprises. Basement, Ale and wine cellar. Ground Floor. Front entrance hall, side entrance hall, dining room (21½ft. by 14½ft.), first drawing room (20½ft. by 18ft.), second drawing room leading from first (28ft. by 17½ft.) including bay windows, library, fire-proof room, kitchen, scullery, butler's pantry, larder, pantry and large store room. First Floor. Small study, six principal bedrooms, two dressing rooms, two servants bedrooms, and two w.c.s. Second Floor. Two attics. Includes a valuable pair of old Dutch iron gates, not included in this lot, but may be taken by the purchaser at £150.

The property was bought by Wm. Bowyer, a retired farmer and brewer, from either Eaton Socon or Southoe. He remained here until his death, in 1913, and was followed by his widow who died in 1919. During this period the Bowyers were always willing to lend the grounds for public events, and they were extensively used for flower shows, Sunday school treats, and annual outings of many kinds.

The property was next bought by F. E. Brightman, farmer and market gardener, who had once had a greengrocer's shop at 26 High Street. He divided the house into two parts, himself living at the west end. He also started to dig gravel from the land at the back, using his farm labour when they had little else to do. It was in the course of this digging that the author noticed pits filled with black soil showing in sections on the gravel face. They contained pottery, animal bones, and objects of bronze, iron and bone. The pottery was of a type at that time not unknown, but never before found in association with objects that could be dated to the late Saxon period. A number of these pit huts were found and after their publication in 1933 (*Proc. Camb. Antiq. Soc.*, vol. 33, p. 133 and vol. 49 (1955), p. 43), the pottery became officially known as 'St. Neots Ware'. It is now known that these sunken pit huts (now known as *Grubenhus*) were not used for living in, but for such purposes as weaving and cooking. In ditches dug across the site were found objects of the Medieval Period, and in the gravel itself flint implements from the Lower Palaeolithic Age.

Present site of two shops. Here was formerly a row of old cottages, with others at the back, forming a small court or 'yard', no doubt once belonging to Old Hall, and perhaps occupied by servants working there.

Present site of Rober's Bakery and Restaurant. (*Hist. Mon. Comm.*, no. 23). Now pulled down. In 1876 this was a baker's premises when 'Teddy' Edwards came here from Prospect Row, opposite, and was still here in 1889.

Present Pashley's garage. This is the site of an old house and shop, kept, in 1888, by W. J. Pearson, watchmaker, who moved here from Huntingdon Street. He was probably followed by his son W. H. Pearson, and it finally became a second-hand furniture and junk shop, the family remaining until about 1914.

Shady Path. A little to the east of this public footpath, and about half way towards Cemetery Lane, was the Pest House, with a small garden. Here people with infectious diseases were put to isolate them from the rest of the community. It is marked on 18th-century maps, and was still there in 1809.

Sandfield Housing Estate. During the building operations on the former Sandfield Allotments, in 1961-63, many signs of former occupation were found, in the form of pits and ditches from the Late Saxon to Medieval periods. A notable find was a silver penny of Harthacnut.

Post Bridge. This carries the road over the Fox Brook, and beyond it was Green End. There are many references to repairs to this bridge, by the parish, in the 17th and 18th century churchwardens' accounts, when it was always spelt Popes Bridge. It may be that in medieval times this stream was made to run through the town, as an open sewer, along the north side of High Street, where there is known to have been a ditch. Later, when the town had its first brick sewers, this brook had a weir made across it where it is crossed by Shady Path, to flush out the sewer through the town.

A row of detached houses, south of the road and east of Post Bridge, were built on new ground only occupied by a small corn-grinding mill run by Arthur Chapman (see below). The earliest is dated 1885. East of these Henry Ashley had a stonemason's yard in 1890, on the site of a former blacksmith's shop. The family and business were still here well into this century.

A terrace of small houses amongst which was a small shop kept by the Tassell family from about 1890 to about 1930.

The *Queen Victoria* inn. Landlords: 1858 probably John Franklin, 1865 Mrs. A. Franklin, 1877 Wm. Newman, 1883, 1893 Geo. White. The *St. Neots Advertiser* reported in 1889: 'A native of St. Neots is now in town seeking work, by name Pettifer, whose parents once kept the *Queen Victoria*. He was in the 77th Foot in the Crimean War, and in the front line at the battle of Alma. His twin brother was a marine in the Baltic campaign'.

The *Bulls Head* **inn.** Originally there was a house of this name in the High Street, somewhere near the *Fighting Cocks* inn, and the first reference to this site is in 1850, when John Storey was landlord, followed by his wife (1858 and 1862), and then John Joyce, 1897.

Shortsands House. * This house, built early in the 19th century, was appropriately named from a field name in the vicinity. The first occupant found recorded was Rev. Balley, pastor of the Old Meeting (Congregational Chapel), who came here on his marriage in 1823. He was followed by Wm. Peppercorn, who had Manor Farm nearby, and died in 1833. In 1847 Rev. Henry Walter Beaufort (1781-1865) retired here after 39 years as vicar of Eaton Socon. His widow, Isabella Elizabeth (1794-1869) continued here with his daughter Isabella Susan (1834-88), and about 1871 the latter married Rev. Simcoe John Budge (1834-1915) a curate. He became vicar of Great Paxton but they remained here until he took the Brampton living in 1883. Many public events were held on the lawn at the back of the house, and the name 'Budge's Lawn' was still being used after the end of the century. In 1893 Alexander McNish, of Paine & Co. Ltd., came here, leaving in 1896 for Cressener House, Huntingdon Street. He was followed by John McNish, of the same firm, who remained until his death, about 1912.

The Shortsands Football Field was originally attached to the house. It was first used by St. Neots Football Club in 1899, when they left the Common for a ground where they could collect gate money.

Morton House. The origin of this small house, tucked away up a short lane between Shortsands House and Manor Farm, is not known. In 1707 and 1720 it belonged to the important Bainton family of St. Neots, and was then called 'Goodlands'. In 1793 it came to Jonathan Gorham (the bachelor surgeon, see 9 Market Square), no doubt because his mother was Elizabeth Bainton before her marriage (see 22 Market Square). At his death in 1794 the property passed to his nephew Geo. James Gorham, father of the local historian, and he, in 1806, sold it to a Mr. Meadows Taylor of Diss in Norfolk. In 1827 it was sold to Saml. Waterhouse of Hayfield, Derby., and in 1828 to Saml. Morton of St. Neots, hence its present name. There was still a Geo. Morton living there in 1858.

From about 1870 to 1884 it was occupied by Chas. Daintree, timber merchant of Eynesbury, and in 1899 by John Adkins.

* See Plate 10

Early this century Mrs. Squire, a widow, from Cross Hall Farm, lived here with her daughters.

Manor Farm. This consists of a red-brick house, probably built in the first half of the 18th century, and was formerly part of the estate of the Earl of Sandwich, when he was Lord of the Manor. Attached, in 1869, was 60 acres of pasture and 169 acres of arable. In 1770 the tenant was Wm. Pamplin who may have lived at 21 High Street, and in 1809, William and Alexander Peppercorn, who also lived elsewhere in the town. They hired 323 acres, besides 142 acres from Saml. Leightonhouse. Wm. Peppercorn, who died in 1833, lived latterly at Shortsands House nearby, and was probably succeeded by his son G. A. Peppercorn.

In 1839 there was a fire of which the following is a contemporary record:

> On January 14th., a dreadful and alarming fire occurred at Mr. Peppercorn's farm. It was first observed by the Watchman going his rounds. Fortunately a north west gale was blowing so the house was saved, and probably the town also, but 7 fine horses and 12 pigs perished. Most of the stacks were threshed out. Men worked all night with a plentiful supply of water. It is thought to have been the work of an incendiary. Next morning groups of little urchins were seen deliberately cutting off flesh from the half roasted pigs, and hungry dogs sharing in the bountiful repast which this melancholy catastrophe offered them. The remains of 7 horses were thrown into the saw pit.

In 1858 John Brown had the farm and lived in the house, leaving in 1874. In 1887 it was advertised to let, and in 1890 was taken by John Howe later of Shirdley House, Eynesbury, who called the house 'The Lawn'. His foreman was living in the house in 1900, and he kept the farm until about 1908, when it was taken by Richard Aughton. At about the same time the land was sold by the Earl of Sandwich to G. F. Rowley of Priory Hill.

The Railway Station. First opened in 1850 as a station on the Great Northern Railway. In 1897/8 it was rebuilt with the addition of extra lines and a waiting room on the centre platform. At the same time a large granary was put up just north of the station buildings (recently pulled down).

An accident occurred just outside the station, opposite the north signal box, on 10 November 1895, when three coaches and the guard's van left the rails. Two people were killed and many injured, one of whom died later.

The *Railway* Hotel. The first mention found of this refers to 1858 when Matthew Cartwright (1807-95) was landlord. He had first

been coachman to Dr. Ward (see 21 Market Square), and then to
the Rowley family at Priory Hill. Later he became head ostler at
the *Cross Keys*, a responsible and important post in coaching days.
Ironically he heard all day the passing trains that had destroyed
his calling. Other landlords were: 1869 W. Pearson, 1885 C.
Bunnage, 1878 John Spencer, 1899 John Gardner and J. T.
Percival.

CAMBRIDGE STREET, NORTH SIDE

From the railway bridge westward is property all built up on
account of the opening of the railway in 1850. The two public
houses probably first served the needs of the railway navvies, and
later the carters going to and from the station.

The *Engine and Tender* inn. This seems, in 1869, to have been
called the *Railway Tavern*.

The *Peacock* inn. The first mention found of this house is in
1855. In 1883 it was sold for £560.

Murphins Granary. This was built in 1856, and was superseded
by the large granary built at the station in 1898. It was used for
many years by Jordan & Addington, millers.

Victoria Terrace. Seven cottages, built about 1883 for railway
workers, and sold for £690 each.

Albert Terrace. Six cottages built about 1883 for railway workers,
and sold for £585 each.

Woodcocks Lane. This short lane just west of Albert Terrace gave
access to a number of small fields at the back. This name occurs
in 1888, but now appears to be lost. Until the recently-built
Longsands Housing Estate there were no buildings, from the above
as far as Kings Lane, with the exception of one cottage, opposite
Shortsands House, which still exists among the houses of the new
estate. Its front approach is across a footbridge or 'trap' spanning
Fox Brook. Tradition has it that it owed its isolated position to
being built as a Pest House. No documentary evidence has been
found for this belief, and it is known that a Pest House did exist
on the site of the present Sandfield Estate (see above). It is, perhaps, not impossible that it might have been used, or kept, for
that purpose as additional accommodation. It has been much
altered and restored in recent times.

Spring Hill. The slight rise in the main road in this neighbourhood
used to be called Spring Hill. This was on account of the spring
which served as a water supply for the poorer inhabitants of Green

End. Before the course of the Fox Brook was altered in 1963/4, to enable Cambridge Road to be widened, just west of the above cottage footbridge steps led down from the pavement, alongside the supporting wall, to the level of the brook. Near the bottom an iron pipe protruded from the wall and from this flowed a supply of water, piped from a spring on the south side of the road. Water could also be dipped from the brook for purposes other than drinking. In 1888 the spring water was analysed by the local M.O.H., and pronounced to be of very good quality, only equalled by two other wells in the town.

The entrance to Kings Lane. Before 1900 only a footbridge crossed the brook here, and vehicles crossed by a ford. In 1888 there had been complaints of the overpowering stench caused by horses and carts stirring up the mud in crossing the ford. In 1899 the Urban District Council adopted Kings Lane and decided to build a road bridge here. This was done to the designs, and under the supervision of, Mr. Blood, their part-time surveyor. Hence its name Blood's Bridge.

The west corner of Cambridge Street and Kings Lane, now occupied by a garage, was previously the site of a terrace of very poor brick cottages, facing the main road, with their back yards running down to the brook, and probably built about mid-19th century. After being condemned they were pulled down to build the present garage.

Row of villa-type houses, built post 1900, on land formerly allotments.

Cambridge Gardens Housing Estate. Built as Council Houses in 1928 to the design of Mr. Weymouth, the Urban District Council surveyor, at a cost of £428 parlour type and £334 non-parlour type. At the time of the above development two semi-detached lath and plaster cottages stood on the west side of the site, and the remainder of the site was cultivated as allotments. At least as early as 1887 there was a wooden hut on the site, used as a photographic studio and dark room by Jas. Phillips, the first in the town. In 1896 he moved to 10 High Street.

Shady Path. Site of two new houses built 1962, replacing *Hist. Mon. Comm.*, no. 22. Here, in 1874 were four cottages occupied by two families, that on the west belonging to Thos. Sharman, butcher, with his shop and slaughterhouse at the back, and the other to Robert Stoughton.

Thos. Sharman was the founder of the present butcher's business at Eynesbury, and a 'character' about whom many stories were told. One concerns his friend Geo. Malling, whom he met in the street after both had been celebrating rather freely. 'Tom' had been reduced to a state of deep depression, and asked his friend if he would hang him. 'George' readily agreed, and they walked to the slaughterhouse. A noose was prepared and placed round Tom's neck, and fastened to the butcher's hoist, and George lifted him off the ground. He then hastily left, but told Tom's wife, on the way out, what he had done. On reaching home he told his own wife, 'I've done for old Tommy, I've hung him in the slaughterhouse, he's a dead'un by now'. Much alarmed she hurried to the scene, but found that Mrs. Sharman had already cut him down, and, with the help of a neighbour, carried him into the house. Here, only just in time, he was revived. Geo. Malling was ever after nicknamed 'Calcraft', the notorious public executioner of that time. Thos. Sharman moved to 10 Berkeley Street, Eynesbury in 1877.

Formerly a small cottage, part of which was used as a sweet shop and kept early this century by Daniel Crow, and later by his son. Either it, or another very near it, was once a Toll Gate for the St. Neots to Cambridge Turnpike Trust. Later the Toll Gate was moved to Wintringham.

Cressener Terrace. Built by John Franks (see High Street).

Prospect Row. Among people living here in the last quarter of last century was Mr. Litchfield, tailor. Mrs. Hale started a laundry business here, afterwards moving to Windmill Row. There was also J. Wright, taxidermist, who was here in 1875.

No. 39. About 1860 the home of George Gray, ropemaker.

No. 37. House and shop of E. E. Ebbutt, tailor, who died 1889. The present house replaced an older cottage in which lived Jas. Stratton, who kept two or three cows, and lived by retailing milk. He had a mentally deficient son who, in the early 1800s, set fire to some of the farm buildings belonging to Cedar House, and was convicted and set to penal servitude.

No. 35. The present *Angel* inn. Formerly the *Wireworker's Arms*, and renamed after the *Angel* inn was pulled down in the Market Square in 1935. The possible origin for this name is the presence of a Jacob Cowan, wireworker, in Cambridge Street in 1839. Landlords included: Thos. Richards, pork butcher 1873, 1875,

Eli Shepherd, watchmaker 1881, and Thos. Dicks 1896. It was
for many years a common lodging house.

Malting and adjacent buildings in red brick, and probably dating
from the early 18th century. These no doubt were originally
attached to the large house next door (Cedar House), and in the
early 19th century belonged to the Peppercorn family. From them
they were purchased by Thos. Chapman, landlord of *The Pigeon*
inn, High Street, and also owner of the *Chequers* and *Plough* inns,
Eynesbury. He no doubt used these premises to brew his beer. At
his death in 1880 it was sold for £680, and then described as a
three-quarter brewery. In 1884 it was occupied by Arthur Chapman, grandson of the above, as a branch of his Eaton Socon milling
business, putting in steam power when he gave up Duloe Windmill
in 1889. He remained here well into this century, and also owned
Blunham Mill. Among A. Chapman's reminiscences of St. Neots,
printed in the *St. Neots Advertiser*, he describes the barn as being
one of the oldest in the town, with walls so thick that the temper-
ature inside varied little in winter or summer. He recalled being told
by Mrs. Huckle, an old woman from Green End, that her mother
remembered John Wesley preaching in the malting at five o'clock in
the morning to catch the men going to work. Others said to have
preached in the malting were Rev. Henry Venn of Yelling (1778),
Rev. John Berridge of Everton (1755), and George Whitefield.

The house attached to the malting was built by Robt. Rich,
builder, of Brookside, for Thos. Chapman, when he bought the
malting.

Cedar House (now pulled down). This was probably built as a
farmer's house in the late 17th or early 18th century, and in
1809 had connected with it a dovehouse, the malting described
above, and 100 acres of land. In 1770 it was occupied by Wm.
Ingersole, who was probably not the owner as in 1802 it was
sold to a Wm. Ingersole, either the same or son of the above, by
Wm. Scarbrow of Old Hall opposite, for £2,675. The Ingersoles
were farmers, merchants, and bankers, one branch of the family
having a business at 26 Market Square. This Wm. Ingersole would
appear to have been involved in the failure of the Rix, Gorham &
Ingersole Bank, in 1824/5, and to have left here soon after.

In 1836 the house was occupied by Edward Toogood of St.
Neots Paper Mill. About 1850 it had been taken by Christopher
Hall, who farmed Cross Hall farm, Eaton Socon. He also had a
business as parcel and goods agent for the Great Northern Railway, was a coal merchant, and carting contractor which included
carting for the Paper Mill, and had his office here.

By 1858 the house and business had been taken by F. J. Wood, who combined this with the offices of Registrar of Births, Marriages and Deaths, and Relieving Officer, and had other business premises at 40 Market Square. The firm failed in 1873.

During part of the above time the farm buildings and yard attached to the house were let to James Brown, butcher and farmer, at St. Neots bridge, and it was during his tenancy that they were set on fire by Jabez Stratton, son of the neighbouring milkman (see above).

About 1874 the house was bought by C. R. Wade Gery, solicitor, then in partnership with his uncle Saml. Day, of Old Hall opposite, where they had their office. In 1880 however he dissolved the partnership, just before Saml. Day went bankrupt in 1881. He then established his own office in New Street (the present Wade Gery & Brackenbury). While living in the house he had already turned the old farmyard area into a garden, and in 1885 considerable alterations and additions were made to the house. It was, however, even later than this, when it became the fashion to name houses, that it was given its name.

About 1901 C. R. Wade Gery left to live at Wornditch Hall, Kimbolton, and the house was taken by Mrs. Meade, widow of Rev. Meade, vicar of St. Neots, who died in 1902. She kept an aviary of cage birds which could be dimly seen through a window of coloured glass facing the street, and were a fascination to passing children. At her death in 1923 the premises were made into a private school for girls under Miss Shepherd Smith, and it remained as a school until 1968.

No. 25. At present a private house but was, in 1854, the *White Hart* inn, kept and owned by Joseph Sale, cooper, who died in 1868. He was probably followed by Mrs. Sale who died in 1899.

No. 23. Private house with an archway leading to a yard at the back. This was a blacksmith's premises, kept, in 1872, by Robert Cuthbert. He sold the business to John King (1814-75), shoeing and jobbing smith. After his death the business was taken over by Thos. Hill, of the blacksmith's firm opposite. In the same yard, in the 1890s, was the workshop of Geo. F. Jones, called by him the 'Umbrella Hospital', where he repaired umbrellas, and reseated cane-bottomed chairs. He was also a birdcatcher, and dealt in wild trapped cage birds, before it was illegal to do so.

No. 19. Here, in 1902, lived R. Hill, who kept a small bicycle shop and was also a postman. In 1910 it was a greengrocer's kept by F. Kemp.

No. 17. Present private house, with builder's yard and workshops (C. G. Evans & Son) at the back. (Part *Hist. Mon. Comm.*, no. 21.) This was formerly the *Plough* inn, kept, in 1839, by Saml. Tomplin, who was also a wheelwright and coachbuilder, with his yard at the back. He was followed by his widow, Sophia, who catered for supper parties. The business was carried on by a son, also Samuel (1842-96), in the same trade, and after his death, by his widow, Mary. Early in the present century the licence was given up and the house and premises taken by Chas. G. Evans, son of the printer of 15 High Street, as a builder's yard.

Nos. 13 and 11. Between these private houses is a right of way through to the builder's yard behind and belonging to no. 17. This also at one time led to a cottage which is almost certainly the one referred to in a sale advertised in 1855 as 'a cottage up the jetty, near the *Plough*, Cambridge Street'. This is the only instance found for the use of the term 'jetty' in the town. The name is common in Oxfordshire, for instance, to denote a small cul-de-sac road leading out of a main road, meaning something jutting or jetting out.

No. 11. The present *Rose and Crown* **inn.** This was a public house at least as long ago as 1809, when Wm. Gale was landlord. John Andrews was the landlord in 1823 and 1855, and in 1858 it was Mrs. Andrews. Before 1860 it was taken by John Andrews, a baker with a large business, who moved here from Huntingdon Street, and in 1860 moved to 47 High Street. Later Wm. Stern was landlord, and about 1890 Alfred Cattell, who was also a baker, and was followed by J. W. Cattell (1840-99), possibly a nephew.

No. 9. The present *Two Brewers* **inn.** Before 1862 this house was called the *Jolly Brewers*, and early last century there were three cottages at the back. Landlords included: 1809, Jas. Waterfall; 1814, 1824, Jas. Savage; 1830, Jos. Sale, cooper, who moved to the *White Hart* in 1854 (see no. 25 above); 1854, 1858, Saml. Page; 1874, 1890, Jas. Illsley. He was also a millwright, and in addition started at the back a small works to manufacture ginger beer and mineral water. In 1884 his son, Herbert, was badly injured here when a bottle burst. In 1890 the inn was taken over by Ben Richardson, and the mineral water business and stock in trade sold to Jordan & Addington for their similar business in St. Mary's Street, Eynesbury. Elizabeth Richardson was the landlord in 1899.

No. 7. Present private house, but probably once part of no. 9.

No. 3. Formerly a small house and shop (*Hist. Mon. Comm.*, no. 20). Now added to the business premises at no. 1, next door.

No. 1. Present large corner house used as solicitor's office of Wilkinson & Butler. It is built of red brick, now plastered over, and the original entrance in Cambridge Street changed recently to the present one in Huntingdon Street. It was probably built in the early 18th century, and used to be known as 'Cross House'. In the late 18th century there was a malting at the back. The earliest reference found to the house is dated 1771, when the owner Wm. Scarbrow of Old Hall, Cambridge Street conveyed it, as part of a marriage settlement, to his daughter Elizabeth and son-in-law John Bellingham, of *St. Martin-in-the-Fields*, described as a limner. They only lived here until 1777, but in 1776 a son was born and named John who was to become notorious in the history of the country.

John Bellingham the younger became a trading agent in Russia, and was unwise enough to expose a real or imagined trade fraud which involved the governor of Archangel. As a result he had his passport confiscated, was committed to prison, and heavily fined. He remained in prison for six months and all his appeals to the British Ambassador for help were ignored. On his return to England he appealed for redress, in vain, to the Prince of Wales, the Marquess of Wellesley, the Privy Council, and to the Treasury for compensation. Finally his application to petition Parliament was rejected by Spencer Percival, the Prime Minister.

On 11 May 1812 he entered the Parliament buildings to wait for the Prime Minister to appear. When he saw him he approached, drew a pistol, and shot him through the heart. Probably in response to the public horror and indignation, the trial started only four days later on 15 May and the judge refused an adjournment to allow the defence, who pleaded insanity, to bring down witnesses from Liverpool to testify as to the defendant's state of mind. He was hanged at the New Drop at Newgate on 18 May.

On leaving the town in 1777, John Bellingham (the elder) sold the house to John Parks, attorney, who remained there at least until 1800. About 1802 it was in the hands of Wm. Day, attorney, who probably lived here, as well as using it as his office, before he moved to the Shrubbery in Church Street.

About 1820 it ceased to be a solicitor's office and was taken by John Mackenzie, who came here from Huntingdon and turned it into a boarding school. He seems to have soon died, for by 1823 the school, advertised as a Ladies Academy, was being run by his widow, Mrs. Elizabeth Mackenzie, who had been left with a family of three sons and three daughters. The eldest son, Charles, born at Huntingdon in 1805, was apprenticed to a cabinet-maker, but would not apply himself to the trade, and spent much of his time with his two wealthy friends, John Palmer, son of the owner of the Ouse Navigation, and Charles Savine, son of the St. Neots surgeon (see 18 Market Square). Eventually he joined Robinson's Theatrical Company, in Lincolnshire, a touring company in which 'T' saw him at Huntingdon. He soon rose to national fame as an actor under the name of Henry Compton. His grandson was the well-known writer Sir Compton Mackenzie, who gives a full account of his family in *My Life and Times* vol. 1, (1963). It is not known when Mrs. Mackenzie left, (she was still there in 1830) but in 1838 the house was taken by Peppercorn & Wilkinson, solicitors, who moved here from the present Church House in Brook Street.

Octavius Robert Wilkinson (1807-92) was born at Stokesly, Yorkshire, and was admitted as a solicitor in 1830. In the same year he came to St. Neots as partner to Wm. Peppercorn, at his Brook Street office, before coming here. After some years the partnership was dissolved, and he remained here alone until 1856. Meanwhile, in 1847, he had been appointed clerk to the Justices, and the Petty Sessions Court was held regularly in his office on these premises. The actual room used as a court was one added by Mrs. Mackenzie as a classroom, but cannot now be positively identified. Formerly the court had been held at the office of John Wells, attorney, at Eynesbury (probably at Church House, Berkeley Street), and it was not moved from Mr. Wilkinson's office until the police station was built in New Street about 1860.

In 1856 O. R. Wilkinson's son-in-law, F. G. Butler, joined the firm as a partner, and later his own son Surtees (1841-96). On qualifying, in 1862, Surtees Wilkinson married the daughter of Wm. Peppercorn, his father's former partner. In 1884 F. G. Butler followed his partner as clerk to the court, retiring in favour of his son, Francis Noel, in 1905. The office remained with a partner of the firm until 1968. The sons of both S. Wilkinson and F. G. Butler qualified as solicitors and practised in this office. Among those articled in this office was Arthur Hughes, son of Judge Thomas Hughes, author of *Tom Brown's Schooldays*, and a nephew of O. R. Wilkinson. No member of either family now remains in the present firm.

HUNTINGDON STREET

This is one of the four planned medieval streets of the town that met at the Cross, and the name goes back at least to the 15th

century. Until the middle of the 19th century it would appear
that there were few houses on the east side, although late medieval
pottery was turned up in making Almond Road, together with
two jettons, one 14th-century North Italian and the other 15th-
century German, in the gardens of the police houses, formerly
Dovehouse Close. On the west side building was probably more
dense and of a slum character. That part of the street from
Rycroft Avenue northwards used to be known until recently as
'The Borough', and was probably the poorest in the town in the
19th and early 20th centuries. It may well have been the same
in earlier times.

East Side
No. 6. About 1905 this was a pork butcher's, kept by S. Wright,
and later continued by Mrs. Wright until about 1914. S. Wright
was nephew-in-law to Mrs. Sly, the famous sausage-maker in the
High Street, and inherited her formula which he sold to J. R.
Smith in 1910. About 1919 the shop was taken by A. Freeman,
watchmaker and jeweller, his sons moving to 42 High Street.

Girls' and Infants' School. This was built in 1841, back from the
street and approached by a passage north of the above. In the 19th
century it was known as the National School, but more recently
as the Church School. It was closed in 1961.
  In 1858 there was also a cottage in the school yard.

No. 8. This is now a private house but was previously the *Blue
Ball* inn, and in 1858 had two cottages in the yard at the back.
  Landlords included: 1809, Wm. Richards, who also had a brewhouse; 1823, Wm. Higgins; 1830, Thos. Wells; 1830, Jas. Dew;
1854, Wm. Robinson; 1875, Jas. W. Cattell, who in 1897 moved
to the *Rose and Crown*, Cambridge Street.

Cressener House. The late Urban District Council offices. This is
a fine 16th-century, or earlier, double cross wing medieval type
house, and, like others in the town, resembling a farmhouse rather
than a town house, and this is probably what it originally was. It
is now cased in local brick but inside has many features of the
original timber-framed house remaining. It is to be hoped that
it can be preserved as one of the very few town farmhouses left.
  The late Saml. Hawkesford of Brook Street once told the author
that members of the once important Hatley family (see memorials
in the south chapel of the church) once lived in this house, but
there is more certain evidence that they were associated with an
equally ancient house in Huntingdon Street that was destroyed
in making Rycroft Avenue. There is however no doubt from the

map of 1770 that at that date it belonged to Mary Leightonhouse, member of another important local family, and that in 1814 it was sold by a Samuel Leightonhouse and his wife to Lt.-Col. Wm. Humbley (1783-1857), a hero of the battle of Waterloo, whose memorial is in the porch of Eynesbury church.

At that time the property is described in the deeds as having 'a close of pasture lying behind, containing one acre two roods, and the toft and scite of a barn called Ropers Barn, containing two acres one rood 24 poles. Bounded on the north by premises belonging to Geo. Jas. Gorham, on the east by a close of pasture called Woodcocks Close [purchased by W. Humbley], and on the south by premises belonging to Jas. Pratt, Wm. Ingersole, Adam Love [see Loves Farm], and the heirs of Ishmael Warren'. It would seem that Col. Humbley lived here, if at all, for only a short time, as on retiring from the army, after his severe wounding at Waterloo, he immediately built Waterloo House, Eynesbury to live in. He probably let this house but bequeathed it to his son, Lt. Col. William Wellington Waterloo Humbley (1815-86).

He, before starting his army career, was educated first at Mr. Elliot's school at Eaton Socon, and then by Rev. John Fell at Huntingdon. His service was mainly in India, in the 9th Queen's Royal Lancers, and he was in action on the North West Frontier. He took part in battles at Moodkee, Ferozeshal, Aluval, and Sobron, and described his experiences in *Journal of a Cavalry Officer* 1854. He left the army about 1850 and came to live here about 1854. He was appointed a J.P., and was chairman of St. Neots bench for 18 years. His memorial is near that of his father in the porch of Eynesbury church.

The first mention of the name 'Cressener House' is in the will of Col. Humbly senr. In 1848 he bought, from the Earl of Sandwich, the Eynesbury manors of Ferrars, Bulkeley, and Cresseners, Robert Cressener giving the manor its name when he acquired it in 1410. This supplies a plausible reason for this name being given to the house.

In 1895 a great storm did much damage in the district; this house suffered badly and one gable was blown down. In the same year Alexander McNish (of Paine & Co.) came to live here, moving from Shortsands House, Cambridge Street, and in 1899 the executors of W. W. W. Humbly tried unsuccessfully to sell the property, which did not reach the reserve of £1,450. A. McNish was shortly followed by his brother John McNish, who came here from The Limes, Huntingdon Street, and left for Shortsands House in 1900. He was followed by Dr. Gardner Hill and then T. W. Thornton, who was here 1909-16.

Meanwhile the house had been bought in 1899 by John Franks, of High Street, and he retired to live here until his death in 1920. It became the St. Neots U.D.C. offices in 1938.

No. 14. Present temporary car park (*Hist. Mon. Comm.*, no. 31). There stood here, until it was pulled down in 1963, another double cross-wing timber-framed house similar to Cressener House.* It had however been for many years in a semi-derelict condition, and divided into a number of tenements. It was apparently in this state in 1809, when owned by Saml. Leightonhouse. When it was pulled down the massive central chimney was found to have been built of re-used stone, much of it moulded, and probably derived from St. Neots Priory. Excavations under the house revealed signs of previous buildings and, at the edge of the present pavement, the medieval street side ditch contained pottery of the 12th century. Early in the 19th century there was said to have been a large barn behind this property probably Ropers Barn (see above), to which were attached legends of Charles Wesley having preached there.

The south end of this house was a butcher's shop early this century, and the north end, at the corner of East Street, a boot-makers. Here, in 1809, lived John Sibley, followed by Chas. Sibley (died 1869), who besides being a bootmaker was Assistant Over-seer and Collector of Taxes, and parish constable before County Police were appointed. He was followed by his son, also Charles, (1834-98) who held the same offices. They employed a number of men at the trade, and used a workshop and loft in East Street. Many of the men were part-time postmen, with irregular post office hours, who worked here in their spare time.

House and shop at north corner of East Street. This house was first built as a private house, probably about 1885, by Alfred Harry Boutall (nicknamed 'Bucky') with the winnings of his race-horse 'Hacklers Pride', after which he named the house (see 43 Market Square).

In 1907 David Smith, greengrocer, came here from 49 High street, making part of the house into a shop.

Present County Library Branch. This replaced an old cottage in the foundations of which were found moulded stones probably from St. Neots Priory. These are preserved in the present building.

Private house and now doctor's surgery, at the south corner of Avenue Road. In 1885 this house was owned by Geo. Day, of

* See plate 14.

Wistaria House nearby, who had as tenant here John N. Kirkham, owner of the Ouse Navigation from Bedford to St. Ives. Day was his agent in St. Neots with John Dew Fairey as chief clerk. From him the ownership passed to his son Thomas Nestian Kirkham M.I.C.E., F.C.S., M.S.A. (1824-1908), of Great Barford.

In 1890 the house was taken by Edward Pearson, coachbuilder, coming from Eynesbury, and formerly at 47 High Street. He made his workshops in the yard and called the house 'The Elms'. He was followed by his son Harry W. Pearson, in the same trade, who also dabbled in the bicycle-making trade, producing his own model 'The Neotia'. He died about 1930.

St. Neots Co-operative Society shop, on the north corner of Avenue Road. This is built on the site, about 1825-30, of a timber yard belonging to one of the Day family. The Society was first formed at Eaton Socon in 1882, and this shop has inscribed on the front '1887 Unity is Strength'. It was built by W. Wade for the Eaton Socon Co-operative Society for £358. At the Annual Festival and dinner, held in the Corn Exchange in 1892, it was reported that the annual turnover was now £5,000, an increase of £1,000 in the past 18 months.

Present private house. This occupies the site of a former old thatched cottage where, about 1835-45, lived Mrs. Taborn, reputed to be the fattest woman for many miles around. When she died her coffin could only be got out by taking down part of the wall of the house.

Pipers Path. This apparently took its name from Pipers Close, alongside which it ran. In records of 1748 and 1757 it is called Pipers Lane, which is interesting in view of later disputes as to its correct width. In 1887 the Local Board complained to Mr. Rowley of Priory Hill and owner of the adjoining close, that his fence was an encroachment on this public right of way. People said that originally the right of way was 10 feet wide, and had been reduced to eight feet six inches, and that now Mr. Rowley was only leaving a three-foot path. In 1892 the matter was raised again when it was stated that the path, which had been nine feet wide for the past 27 years was now being reduced by about four feet. Research established that it had been diverted, some time back, by Geo. Day (of Wistaria House) and that the true path ran under his stables. No record of a legal diversion could be found in either Vestry or Quarter Sessions Minutes.

Present garage occupying the site of Wistaria House, pulled down 1959. This was built as a wealthy farmer's house, probably early in the 18th century, and possibly by the locally important Wye family. In 1743 it was occupied by Wm. Wye, and had a homestead and rickyard. In 1757 it was owned, and probably occupied, by John Waller, described as gentleman, and called 'The White House'.

In 1770 it belonged to the Laundy family, and became a school under Thos. Laundy (1766-1840), who is buried in the Baptist cemetery. In 1823, when he may have retired, it was described as a 'Ladies Academy', under Ann Laundy, presumably his daughter. There was a Thomas Laundy Franklin, who may have lived here for a while, but the next certain occupant was Geo. Day, who was a man with many interests. Besides being in partnership with his brother Wm. Day, the solicitor, he had a saw mill in Huntingdon Street, was an auctioneer and estate agent, and chief business agent to the owner of the Ouse Navigation. His office, run by his chief clerk John Dew Fairey, was on the opposite side of the street on the site of the present house, no. 61. To walk dry-shod to his office he had a cobbled path laid across the street. He died in 1872 and the house was sold for £1,400.

In 1873 John McNish (of Paine & Co.) came here when he married, moving to the Limes next door in 1882. It was probably at that time, or soon after, that Alfred Jordan (1856-1931), came here, and remained until his death. He was a bluff, generous, forthright character, held in great respect and esteem in the district.

He was born at the *Golden Ball* inn on the Market Square, of which his father Wm. Jordan was landlord and Collector of Market Tolls. He became a corn merchant, first at Eaton Ford, then moving in 1883 to New Street, with offices in part of the building now occupied by Wade Gery & Brackenbury, at the corner of Back Lane. While here he took as partner his brother-in-law, John Addington, and in 1919 Jordan & Addington moved from here to 24 Market Square. As a young and middle-aged man he was a great horseman, hunting with the Cambridgeshire and FitzWilliam Hunts, playing polo at Eaton Socon, and riding out to his farms at Hail Weston, Bolnhurst and Eaton Socon (Cobalden). About 1895 he was captain of St. Neots Fire Brigade, and annually entertained members of the brigade on his lawn (see 48-56 Luke Street, Eynesbury). He was also, for many years, a member of the U.D.C. His widow lived on here until her death in 1940.

The Limes. Now divided into two houses. Like the preceding property this was built as a wealthy farmer's house, probably early in the 18th century or before, and attached to the land now occupied by Priory Park, before it ceased to be farmland in 1795. In 1706 Stephen Bainton (or Baynton) had Priory Farm (36 acres) and this house may therefore have been the home of this wealthy and important local family. In the map of 1757 the house is shown as belonging to Sir Stephen Anderson, and is called Priory Farm, with Dovehouse Close at the back.

Late in the 18th century the house was occupied by Wm. King, an attorney and wealthy local landowner. Joseph Wright of East Street recorded his mother's recollections of him, which must date back to about 1800, as follows: 'The Limes was occupied by Wm. King who had the reputation of being a crafty old fellow, and was nicknamed 'Lawyer King' or 'Squire King'. He lived very humbly with only one general servant but managed to get together £30,000, which his only daughter came into. She was a little deformed person, supposed to be left on the shelf, but it was commonly said that she would bring her weight in gold to a husband. It was even said that a husband was advertised for. Correct or not Ousley Rowley of Huntingdon married her [he was the founder of Priory Hill House and Park]. Old King, on a summer evening, would sit outside his front door in the shade of the Lime trees, with a large tankard of beer on the ground, and long 'churchwarden' pipe, enjoying his 'bacca'. Often he had a group of children around him telling them tales. He had knee breeches and stockings, low ankle jack shoes, buckles on his knees and shoes, and wore what was called a 'spencer', a kind of long jacket with a band round the waist and made of serge cloth.

However honest a lawyer may be there are always many who will doubt his honesty. It was common report about King that he had forged a will, depriving certain persons of their rights and engulfing it himself. It was said that after the death of a person a pen was put in the dead hand to mark the will so that he could swear that the hand had marked the will. It was said also that he confessed to this act on his death bed, his last hours being embittered by the recollection. He was a little man in stature. Wm. King was still living here in 1809, and died in 1814.

The next occupier was John Smith, nicknamed 'Black Jack'. He was described as 'having control of all the carriage of goods from St. Neots to London before the railway came'. He was still here in 1836, and was followed by Rev. John Green, while waiting for a new vicarage to be built at St. Neots. This was completed in 1848/9.

The next occupants were the Misses Fanny and Laura Beaumont who had here a girls' school advertised as a 'Ladies Boarding Establishment'. They were still here in 1862, but by 1873 the school had been taken over by a Miss Chapman, who became insolvent in 1878. In 1882 John McNish moved here from Wistaria

House, next door, leaving again in 1890 for Cressener House. In 1893 the new occupant was Chas. Malden, manager of Day & Sons, Priory brewery.

At about the end of the century the house was divided into two properties, and only at this time does the name 'the Limes' seem to have been first used for the northern half.

A small two-room cottage stood, until 1966, just north of the Limes. This was probably all that remained of 'Rowleys Court', a slum condemned in the 19th century.

HUNTINGDON STREET

WEST SIDE. From the Cross northward.

Present Co-operative Society property, site of house pulled down 1960. This was originally a timber-framed house, probably of the 16th century, that had been faced with red brick about the middle of the 18th century. The date of this work was almost certainly indicated by the inscription 'J.E. 1754' cut on the stone lintel over the middle first-storey window. At this date the whole corner site belonged to Joseph Eayre, the bell founder, and on it he built the *George* inn (the present Co-operative Society shop). From the deeds of the property it is apparent that he restored a house on this site. Tradition says that he lived here, but no documentary proof for this has been found, although it may well be true, and some support for this theory is the fact of his putting his initials on the lintel stone. He is also said to have sunk a large valuted well, or underground cistern, under the roadway opposite this house. From this water was drawn, by a public pump, for the benefit of inhabitants of the neighbourhood. This was found and destroyed during trenching for public service pipe-laying in the 1950s.

The inscribed stone was rescued by the author and later given to an American, a descendant of a branch of the Eayre family who had emigrated in the 18th century. He had come to St. Neots to see if there were any traces of the family left, just too late to see the house. The stone was taken to America.

For many years this house was the home of the Rutter family, who probably originated from Geo. Rutter (1740-1803), a barber and peruke-maker, who came from St. Ives. In 1809 Mary Rutter had a shop here, and in 1823 John Rutter a baker's shop. About 1860 there was still a John Rutter, baker, here, but by about 1870 he had moved to 11 Cambridge Street.

About 1925 the house became the last home of Chas. Gill (see 11 South Street) and he lived here until his death, aged 90, in 1953. In 1935 his decoration of the house at the time of the King George V Jubilee won him first prize for the town.

The Public Pump. As mentioned above this had probably been provided, sometime about the middle of the 18th century, by Joseph Eayre. In 1877 the Local Board received bitter complaints from Rev. Hepplewhite, of the Wesleyan Manse, on account of the nuisance caused by people and watercarts coming here for water, and asking for its removal. In 1878 the Local Board decided to remove the pump to Brookside, Cambridge Street, but to preserve access to the well for fire-fighting purposes only.

The Wesleyan Chapel. The Wesleyans seem to have been established in the town between 1792 and 1797, and the chapel probably dates from that time. Its original pews were removed in 1868.

Two cottages in the chapel yard. One of these was probably always occupied by the chapel caretaker. The other in 1809 was the home of Thomas Wells, probably a basket-maker as he hired the Flag-holme osier beds at the north end of the Common. His son Samuel Wells was living here about 1860-70, and was father to Zachariah Wells the printer (see 15 High Street).

House, formerly the Wesleyan Manse, pulled down 1964. This had been one of a pair of semi-detached houses, end-on to the street, of which the other had been pulled down to make room to build the Wesleyan Chapel. It was of red brick, with reed plaster, and was probably built early in the 18th century. Alongside it there used to be a passage leading to two cottages at the back. In one of these, in 1887, lived Robt. Smith, chimney-sweep (see High Street, south side).

No. 7. House pulled down 1964. This was formerly the site of two cottages in one of which, about 1860, lived Oliver Kinn, basket-maker. The house recently pulled down was probably built for himself by Josiah Parker Piggot, builder, and he was living there about 1870-90. Later it was occupied by Geo. Wrycroft, builder.

No. 11. The *Old Sun* or *Sun* inn. (*Hist. Mon. Comm.*, no. 28). This house probably dates back to the late 17th century, being timber-framed with a red-brick chimney, and originally had four rooms. It seems to have been originally thatched. Additions to the back were probably made in the 18th and 19th centuries. Deeds of property on the south (Joseph Eayre's trustees) mention the inn in 1791. Wm. Lucas was the landlord 1809, when there was a cottage at the back, and either he or his son was here in 1836.

In 1839 it was Mary Lucas, who had also a butcher's shop, and was still here in 1850. In 1858 John Knight was landlord.

House made into offices and showroom for G. Wrycroft & Sons Ltd. This was built on the site of the *White Lion* or *Lion* public house. During much of the last half of last century (from at least 1858) this house was kept by two well-known characters, Mr. and Mrs. Thos. Gale. Thos. Gale was for many years herdsman to the Common Proprietors. One of his duties, besides counting and looking after the cattle, was spreading their manure. This accounted for his nickname 'Turd knocker' Gale. His wife added to the joint income by making pork pies, to sell at 2d. each, to the Saturday night customers. She also catered for harvest suppers, and, in 1884, 14 men sat down to such a festival ordered by Mrs. Rowley of Priory Hill.
W W. Stocker was landlord in 1896 when the licence was transferred to G. Flowerdue. The house was closed in 1915, £427 being paid in compensation, and sold to Geo. Wrycroft for £195.

Geo. Wrycroft was a bricklayer, formerly employed by Wm. Osborne of 17 Church Street, where he gained experience of high-class building work, and set up for himself at 38 Russell Street, in 1866 or 1867. Later he was joined by his brother Arthur and his own two sons and a daughter, and a prosperous firm was built up, employing a large labour force and gaining a wide reputation for high-class work. It finally went into liquidation in 1968.

Present open space, formerly occupied by three or four cottages, with a passageway to another at the back. In one of these, in the last half of last century, lived 'postman' Lovitt. One of his duties was to take a mail bag up Duck Lane to the railway line to be picked up by the express train by means of the catching apparatus. As sidelines he did cobbling and had junk and antiques displayed in his window.

House and premises built for use in corn and coal merchanting. About 1860-70 the site was occupied by a cottage and a small seedsman's shop, kept by John Baxter, gardener to J. H. Day of the Priory.

In 1879 Wm. Wildman of Eynesbury built the present premises for J. & S. Hinsby, who established here a corn, coal and mineral water business, with a corn mill at the back, which remained well into the present century.

The Hinsby brothers were, however, better known and remembered for their pioneer venture into public transport. This seems to have developed from a carrier's business which Samuel Hinsby

was running to and from Bedford, four times a week, in 1870.
In 1873 this was extended to St. Ives on Monday, and Cambridge
on Saturday. From this developed, at least in the early years of
this century, a two-horse 'bus, running to Bedford every Wednesday and Saturday, and carrying partly passengers and partly goods.
Sometime before 1914 a motor 'bus was put on the road, causing
great excitement in the district (its number was said to have been
EW9). The first week of operations was apparently not without
incident, and inspired the following:

> Hinsby had a motor bus,
> For the benefit of us,
> The first day he had a loss,
> Four cats, three dogs, and poor old Cookie's horse

Cook was the grocer in Church Street and his horse and cart were
run into by the bus. The old horse 'bus, laid up in 1912, was
commandeered in 1914 and sent to France, but the motor 'bus
continued to run to Bedford throughout the War.

No. 25. Butcher's shop. This is another of the butcher's shops
in the town associated with the Bartlett family, others being at
corner of Church Street and Brook Street, and at 9 South Street.
Mr. Geo. Bartlett, the present owner and occupier, thinks that
this shop was the main one. Family tradition says that the family
business dates back 300 years, records certainly confirm this up
to 200 years. Wm. Bartlett was probably here in 1809, Geo.
Bartlett in 1858, John Bartlett in 1879, and in 1908 it was
Bartlett & Son.

No. 35. Present house and shop. Joseph Wright of East Street
recalled being told by his mother that in this house lived Taylor
the weaver (perhaps about 1820). 'He used to weave linen sheets,
table cloths etc. on his loom. Many of the cottagers used to spin
flax from the yarn into threads by hand, then run it from the
reel or bobbin into balls for sale to the weaver; or send the threads
to be spun into sheets for themselves'. In 1854 this had become
the house and butcher's shop of Geo. Robt. Banks (1820-76),
followed very soon after that by John Banks, in the same trade.
He remained until declared bankrupt in 1873.

An undated newspaper cutting records that John Banks had
a handsome two-handled silver cup inscribed 'Reuben Banks (with
the aid of his brother George) secur'd Jno. Maxwell, a desperate
Footpad, in Great Staughton Field, Huntingdonshire, 11 March
1808. This cup (with 20 guineas in money) was presented to him
by subscriptions of his countrymen as a reward for his heroic
action'. Reuben Banks was Mr. J. Banks's grandfather. The government in recognition of their conduct made the two young men

free of all toll on all roads of the country, and free of all taxes, for the rest of their lives. The cup is in the British Museum. Mr. Banks also possesses a copy of a printed handbill, of which the following is a copy:

March 18th. 1808. St. Neots. HIGHWAY ROBBERS.
Whereas on Friday night the 11th. instant, two desperate Footpads stopped and robbed several Persons upon the road between St. Neots and Gt. Staughton; one of whome was taken into custody by **George Banks** aged 23 years, and **Reuben Banks** aged 17 years both of Hail Weston, (whom they stopped) after a violent resistance, which was ineffectual by the Heroic and almost unparalleled efforts of the said **George** and **Reuben Banks**, who (tho' unarmed) engaged, fought, and secured a Villain armed with a Brace of loaded Pistols: his Associate they deterred from assisting, by presenting a Pistol at him, which they had but the moment before wrested from the Hand of the Villain with whom they were then struggling.
On the following Morning some Persons of St. Neots, armed themselves, and went in pursuit of the Accomplice, and took him in the Parish of Eaton Socon.
The principal Robber was tried at Huntingdon Assizes, on March 15th., and sentence of Death passed upon him, the other is committed to Bedford Gaol, for trial at the next Assizes.
Notice is Hereby Given
That a subscription is opened for the purpose of rewarding the said **George and Reuben Banks**, for their heroic Conduct, and for making some acknowledgment to other Persons most active in securing the Robbers. That a Committee of the Subscribers of Half-a-Guinea and upwards, will meet at the Cross Keys Inn, in St. Neots, on Thursday the 7th. April next at Four o'Clock (when the Subscription will be closed) to receive the Report of the Sums subscribed, and to dispose of the same in such a manner as shall be thought proper, and that a List of the Subscriptions, and an account of the Disposal of the Money will be published in the Cambridge Newspaper.
Subscriptions will be received by the Bankers at Huntingdon, St. Neots, and St. Ives and by Mr. Tomlinson at Kimbolton'.

The property seems also to have been used by Thos. Banks, builder, and was sold by Mrs. Banks in 1877.

No. 37 or 39. A cottage adjoining the above, and subsequently burnt down, was, about 1860, a 'Dame School' run by Dame Holland.

Present shop at south corner of Russell Street. (*Hist. Mon. Comm.*, no. 29). In 1850 this was probably the house and shop of Wm. Stoton (1785-1855), tailor. In 1864 it was a grocer's shop kept by John Dalzell senr., who left here about 1874 to move to 56 High Street. Besides the house and shop there were cottages in the yard at the back. Towards the end of the century Fred Lovitt had a grocer's shop here.

House and bakery, at the north corner of Russell Street. Pulled down in 1960 to build Russell Court flats. In 1850 this was the house and bakery of James Abraham, who, about 1878, was followed by his son Geo. Abraham, a locally famous athlete and runner. He was succeeded, about the end of the century, by Thos. Andrews, baker, who moved to 47 High Street early in the new century. He may have kept on these premises, or they may then have been taken by A. Abraham, baker. About 1916 Bert Baker, a baker from Great Gransden, moved here staying until his death about 1959. This brought the trade to an end after well over 100 years.

While excavating to lay the foundations of Russell Court a deep filled-in ditch or watercourse was found, running east and west. From this came an almost whole 13th-century cooking pot, now in the Norris Museum, St. Ives.

House and premises at the south corner of Bedford Street. About 1860 this was the home of James Banks, builder, who went bankrupt in 1897.

No. 55. House at the north corner of Bedford Street. This replaced two old cottages, in one of which, in the last quarter of last century, lived Chas. Baldock, rat-catcher, a very well-known local character, with a wife who was a dressmaker. He must have been descended from a family of rat-catchers, for in 1825 Day & Son of the Priory were paying £1 3s. 3d. a quarter to Baldock, rat-catcher. He himself became tenant of Bell Rope field, Eynesbury, from Day & Sons, on condition he kept them free of rats. In his early days he acquired fame as a comic singer at local concerts, and was the first treasurer to St. Neots Co-operative Society. Many will remember him in his latter days, a bearded figure in very old and dirty clothes, whose fund of 'rat stories' was inexhaustible. He drove through the town in his ramshackle cart drawn by a decrepit pony in worn-out harness fastened with string. A story about him lingered for many years. On one occasion his ricketty cart collapsed, pinning himself and the pony to the ground. Bystanders quickly started to detach the harness to get the pony away from the wreckage. Baldock, fearing for his precious harness, was heard from beneath the cart to protest 'Don't cut it. It all unties'. He died in 1936. (See also Tebbutt, *Huntingdonshire Folklore* 1951.)

No. 61. Private house. There had been a horse pond here in the 18th century, and about the middle of the 19th century Geo. Day, who lived opposite at Wistaria House, built an office here, where his chief clerk, J. Dew Fairey, attended to his business as chief agent to the Ouse Navigation Co. He had a pebble crossing laid down across the road from his house to this office. After the death of Geo. Day in 1872 J. D. Fairey set up as an estate agent at this office, moving to South Street in 1877. About 1887 the present house was built as a wedding present from his bride's family to A. J. Wakefield, a member of the staff of the Vulcan Ironworks on the Market Square. In 1894 Mrs. Good, widow of Dr. Good of 20 Market Square, came here to live, and remained until her death in 1937.

Rycroft Avenue. This site was bought by G. Wrycroft & Sons, builders, in 1911, and developed by that firm in subsequent years. Along the north side of the site was once a private occupation access called Well Lane.

On the frontage, when it was first acquired, was an old semi-detached timber-framed house, with a jettied upper storey, which was demolished. It seems to have been of single cross-wing farmhouse type, and probably dated from the 16th century. A drawing of this house is preserved in the Norris Library at St. Ives, and a note on the drawing says that it was the home of the Hatley family, although they were also said to have been associated with Cressener House in the same street. The wealthy and locally important Hatley family appear frequently in local records of the 16th, 17th, and 18th centuries. Indeed the *Antelope* inn, on the Market Square (see no. 22) was in the hands of the executors of Wm. Hatley of Southoe in 1770, and the inn sign was said to have been taken from the Hatley crest or coat of arms. Loftus Hatley (1688-1757), son of Richard Hatley, left money to support the St. Neots Charity School, and his son Richard, (1723-89) in his will, added to this, as well as leaving a sum to the church organist. There are a number of memorials to the family in the church, and their gifts are recorded on the Charity Board.

The Borough. This part of the street, and northward as far as what used to be the end of the town, was always known until recently as the Borough. A row of very poor slummy cottages used to occupy the space as far as the *Globe* inn, many of which used to be tenanted by workers at the Paper Mill.

About the turn of the century one of these cottages was in such a deplorable condition that the owner wished to pull it down. It was however occupied by a chimney-sweep, Jesse (Sooty) Chapman and his family, who refused to vacate the house. The owner 'Andy' Baxter removed the doors and windows, to no effect, and finally took all the tiles from the roof. As the family still remained, his last stratagem was to give them vouchers for free groceries and beer to be had for the fetching. Directly the family was out of the house he and his men quickly pulled it down with ropes. On finding their house gone the Chapmans, including the children, walked to a spinney that used to exist on the west side of the Great North Road opposite Paper Mill Lane, and camped there for several months in a hole in the ground.

No. 77. The *Globe* **inn,** (*Hist. Mon. Comm.*, no. 30). This house was chiefly distinguished for its pictorial sign. On one side was painted the earth as a globe from which protruded the head and shoulders of the 'Struggler'. On the reverse side were the lines:

> Assist the Struggler,
> My friend and brother,
> And through this World
> We'll help each other.

In 1874 the landlord was John or Francis Day, also higgler and watercart driver for the Town Commissioners. In 1898 it was Fred. Ray, when G. F. Rowley's Harvest Supper for 40 men was held here.

House formerly *The Three Horseshoes* **public house.** About 1860 the house was kept by Saml. Page, but in 1870 a renewal of the licence was refused, the chairman of the bench saying that there was in the town one public house for every 60 of the population. S. Page was also a knacker and horse-slaughterer, and started this business in 1871, in a yard some way back from the house.

He was followed in the same trade by Chas. Beeson, who was there in 1887, and extended his business by selling artificial manures. In 1899 he bought Blunham Mill on the Ivel. The business here was continued by Beeson Bros., and closed down in 1962.

A pair of semi-detached thatched cottages. Once standing alone and detached from the town, but now hemmed in by council houses. They were built for employees of the Rowley family of Priory Hill, and bear the date 1815.

St. Ives Way or Lane. St. Ives Way entered Huntingdon Street at the south-west corner of Priory Park, and followed the line of the present public footpath skirting the park to Priory Hill, thence to Hawkesden Leys common, and leaving by its north-east corner across the fields, where its line has now been largely lost, to Toseland. It is probable that it was only a bridle road, seldom used for wheeled traffic. It went out of use, except as a footpath, when the road from Paxton Hill to Toseland was made at the Inclosure of Great Paxton in 1811.

The St. Neots to Cambridge turnpike trust. This originated in an Act of Parliament of 1776 which expired in 1874. It is always described as running from St. Ives Lane to Huntingdon Street to Bell Lane, Cambridge. There were Toll Gates in Cambridge Street (somewhere between Cressener Terrace and Shady Path), Eltisley, and Coton. The site of the St. Neots Gate was, at some time before 1850, moved to the Toll Gate Cottage still existing at Wintringham.* This was said to have been a costly decision for the trustees as when the railway was built they lost all the tolls on traffic going to the station. The St. Neots Toll Board,** long preserved at Wintringham Hall, was removed to an unknown destination in the 1940s.

Bullens Bridge. This is mentioned in a reference dated 1874, and probably refers to the bridge over Gallow Brook, at the parish boundary with Great Paxton.

NEW STREET

New Street or New Lane, as it used to be called, must originally have been merely a track leading to the Common and the corn mill (the present Paper Mill site) beyond, but there was almost certainly no bridge over the river there before the early 17th century. There is a reference to a 'Neystrete' in the Priory rents of 1505, and this may relate to the short length of road from the High Street to Back Lane. Recently, when the street was excavated for new public services, it was noted that the medieval road metalling, associated with that of the High Street, did not extend up New Street further than the entrance to Back Lane. This may have led to an entrance to the Priory, whose east precinct wall is presumed to have run along the west side of the street.

There is a puzzling item in the churchwardens' minutes of 1696, when money was voted for the repair of New Lane bridge. It is just possible that this refers to a now vanished ditch or watercourse that crossed the street and was once designed to flush the Priory rere dorter sewer. It might even be the same ditch found under the Russell Court flats.

The 1770 map seems to show no houses at all in New Lane, and 'T', writing of the period about 1820, says that then the only ones were the *Old Cannon* inn, the Baptist Meeting House, and a malting and some cottages at the south end, on the site of the old Police Station. The ordnance map of 1835 shows some

* See Plate 20
** See Plate 21

buildings on the west side as far north as West Street, a.id a few on the east side between the entrances to Bedford Street and Russell Street.

From that time on, until Avenue Road was opened up in the early 1880s, this street became the main development area for middle-class houses in the town. The old name persisted until about 1860.

WEST SIDE

Present block of offices, Wade Gery & Brackenbury, as far as Back Lane. These interesting buildings were built by the Town Commissioners and completed in 1846 to the plans of Medbury Joyce, whose reminiscences, published under the pseudonym of 'Townborn', have been so freely drawn on by the writer. To prepare for the development of New Lane as a residential street the commissioners purchased land on the west side from the Earl of Sandwich to widen the entrance to High Street. Old property on the site was pulled down, and on the remaining land they decided to build Public Rooms in which to hold their own meetings, to let to other official bodies, and for sales and public meetings. The meeting rooms (now subdivided) were on the first floor, and the ground floor was designed as a fire engine house, lamp room, and store.

In 1852 Mr. Medland told the commissioners of his plan to build a larger Public Room, on the Market Square next to the bridge, on condition that the Commissioners agreed to sell their Rooms. This they did, and the property was sold to Geo. Day in 1853 for £315. In 1871 he sold it to Jas. Kirby, of 1 High Street, for £320. In 1877 it was leased, for five years, to Joseph Topham, at £50 a year, and in 1880 to C. R. Wade Gery, solicitor, at £40. In 1890 he purchased the property from Jas. Kirby for £700.

In 1883 the north end of the building was leased to Alfred Jordan and in 1890 to Jordan & Addington, corn merchants, who had their offices here until moving to 24 Market Square about 1920.

BACK LANE ENTRANCE

The *Falcon* inn. The landlord of this house combined it with a blacksmith's business in premises at the back, with an entrance in Back Lane. It seems to have been started by Thos. Lewis (1800-1881), who succeeded his father John Lewis as blacksmith on the Market Square at the north end of South Street, and lived in a house on the Corn Exchange site. The business was in New Street in 1854, and may by then have moved here, or was using both premises. Thos. Lewis was a keen fisherman and in 1880, when he was 80, he caught nine pike at Wray House, Little Paxton, including, it was reported in the *St. Neots Chronicle*, one of 50lbs. and another of 22lbs.

He was succeeded by his son-in-law, Jabez Jefferies, who died in 1888 aged 43. The public house and business was then carried on by his widow, Lucretia Jefferies (1846-96), and at her death by her son-in-law Walter Wright. He was still there in 1914.

Present Ireland Bros. Motor Engineers. Probably the oldest garage in the town, that moved here from 24 and 28 High Street. The site, and also that to the north, was once the garden to Wm. Medland's house opposite. It was remembered as a beautiful garden with many fine trees and shrubs, and particularly as having a magnificent weeping ash. In 1896 the garden was bought by Chas. Redman (1874-1939), a native of Eynesbury who trained as a gardener at Hatfield House. Here he started as a seedman and nursery gardener, adding a shop when the post office block was built next door in 1913. He had a great commercial success. On an unidentified part of this site Zachariah Wells (see 15 High Street) had his printing works from some time in the 1890s to about 1911.

The Present Post Office. Moved here from 36 Market Square in 1913.

Nos. 23-25. Present terrace of houses with an archway. At the back of this terrace, before 1890, was a ropewalk used by Chas. Gray (1815-90), who had moved here from 78 Luke Street, Eynesbury, and lived in one of the houses of the terrace. In another house lived John Basford, builder, who sold his business and premises there to Geo. Middleton in 1894.

Baptist Cemetery.

West Street entrance. This was the site of both a tanyard and ropewalk. Public service trenches dug along West Street in 1964 revealed, at a depth of one and a half feet, a thick layer of decayed bark. The tanyard was probably that of Thos. Lovell, tanner and currier, who had premises in this street, as well as at 15 Market Square, in the first half of last century.

No. 27. House, now offices, at the north corner of West Street. This house was taken by Mr. and Mrs. Miles to accommodate their quads, born 28 November 1935, and enlarged by them with the help of advertising fees and subscriptions (see also 26 Caldecot Road, Eynesbury).

The Gospel Hall, now a factory of Transfer Tools Ltd. The author has been unable to identify the small sect that opened a chapel here in 1867 under the pastor Rev. F. Newman, who had once been a Church of England parson. For a time the community must have gathered strength as chapels were established at Staploe and Southoe. Rev. Newman was still here in the early years of this century, and living at The Lilacs, East Street.

The present sale and auction yard, next to the Common. In Wrycroft's Almanack 1902, it is stated that before the parish workhouse was built in Church Street, in 1768, it was formerly at the north end of New Street near the Common gate. It may well therefore have been on this site if the record is correct. The first auction yard here seems to have been that of Frank Maddison (1820-78), who was here in 1864. He was followed by F. J. Maddison, and by 1905 it had become Maddison & Son. In 1912 the business was taken over by Dilley, Son & Read, of Huntingdon and St. Ives.

The Common Gate. Before about 1950 there was no cattle grid here but a wide gate barring the main road. This was taken away, or fastened back, during the non-stocking season, but was kept closed when the cattle were on the Common. On the west side of the gate was a small flat-roofed hut or cabin used as a shelter for the Common gateman, who spent the entire day there opening the gate when vehicles wished to pass through. For this service he expected to receive a tip, or from those who used the gate regularly, an annual sum. On each 1 November when the cattle were taken off he, accompanied by the gateman from the other end of the Common, went round the town collecting this. Old Age Pensioners of tough constitution would apply to the Common Right Proprietors for these jobs (at no wage). Being nearest the town, and the *Cannon* inn, this gate was considered the superior job, and new applicants graduated from the far gate to this one.

Some gatekeepers were notoriously cantankerous and would slam the gate in a driver's face if they were given no tip, or an insufficient one.

There used to be a St. Neots saying when a particularly bitter wind was blowing, 'Someone has left the Common Gate open'.

EAST SIDE

The Pound. On the east side of the Common Gate stood the Town Pound. It was a brick structure and is now filled by an electricity transformer. About 1925 G. F. Rowley of Priory Hill, claiming that as Lord of the Manor it was his property, sold it to St. Neots Gas Co.

The *Cannon* **inn.** This inn stands at the south corner of Bedford Street, which, in 1878, was known as Hyde Park Corner. An official name plate with this name was visible until recently. The inn was certainly there in 1809, and until about 1850 it seems to have been called *The Old Cannon*. There was, as usual, an attached cottage. Landlords included: 1809, Joseph Norman; 1823, John Hilton; 1830, 1859, Geo. Hilton, who also drove a carrier's cart to Bedford on Tuesdays; 1883, Wm. Last, formerly gardener to Sir Williamson Booth and later to Lord Esmé Gordon of Little Paxton Park; 1896 W. W. Brittain, who catered for market dinners; 1897, A. Strudwick; 1908, 1912, W. S. Crossman.

At some time during the 19th century the inn, formerly quite small, was rebuilt with extensive stabling to accommodate the horses and vehicles of farmers and others coming to market, and the numerous carriers' carts, all of whom found this a convenient stop for the New Street sale yards.

Its proximity to the Common made this inn the rendezvous of the town milkmen, many of whom, during the grazing season, kept their cows there. After milking time they would gather here before distributing their milk round the town. Stories of the milkmen and the *Cannon* have passed into the folklore of the town. 1 May, the traditional day for opening the Commons for grazing, was, for the milkmen, a full day of celebration in the inn, and the afternoon milk round a precarious affair. Many stories are told of the 'iron cow' in the *Cannon* yard from which shortages were made good. A practical joker once sent an urgent message to a notorious milkman urging him to come quickly as one of his cows had a mangel-wurzel stuck in its throat. On arrival he was shown the blocked pump spout!

No. 44. Denmark House. In 1862 and 1867 this was the home and business premises of Mrs. Lucy Paxton (1818-88) who made and advertised millinery, cloaks, shawls, etc. Her father was Mr. Mole of the Manor House, Little Barford and she married John Paxton, who died young, as did her only child. In 1876 Mrs. Tingey obtained a licence to keep a lunatic asylum here.

In 1887 a school was established here for a short time by Edward Clifden, and in 1889 P. C. Tomson editor of *St. Neots*

Advertiser lived here for about a year. Having fetched £680 in 1888 the house was sold for £380 in 1894.

In 1899 Dr. Bowe came to live here, having taken over the practice of Dr. Campbell Grey, who had moved here from Brook Street the previous year. He stayed here until he went to Priory Lane in 1912.

No. 42. Small shop at the north corner of Russell Street. Here in 1884, was E. Elphic, grocer and Miss Elphic, dressmaker.

House at the south corner of Russell Street. This was once the *Prince of Wales* inn. In 1877 the landlord was Mr. Peacock, and later Jack Sergeant, milkman. The licence was given up in 1892.

Prospect House. Now divided into flats. This house was built about 1838, as a school, by Joseph Oliver, furniture dealer, who lived on the site of the late Corn Exchange in the High Street. For about two years it was run by a Miss Gale, but in 1840 the management was taken over by Joseph Oliver's eldest daughter Ann. At that time there were no houses on the west side of the street opposite, and Ann Oliver named the school Prospect House because of its view across the meadows to the river, and beyond, as far as Cross Hall. Directly opposite was Arnold's Close, hired from the *Cross Keys* as the school playing field. Ann subsequently married a Mr. Adkins and the school was taken over by one of her sisters, who, in her turn, in 1856, married James Paine, then a partner in the well known St. Neots firm.

From 1855 to 1863 the school was managed by the Misses Geard, but after that date another Oliver sister, Elizabeth (1829-1912), took charge. She retired in 1906, selling the school to Miss Prentice. It ceased to be a school about 1939, after giving 100 years of good educational service to many generations of middle-class girls.

House next to the auction yard. This was the home of three generations of the Ennals family. In 1864 Mr. Ennals senr. was in partnership with his son John H. Ennals, as Ennals & Son, auctioneers, and using the premises next door on the south as a sale yard. He had also been clerk to the Poor Law Guardians since 1835. The sale yard was given up in 1875, but some sale rooms in Russell Street were retained. J. H. Ennals followed his father in his official jobs and was also collector of Taxes and Registrar of Births, Marriages and Deaths. He died in 1887. His son John A. Ennals succeeded to all his father's official jobs and also became clerk to the St. Neots Rural District Council. He died about 1940.

Auction Yard. No records have come to light to show when this land was first used as an auction yard, but it was certainly in use by Ennals & Son in 1864, and given up by them in 1875 (see above). They were then taken over by another partnership of father and son, J. Brown senr. and J. Brown junr., which firm was there until about 1903. The beginning of their period coincided with a local boom in the pig trade. Buyers came to St. Neots market from as far away as Nottingham, Leicester and Birmingham, and it was a common sight to see 100 pigs being driven, on foot, to the railway station.

Following the Browns the yard was taken by S. V. Ekins, who moved here from the Market Square; the present business is still being carried on by his son V. H. Ekins.

Private road and footpath leading to the Congregational Old Meeting and High Street. A terrace of houses on this road was originally built for policemen, and the area was known as 'Policemen's Yard'. The footpath, normally closed to the public by a locked gate, used to be opened in times of high floods to enable New Street people to get to the High Street, when the Market Square and the south end of New Street were under water.

The Baptist Chapel. Formerly called the Baptist Meeting House. This chapel was built in 1816, and was one of the first buildings in this part of New Street.

Terrace of small houses. In one of these lived R. M. ('Mont') Ridlington (1844-96) veterinary surgeon. He came to the town in 1877, and was first at 43 High Street, and here in 1885.

Present Constitutional Club. This large house was the home of, and was almost certainly built by, William Medland (1804-72). He was a wealthy and important man in the town, in business as auctioneer, estate agent, surveyor, and manager of a branch bank of Wells & Co. of Biggleswade. His office and bank was on the east side of the Market Square. He was also a Town Commissioner. His garden opposite, on the west side of New Street, was greatly admired (see above), and he collected, as garden ornaments, much medieval carved stonework, most of which probably came from the Priory. Some of this is now in the garden of the late U.D.C. offices, Huntingdon Street. His widow lived on in the house until the 1890s.

In 1895 the house was bought for the Conservative Club, which the previous year had changed its name from the Working Men's Club, and changed it yet again to the Constitutional Club. The club had been started by Geo. Bower of the Vulcan Iron Works, in premises in the High Street (see nos. 60, 58) in 1882. When it first opened here members paid a subscription of 10s. a year, or working men earning up to 30s. a week, 1½d. a week. Quoits was then a popular game, and quoit beds were laid out.

The *Wrestlers* inn. The origins of this inn go back to the early 18th century, when it was in South Street (see nos. 5, 7) and called the *Wrestlers and Crown*. It seems probable that sometime between 1830 and 1838 J. H. Day, of the Priory brewery, built the present inn and had the licence transferred from South Street.

Landlords include: 1850, Chas. Munsey, also bootmaker; 1862, Wm. Shelton; 1875, Mrs. Shelton; 1887 G. Cane, who went bankrupt; 1887 A. W. Gilbert, who came here from the *Wheatsheaf* in Church Street. In 1897 he was running a wagonette break to Bedford every Saturday, at a return fare of 2s. 6d. Mrs. Gilbert was landlord in 1908 and 1914.

The Police Station and Magistrates' Court. Previous to 1850 this site was part of an area occupied by a malting and the wagon yard of Day & Son's Priory Brewery.

The exact date of the building of the police station, inspector's house and court is uncertain, but the *St. Neots Almanack* of 1865 refers to them as 'lately erected'. In 1871 improvements were made in the magistrates' room, which included a platform, and in 1900 the layout of the court was reversed, and what had before been the magistrates' retiring room became the witnesses' room (at the north end). Apparently before that witnesses had to wait in the street. A new magistrates' room was built at the south end.

In 1877 the Local Board were holding their meetings in the court room, and the U.D.C. in 1900. It became the headquarters of A.R.P. in St. Neots Urban and Rural Districts during the first part of the Second World War.

Small shop. A small draper's shop was opened here, about 1880, by Geo. Spencer Riseley. He had previously been a packman, travelling round the district selling clothes which he obtained wholesale from W. Norris of 7 High Street. In 1893 he handed over the business to his son George. In 1899 the firm were able to rent, and move to, a newly-built shop at 28 High Street, where the family remained until 1957.

For a few years the shop became offices of F. J. Maddison, auctioneer, and about 1902 were taken as a branch of the Capital & Counties Bank. This bank had absorbed the Wells, Hogg, and Lindsell Bank, formerly kept by Wm. Medland in the Market Square. They were here at least until 1917.

BEDFORD STREET

In 1726 this street was called John Nutters Lane, afterwards contracted to Nutters Lane, until officially (and pretentiously) changed to Bedford Street by the Local Board in 1878. During the 19th century it became, by design or accident, the area of new industrial development in the town.

WEST END, NORTH SIDE

The 'Gas House'. St. Neots Gas & Coke Co. In 1845 a prospectus of the proposed St. Neots Gas & Coke Co., with a capital of £2,500 in £10 shares, was issued by a provisional committee of leading citizens of the town. They were: J. Carrington,* Wm. Day,* G. Squire,* J. D. McKenzie, O. R. Wilkinson,* J. Savill,* F. Toogood, Saml. Day, Mrs. Squire, W. G. Habershon, T. S. Darnell, Wm. Islip,* Thos. Lovell,* Jas. Paine,* J. Medlock,* E. Mackaness, E. T. Geard,* J. Stott, J. Ingersole, Thos. Elgood,* W. Medland, M. Thornton, W. T. Mole, Jas. Shepherd, J. T. Goodgames,* J. Wilcox, J. Wilson, Jos. Oliver senr., F. Emery. Treasurer, Wm. Paine. Solicitor, Saml. Day. Of the provisional committee those indicated by an asterisk became the first board of directors.

The gas plant was quickly erected and started operations on 30 July 1846, the town commissioners having given the company a contract for street lighting. The first balance sheet was prepared in 1847, a profit of £140 was made and a dividend of five per cent paid. In 1877 an additional gas-holder was erected, and in 1884 the capital was increased. In 1889 £10 shares were worth £18, and in 1897 they reached a record price of £20, when a 10 per cent dividend was paid. When the manager, F. Maddison, died in 1879, James Linford was appointed, and acted until about 1910. In 1948 the company was nationalised and placed under the Eastern Gas Board, who closed it about 1958.

Flour Mill, Paine Co. Ltd. It is not quite certain if there was a steam mill on this site before the mill that was built (or rebuilt) here by John Medlock, after his existing mill in Back Lane was burnt down in 1846. When he proposed to rebuild it on the same site there was an outcry among his neighbours, who included the Town Commissioners, on account of the noise. On payment of £50 from the commissioners, and £70 collected from the neighbours he agreed to build his new mill in Bedford Street (then Nutters Lane), and it became known as Nutters Mill.

In 1855 he sold the mill to Joshua Malden for £740, and he, in turn, sold it, in 1859, to Thos. Smith of Tilbrook for £921. In

1865 it was sold to Wm. Paine for £800. Wm. Paine also had a timber and builders merchant's business, with sawmill, almost certainly in Bedford Street and probably at this same site. Sometime in the late 1870s he sold this to Chas. Daintree of Fenton, who moved this business, including the steam engine, to Navigation Wharf, Eynesbury. One of Wm. Paine's apprentices in the timber trade was Geo. Jewson of Earith, later founder of the well-known Norwich firm.

Wm. Paine then concentrated his milling and brewing businesses, and this mill was greatly enlarged and developed during the 19th century. In 1910 it was totally destroyed by fire, and the present mill built in its place.

Phoenix Engineering Works. John Bennett & Sons. This business was started about 1888 by John Bennett, who had been an engineer at Bowers Vulcan Iron Works. When the latter was sold up he purchased much of the stock and patterns. He was followed by his two sons John and 'Bate', who both remained bachelors, and lived in the house adjoining the works.

Malting. Paine & Co. This was probably built by Wm. Paine. 'G.H.' recalled that in the 1880s he, with other children, used to be employed, during the school holidays, in picking out and unblocking, with awls, the holes in the stone or brick floor of the malting chamber, at the rate of 4s. a week. From the height of the malting windows they watched the new Co-operative Society shop being built in Huntingdon Street (1887), and to the north could sometimes see horses being killed in Beeson's yard.

SOUTH SIDE

Houses on the south side of Bedford Street were built mainly in the latter part of the 19th century. Some dated ones range from 1876 to 1898.

RUSSELL STREET

This street was called Russell Row, until given the present name by the Local Board in 1878. It was laid out in the early part of last century on low ground that was below the town's drainage and sewers, and intended to provide the cheapest type of dwelling for workers in the new industries then springing up in the town. In 1836 there were only 22 houses in the street. These nearly all belonged to W. Abbott of Berkeley House, Eynesbury, and it may well be that the original development was his. The long

terrace of small houses on the north side of the street was typical
of workmen's slum-type dwellings of that period. Even at the end
of the century the rent was only 1s. 6d. a week.

It is presumed that the street was named after Lord John Russell
(1792-1878), the great radical and Parliamentary reformer, who
had represented one of the Huntingdonshire Parliamentary divisions
in 1820. However the inn in the street, the *Lord John Russell*,
was not so named until about 1870, being known previously as
The Boot.

During the last century there were a great number of small
business owners, shopkeepers, and craftsmen, living in this street,
whose actual houses it has not always been possible to identify,
especially as there is some doubt if the numbering, at present from
the New Street end, was not once done from the Huntingdon
Street end. Among those living in this street were:

Joseph Sleigh, clay pipe maker. He was born at Hunslet, Leeds
in 1823, and as a boy moved to Bedford. In 1837 he was apprenticed to Thos. Page, pipe-maker, Eynesbury (see 14 St. Mary's
Street). After completing his apprenticeship he went away as a
journeyman, but returned to St. Neots in 1847 and built himself
a pipe kiln behind his house at 1 Russell Street. The kiln was
dome-shaped, six feet high and four and a half feet across and
held 150 gross of pipes for firing. The pipe clay came from Poole
in Dorset to King's Lynn by sea, and thence by barge to St. Neots,
where it was landed at Brookside. It was in square dry lumps
about 12 inches across, weighing 72 to the ton. The pipe-maker
had to process it by further drying it to a flour-like powder, and
then adding water to make a kind of dough. This was then pressed
into moulds by hand.

The chief trade was in 'churchwardens', which were sold to
public houses, and fetched ½d. each, or three for a 1d. The landlords supplied them free to regular customers. Foul pipes were
returned for refiring to clean them. Sleigh gave up his trade in
the early 1850s to work at the Paper Mill. It was said that after
the Great Exhibition of 1851, wooden and meerschaum pipes
became fashionable and the trade in clay pipes declined.

Other inhabitants were in 1855, Miss Franklin, who kept a day
school; 1855, Peter Chandler, shoemaker; 1858, Miss Little,
dressmaker; 1867, Geo. Piggott, builder; 1870, 1893, W. Chamberlain, taxidermist. He was considered an outstanding craftsman and
prepared many of the cases of stuffed animals in St. Neots
museum. 1850, Jeremiah Moss, baker (1801-89). (See 47 High
Street) He had his bakehouse at the back of no. 45, next to *The
Blue Ball* inn. About 1889 the above premises were taken by

T. Andrews, baker, followed by 'Bert' Baker, before the latter moved to Huntingdon Street.

1872, James Jones, shoemaker; Mrs. Wells, dressmaker; 1871, 1878, Wm. Parish Stocker, butcher (1829-91), with a brother in the same trade at Eynesbury. Prosecuted in 1878 for selling bad meat. 1886, Geo. Peacock, whip-maker (1846-86); 1888, Joseph Whitbread, gunsmith, whitesmith, locksmith, and bell-hanger; 1893, J. Hensman, fishmonger; 1899, B. Bruce, shoemaker.

No. 25. The *Lord John Russell* **inn, formerly** *The Boot* (see above). Landlords included: 1849, 1880, Geo. Richardson; 1881, 1897, J. Boddington.

No. 44. The (Old) *Blue Ball* **inn.** Landlords included: 1858, Wm. Robinson; 1892, Mrs. Matthews; 1898, J. Love.

No. 38. Here, in 1887, Geo. Wrycroft started business on his own account, after working as foreman for Wm. Osborne of 17 Church Street.

Thrift Place. A terrace of houses on the south side dated 1877. Here, at no. 4, in 1883, lived Mrs. Hunt, dressmaker.

PRIORY ROAD

Wesleyan, or Council School. This school was built and maintained by the Wesleyans in 1858, and was taken over by the County Council about 1926 (see Schools).

Business premises across the road opposite the west end of the above school. This was probably the premises of John Edey & Son, builders, in 1849, who had 'Steam Joinery Works' in this road in 1887. A Thos. Edey of this firm died in 1885, but the firm carried on at least until 1893. They were probably followed by Furnace Fisher, carpenter, who retired in 1900. Next came W. Frost, 'Coach, Van, Cart, and Lorry Builder'. He was succeeded by T. L. Williamson, a native of Lincolnshire, in the same trade. His son Ralph was almost the last wheelwright to survive in the district.

AVENUE ROAD

This road was laid out and building plots made available chiefly through the initiative of Geo. Bower of the Vulcan Iron Works, in the early 1880s. First it seems to have been called Nutter Street, but in 1886 the present name was decided on. In that year the sewer was put in, and in the course of digging it, at a depth of four feet, skeletons belonging to a pagan Saxon cemetery were found at the west end and on the south side. Others were also found nearby in building the first houses on that side, which are still to be seen dated 1886. Prices for building plots averaged £1 a foot frontage.

Kings Lane must have existed in some form at this time, and certainly had part use as a ropewalk. Until the present bridge was built in 1900 there was a ford over the brook for carts and a footbridge leading to Cambridge Street.

EAST STREET

This was a previous development to Avenue Road, and the first building plots here were advertised in 1866. Previously the site was occupied by allotments. Building seems to have gone on rapidly for in 1871 it was stated that an entirely new street had grown up, and in 1872 the inhabitants were complaining that they had no lighting or paving, and were refusing to pay rates.

The present Roman Catholic church, was built as a Baptist chapel in 1873 (see Nonconformity).

No. 7. This cottage, pulled down in 1962, stood on the north side a short way from Huntingdon Street. It was built of 'stud and mud' and must have been there before the street. In it lived Joseph Wright the antiquary, who died in a fire in this cottage in 1934, aged about 90. He had the ambition to write a history of St. Neots, and spent much of his life collecting printed material, manuscripts and notes for this purpose. By trade he had been a skilled paper-maker at the Paper Mill, and as far as the author is aware never married. He is remembered as a kindly old man living alone in some squalor, amidst stacks of books and old newspapers. He was never jealous of his collection and always ready to show it to anyone interested, or give information from his long memory. Much of what he told the author is in this book. At his death a large part of his papers were burnt or ruined by water, but most of what remained found its way to the Norris Library, St. Ives. One particularly valuable item is a complete copy of the minutes of the Town Commissioners which he made from the original, which has now disappeared.

MONKS HARDWICK

This must be the site of the Monks Hardwick manor, surrounded by its demesne farm, originally in secular hands but later acquired by St. Neots Priory, probably in the 14th century.

At the Dissolution it passed, like the rest of the Priory property, in 1542, to Sir Richard Cromwell, remaining in his family until sold to Sir Edmund Anderson in 1600. Ousley Rowley bought it from the Anderson family in 1793, reselling it in 1812. It was in the hands of John Holland in 1859 when it was bought back by G. W. Rowley of Priory Hill, for £30,000.

The house, dating back to the late 16th century, is thought to be only the wing of a much larger mansion. Gorham suggests that it was not only the possession but the home of Henry Cromwell, second cousin of the Protector.

In 1688, under the Toleration Act, a Quaker Meeting was registered here by Thos. Loundies.

Tenants included: 1775, Mr. Smith; about 1780, Mr. Peppercorn; 1809, G. & W. Fowler of the Priory Brewery; about 1815, W. S. Maine; 1836, Wm. Saunderson. It was being farmed by the owner, John Holland, before the sale to G. W. Rowley in 1859 (see Brook House, Brook Street). In the early 1870s the tenant was Isaac Bradshaw. In 1872 a labourer returning home late from the Michaelmas night celebrations discovered a fire which burnt the whole of the year's harvest, but a chimney fire in the house in the same year was fortunately put out.

Bradshaw left for Caldecot, Eynesbury, in 1875, selling 670 long-wool sheep, 41 shorthorns, and 31 cart and nag horses. In 1900, and for many years after, the tenant was C. Beaumont.

A farm road eastward from Monks Hardwick leads to High Barns, on the same farm, and thence to the parish and county boundary at Hail Lane. This was claimed as a public right of way, and it was said that Mr. Newton of Croxton Park used, several times a year, to drive this way to attend St. Neots Bench, much to the annoyance of his colleague G. F. Rowley, who strove to disallow the public right.

LOVES FARM

The name of this farm came from Adam Love, who probably both owned and farmed it. He may have lived there or somewhere in Cambridge Street. A tablet on the south side of the belfry chamber of the church records 'Thomas Cotton, late of this parish died 1793 aged 70, also Ann wife of Adam Love died 1806 aged 77, and Adam Love late of this parish gent, nephew of Thomas Cotton, died 1825 aged 75'. On Adam Love's tombstone in the churchyard is inscribed:

Why wonder we that man no more
Is by affection led,
When this sad stone declares to all
Alas, that Love is dead,
Why what the history of the past
Is cruelty and pride,
When this same monument records
That Love with Adam died.

In 1809 the farm was of 95 acres, and at some time in the 19th century it was acquired by the Rowley family. Occupiers include: 1862, 1867, Henry Howitt; 1877, Robt. Lawrence; 1893, Henry Catmull; 1893, Saml. Hinsby; 1911, J. Hinsby.

TITHE FARM

At the Inclosure of the parish in 1770 this farm was awarded to Geo. Smith Inpropriator of the Great Tithes, in order that the farmland of the parish might, in future, be free of tithe. It was of 303 acres.

In 1842 it was bought by John Hill Day of the Priory Brewery, and was left to his grandsons at his death in 1868. In 1880 it was bought for £10,300 by Mrs. C. Rowley, widow of G. W. Rowley, and remained in the hands of that family to the present century.

Tenants included: 1800, John Smith; 1825, Moss Bros; 1836, Simon Maine; 1855, 1859, Thos. Powter; 1874, John Knighton; 1880-88, James Day (1857-1933) son of Thos. Day of Wintringham, who left here for Roxton Park; 1897, Eliza. Warrington.

UPPER WINTRINGHAM FARM and HALL

This was once the site of a hamlet and there are almost certainly the signs of a deserted village here. The present house is surrounded by a rectangular moat. From about 1566 to 1672 it was the home and possession of the Payne family, prominent in the life of the town during that period. In 1809 it belonged to Saml. Leighton-house and in 1836 to John Chamberlain. The farm is of about 320 acres.

In 1800 Lewis Flint was the tenant, and he remained until 1814. By 1836 James Day was there having almost certainly bought the farm and it is probable that Thos. Day (1827-86), who followed, was his son. He took over the farm about 1864. He was also a land agent, in charge of estates of the Duke of Manchester at Kimbolton, and of Mr. G. O. Newton at Croxton. He was also a keen supporter of the Wesleyan cause. His two sons were also in the land agency profession. One, James, farmed at Tithe Farm (see above). The other son, W. H. Day, went bankrupt in 1890.

In 1871 a new house, the present one, was built by Edey & Wildman of St. Neots for £1,771. There is no record of the house that it replaced, but it was probably the Elizabethan mansion of the Paynes, and some panelling from it is preserved in the present house.

The death of Thos. Day, in 1886, coincided with that of Catharine, widow of G. W. Rowley, with whom, at Priory Hill, lived her bachelor son Chas. Percival Rowley (1827-1904).* When his nephew Geo. Fydell Rowley then came to live at Priory Hill he moved to Wintringham Hall, as it was then called, which he bought from the Day family, and remained there until his death. The farm was left to his nephew.

LOWER WINTRINGHAM

This farm of about 320 acres is also a possession of the Rowley family and may have been acquired by Ousley Rowley on first coming to the district.

It is chiefly notable for its long association with the family of Achurch, as tenants. There was a Mr. Achurch at Wintringham in 1775, and Samuel (1775-1831) and Robert Achurch farming here in 1809. A Robert Achurch was here at least from 1858-78, followed by a Henry Achurch. His son Stanley, the last of the family to live and farm here, died unmarried in 1921.

* See Plate 29.

EYNESBURY ORIGINS

Eynesbury, and here we are confining it to the present parish and not the ancient one that included St. Neots, can be said to be one of the oldest inhabited sites in the country. Polished stone axes and Beaker pottery found when gravel was dug behind Red House in Montague Square (*Antiquaries Journal*, Oct. 1930) indicates that people were living here in the early Bronze Age, about 2000-1500 B.C. A pit of the early part of the Iron Age, probably about 400 B.C., was found by the author when the former Rectory Meadow was being levelled as a playing field for Eynesbury School (Grid. ref. TL. 182600). In the later part of the early Iron Age, immediately before the Roman conquest, this district was occupied by Belgic invaders from the Continent and Mr. Colin Dains has found a settlement of this period on land now being built over near the cemetery in Howitts Lane (Grid. ref. TL 189593). (See *Proc. Cambs. Antiq. Soc.*, vol. 61/1968.)

In the great developments, including a steep increase in population, that took place during the Roman period, the above mentioned Belgic settlement, probably mainly concerned with farming, remained, at least for a time. It would appear, however, from a lack of evidence to the contrary that a new centre of population or small village was started after the Roman conquest in the area of, and south of, the Coneygear. The 1835 ordnance map shows a complete rectangular bank and ditch earthwork on the cultivated allotment land immediately south of the recreation ground. Since that date this has been almost completely destroyed by gravel digging, but an excavation by the author in 1933 (*Cambs. Hunts. Arch. Soc.*, vol. 5, Part V (1935)) showed this to be of Roman date and probably late 3rd century, a time when defences were ordered to be constructed all over the country. A mound just outside the south-west corner of the above earthwork (Grid. ref. TL 180594) excavated by Mr. G. Rudd, has revealed remains of a Roman building with hypocaust heating. Nearby (Grid. ref. TL 180592) Roman building material scattered on a cultivated field suggest the presence of another building, while aerial photographs of the area south of the recent housing development (centred round Grid. ref. TL 183593) show cropmarks that may represent a further settlement. Little is known of the depth or navigability of the Ouse (itself a Celtic name) before the mills and locks were made, but it may well be that there was a small trading post here in connection with the navigation, with perhaps a ford or even a bridge.

Land communications with these settlements are also of interest. Two known Roman roads crossing the parish seem to be alternatives of the same road from Sandy to Godmanchester. Probably somewhere just south of Highfield Farm (in Waresley parish) this northbound road divides, one half taking a line east of the farm, becoming the present bridle road past Abbotsley Downs known as Hail Lane. The other half follows a course along the west side of Highfield Spinney, joins the present highway for a short distance and then follows a straight hedge-line west of Eynesbury Hardwick Farm until the Abbotsley road is reached near Lansbury. This section across the fields is set out as a public footpath in the Inclosure Award. From here its course can only be traced by aerial photography past the west side of Lansbury moat towards Tithe Farm, St. Neots and so on to Godmanchester.

At Lansbury, where this road meets the present highway, is the exact place where the present footpath, known as Half Mile Meadow Path, a continuation of Howitts Lane, ends. The author is personally convinced that Howitts Lane and Half Mile Meadow Path are based on a branch Roman road to the Eynesbury settlements ending somewhere near the Coneygear and passing close by the old Eynesbury cemetery site. A probable confirmation of this was seen by the author a few years ago when a pipe trench was dug from Howitts Lane along the outside of the south boundary garden wall of Eynesbury House (Grid. ref. TL 187594). Just south of this place the lane bends slightly to the east to pass outside the east wall of the garden. Had a straight line northward been maintained the lane would have passed inside the wall. At this theoretical place a metalled road surface could be seen in sections in the pipe trench, about three feet below the present land level, with an 11-foot wide cambered surface passing under the south garden wall. This road was obviously ancient and although there was no proof that it was Roman it is probable that it was. Again, in street excavations in the present highway opposite Shirdley House, at a depth of about two feet, six inches, an ancient cobbled road surface could be seen, perhaps another part of the above road.

Besides producing Roman remains, gravel digging in the vicinity of the Coneygear and Willow Bank last century also provided evidence of settlement in the early Saxon period in the form of several fired clay loom weights of the early annular type, now in the Norris Museum, St. Ives. Gorham figures (page 13) a rare type of decorated pottery vessel from this area, now in the Museum of Archaeology, Cambridge, and attributed by Dr. J. N. L. Myers to the 7th century. No cemetery of the Pagan Saxon period has been found at Eynesbury and no settlement at St. Neots, so it may well be that the cremation and inhumation cemetery found between the west end of Avenue Road and East Street belonged to these Eynesbury Saxons.

In the Late Saxon period there were settlements on both sides of Hen Brook, evidence for that at Eynesbury being found by the author in shallow ditches containing the characteristic 'St. Neots Ware' pottery of that period revealed when the former Rectory Meadow was developed as Eynesbury School playing field (Grid. ref. TL 182600).

Medieval period

It is impossible to be certain if the form of the old part of the present village is of pre-Conquest or post-Conquest date, but it is certainly of early origin and of a not uncommon plan. The original medieval village must have comprised a central Green extending from the present Green to Montague Square (still sometimes called the Green) and including all the land between Luke Street and Berkeley Street, with the houses built only on the outsides of these streets. It is probable that up to the 16th century all that was built on this central area was the parish church, the adjoining *Nags Head* inn, and perhaps a blacksmith's shop at the south end. On the Inclosure map of 1800, and even on the Ordnance map of 1835, there are hardly any buildings on the east side of Luke Street or the west side of Berkeley Street, and of course Buckley Road and Silver Street did not exist. With this large open Green Eynesbury must have looked rather like Eltisley (Cambs.) at the present time. When this central area came into private hands and by what means is not known.

From the church, towards St. Neots and the Hen Brook Crossing, runs St. Mary's Street, once sometimes called High Street. At the south end of this street against the churchyard wall an old print shows the Stocks and Whipping Post. From observation of street excavations along this street the author has noticed that from a short distance north of the church the street level and that of the houses along it has been artificially raised, to give some immunity from floods, by as much as two feet, as one approaches the bridge. As shown in the case of St. Neots, the tendency at the end of the Middle Ages, and after, was for the business population to move nearer the river, or its navigable tributaries, even at the risk of occasional flooding, and to build up the land surface to minimise this danger. Actually in recent years houses along this street have been the first to be inundated when flooding has occurred, and in 1947 the water was over two feet six inches deep in places here. It should be noted that, with the possible exception of the *Chequers* inn, no houses in this street are earlier than the 17th century, and this may be a clue as to when the level-raising took place. It was also early in this same century that the navigation locks were built on the Ouse as far up as St. Neots.

Southward from the Green the village ended at Townsend Pond, now filled in.

LOCAL GOVERNMENT

In 1800 Eynesbury, like St. Neots, was governed by its Vestry Meeting, but remained unaffected when, in 1819, commissioners appointed by Act of Parliament took over the running of St. Neots. The Vestry continued to govern Eynesbury until the appointment of a Local Board for both parishes in 1876.

Those entitled to take part in Vestry meetings had to own property in the parish. If it was under £50 ratable value they had one vote, with an additional vote for every £25 value over £50, to a limit of six votes. The usual attendance at a Vestry Meeting was under 10 but very occasionally as many as 30 attended. The rector was the ex-officio chairman. Their most important duties were to fix and collect a rate on property, including land, and appoint the parish officials from among the inhabitants. These were the Constable, Pinder, Surveyor of the Highways (or Waywarden), Overseer of the Poor, and Clerk. A number of the Vestry minute books and accounts are still preserved in the church safe and go back to the late 16th century.

One of the most onerous parish duties was the relief of the poor, sick, and unemployed, which necessitated maintaining a Workhouse in the parish. This burden was removed (except in respect of paying a rate) about 1838 when Unions of Parishes were formed to administer the Poor Law under a Board of Guardians, and accommodation was provided at Eaton Socon. Eynesbury Workhouse was sold in 1838. As an example of how few public amenities were provided, the Vestry never apparently even contemplated street lighting, and only in 1854 was a public sewer discussed, with no evidence that it was ever proceeded with. On the other hand it protested vigorously, but unavailingly, at being included with St. Neots in the new Local Board in 1876.

GAZETTEER

ST. MARY'S STREET

This name was officially adopted by the Local Board in 1878. Formerly also called High Street and Bridge Street (1746).

West side

Eynesbury bridge (called St. Neots bridge in a deed of 1746). From the underside of the arch crossing Hen Brook it can be seen to have been twice widened. The original bridge, approximately 10 feet wide and built of red sandstone, occupies the centre of the present bridge and may be medieval. It was subsequently widened on each side by five feet and the arch rebuilt. This was done in local grey bricks which cannot be earlier than about 1740. About 1922 it was again widened in concrete, adding four feet on each side to form the present footpaths.

St. Neots churchwardens' accounts record repairs in 1710 but do not state whether the work was done jointly with Eynesbury churchwardens.

On the SE. side there are steps leading down to the brook for dipping water or access to boats and the brook wall on that side is of sandstone like the original bridge. The approaches to the bridge have been made up by several feet and it is likely that there may once have been only a packhorse bridge and a ford before St. Mary's Street was raised, probably in the 17th century.

No. 2. Navigation Wharf. C. G. Tebbutt Ltd., Timber and Builders Merchant. Formerly the yard and depot of the company owning the Ouse Navigation made on land reclaimed from water meadow by dumping building and other rubbish, probably in the 18th century. The first record found of its occupation by the navigation company was in 1793 when Suzanna Palmer was admitted to Eynesbury Manor, and again in 1816 when Palmer & Franklin, navigation owners, had it. Francis Rix, merchant, was their local agent and Jas. Brown, carpenter, their foreman. Here barges were repaired and possibly built, and goods landed, loaded and stored for customers without private wharfs. The two adjoining houses (nos. 4 and 6) also belonged and probably housed their workmen.

The present small office attached to the bridge is on the site of a blacksmith's shop. Here ironwork connected with the barges and lock gates would be made and repaired and the barge horses shod.

It is not known exactly when the yard ceased to be used by the navigation company. Suzanna Palmer died in 1829 leaving her interests in it to her nephew Rev. Sir Thomas Grey Cullum. In 1855 he died, leaving the property to his wife, but by then it was let to Geo. Austin, carpenter, and Wm. Taylor, blacksmith. Taylor may have once worked for the company but now he had his own business. In 1864 Lady (Anne) Cullum sold the whole property, including the two houses, to Austin for £400.

It is not known what use Austin made of the yard but Taylor was still remembered in the author's early days as a figure of muscle and brawn embodying all the legendary blacksmith virtues, and who had the distinction of having his almost perfect likeness depicted on the sign of the *Village Blacksmith* inn, which he took on his retirement (no. 8), painted by Edward Mackaness (see Market Square, N. side, no. 34).

He retired in 1873 when his business (not premises) was sold to Thos. Ibbett the South Street blacksmith. A relative, possibly a son, was blacksmith at Abbotsley and kept the *Plough* there, making the model plough still used as the sign.

In 1878 Austin let part of the yard, which included a carpenter's workshop, saw pit, and wharf, to the Local Board, and in 1879 another part, which included a lime kiln, to Daintree & Jewson, a new firm of timber merchants, with the offer to buy the whole for £700, which they subsequently did. The present office, replacing the blacksmith's shop, was built in 1880. The business, however, did not prosper and in 1889 was sold together with the premises to Chas. G. Tebbutt in whose name and family it has remained (see also under C. G. Tebbutt, Ltd., p. 159).

No. 4. This house was attached to the navigation yard (see above) and 'A.C.' says that Austin, an agent of the company, lived here. Later he hired the yard. From about 1884-7 Chas. Daintree, of the above yard, was here. This house is part of a terrace of four houses (no. 9 *Hist. Mon. Comm.*) built probably in the early 18th century. They are timber-framed buildings afterwards faced with brick and have at times suffered badly from flooding. The front top room has wide oak floor boards nailed to re-used joists with a face showing geometric wall painting in red and blue.

No. 6. 'G.H.' remembers E. Clifton, a retired schoolmaster, living here, moving from Denmark Cottage, New Street, St. Neots. He was a kindly, generous old bachelor coaching a few pupils and sailing a dinghy on the river.

No. 8. The *Village Blacksmith* **inn.** In 1860 this was occupied by Mrs. Mehew but there is no record of it being an inn until 1873 when it is first mentioned in Paine's books, with Wm. Taylor as tenant, in the same year that he sold his blacksmithing business (see above). The sign, a portrait likeness by Ed. Mackaness, remained long after his death in 1878. In 1880 it was kept by Wm. Ringham who wore moleskin trousers. The licence was surrendered in 1961.

No. 10 (end of terrace). Here lived Ann (or Susan) Woods (1821-93) who ran a carrier's cart, taking over from her father (probably the J. Woods of Robson's 1839 *Directory*) who started the business in 1814. The cart went to Cambridge every Thursday and Saturday. 'G.H.' remembered her as an old woman, mean and witch-like, riding inside her covered cart with her driver Billie Gregory outside. It was said that after her death Sharman, the next tenant, swept the chimney and £200 in gold fell into the grate, only to be claimed by her executors. Geo. 'Ferrety' Sharman was a fish curer and came here when his premises in St. Neots High Street were pulled down by J. Franks to make his new shop. He had a herring-smoking shed at the back.

Open Space in front of Kayser Bondor. Here were two timber-framed tenements which were pulled down in 1938. (*Hist. Mon. Comm..*, no. 8).

No. 12. (*Hist. Mon. Comm.*, no. 7.) A house with two storeys and attics built in the late 17th or early 18th century and having an 18th century cornice and fascia below the eaves.

1866-71 the tenant was Alfred Worthy. 1871-90, it was occupied by Richard (Dick) Burgin, a flamboyant and much talked-of character who was by trade gunsmith, cartridge-maker, brazier, tinsmith and gas-fitter, and whose father had been landlord of the *King's Head*, St. Neots. He organised and took part in all kinds of local sports including quoits. He also kept greyhounds and bet heavily. He ended his days a ruined man to which was added tragedy when in 1895 his 20-year-old daughter Effie was murdered by shooting at Bedford. He is said to have ended his days in the workhouse, after being ejected from here in 1890. (See also no. 9, *Chequers.*)

He was followed by Wm. Chapman, tailor, working for his father next door.

No. 14. From 1862 Geo. Chapman, tailor, lived here, employing his son and several assistants. He was followed by his son William who, as trade declined, took a part-time job as County Court bailiff. He gave up business about 1925.

Yard entered between nos. 12 & 14. This large area, now occupied by Kayser Bondor factory, extends as far back as the rectory garden and the navigation yard. It had extensive buildings for brewing and malting including a circular barley-drying kiln in red brick of the 17th or early 18th century. In 1858 it belonged to Paine & Son, brewers, and was sold in 1875, for £775, to Geo. Taylor, landlord of the *Chequers* inn (opposite). He used it as a coalyard and ginger beer and mineral water factory, Jordan & Addington taking over on his retirement in 1887. (See *Half Moon* inn, Market Square, St. Neots.) The factory closed early this century.

Besides those described above smaller industries occupied part of this yard. In the early 19th century a Mr. Harvey had a kiln for making clay tobacco pipes here, later taken over by Thos. Page. In 1837 Jos. Sleigh became apprentice to Page and later built his own kiln in Russell Street, St. Neots, in 1847. Clay pipes, evidently wasters from this kiln, have been found in this area but unfortunately the makers did not include a trademark on their moulds. Page gave up in the late 1850s.

About 1899 Chas. Clark, bootmaker, set up shop in this yard. He advertised himself as 'retired after 16 years as Master Shoemaker to the Kings Own Hussars and Officers of the Indian Army, and having the Crimean, Turkish, Lucknow, and N.W. Provinces medals'.

No. 22. Here in 1850 lived Wm. Stoton, tailor, who died in 1875.

No. 24. (*Hist. Mon. Comm.*, no. 5.) Recently named the Manor House, but the author can find no evidence of it having any connection with any of the Eynesbury manors. The house is, however, of late 17th-century date and very pleasing architecturally with its shell hood over the central front door and original panelling inside. It has been carefully and tastefully restored by the late owner, Mr. G. Wrycroft, and a fuller architectural description is given in the *Royal Commission Report*.

Like a number of other houses facing the main street it had at the back a yard with a terrace of small tenements, in this case nine, of two rooms each, facing the back of the main house. They appear to have been built after the house (see below) and were pulled down about 1937. This row used to be called the Barrack

Yard and was supposed to have had something to do with the billeting of soldiers, but no evidence has been found for this story.

The deeds record that in 1738 Martha Leithe, widow, of Bedford, sold the property to Thos. Berkeley of Gamlingay for £150, and he apparently came to live here. It is then described as a messuage, formerly two messuages, with dovehouse, orchard, and garden, with a stone yard and green yard, formerly in the occupation of Rev. Thos. Selden and Ann Harvey, widow.

In 1746 Thos. Berkeley died, leaving the property to his widow Grace, of Lambeth, and his three daughters, Elizabeth, wife of Thos. Joyce of Eynesbury, hempdresser, Penelope, wife of Samuel Wherritt of Clerkenwell, oilman, and Katharine, wife of Nicholas Apethorpe of Gamlingay, gentleman. They sold the main property to Edward Billett the younger of Eynesbury, gentleman, and some of the back land on which stood a cottage to Levitt Dixie, comb-maker. Dixie died in 1783 and was followed in his trade by his son Christopher, to whom he left the cottage. It was sold to Edward Billett (son of the above) for £45 in 1787 and probably pulled down. (For other members of the Billett family, see Hall Place, Cambridge Street, St. Neots.)

Edward Billett the younger died in 1748 and his son Edward lived here until or just before his death in 1813. At this time the premises, for the first time, are described as divided into 10 tenements, which must refer to the row at the back, which does not appear in a description of 1746. At the actual time of Edward Billett's death the house had been let, first to Elizabeth Hedding, widow, and then to Mrs. Willoughby Ebenezer Cole. The Hedding family were Lords of the Manor of Little Paxton and Wm. Hedding (d. 1729) had a daughter Ann (Cole). The Mrs. Cole here was perhaps the widow of Rev. Cole, Rector of Eynesbury, who died in 1808.

In the two-room cottages at the back were then living people with well known local names: Thos. Edey, John Dixie, Wm. Miers, Robt. Radwall, Thos. Wells, Wm. Jones, John Nicholson, and Thos. Atkinson.

In 1813 the trustees of Ed. Billett sold the property (with two other cottages) to Dr. Alvey of Old Hall (now Hall Place) Cambridge Street, St. Neots, for £500, who, it would appear, bought it as an investment. Dr. Alvey died in 1826 and at the death of his widow, in 1837, the property was sold to Wm. Paxton, clockmaker of St. Neots, who owned it at least until 1858 but probably did not live here.

By 1854 it was occupied by James Wildman as a dwelling-house and general hardward shop. He was followed, about the turn of the century, by his son Cecil whose wife kept the shop while he had a barber's shop in one room. The author remembers it as one of those gloriously untidy village shops with high shelves full of an enormous variety of dusty goods that had not been handled for years, and where all the small boys took their pennies to buy marbles. Cecil was a small dark vivacious man who spent most of his time at his trade and would call on favoured customers at home for haircutting. 'G.H.' vividly recalled the scene at the shop on Saturday nights when it would often be open until midnight. It was the custom for the working class to come in for their weekly shave, costing 1d., after the pubs closed at 10.30 or 11 p.m., so as to look respectable for Sunday. The shop was often full of drunken and truculent men impatient to be served. Besides his cut-throat razor, Cecil's implements for shaving were a saucepan of hot water on an oil stove and the soap in a half coconut shell.

In one of the cottages at the back lived John Jones (1810-94), probably the son of Wm. Jones (see above). He was a chimney sweep, grave-digger, sexton, bell-ringer, and church caretaker. One of his sons Fred (or more popularly 'Lulu'), followed in his father's occupations, another, Chas. (1847-1937) worked for 32 years as stoker at Bowers Vulcan Iron Works and then 35 years at Jordan & Addington's coalyard. He recalled as a boy helping his father sweep the Paper Mill chimney, climbing up inside, and when it was finished diving into the river.

No. 26. Here lived at least three generations of the Radwall family, all in the building trade. Indeed it might have been even longer for there was a Radwall, builder, in Eynesbury in 1753. In 1746 these premises comprised a house, garden, workshop, and Rope Yard, occupied by Thos. Joyce. John Bigmore Radwall (1803-69) came here between 1826 and 1847 and in 1848 his billhead advertised 'plumber, glazier, ornamental painter, water closets, engine pumps, and paper hanger'. He was followed by his son Charles (1836-1908) in the same trade, and he by a son, another Charles. This latter was, however, a joiner and later moved to Gamlingay where he did much fine work such as making museum cases for the Sidgwick Museum, Cambridge. In his younger days he made a name locally as a footballer and speed-skater.

Nos. 28-34. Here was a terrace of five timber-framed tenements, probably of the late 17th century, (*Hist. Mon. Comm.*, no. 4) that reached as far as Rectory Lane and was pulled down in 1960 to give place to a shop and flats. Excavation showed that the original ground floors had been of clay afterwards covered by nine inch square local floor tiles.

The first house, no. 28, was a small shop occupied in 1878 by Edward Stocker, butcher (1833-91), with a slaughterhouse at the back that was condemned by the Local Board in 1880. He was followed in the same trade by his son Edward ('Happy') Stocker who about 1910 moved to no. 21 across the road.

The shop was then taken by Mr. and Mrs. Petchey selling sweets and greengrocery, and also became the new post office, moved from no. 21 opposite.

Rectory Lane. A row of three very low timber-framed cottages along the north side of this lane was really a wing of nos. 28-34 pulled down with the others in 1960, and included with them in *Hist. Mon. Comm.*, no. 4.

In the last one of these, according to tradition, lived James Toller, the Eynesbury Giant, who became internationally famous in an age when natural prodigies were the subject of enormous public wonder and interest. Little has been recorded about his parents, but Pigot's *Directory* 1830 gives a Wm. Toller merchant, Market Square, St. Neots. This is probably the man of the same name whose death, aged 45 in 1831, together with that of his wife Jemima, aged 47 in 1842, is recorded on a memorial at the door of the Baptist chapel, New Street, St. Neots. These, however, could not have been the parents of James Toller who was born at Eynesbury on 28 August 1798. At the age of 10 he was already 5 ft. 5 in. in height, reaching his full height of 8 ft. 1½ in. at the age of 18. Wm. Noble Bewsher, his constant friend and companion in youth, recorded that from foot to knee he measured 26 in. and that his foot was 15 in. long; also that his two sisters appeared to partake of his unusual growth. One at the age of 15 was 5 ft. 8½ in. and the other at seven was nearly 5 ft., while his brother and parents were of ordinary stature. His appetite was little more than ordinary.

In 1815 he was exhibited in London and presented to the Emperor of Russia and the King of Prussia, and also toured the country. In 1816 he was on show at no. 34 Piccadilly with Simon Paap a 28 in. dwarf. Soon after this he enlisted in the Life Guards where he was much noticed by H.R.H. Duke of York. It was probably at this time that he was described in London as 'a pleasing good natured country looking lad' and had the following verses written about him:

James Toller

To see him hundreds day by day did throng,
As he from place to place did pass along.
His 'bode uncertain for to think 'tis vain
One place so tall a wonder to contain.
His whole proportion was upright and straight
'Twas eight foot fully and a half in height
Not much in debt to age, his body clean
Up to his stature and not fat nor lean.

Very soon his health declined and he left the army and returned to Eynesbury to live with his mother in Rectory Lane. It was probably at this time that he had a gig specially made with a well to take his feet and would astonish strangers when he suddenly stood up. To avoid annoyance by the public Rev. Palmer allowed him to walk in the rectory garden, which adjoined his mother's house, and here he carved his initials on a fine chestnut tree.

This tree was cut down by Rev. Maule and used to make a new altar table for Eynesbury Church.

He died on 4 February 1818 at the age of 20 and was said to have been 8 ft. 6 in. tall when he died. It was rumoured that £20 had been offered for his body by the medical profession and as a precaution against body snatchers he was buried in the middle aisle of Eynesbury church.

In one of these cottages lived Nurse Goodman, the first and much loved District Nurse appointed for Eynesbury, probably about 1910.

Eynesbury Rectory. This is one of the most interesting houses in the village. It was built in the early 17th century and is described architecturally under *Hist. Mon. Comm.*, no. 3. The extensive stables were once used as a school (see Eynesbury School). It used to be pleasantly surrounded by a park-like glebe in the angle of the Ouse and the Hen Brook extending as far up the river as the footpath to the old cemetery and along the brook to Navigation Yard. The remaining glebe, together with the house, was disposed of in 1961.

Rev. Wm. Maule was probably the most colourful parson who lived here in the 19th century, and the one who made the most impact on the parish. He was rector from 1851 to 1890 and was still remembered and admired by many old friends of the author. He was the son of a former Secretary to the Treasury and was presented by his father's executors to the living. His brother was the Public Prosecutor. Educated at Winchester he went to Trinity College, Cambridge where he became President of the University Boat Club and won the Diamond Sculls at Henley. He came to Eynesbury after occupying curacies at Cookham and Fletton.

When he was instituted the church was stated to have been in a state of dilapidation and he had it thoroughly restored by his friend Sir A. Bloomfield, then just out of his articles with Sir G. Gilbert Scott. On part of the south side of the glebe he provided land and raised funds for a new village school and the first allotments.

His interest in rowing inspired him to start a Rowing Club in St. Neots in 1873 and he became the first president. Although opposed to the union of the two parishes under a Local Board, he became the first elected representative for Eynesbury. He was also described as a fluent speaker, a popular preacher, a musician of distinction, but something of a martinet in his sense of duty.

Among his sporting accomplishments was that of a good amateur boxer, and he is remembered as patrolling the streets on Saturday nights breaking up drunken fights and brawls. One story of his prowess in this field tells of a challenge of a young bargee, who persisted in camping on the Rectory Meadow in spite of several warnings of trespass. Finding him there again the Rector imme-diately agreed to fight it out, took off his jacket, and they set to on the banks of the Ouse. The bargee received a severe drubbing and promised never to trespass there again. This story was con-firmed, many years later, by the man himself, then old and dying, in Huntingdon Hospital, when visited by a later rector, Rev. South Phillips. Rev. Maule died in 1898.

RECTORY LANE, SOUTH SIDE

No. 36. Eynesbury Cottage. At the latter end of the century a succession of curates had lodgings here.

No. 38. Once *Blue Ball* inn, also once included a small shop. Land-lords: 1830 John Hunt; 1854 Wm. Emery (carpenter); 1861 J. Forskett. In 1863 and to about 1898 G. Howard. He had a son, J. W. Howard who fought in the Matebele War and sent a series of letters to *St. Neots Advertiser* in 1896 describing his experi-ences. Soon after he emigrated to America, took part in the Klondyke Gold Rush, and was supposed to have become a million-aire. 1898 Wm. Freshwater, then Fred Ford.

No. 40. Shop, now Cooper's Stores. The home and business of a branch of the old Eynesbury family of Broughton for nearly 100 years.

1839 Betsy Broughton, straw hat maker (probably 1803-79); 1850, 1862 John Broughton, tailor; 1866 S. C. Broughton, tailor and woollen draper; 1899 — Broughton.

Behind no. 48 was a yard known as School Yard, in which were a number of small cottages pulled down during this century. Some-where in the yard in the first half of last century was the firm of Freeman and Dixie, lantern leaf and comb makers.

Between nos. 38 and 40 there was a public right of way to the river, running through the rectory glebe along what is now called the Box Walk. This was closed, with the agreement of the Vestry, by Rev. Maule in 1862. In return he gave land for an alternative path 60 yards further south, the present Cemetery Path.

Eynesbury School (See page 55).

ST. MARY'S STREET, EAST SIDE

No. 35. Private house. Has a shield with arms of unknown origin cut in stone and let into the north wall. Here lived Clark Charles

(1824-1905) who was said to have changed his name from Charles Clark. He was a builder and undertaker and sold his business to Jas. Pearson, of Montague Street, in 1883. He also practised money-lending on a small scale, charging 1s. a week interest on £1.

No. 33. Baker's shop and house. Before 1876 it had been in the occupation of Jos. Mehew. At that date it was taken over by Ed. Page and had a 12-bushel oven and three small cottages in the yard. In 1896 he was succeeded by Wm. F. Love.

No. 27. Shop and house. At present F. K. Lee, grocers. In 1854 it was occupied by Abraham Staines (1801-55), shoemaker and leather seller. The business was carried on by his wife until about 1867. In 1868 Wm. Edwards of the same trade took it, moving to 17 High Street, St. Neots in 1895. He was followed by 'Jim' Bingham who turned it into a hardware shop. He was followed by his widow who was there well into this century.

No. 25. Now a private house. Here used to be Fred. Favill (1833-84), harness-maker and leather worker. He was followed by his son Henry in the same trade. It is recalled that, accompanied by his apprentice nicknamed a 'nacky boy' he travelled round the local factories repairing the machinery driving belts.

No. 23. Shop and house. Now T. K. Payne, fishmonger. From sometime soon after 1860 until about 1895 this was a butcher's business owned by W. Fowler, noted for his good meat. He then sold the business to Geo. Sharman who remained here for a few years before building and moving to a new shop at no. 11.

No. 21. Shop and house, of timber frame with hazel wattle and daub, brick-faced. Geo. Flanders (1837-89) came here and kept a grocer's shop which his widow carried on after his death, until about 1910. This shop also became the first Eynesbury post office of which the earliest mention found is in 1893. When the Flanders left it was moved to no. 28 opposite. The next occupier was Ed. Stocker, butcher, from no. 28, followed by his son Frank, and later by his grandson L. F. Stocker (who died in 1961), all butchers.

No. 19. House (pulled down 1963) and large yard. This was probably originally a farmhouse. In 1854 and 1860 it is recorded as being in the occupation of Robt. King, farmer and cattle dealer. Afterwards John How lived here before moving to Shirdley House, Berkeley Street. He used the yard for cattle and pigs, and other farm purposes. In 1888 Jas. Osborne moved in. He was an engineer, millwright, brass founder and threshing tackle proprietor, who found he had not enough room in the old Fellmongers Yard across the bridge where he had formerly been. He stayed here until about 1912 and the author can remember the yard full of great threshing and steam cultivating engines, drums and elevators.

Noah Hull then erected a ramshackle wooden shed with a tarpaulin roof in the yard, and thus opened the first cinema in the district. The lantern was lit by an electric arc lamp from a fairground steam engine, driving a dynamo. There were few seats and most of the audience had to stand. John Franks (High Street, St. Neots) took over and ran the cinema for a short time until 1914 when the yard was occupied by the military.

Nos. 17, 15, 13. The site of two cottages (*Hist. Mon. Comm.*, no. 11) pulled down to build the present public convenience.

No. 11. Present Wiles, greengrocer. In 1873 this was a small grocer's and sweet shop kept by J. Gray. Soon after 1895 it was bought by Geo. Sharman (see no. 23) who built the present shop for his butcher's business, and moved here about 1898. He remained until about 1904 when he emigrated to Canada. He returned to St. Neots in his old age and died there in 1962.

In 1904 J. S. Mortimer, butcher, came here from Shefford, moving to High Street, St. Neots in 1911. After this it was unoccupied for many years except as greyhound kennels.

No. 9. The *Chequers* inn. (*Hist. Mon. Comm.*, no. 10.) This picturesque old inn probably dates back to the early 16th century, although there have been many later additions and much restoration. It has a T-shaped plan with a cross wing at the west end. It is probably the oldest house in Eynesbury. Manor Courts of the Eynesbury Manor of Buckley, Berkeley, Ferrars and Cresner, were held here in the 18th century and there is specific record of one in 1785 when the Earl of Sandwich held the Manor.

In 1848 the premises are described as having 'a parlour, club room, tap room, three sleeping-rooms, kitchen, back kitchen, cellar, dairy, stabling, and with two cottages' (see below). In 1894 there was at the back a quoit ground, much used by local people, and matches with visiting teams were held here. It was remembered at the end of the century as a 'gentleman's pub', where working men were not welcomed.

Landlords were: 1783 Jane Briggs, 1785 Andrew Simons, 1821 Widow Mays, 1830-72 John Mays (1797-1872), who bought it in 1848 for £640, 1875 Mrs. Gray, 1880 sold on the death of Thos. Chapman, brewer, Cambridge Street, St. Neots, to Geo. Taylor for £700, and he moved here from the *Half Moon* hotel, Market

Square, St. Neots (see this item) and also had a mineral water factory opposite (see above). He retired to 24 Market Square, St. Neots in 1887. In 1890 the landlord was J. Marshall from Eaton Socon, 1892 Mrs. Marshall, 1893 D. Parlett, 1894 probably 'Dick' Burgin (see no. 12 above) who made the quoit ground at the back, 1895 Eben. Corn, 1896 A. W. Lane, 1897 Susan Bennett followed by G. Wyatt, 1899 H. Warner, 1899-1910 Geo. F. Ashley.

Nos. 7 & 5. Old cottages pulled down to make the present *Chequers* car park and originally part of the premises. G.H. remembers a small shop in one of these kept by Joshua Bass senr., who was also a land measurer.

No. 3. Present Post Office and shop. 1854 John Smith. About 1879 John Whitbread and his son Arthur, tailors, were living and working here. Arthur followed his father and the present lean-to was built as a workshop, after 1880. Sitting cross-legged on his table he was a familiar sight to everyone coming over the bridge to Eynesbury, and no-one came over unobserved by him. He died about 1930.

No. 1. The former *Dog and Duck* inn and yard. The last painted sign showed a liver and white spaniel flushing a mallard duck from the banks of a stream. From its position on Hen Brook it seems likely that at or near this house was once practised the old cruel sport of 'dog and duck', at which spaniels chased pinioned ducks on an enclosed piece of water.

There is a large yard at the back which had a wharf on the brook. In 1848 this property belonged to W. W. Abbott of Berkeley House, Eynesbury, and in 1860 the yard was let at £10 a year to Paine & Son (see Paine & Co. separate item). They had a sawmill here and timber storage sheds. However in 1865 Geo. Bower (see separate item) of the Vulcan Iron Works was using it for storing his carts, wagons, and rafts. In 1870 Paine & Son bought it at the death of W. W. Abbott. About 1880 it was acquired by Daintree & Jewson of the Navigation Yard opposite who soon after resold to the Local Board to enable them to vacate that part of the Navigation Yard they occupied. The Local Board established their Fire Station here and it was used for this purpose until about 1959. In 1890 the engine housed here had been an exhibit at the 1851 Great Exhibition. The inn licence was surrendered about 1945.

BERKELEY STREET

This name was officially adopted by the Local Board in 1878, and it was stated to extend 'from the church to the wash pond at the end of the district'. That would be Townsend Pond that used to exist at the junction of Little Barford and Potton roads. The older name for this street was Front Street and it was still so called in 1888.

WEST SIDE NEXT TO THE CHURCH

No. 2. *Nags Head* **inn.** The present house **replaces** the old 15th-century inn, (*Hist. Mon. Comm.*, no. 13), pulled down in 1927. It was of the type with central hall and cross-wings. Situated on what, at the time it was built, must have been the village green and not a site for an ordinary building, this inn could well have had an association with the church as a 'church house' where semi-religious feasts and functions took place. Even at the end of the century, people coming to church from outlying parts of the parish would go there for meals and refreshment. In 1706 there was a 'church house ground' near the church (see also under 'Eynesbury Hardwick').

In 1848 Capt. W. W. W. Humbley bought the Manors of Eynesbury from Lord Sandwich (see the *Chequers* above) and at least from 1870 to 1900 the Manor Court was held here on 31 May by the steward, latterly O. N. Wilkinson, solicitor, of St. Neots.

Landlords were: before 1567 Raife Pattinson, 1567 Thos. Bull, before 1743 Francis Bull, 1743 Simon Staughton, before 1814 Wm. Pye then Wm. Dixie, 1814 John Smith, 1830 Henry Smith, 1854 Stephen Clarke, mason, 1862 John Evans, 1870 Saml. Nurrisk, 1877 Wm. 'Skinny' Bull (1806-89). He was a milkman and kept 20-30 cows in a yard at the back and made butter in a large way. It was said that he had been cowman to Mr. Staughton, a well-to-do farmer in Eynesbury. He, however, did not prosper and Wm. Bull did, eventually buying up all his master's cows. From this arose a local saying that 'all Staughton's cows have turned into Bull's'. 1889 Naomi, widow of Wm. Bull (1822-1908), 1897 Henry G. Gilbert, 1899 Wm. Stanley.

As was usual at the back of the inn there was a small cottage in which lived, G.H. remembers, John Gaunt, a Crimean War veteran, with a wooden leg, who made a meagre living selling oranges from door to door from a basket.

Methodist Chapel. It was built in 1928 and replaced two little thatched cottages in one of which was a small sweet shop.

No. 10. Butcher's shop and house. Before 1877 these premises were occupied by John Gorham Bingham, a cooper of 50 years' standing. At that date he disposed of his business to his son,

John Edmund Bingham and the premises were taken over by Tom Sharman, butcher, who moved here from St. Neots (see Cambridge Street). He died early this century and was succeeded by his son Wm. 'Jobber' Sharman who died in 1961 at the age of about 90. 'Jobber' also had an extensive cattle-dealing business and was a well-known character in all the local markets. Many tales are told of his exploits of which one must suffice. Sometime, pre-1914, he challenged H. Mortimer, another butcher, to a race along St. Neots High Street for a wager. Mortimer was to run 100 yards and he only 50 yards, but carrying 15 stone of shot. Mortimer arranged to have his horse and trap ready and, when the signal to start was given, a helper started it up and he ran holding on behind. 'Jobber' however won by 15 yards. He retired and was succeeded by his son Bill who died early leaving the business to be carried on by his widow. It had been in one family for about 100 years.

No. 12. One of two semi-detached cottages. G.H. remembers that in one of these lived Mrs. Nichols with her daughter Annie, who had a wooden leg, and her bachelor son Fred. She did high-class washing and laundry for the gentry, helped by her son and daughter. Fred had been a skilled engineer at Bower's ironworks at St. Neots, but when they closed he decided to help his mother with the washing rather than leave the town to seek work at his trade. He was also a musician, playing the dulcimer, and was in great demand at public house parties. At Christmas he would go round playing carols, his friend Dilley holding the lantern and collecting box.

A regular Monday morning sight in the village was a donkey cart arriving from Southoe with Rev. Moorsom's linen basket. The field at the back of the *Merry Boys* inn was hired as a drying ground. Fred and Annie carried on the business after their mother's death.

No. 14. One of two semi-detached cottages. This was a small shop kept by Chas. Moore (1829-96), who came here in 1882 and dealt in tea and coffee and general groceries. He was always known as 'General' Moore, and was also a piano tuner. He was reputed to be 'psychic', and to see spirits in the fire. His wife carried on the shop after his death.

Old Methodist Chapel. This was built to plans by Mr. Littlewood, architect, of St. Neots, probably in 1855 when tenders were advertised for. The foundation stone was laid by Rev. J. Baker, Wesleyan minister from St. Neots. After the new chapel was built in 1928 it was used for a time as the Sunday School and later sold.

No. 24. Semi-detached villa. Here lived Thos. H. 'Gentleman' White, who retired from being landlord of the *King's Head*, St. Neots in 1878. About 1905 he had the first and only motor boat on the river.

No. 32. At the south corner of Silver Street. Formerly the *Gardener's Arms* inn. Renewal of licence was refused in 1913.

No. 44. Site of present Co-operative Society shop. Here lived three generations of the carpenter family of Green, who also kept a small shop. John Green (1820-76), master carpenter was followed by his son John jun. whose own son followed the trade. John jun. left here about 1903, when the shop was taken by Geo. Harvey in connection with the bakery behind the terrace nos. 48-60, followed by Mrs. Stevens who was there at least until 1914.

No. 46. Thatched cottage with wattle and daub walls. (*Hist. Mon. Comm.*, no. 14) built probably in the early 18th century. Pulled down in 1969.

Nos. 48-60. Terrace of six cottages with an archway in the centre giving access to the back doors and baker's premises. This is typical 'industrial revolution' building comparable with Russell Street, St. Neots and can probably be dated 1820-30

In the end house lived a widow, Mrs. Sly (probably Mary Anne Sly, 1831-90) who used the bakery to make her famous sausages before moving to St. Neots (see High Street). The bakehouse was used afterwards by Mr. Page, then John Jarvis (1835-97) followed later by Geo. Harvey about 1903-06.

No. 64. Corner house facing the Green. Formerly the *Golden Ball* inn. In 1814 it had two cottages attached, and a lime kiln and coke kiln.

Landlords: before 1814-30 Wm. & Mary Charlton, straw hat makers; 1854 Wm. Stratton; 1871 Wm. Slinn, tailor; John Mason; Fred Ford (1899). About 1900 Wm. 'Brushy' Freshwater came here from Waterloo Farm when it was burnt down. He was a small farmer and cattle dealer and notoriously eccentric character. For a short time he was a member of the St. Neots U.D.C. where on one occasion he exchanged blows with Saml. Flint, another member, during a meeting.

No. 66. Now a shop rebuilt from an old cottage (*Hist. Mon. Comm.*, no. 15). G.H. remembered Leonard Baines, poultry dealer, living here.

Site of Ferrars Avenue council houses built 1919/20 to designs of architect Barry Parker of Letchworth. Previously this site was a grass field with a gate in the middle of the side facing the Green. In the north-west corner was a pond half in the field and half in the Green, with a fence across the middle. On this the author learned to skate. When land at the back of Luke Street was no longer available Eynesbury Feast was held in this field.

At 13 Ferrars Avenue (now 26 Caldecote Road) the St. Neots quads were born to Mr. and Mrs. Miles on 28 November 1935.

Hare & Hounds inn. This was really also a smallholder's or market gardener's house, with a cottage and farm buildings, later burnt down, at the back. Landlords: 1854 Saml. Flint, market gardener (1838-83) followed by Susan Flint, 1898 Ed. Taylor, 1899 Alf. Wright.

No. 64. Mansden House. There used to be a vague tradition that this house was rebuilt from, or on the site of, the parish workhouse, sold in 1838, and the author remembers as a child it being rudely called 'Bug Hall'. It was parish property at the time of the Inclosure. From at least 1880 it was known as Vine Cottage and from about 1890 became the home of Zachariah Wells, printer and publisher, of the *St. Neots Chronicle*, High Street, St. Neots, followed by his son Frank.

No. 66. Now a private house formerly the *Swan* inn, whose licence renewal was refused in 1913. As usual it had a cottage at the back. Landlords: before 1885 John Bennett, 1885 Henry Cade, 1897 J. T. Bull, dairyman.

No. 68. Halls Farm. Here formerly was a farmhouse with another small house attached, that belonged to Simon Staughton in 1800. They were called Rose Villa and Rose Cottage in 1884, and had 61 acres of land. In 1848 it belonged to James Paine (see Paine & Co. Ltd.) and in 1880 to John Sharp and was let to Brightman & Cooper, who, however, gave it up in that year. It was then let to Thos. Glenn, dairyman. About 1890 or soon after, Isaac Hall, (1846-1904) a farmer and market gardener from Sandy, bought the farm and built a farmhouse from the two old houses in 1894. He had previously been at nearby Low Farm for a time, and was a skilled and successful farmer and market gardener. He was followed by his son Alfred, and later by his grandson and granddaughter.

No. 70. The *Cambridgeshire Hunter* inn, which also had a cottage at the back. Landlords, for about the last 20 years of the century, were various members of the Trolley family.

Low Farm (*Hist. Mon. Comm.*, no. 20). In 1848 the house and attached land belonged to Lord Sandwich with a Mr. Flint as tenant. In 1880 this farm was occupied by Christopher Hall and later Isaac Hall, before moving to Halls Farm (see above), when he put a foreman in here.

The corner field, (now built on) at the junction of Little Barford and Potton roads was known as Pound Close. Also at the junction adjoining the roads was Townsend Pond, filled in about 1950.

EAST SIDE, FROM THE SOUTH END

Waterloo House. Present site of houses called Waterloo Drive. This house was built by Lt.-Col. Wm. Humbley (1783-1857) late of the Rifle Brigade, who saw active service in the Peninsular War, and Walcheren Expedition, and the Battle of Waterloo, where he was wounded by a ball in each shoulder. He seems to have had family connections with the district (in Eynesbury churchyard there is a stone to Eliza, wife of Wm. Humbley who died in 1780) and built this house on his retirement probably first calling it Waterloo Cottage. In 1848 he bought from Lord Sandwich the Lordship of the Eynesbury Manors (see the *Nag's Head* above). He was buried in Eynesbury church and a memorial to him can be seen in the porch. This describes him as 'a gallant and distinguished officer in the Rifle Brigade (old 95th.) who after serving faithfully his King and Country on many battlefields in Denmark, Spain, Portugal, France, and Holland, wherein the British were always victorious, was himself overcome and conquered by the Last Great Enemy in the quiet retirement of this village'. His widow Mary remained at Eynesbury until her death at the age of 86 in 1871.

Col. Humbley had a son Lt.-Col. William Wellington Waterloo Humbley (1815-86) who after his retirement from the army lived in St. Neots (see Cressener House, Huntingdon Street). His only daughter Vimiera Vittoria Violetta Stampers (1829-99) died at 'The Firs', Sandy, and her son took the name of Humbley.

In 1887 it was let to Eliza C. Baker, widow of the rector of Old Warden, Beds. In 1890 it was occupied by Thos. A. Wagstaff surveyor to Toseland Division Highway Board. In 1899 it was described as having three lofty reception rooms, hall, kitchen, seven bedrooms and stables. When put up for sale by the executors of W. W. W. Humbley it was withdrawn at £690. From about 1893 to 1908 it was run as a home for elderly people, and about 1911-14 was occupied by Mr. Tom Armstrong, draper of St. Neots.

At about this time it was bought by Harry Underwood Bishop (1869-1935) a large farmer and market gardener. He was a well-known and popular figure in the district, tall, burly, and robust and often described as a typical 'John Bull'. His grandfather, John Bishop, was said to have been a wagoner, making a living by taking market garden produce to London and, among the other wagoners, was acknowledged as 'King of the Road'. Equal in physique to his grandson he had gained the title by fighting all others who had challenged his right to drive down the middle of the road, putting all other wagons on the grass. At last he was challenged by a younger man and neither would give way. They fought it out on the grass verge and the old champion was at last beaten. The house was pulled down about 1947.

Waterloo Farm. The present house was built about 1913 by Samuel Flint, farmer, to replace an old farmhouse burnt down at that time. In 1854 it was occupied by the Marshall family, farmers and market gardeners who were here at least until the 1870s.

Eynesbury House. This house was built by a Mrs. Newton about 1870, and who left in 1875. About 1889 it was bought by James Paine (1825-1912) (see Paine & Co. Ltd.). In 1895, during a great storm, the large tall chimney fell and crashed through all floors to the ground without anyone in the house being hurt. In 1898 it was bought by Wm. Emery (died 1915), banker and bookseller, (see Market Square, St. Neots) on his retirement, and his widow lived here until 1931.

The Ferns. This was originally a timber-framed and thatched farmhouse, probably of the 17th century, part of which was pulled down, and a square block one room deep added to form the front about 1700. This was done in red brick and tile and still has the original iron-framed windows with leaded lights. The kitchen is part of the first house and its original rafters for thatch are under the present roof. In the hall is a reset plaster panel depicting 'amorine'. This came from a farmhouse on the south side of Adams Lane, Great Paxton, pulled down about 1930. Its date is about 1600 and it was probably made by itinerant Italian craftsmen. Another from the same mould was in the *Angel Arms*, Market Square, St. Neots and reset in the present *Golden Ball*. Outside the present back door was once a pond and the still existing wood and thatched sheds bordering Howitts Lane were once cow sheds. Belonging to the house is a small thatched cottage, William John Chapman was living here about 1850 and his son William was born here (see Alma Cottage below).

In 1876 a Miss Evans lived here, who in 1876 married Rev. E. Evans of Marshfield. After her came Rev. Townley, curate, who in 1889 became rector of Christchurch, Cambs.

In 1896 the house was bought by C. G. Tebbutt who lived here as a bachelor until his marriage to Katharine Mary Warren of St. Ives in 1899. He founded the present firm of C. G. Tebbutt Ltd. (see separate item) and on coming to the district in 1889 at once took a leading part in its sporting life. He played with and captained local cricket and football teams, rode at Brampton Races and hunted with the Cambridgeshire. He was internationally known as a speed skater and writer on speed skating and the original form of ice hockey, called Bandy, which he introduced into many European countries. He left here to live at Bluntisham in 1910. The author, his eldest son, was born here in 1900, and returned to live here from 1926 to 1966.

Shirdley House. This fine Georgian farmhouse, facing the Green, was bought by St. Neots Urban District Council and restored with taste. The large thatched barn that stood on its north side was pulled down in recent years.

In 1800 it belonged to Paul Pattison, a large local farmer, but by 1825 had passed to Ed. Peck (1802-67), probably through his wife Jane Pattison Peck (1803-84). His son was named Edward and probably his grandson also. Wm. Peck, probably another grandson, carved his name on a rafter of the old barn in 1857. It is still preserved by Mr. Wm. Chapman of Alma Cottage, Howitts Lane. William met a tragic death by poisoning in 1871 at the age of 31. After selling some scrap silver to Wm. Chambers, watchmaker, at his shop in St. Neots, Market Square, he was given a glass of beer which accidentally contained cyanide, and died within a few minutes of drinking it.

In 1855 Eliza, third daughter of Ed. Peck, married a Wm. Chapman, cattle dealer, which may account for the premises being occupied by John Chapman about 1890. Soon after, John How, farmer and cattle dealer, moved here from 19 St. Mary's Street. He was a rough, hard man whose ruthless character made him unpopular in the village. His first wife had died in 1878 leaving two small children, and he then married a widow with one son. The new wife did not get on with her stepchildren and one night the two, aged about 7 and 9, were turned out of doors. The village showed its strong disapproval by burning him in effigy on the Green in front of his house. He finally went bankrupt and died in 1916.

No. 27. New Darringtons Garage. This replaced old cottages in one of which, about 1887, lived Bonner, a master tinsmith and once an employee at Bower's ironworks, St. Neots.

No. 21. Private house, but once a pork butcher's premises kept by James Kirby (1826-99).

Merry Boys **inn.** This had three cottages attached. Landlords: before 1879 to the 1890s, 'Billie' Lamb. an 18-stone character who occasionally killed a pig and sold pork, and was also a coal merchant. G.H. remembers the price was 1s. cwt. delivered, 10d. from the yard, and 8d. from the station. He was followed by Jonathan (or 'Shont', as all Jonathans were called) Partridge who was a rod (osier) cutter for Newman (see Market Square, St. Neots). 1899 to 1912, Benj. Hackett.

No. 15. Private house now 'Five Gables' formerly 'Strathfield'. Before 1887 this house was occupied by Rev. Newman, minister of one of the St. Neots nonconformist chapels, who kept cows in the field at the back and sold milk. About 1887 John Sibley (see Paine & Co. Ltd.) came here from East Street, St. Neots, staying until 1898 when he moved to the Market Square. The house was then called Ivy Bank. In that year James Paine, whose fortunes had fallen somewhat, moved here from Eynesbury House (see above), remaining until he died in 1912. Two of his daughters remained, the last one dying about 1960.

Eynesbury Church Room. Built on a vacant site in 1901. Inside is a tablet inscribed 'In memory of John Hipwell Goodgames and Harriet his wife, also Frederick Emery and Charlotte his wife, by their children Harriet Goodgames, Elizabeth and Wm. Emery, 1901'.

No. 7. Manor Cottage. In the 1890s this was occupied by Arthur Elgood, miller (see Market Square) followed by Tom Armstrong, draper (see Market Square), before going to Waterloo House (see above).

No. 5. In this small cottage lived Geo. Redman whose son Charles was apprenticed as gardener to Lord Salisbury at Hatfield. He returned to St. Neots in 1896 and started a nursery garden business in New Street, with conspicuous success. His sons went into the brewery trade becoming directors of Wells & Winch Ltd., Biggleswade.

No. 3. Church House. In the early 19th century this was almost certainly the home of John Wells, conveyancer and clerk to the Toseland Petty Sessions which were held at this house, at least up to 1834. 'T' writing in 1891 says '70 years ago there were no Bench Magistrates then in the town . . . and Ousley Rowley would walk down on Thursdays to the office of Mr. Wells the

Conveyancer at Eynesbury where he would meet the rector, Rev. Palmer, and conclude the magisterial business within the hour'. *St. Neots Chronicle* in 1870 recorded that the body of Wm. Wells, aged 67 or 68, was found on the railway. He had been an inmate of the workhouse and was the son of a solicitor of Eynesbury, clerk of the Magistrates Court. The family had become reduced. A John Wells of Eynesbury, probably the above, was clerk for the ballot for the Provincial Cavalry in 1797.

Later Jas. Wilkinson (1788-1862) lived here and it is recorded that in 1853 Mrs. Wilkinson, who had been totally blind for 20 years, accidentally fell down the stairs and as a result of the shock completely recovered her sight.

Probably about 1860 James Brown (1822-99) came to live here. He was a wealthy butcher and farmer with a shop on the Market Square, next to the bridge. He married a Mrs. Carter, daughter of T. Jennings, a well-known Newmarket trainer, whose first husband had been trainer to the King of Italy at Turin. They were remembered in the village as being generous and good to the poor. His son Harry and daughter Cissie continued to live here for some years after he died.

No. 1. Berkeley House. A large and probably old house with groom's cottages, stables, garden, and grass paddock at the back extending down to the brook. It was for many years the home of the Abbott family, and Wm. Ward Abbott (1793-1870) was here at least as early as 1823. He was described as an auctioneer and surveyor. He was also a property owner in the district and had a foundry somewhere in St. Neots. His daughter Mary (born 1818) married Wm. Paine of St. Neots (see Paine & Co.) and his portrait hangs in the present boardroom of that company. Some action of his must have incurred severe public disapproval. In 1828 it was alleged at Quarter Sessions that 15 men, mainly of St. Neots and Eaton Socon 'with others as yet unknown to the number of 100 or more, did unlawfully . . . and tumultuously assemble . . . and gather together a certain Wooden Gibbet in a common highway near the dwelling house of one Wm. Ward Abbott, did erect and carry about and exhibit . . . a certain figure resembling a Man . . . as the effigy of the said Wm. Ward Abbott . . . and did hang on the said gibbet and did make a great noise and disturbance for a long time to wit for the space of one hour to the damage and disturbance of the said Wm. Ward Abbott'. At his death, in 1870, the property was sold and almost certainly was then bought by John Hipwell Goodgames, draper of St. Neots, (see 37 Market Square) who died at a great age in 1896, and his wife Harriet, born 1816, dying a

year earlier. His daughter, Harriet, continued to live here until her
death in 1922. She was followed by Dr. Cross, on his retirement
from practice in the Market Square.

MONTAGUE STREET

West side, next to the School. A public path and right of way to
the river, given in 1862 by Rev. Maule in place of another path 60
yards further north which was then stopped up. It also gave access
to Eynesbury cemetery laid out from land in Dovehouse Close
under a Burial Board in 1856. The first members were: Rev. Maule,
Henry Wigginton, Wm. Paine, Wm. Peppercorn, Ed. Peck, Robt.
King, John Bishop.

House and builder's premises. Now called 'The Cottage'. Built
in 1874 for £195 and occupied by Piggot & Banks (probably
builders). In 1883 it was taken by Jas. Pearson, when he bought
the builder's and undertaker's business of Clark Charles (see 35
St. Mary's Street), and he was here at least until about the end
of the century.

Old timber-framed house facing Montague Square, at the junction
of Montague Street and Washbank Road (*Hist. Mon. Comm.*, no.
12). Now partly pulled down, and called 'Coneygarth'. This was
a farmhouse and once the home of the Luke family, after whom
Luke Street is named. In 1677 it was divided into two houses
in which lived Nicholas Luke the elder (died 1681) and Nicholas
Luke the younger. His son Samuel (1685-1754) left no male heir.
With this house went 86 acres of land in the Coneygear and
Eynesbury open fields, and Ray or Horse Mill close, on which is
now Eynesbury School and the old cemetery.

MONTAGUE STREET, EAST SIDE NEXT TO THE CHURCH

Private house formerly bakehouse and shop. From about 1865
this was occupied by Robt. Smith, baker and grocer, until his
death in 1895. After this the grocer's shop was given up and the
baker's business carried on by Chas. Brown until 1947. He was
the son of a foreman pattern-maker at Bowers Vulcan Iron Works,
St. Neots, and himself an apprentice with Ekins, baker, in South
Street.

Site of T. W. Wren Ltd. Fried Fish Depot. Part of this site was
once occupied by a terrace of small 'mud and stud' cottages known
as 'Fishpond Row', said to be named on account of a fishpond at
the back, long ago filled in, and perhaps used to store fish netted

in the river. It may not have been a coincidence that G.H. remembers, living in one of these, Wm. Harlot, known as 'Popson Jonnie' who had a drag-net which he used to catch fish in the river to sell by hawking round the district. In another cottage he remembered Ephraim Crow, a rat catcher, with kennels and pens for his dogs and ferrets at the back.

Also on this site were a pair of semi-detached rather high thatched cottages with a plaster front decorated at first floor level with a large letter A.

MONTAGUE SQUARE or GREEN

The Red House. A Georgian-type house in which red brick was used probably after it became unfashionable or unusual hence the name. G.H. said that it was by tradition built by a doctor and never finished. This may be borne out by the fact that it had a semi-turret built outside to take the stairs and was only one room in depth. A curious feature is a fireplace in the capacious cellar.

It was probably lived in by a family called Bettles or Bewley, who had the adjoining business premises up to about the middle of last century or soon after. About 1850 Henry Harvey, (1826-95) a journeyman parchment-maker, came to the district and found work at the fellmonger's yard in Church Street, St. Neots, next to Eynesbury Bridge, then probably belonging to John Fairey. After a short time he decided to set up himself and his wife and family joined him, first at Elm Lodge, Potten Road and soon after at these premises where he lived until his death, and where his widow survived him by nine years. After this it was empty for about 10 years.

The Skin Yard. Industrial premises adjoining the above house were pulled down and built over by the U.D.C. in 1960 after being derelict for a number of years. The first known occupant of the premises was a corn and general merchant either named Bettles or Thos. Gibson Bewley, who may have built the premises in that position as being convenient to the navigation. Some time soon after the middle of the century they were taken over by Henry Harvey (see above) and adapted for parchment-making. From humble beginnings he became a prominent and respected member of local society and served on the Local Board during the whole of its existence. At his death the yard was divided, part being left to his son Harry (1849-1932) and part to his grandson Albert Harvey, both being parchment-makers. The last of the family to work there was Albert's brother Alfred, who carried on in a small way until about 1945, by which time the demand for parchment had almost ceased.

Sheepskins were either bought from the local butchers and split or obtained already split from the fellmongers. They then had to be boiled and stretched on frames for the delicate process of scraping with half-moon-shaped blades to remove all the fat and reduce them to the finest quality parchment required by the well-known firm, Waterlow of London, who took much of the firm's output.

In the small grass close at the back of the Skin Yard Henry Harvey dug gravel, investing the proceeds in building Montague Terrace next to the Red House. In the course of this digging, in 1890, two skeletons were found in graves four feet apart and lying east and west. Earlier, in 1889, Mr. Harvey had deposited in the Victoria Museum, St. Neots a box containing human bones and pottery sherds representing two early Bronze Age beakers found in his gravel pit. In 1930 Mr. Albert Harvey produced to the author, from his office at the Skin Yard, two polished stone axes also from the same site (see *Antiquaries Journal*, October 1930). All are now in the Norris Museum, St. Ives. In 1960 the ground under the demolished building was trenched by the author in the hope of making further finds. Under the wing facing Montague Square at 2 ft. 6 inches below the floor was found the clay floor and walls of a single room building, possibly part of a larger house, dated by its associated pottery to the early 12th century. Above it, but under the existing floor, was the floor of an 18th-century building (see *Proc. Camb. Ant. Soc.*, Vol. LIV, 1961). The finds are in the Cambridge Museum of Archaeology.

The Coneygear. The name is said to mean a rabbit warren. G.H. remembers it as private land through which ran the present public footpath to 'Eaton Dams'. The present recreation ground is marked as a gravel pit in the 1830 Inclosure Map and Gorham says that it had long been used for that purpose. He records that pottery he calls Roman had been found there, and illustrates an unusual bottle necked Saxon pottery vessel found in 1816 that is probably of the 7th century A.D. It is now in the Museum of Archaeology, Cambridge. Also from this area, in the Norris Museum, St. Ives, are some early Saxon clay loom weights, indicating a settlement.

On the cultivated allotment ground south of the footpath gravel-digging last century destroyed most of the earthworks of a small Roman ditched and banked rectangular enclosure marked as complete on the one-inch Ordnance map of 1835. Excavations by the author showed it to be a Roman work, probably of the second half of the 3rd century (see *Trans. Cambs. and Hunts. Arch. Soc.*, Vol. V, Part 5, 1935). Mr. Rudd has recently discovered a Roman building with hypocaust heating under a mound near the footpath just outside the south-west corner of the earthwork site (grid. ref. TL 180594).

The Pound. There are references to a Pound near the Coneygear, perhaps an earlier site than that on Eynesbury Green.

Cottages between the Coneygear and Montague Square were pulled down about 1960.

The *Woolpack* **inn.** Kept for many years by the Shepherd family. Landlords: Mrs. Eliza. Shepherd (1798-1879) whose husband was a wool stapler. In 1879 the annual dinner of the Association for the Prosecution of Garden Robbers was held here. Her daughter Anne Tomblin, who died in 1903, was then stated to have been the last of the Eynesbury May Queens, during Rev. Maule's incumbency. She was followed by her son Charles Shepherd (1840-99) and he by his widow Emma. She was there until about 1912 and was followed by H. Shepherd.

River Terrace. Nos. 1-10. Built 1899 by Peter Wildman. In one of these G.H. remembers that there lived Mark Freeston. He made a part living by buying pig's trotters from the butchers, taking them to the Skin Yard (see above) to beg hot water in which to skin them, and then hawked them round the district.

The Wash Bank. This was a cart way to the river where horses were taken for watering, carts washed, and watercarts filled. For much of the way across the river the bottom is hard and shallow, and it may once have been a ford. On a map of Lord Sandwich's land, dated 1848, this road is called Mill Lane, and the little field along the river bank to the south belonged to the navigation company. It is probable therefore that riverborne goods for Eynesbury were unloaded here.

Willow Bank. Probably built by Frank Wallis, a gentleman of independent means, who lived here at least from 1872 until the end of the century.

LUKE STREET

South Side

Montague Terrace. Nos. 47-65, next to the Red House. Built by Henry Harvey (see above) in 1893 at a cost of £100 each from the proceeds of gravel digging behind his house. Before they were built, three old thatched cottages were pulled down on the west side of the site. The field was then known as Britain's Field and had a hedge along the frontage and a wide footpath much narrowed when the present terrace was built. Britain's Field was used for the annual Eynesbury Feast. G.H. remembered seeing 'Harris's Roundabouts' there with 'penny farthing' bicycles alternating with horses in the circle.

Nos. 31-45. Terrace of eight cottages. These once belonged to the Forester's Club, as did the field in which they were built. G.H. remembered a Robt. Wye, bootmaker, living in one of these. He may have been the last local representative of the once wealthy 18th-century St. Neots family of that name. An Eliza Wye died in the workhouse, aged 91, in 1891.

Two semi-detached cottages, with formerly two more up the yard. After Montague Terrace was built (see above) the Feast was held in the field behind these.

Just east of this site and back from the road G.H. remembered a large barn, built with red brick up the first floor and then tarred weather boards up to the eaves. Inside it had a loft over the whole area and at ground level a stone floor used by people to thresh out their harvest gleanings.

It was here that the first indoor services of the Salvation Army were held in the district before the Citadel was built in St. Neots in 1891. Either this barn, or one on the opposite side of the street (see below) was used as a school for Eynesbury children sometime previous to 1861. It was owned, G.H. remembered, by Dick Shepherd, a small 'wheelbarrow' builder.

No. 15. Detached house. Here lived W. Ashley, who was appointed clerk to Toogood Bros. at St. Neots Paper Mill in 1876, and later became clerk and treasurer to the Starr-Bowkett Building Society, in which many local people had invested money. In 1892 the society became insolvent and Ashley disappeared. A warrant was issued for his arrest and in 1893 he was arrested on his return from Canada, where he had fled. He was sentenced to three years' penal servitude for larceny and fraud. This caused a great stir locally as many small savings were involved and he had been looked on as a gentleman.

Nos. 3, 5. A red-brick house, (*Hist. Mon. Comm.*, no. 19) now divided into two. This must once have been a farmhouse. In 1785 it had a close of eight acres attached (Old Close), had been occupied by Geo. Villers, and was then taken by Simon Pattison. In 1800 Paul Pattison had it. G.H. remembered it occupied by first John and then Tom Emery, both carpenters.

Old School Yard. This terrace of six squalid brick and tiled tenements (later made into four) each having only one room up and down was pulled down in 1960. It was built at right-angles to the street and faced north across a yard. Its history is obscure but there can be no doubt that at one time it was a school. Once when repairs were being carried out, the author saw, previously covered by plaster, an inscription 'Suffer the Little Children to Come unto Me', painted over the end doorway to the west. From the evidence of a number of wills and property transfers, in which the boundaries of adjoining properties are described, there is little doubt that this was the workhouse in 1785, but had become Rev. Palmer's school in 1825.

North side, next the Green.

Nos. 2-28. Terrace of 14 houses. G.H. remembers that in one of these lived Mrs. F. H. Martin ('Black Sal') hosier and dealer in second-hand clothes.

No. 30. *Crown* inn, at the corner of Silver Street, which no doubt gave the alternative name of Crown Street to this end of Luke Street. Landlords: 1889 — Gaunt, also blacksmith, followed by Martha Gaunt. 1893 Ernest Stocker, who was there until after the end of the century.

No. 44. House with blacksmith's shop at the corner of Silver Street. Very probably the business of Ed. Dixie, mentioned in *Directories* of 1824 and 1830, and afterwards, perhaps, Chas. Disher (1799-1880). Later there was here John Peters, probably son of Wm. Peters, blacksmith (died 1876) and some of whose tools together with his account books for 1855 and 1865-75 were found when an old lady named Mrs. Peters died in East Street in 1963. The books are now in the county archives. The last blacksmith, Fred John ('Shuny') Haynes was there in the 1890s and up to 1914.

Nos. 48-56. Walnut Tree Terrace. Was so named because when built there was an orchard of walnut trees at the back. G.H. remembered that in no. 56 lived Mrs. Disher with two grown-up bachelor sons. They kept cows, using all the milk for butter making. The two sons played the fiddle and banjo and were in constant demand at all local shows, fetes and parties. At outdoor events they played from a shelter of tarpaulin which they kept and erected, and which was known as Disher's Booth. The *Chronicle* of 1876 reported that Disher's Band played country dances and the polka at Eynesbury Choir Annual Ball in the schoolroom.

Behind this terrace stood a large barn with stables on the ground floor and a loft above. G.H. remembers that it belonged to Wm. Whittet, baker, Market Square, and was let to C. Newman, grocer of Market Square, who used it for 'rod' peeling. Women were employed to peel the freshly-cut osiers which were then stored in the loft and sold to basket-makers. Either this barn, or more likely the one opposite (see above) was once used as a school. G.H. was the first to discover, in about 1898, that the barn was on fire, and ran to St. Neots to summon the fire brigade. He found them in the course of being entertained by their captain, Aldred Jordan, on his lawn at Wistaria House, Huntingdon Street, and very reluctant to leave or believe in the authenticity of the fire. When at last the horse-drawn manual fire engine approached by way of Montague Street, and the horse saw the smoke and flames, it refused to go on. It then had to be driven back to the church, turned down Berkeley Street, and unhitched by the pond on the Green, from which water was pumped on the fire. The barn was totally burnt but adjoining property saved.

BUCKLEY ROAD

G.H. remembers this as a private way, known as Brittain's Path, with a gate at each end, having on the south side a walnut orchard belonging to Ulysses Brittain (see below). The public, however, often used it as a short cut to and from the *Nag's Head* in Berkeley Street.

No. 58. House, bakehouse, and shop. The home and business of Ulysses Brittain, baker. He was here in 1854 and was followed in the 1890s by his son-in-law W. Edwards, and he by his son of the same name, all bakers.

No. 78. House with small shop and bakehouse. Here lived Chas. Gray, rope-maker (1815-90) who afterward moved to the ropewalk in New Street, St. Neots. G.H. did not remember the bakehouse in regular use but often let to bakers when their own ovens were being relined.

SILVER STREET

This street does not appear on the 1835 Ordnance map, but was there in 1878 when the Local Board confirmed the name. G.H. remembers Geo. Baldock (1822-99), rat-catcher, stack-dresser, and smallholder, who lived next to the blacksmith's shop at the north-west corner of this street. It is almost certainly his father who appears in the accounts of Day & Son, the Priory, St. Neots as contracting for rat-catching there at £1 3s. 3d. a quarter, from 1830 to 1840. His son Charles followed the same profession but lived in Huntingdon Street.

HOWITTS LANE

This may have been named from John or Joseph Howitt who is referred to in 1794, and as Surveyor of Highways in 1812 (see also under 'The Laurels' below). It was also called Brickkiln Lane in 1825. J.L. remembered that in the 1860s it had a gate across the road just beyond Ferns Cottage and another at the entrance to 'Dark Lane', that is the junction leading north at Eynesbury cemetery.

Ferns Cottage. On the west side at the edge of the Green (*Hist. Mon. Comm.*, No. 18). One of the very few thatched cottages left and built of 'wattle and daub' with wood framing. It dates probably from the early 17th century and was attached to the nearby farmhouse (now the 'Ferns', see above).

Alma Cottage. On the east side, opposite the Green (*Hist. Mon. Comm.*, no. 17). Also thatched and probably of the 17th century. In the early part of last century belonged to the Pattison family and Paul Pattison may have lived here. Inherited by the Peck family, it was sold at the death of Jane Pattison Peck to Wm. John Chapman in 1884, her son-in-law. He may have lived here, but certainly his son William (1853-1923) did. He did business from here as dealer in pigs and agent for agricultural supplies, and his son still lives here (see also the 'Ferns' above).

The Laurels. This was once a farmhouse and had attached land at the back along the east side of Howitts Lane as far as the railway. In 1800 and 1825 it was occupied by Joseph Howitt, described as late of St. Neots, innkeeper, and he no doubt gave his name to the lane. He was followed by Rev. Geo. Freer, probably a curate. In 1877 John Lenton (1829-90) was here until his death. He came from an old Abbotsley family and was regarded as well-off. He weighed about 20 stone. G.H. remembers the field behind being used for school treats.

Mortar Pit. A short way up the lane, on the west side (grid ref. TL. 187594) a long narrow field running along the lane, and now built over, was awarded at the 1800 Inclosure as a public mortar pit. From here any parishioner could dig clay for building or repairing 'wattle and daub' cottages.

POTTON ROAD

Also used to be known as Drove Road, possibly because cattle
were driven along it to join the known cattle drove way towards
London which follows a Roman road and is known locally as
Hail Lane. This road joins it as Highfield. The only development
on this road in the 19th century was the brickworks on the east
side (grid ref. TL. 189592) with a small group of cottages for a
foreman and workmen, and a rather larger house called Elm Lodge.

The Brickworks. These first appear on the 1835 Ordnance map
(but not at the Inclosure of 1800) but seem to have been developed
and extended by Jas. Paine in 1853. He built and occupied
Elm Lodge on his marriage to Miss Oliver in 1855. He left here
to live in Eynesbury House about 1889. His main trade at the
outset was with the Great Northern Railway Company, then
working on their main line. In 1883 he sold the business 'in
consequence of the end of the tenancy', together with the stock
which comprised: '500,000 building bricks, 15,000 roofing tiles,
326,000 draining tiles of various sizes, 2,000 culvert tiles, 1,200
octagonal chimney bricks, 1,500 garden tiles, 50 headstones, 2,000
ridge and hip tiles, 176 open gateways, 15in. and 12in. lead pump,
piping, wheelbarrows, planks, shelves, pug mills, three tiles
machines, kilns, drying and other sheds'. It seems probable that the
business was then taken over by A. W. Atkinson of St. Neots,
who appears to have already established a brickyard on an adjoining site by 1865. This firm continued to make bricks here until
about 1920. The bricking business was a seasonal one. The winter
months October to May were used to dig clay, which was done
with wooden shovels, and a small windmill pumped up water to
mix with the clay to 'make' it. Silver or seashore sand was imported
by barge and carted from Brookside and used to prevent the clay
from sticking to the moulds. The kilns were only in use during the
remainder of the year and the chief products were building bricks:
plain, pan, corrugated and ridge tiles, 9 in. by 9 in., and 12 in.
by 12 in. floor tiles, and field 'tiles' (pipes), then mainly two inch.
G.H. remembers that three or four men were employed in the winter and six or eight in the summer. The foreman was Eli Andrews
(1849-1912) who lived in one of the brickyard cottages.

Brickfield House. This had a fellmonger's premises attached adjoining the brickyard. Probably occupied by W. Whitley before 1879,
one of a firm of fellmongers that also had premises in Church
Street, St. Neots. At that date it was taken over by Ebenezer
Watson, fellmonger, and he was followed by his son John who

gave up about 1930. His was a one-man business and he would fetch the hides from the butcher in a wheelbarrow. Leather was supplied to the shoemakers and hair to the builders for plastering.

Also in an open space here, in the early years of this century, Jarvis Peacock, formerly farm foreman to Isaac Bradshaw of Caldecot, had his business of agricultural contractor and kept here his teams of steam ploughing and threshing engines and their tackle.

Toll Gate. The 1835 Ordnance map marks a Toll Gate along this road about 200 yards north of the Abbotsley road junction. (Grid. ref. TL. 194571).

Eynesbury Fields Farm. There is liable to be some confusion of names here as both this and the following one are marked 'Eynesbury Fields' on the 1835 Ordnance Map. However this farm retained the name at the end of the century. It was, of course, a post-enclosure (1800) farm, awarded to the Earl of Sandwich, consisting of 304 acres in the former open Brook Field. At his death Jas. Brown (1792-1878) was farming it, and he was followed by Walter Brown, Jas. Peck was there in 1883 and he was succeeded by Frank Bishop, brother of Harry Bishop of Waterloo House (see above), who remained here until his death.

Parkers, Brittains or High Farm. This post-enclosure farm was formed from land in the former open Middle Field, awarded to Samuel Luke, Wm. Fowler, and Simon Staughton in 1800. 'T' remembered it being farmed by Wm. Simpson. In 1860 D. Brittain was there and was followed by his son F. W. Brittain, who was there in 1890 and until about 1909. Being owner-occupied the latter had the shooting rights, and he and his friends enjoyed much sport on account of the farm's situation on the borders of the Pym, Alington, and Rowley estates, where game was reared and preserved. It was said that some crops were grown specially to attract game.

Eynesbury, or Puttocks, Hardwick Farm. An ancient enclosed manor farm, actually part of a separate parish of that name that includes Caldecot, Lansbury, and Weald. It has been in the ownership of the Pym family for about 200 years.

The house (*Hist. Mon. Comm.*, no. 3), which is still largely surrounded by a wet square moat, dates from the 17th century, or possibly slightly earlier. It had probably been a double cross wing house with the south wing pulled down and rebuilt, or a new wing added. The present north wing and central hall part is wooden framed, now cased in brick with a massive stone and brick chimney at the junction of the hall and north wing. The cross wing is in 12-foot bays. When the west wall of the north wing was rebuilt, within living memory, faced Barnack stones, some with Norman dog-tooth moulding (now in the garden) were found in the sub-wall supporting the timber-framing of what was then the dairy. The farm buildings just outside the moat on the west side have courses of building stone in their walls, and this probably all comes from the chapel of St. Thomas, which was still being disposed of as a property there in 1549. There are more faced stones in the bank outside the moat at the north-west corner under an oak tree, and the grass field immediately north of the moat has a very irregular surface. It seems likely that somewhere on this area was the chapel and small village of Eynesbury Hardwick. It is also of interest that one of the posses-sions of the chapel, at its dissolution, was a cottage at Eynesbury called 'church house' which may have been the *Nag's Head* (see above) used for refreshment by these remote inhabitants when they visited the mother church. In 1706 there was a 'church house ground' on the street near the church.

Known tenants of this farm are: 1799 Wm. Kidman. In Georg-ham churchyard in Devon is a memorial to: 'W. Kidman aged 23, son of Wm. and Mary Kidman of Eynesberry Hardwick in Co. Huntingdon who lost his life near the rocks of Baggy. H.M.S. Weazle. February 10th. 1799. The sloop Weazle was sunk with all hands (105 men and 1 woman) on a voyage from Appledore to Falmouth'. In 1854 the tenant was Ed. Peck. The author was told by his old sawyer, Fred Cade, in 1934, that his father, as a young man, engaged himself to Ed. Peck for a year as labourer, and lived in the house with other hired servants. The farmer was mortally afraid of robbers and had the bridge over the moat made into a drawbridge which he pulled up every night, leaving the house completely surrounded by water. 1860, 1875, Peck and Hill; 1879-99 R. S. Taylor; 1902 Richard Anthony followed by his son, Reginald Anthony, the present tenant.

Lansbury. Another ancient enclosed farm belonging to the Pym family and called, on the Inclosure map (1800) the 'Hamlet of Lansbury'. Its name comes from the family of Launcelyn, medi-eval owners of this manor, with whom must be associated the moated site (grid. ref. TL. 209580), and whose memorial brasses can be seen in Cople church, Bedfordshire.

Tenants have been: 1841, 1854 John Wiggington (died probably in 1856 at an advanced age) followed by Henry Wiggington, who left 1879. John Browning (died about 1890), became a tenant and it has been farmed by members of the Browning family ever since.

LITTLE BARFORD ROAD

Day's Brickyard. On the east side of this road, almost on the parish and county boundary, was Day's Brickyard, at a place called Galley Hill. There was probably an early brickworks here as a 'Brickkiln Field, adjacent to Galley Hill', is mentioned in 1838. There is no mention of a brickyard in Day & Sons' account books, 1823-42, but they were rated for it in 1860. It was sold to Harry Bishop at Day's sale in 1919 but he sold the stock and discontinued the business. Some of the moulds and brick-making tools were salvaged by the author and are now in the Norris Museum, St. Ives. Two cottages, built for workmen, still exist on the road frontage.

The Parish Boundary. Among the Little Barford parish records are a number of accounts of the annual Perambulation or Beating of the Bounds, dating from 1693. This took place in May on Rogation Tuesday and it was apparently usual to meet the Eynesbury party on the same errand, so that differences could be settled on the spot. There was apparently a farmhouse built actually across the boundary at one place, and it was the custom for a member of one parish to put a stick in at the window of the house and a member of the other parish to pull it through another window; the same was done when a dense 'briery' was encountered on the boundary. In 1829 Joseph Andrews, aged 81, who had witnessed the last Perambulation, pointed out the boundary to Rev. Alington and W. Peppercorn.

Bishop's Farm. This is of course a post enclosure farm that almost certainly took its name from John Bishop (1819-88).

Caldecot Manor Farm. Long a possession of the Pym family, and actually in the parish of Eynesbury Hardwick. The house (*Hist. Mon. Comm.*, no. 2) dates from the early 17th century and still has a moat partly surrounding it. Irregularities of ground nearby suggest other buildings and it is probably a deserted village site.

The name is of interest as there are many Caldecots on or near the old cattle droving roads, of which the nearby Hail Lane of Roman origin is one. 'Caldecots' are said to have been shelters, as opposed to inns, where drovers could find shelter for the night but with no fire or food. The author was told by F. Cade in 1934 (then aged about 75), that his father used to drive cattle along this road to London as a young man.

Tenants of this farm were: 1854, 1860 Henry Wiggington; 1875 Thos. Fuller (leaving); 1875 Isaac Bradshaw, who came here from Monks Hardwick. He had a set of Fowlers steam engines and undertook ploughing and threshing contracts. He went bankrupt and had left by 1888, when he was at Great Paxton. In 1892 and at least until the end of the century, Frederick Preedy (1860-1928) was here.

Weald Farm. This again was the site of a small medieval hamlet, and earthworks can be seen around the area marked 'Chapel Yard' on the Ordnance map. This small ditched area was tested by excavation by E. F. Newton in 1941 with scant results, but nearby he found the foundations of the 12th-century chapel measuring, internally, 43 feet by 11 feet (*Cambs. Hunts. Arch. Soc.*, vol. VI, Part VI). The finds are in the Norris Museum, St. Ives.

There were at times two farms here and it is difficult to differentiate the tenancies. In 1743 Job. Charlton had a house with 100 acres of land here from Mary Charlton, and in 1775 a Mr. Lenton was here. In 1854 one farm was occupied by Jas. Hagger, followed by R. Hagger who was there until 1894. The other farm was in the occupation in 1854 of Wm. Pentelow (1800-63), followed by Jos. Pentelow, who left in 1879. In 1898 there was Elijah Newell and John G. Ganderson. Wm. Ganderson, son of the above, wrote letters to the *St. Neots Advertiser* in 1898 describing his adventures on the White Pass Trail on the way to Klondyke in the great gold rush of that year.

Weald House. In 1898 this was occupied by the Countess of Dysart.

Eynesbury Church. The church is well described in both the *Victoria County History*, and the *Royal Commission on Historic Monuments*. In the last century there were elm trees round the perimeter of the church yard on the street side and its area was larger than at present. In recent years, the roadside footpath was widened facing Berkeley Street and St. Mary's Street and the wall set back.

A print of 1824 shows the stocks and whipping post just outside the wall facing St. Mary's Street.

The base of a cross stands in the churchyard just west of the north porch. This was returned to Eynesbury from Ramsey in 1935 by Dr. Fisher on the tradition that it had originated from there. It had been given to him by Mrs. Payne who had it from the garden of her father, Wm. Medland, in New Street, St. Neots. It may well have been the base of the pre-Reformation churchyard cross or equally could have come from the St. Neots Cross, known to have existed at the junction of High Street and Huntingdon Street.

A footpath which used to cross the churchyard along the south side was closed in 1874.

In 1946 excavations in connection with a new heating boiler, on the east side of the tower, revealed at 18 inches depth and six inches from the tower foundations a large whole medieval cooking pot (probably of the 13th century) lying on top of two crushed human skulls. There was nothing recognisable inside the pot. There have been a number of recorded instances of medieval pots buried in churchyards but with no known explanation.

THE GREEN

The Green, and here we refer to the one at the junction of Berkeley Street and Luke Street, was in many ways the heart and centre of the village. We have seen in the chapter 'The Origin of the Village' that it once probably extended as far as the church and included all the land between Berkeley Street and Luke Street, as well as Montague Street (sometimes called Montague Green).

Here the boys played football and cricket and the girls their traditional round and singing games. On summer evenings the adults, more particularly the men, met and gossiped, leaning on the railings on the east side of the road.

John Irons, remembering back to the 1850s, described to me how on dry and windy late summer evenings families would bring their sacks of gleanings on to the Green. These had already been threshed at home with a short stick, for want of a flail, and were now sieved on the Green to winnow out the chaff in the breeze. Later the corn grains would be taken to Duloe windmill or Eaton Socon water-mill to be ground for making home-made bread, the miller keeping the bran for payment.

At the time of general elections political meetings were held on the Green and caused great excitement, as Eynesbury was considered to be violently radical and St. Neots conservative. In June 1892 John McNish took the chair at such a meeting, supporting Samuel Howard Whitbread, the Liberal candidate. It was reported that a large audience sang 'Clear the Way for Gladstone's Coming' and 'Hold the Fort', but later became decidedly disorderly.

A number of communal institutions were also placed on or around the Green, and they probably included the workhouse (see Luke Street). Others were:

The Pond. Until 1919 the west side of the Green was not built on and looked out on to a grass meadow called Old Close, with a gate on to the Green and a pond in its north-east corner near the present footpath to Ferrars Avenue. The pond had a fence across it leaving half of it in the field and half on the Green. Horses would be brought down to be watered here and the public would dip the soft water for wash days. It also provided a necessary reservoir for fire fighting. Here the author, as a very small boy, learnt to skate, but on the field side of the pond, where the village boys had not broken or thrown stones on the ice.

The Pound. The pound was on the south side of the pond where now are the gates of nos. 48 and 49 Council houses. Here straying cattle were impounded, and only redeemed by their owners on payment of a fine. Before the Inclosure (1800) when cattle were allowed to stray at fixed times over the Open Fields and Commons the Pound was a very necessary sanction and the pound keeper or pinder (pound herd) an important village official. After the Inclosure his duties became less onerous but the office did not fall into decay until the second half of the century. Indeed in 1859 the vestry ordered a new pound to be built, 15 feet square with walls six feet high and an oak door with lock. The new pound did not have a long life and was last used about 1865. The last pinder was remembered as being named Moore, and the fine to redeem a cow 5s.

In 1881 the Vestry Meeting considered the condition of the pound and a report that David Brittain had removed bricks and a gate illegally. He was given 14 days to return them. In three weeks' time it reported that he had returned six loads of bricks and a gate and posts and the overseers were instructed to sell them for the relief of the Poor Rate.

The Pump. A public well and pump for drinking water was not put on the green until 1895 (near the present telephone booth), and then only in spite of the protests of nearby house-owners who were convinced that their own private wells would suffer. Previously cottagers without wells had to carry water from the pump in Montague Square.

SELECT BIBLIOGRAPHY

Victoria County History, Huntingdonshire, 3 vols.
Royal Commission on Historic Monuments, Huntingdonshire.
Pigot's Directory, Huntingdonshire (1823/4, 1830).
Slater's Directory, Huntingdonshire (1850).
History and Gazetteer: Huntingdonshire (1854).
C. F. Tebbutt, *Diamond Jubilee of C. G. Tebbutt, Ltd., 1889-1949.*
W. Emery, 'Priory and Church of St. Neots', *Cambs. and Hunts. Arch. Soc.* vol. 2 (1908), pp. 16-24.
W. Emery, 'Eynesbury and its Church', *Cambs. and Hunts. Arch. Soc.*, vol. 2 (1908), pp. 29-32.
S. I. Ladds, 'Old Door at St. Neots', *Cambs. and Hunts. Arch. Soc.*, vol. 5 (1934), p. 245.
C. F. Tebbutt, 'Finds on Rebuilding Post Bridge, St. Neots', *Cambs. and Hunts. Arch. Soc.* vol. 5 (1934), p. 102.
C. F. Tebbutt, 'Beakers from Huntingdonshire', *Antiquaries Journal*, vol. 10 (1930), p. 384.
T. C. Lethbridge and C. F. Tebbutt, 'Huts of the Anglo-Saxon Period', *Camb. Antiq. Soc.*, vol. 33 (1932), pp. 133-151.
C. F. Tebbutt, 'Excavations at Eynesbury Coneygear', *Cambs. and Hunts. Arch. Soc.*, vol. 5 (1935), pp. 266-8.
E. F. Newton, 'Late Saxon Sites and a Medieval Chapel at Weald', *Cambs. and Hunts. Arch. Soc.*, vol. 6 (1943), pp. 167-75.
C. F. Tebbutt, 'St. Neots Priory', *Cambs. and Hunts. Arch. Soc.*, vol. 6 (1947), pp, 255-6.
C. F. Tebbutt, 'Roman Coin Hoard from St. Neots', *Cambs. and Hunts. Arch. Soc.*, vol. 7 (1948), p. 17.
C. F. Tebbutt, 'Excavations at St. Neots', *Camb. Antiq. Soc.*, vql. 49 (1956), pp. 79-87.
C. F. Tebbutt, *Folklore of Huntingdonshire* (1951).
C. F. Tebbutt, 'St. Neots Priory', *Camb. Antiq. Soc.*, vol. 59 (1966), pp. 33-74.
C. F. Tebbutt and G. T. Rudd, '13th century Buildings and Metal Workings at St. Neots', *Medieval Arch.*, vol. 10 (1966), pp. 158-60.
J. G. Hurst, 'Saxon-Norman Pottery in East Anglia', *Camb. Antiq. Soc.* vol. 49 (1956), pp. 43-70.
G. T. Rudd and C. Daines, 'Romano-British Settlement at Brickills Estate, Eynesbury', *Camb. Antiq. Soc.*, vol. 61 (1968), pp. 15-18.
R. U. Sayce, 'A May Day Garland from St. Neots', *Camb. Antiq. Soc.*, vol. 32 (1932), pp. 57-8.
P. V. Addyman and J. Marjoram, 'An 18th-century Mansion, a Fishpond, and Post-Medieval Finds at St. Neots, Huntingdonshire', *Post-Medieval Arch.*, vol. 6 (1972), pp. 69-106, and pl. VI-XI.
P. V. Addyman, 'Late Saxon Settlements in the St. Neots Area 111. The Village and Township at St. Neots', *Camb. Antiq. Soc.*, vol. 64 (1971).
G. T. M. Beresford, 'Wintringham', *Medieval Archaeology*, vol. 16 (1972) p. 201, ibid vol. 17 (1973) pp. 179-80.
C. F. Tebbutt, 'An Early 12th-century Building at Eynesbury, Hunts.', *Camb. Antiq. Soc.*, vol. 54 (1961), pp. 85-9.

INDEX

The spelling of surnames in the text has come mainly from original sources such as newspaper articles and rate books, and it has been found, in some cases, to differ while obviously referring to the same person (e.g. 'Osborn' and 'Osborne'). Where this occurs one form only has been used in the index.

Jones, Samuel, Ltd., 133
Jordan, 82, 225, 230, 258, 283, 342
Jordan & Addington, 94, 129, 276, 294, 317
Joyce, 30, 70, 71, 199, 269, 318
Jubilee, 101, 116, 150
Jupp, 169

Keeling, 185, 208, 224, 239
Kemp, 275
Kendal, 171
Kidman, 253, 346
Kidman's Yard, 253
King, 26, 30, 73, 151, 152, 181, 186, 227, 244, 248, 252, 258, 275, 284, 324, 336
King's Lane, 305
Kinn, 286
Kinsley, 245
Kirby, 26, 28, 72, 232, 294, 334
Kirkham, 87, 185, 282
Knight, 287
Knightley, 196
Knighton, 307
Kurr, 253
Kynge, 190

Ladds, 202
Lagoons, 101
Lamb, 334
Lammas Meadow, 118, 119, 120
Lane, 326
Lanning, 147, 193, 196
Lansbury, 346
Larkinson, 257
Launcelyn, 346
Laundey, 74, 283
Law, 72
Lawrence, 307
Lawson, 161
Lee, 200, 250, 264
Leightonhouse, 280, 281, 307
Leithe, 318
Leng, 186
Lenton, 343, 348
Le Tans'ur, 212
Lettice, 85
Lewis, 28, 186, 225, 260, 294
Liberal Club, 186, 199, 259
Limes, The, 125, 283
Linford, 49, 170, 301
Litchfield, 273

Literary Institute, 186, 260
Little, 303
Little Barford Road, 347
Little Bridge Street, 169
Liversage, 74
Livett, 22
Local Board, 17, 37, 87, 93, 150
Local Defence Association, 45
Locks, Navigation, 13
Lockup, 34, 258
London Central Meat Co., 229
London & County Bank, 198
Long, 185
Longland, 178
Love, 280, 304, 306, 324
Love's Farm, 306
Lovell, 184, 212, 233, 236, 237, 295, 301
Lovitt, 40, 232, 251, 287, 289
Low Farm, 124, 330
Lucas, 165, 286, 287
Luff, 161, 211
Lugsden, 161
Luke, 66, 67, 68, 336, 345
Luke Street, 339-342
Lummock, 249
Lynn, 34, 254

Machin, 252
Mackaness, 219, 301, 315
Mackenzie, 277
Maddison, 34, 35, 228, 296, 300, 301
Maddy, 197
Madox, 173
Magistrates' Court, 300
Maile, 218
Maine, 306, 307
Malden, 40, 141, 285, 301
Malling, 273
Malting kiln, 231
Manning, 178
Manor Farm, 14, 15, 270
Marie & Francis, 210
Market House, 229
Market Square, 10, 14, 15, 186-231
Market Tolls, 107
Markham, 162, 243
Marlow, 244
Marshall, 218, 229, 326, 332
Martin, 35, 37, 341
Mason, 329
Mathematical tiles, 250

Stevens, 16, 189, 196, 247
Stocker, 190, 304, 320, 324, 341
Stocks, 168, 169
Stone, 206
Storey, 209, 287
Stoton, 289, 317
Stott, 227, 301
Stratton, 273, 275, 329
Street, 191
Strudwick, 297
Stuckey, 58
Summers, 189, 209, 237
Swann, 223, 237

Taborn, 282
Tassell, 268
Taylor, 60, 135, 138, 142, 180, 188,
   194, 195, 206, 211, 269, 288,
   315, 316, 317, 325, 330, 346
Tebbutt, 88, 89, 118, 120, 145-47,
   159, 160, 173, 175, 209, 241,
   314, 333
Thittle, 217
Thomas, 188
Thompson, 60
Thorley, 211
Thorns, 22, 72, 73, 208
Thornton, 200, 211, 280, 301
Thrift Place, 304
Throughgood, 197
Tingey, 297
Tithe Farm, 307
Tokins, 29, 250
Toller, 320
Tomplin, 276, 339
Tomson, 37, 40, 143, 189, 228,
   229, 235, 297
Tomson & Lendrum, 107
Toogood, 22, 25, 36, 117, 119, 120,
   130, 131, 274, 301
Top Boardings, 118, 119
Topham, 73, 170, 224, 235, 294
Tovey, 175
Town Commissioners, 16, 21-37, 46
Town Crier, 248, 251, 252
Town Pump, 31, 136, 286
Towndrow, 230
Townley, 332
Townsend, 156, 157, 262
Townsend Pond, 312, 331
Trap Close, 169
Tristham, 262
Triston, 173

Trolley, 330
Tuckfield, 175, 236
Turner, 215, 228, 230
Turnpike Trusts, 27, 33, 36, 188,
   243, 273, 293, 345
Tyler, 256

Ubsdell, 236
Upchurch, 176
Urban District Council, 17, 40, 46,
   157, 158

Vaughan, 61, 162
Veasey Desborough Bank, 208
Veitch, 197
Venn, 274
Vicarage, 161
Vickary, 188
Victoria Terrace, 271
Victorian society, 14
Villers, 340
Vine, 235
Vulcan Iron Works, 77, 147-50,
   194

Wade, 165
Wade Gery, 34, 37, 41, 117, 132,
   167, 266, 275, 294
Wade Gery & Brackenbury, 126
Wady, 256
Waggon Yard, 128
Wagstaff, 331
Wagstaff & Turner, 243
Waite, 218
Wakefield, 291
Waller, 173, 191, 283
Wallis, 254, 339
Walnut Tree Square, 177
Walters, 249
Walton, 48
Ward, 68, 190, 209, 215, 271
Waresley Charity, 165
Warner, 252, 326
Warren, 27, 238, 257, 280
Warrington, 307
Warwick, 165
Wash Bank, 339
Watchorn, 207
Water Company, 225
Waterfall, 276
Waterhouse, 269
Waterloo Farm, 332
Waterloo House, 331